CH00920671

C153043471

de Havilland
Mosquito

AN ILLUSTRATED HISTORY

Volume 2

de Havilland
Mosquito

An Illustrated History

Volume 2

Ian Thirsk

Foreword by R. M. Hare
Formerly Head of Structures, British Aerospace,
and one of the original members of the Mosquito design team

Crécy Publishing Limited
www.crecy.co.uk

First published in 2006 by Crécy Publishing Limited
Reprinted 2007

A CIP record for this book is available from the British Library

de Havilland
Mosquito
AN ILLUSTRATED HISTORY
Volume 2

ISBN 085979 115 7   9 780859 791151

Printed in England by J H Haynes & Co Ltd

Photographs
front cover:
(top) *Richard Riding Collection*
(bottom) *W.Cottrell, Alberta Aviation Museum Collection*
back cover:
BAE SYSTEMS
(colour) *Richard Paver*

Crécy Publishing Limited
1a Ringway Trading Estate, Shadowmoss Road, Manchester M22 5LH
www.crecy.co.uk

Contents

For my Mum, Shirley Ann Thirsk, 1937-2002

Memorable Mosquito: British Aerospace test pilot Kevin Moorhouse displays T.3 RR299 over the Mosquito Museum, Salisbury Hall, during the summer of 1995. Engineer Steve Watson is in the right hand seat. (Neil Thirsk)

Foreword

By R. M. Hare

Formerly Head of Structures, British Aerospace,
and one of the original members of the Mosquito design team

This book gives the story of one of the most remarkable aircraft of the Second World War. Based on the premise that speed could be the major form of defence, the Mosquito Bomber and Reconnaissance versions were designed around two Merlin engines and 'clean' external surfaces of the airframe. The only defensive armaments were two bullet-proof bulkheads behind each crew member.

de Havilland had been well experienced in the use of timber airframes, so little demands on metals, which were in short supply at the time, would be made. The firm was told verbally by Lord Beaverbrook to stop work on the aircraft. This, however, brought the straightforward comment from Captain (later Sir Geoffrey) de Havilland: 'They don't want it now but they will want it, we will do it anyway, as a private venture' – so the history books were written!

Designed, built and flown during a period of 11 months during 1940, the prototype aircraft, W4050, can still be viewed in its birthplace at Salisbury Hall, London Colney, now the Mosquito Museum. Ease of construction, modification and repair enabled an otherwise untapped source of labour and skills to be gainfully employed in producing nearly 8,000 of various versions, mainly in England but also in Canada and Australia. In virtually every role fulfilled by British aircraft, a version of the Mosquito was to be found.

Ian Thirsk has done much research into the subject, had many interviews with appropriate people and studied many documents. He is now a well-versed authority on the Mosquito project. The following account is well worth perusing carefully.

Ralph Hare

Glossary

A&AEE	Aeroplane & Armament Experimental Establishment	FTU	Ferry Training Unit
		GSU	Group Support Unit
ACSEA	Air Command South East Asia	HCEU	Home Command Examining Unit
AD	Aircraft Depot	IDFAF	Israeli Defence Force Air Force
ADLS	Air Delivery Letter Service	JRV	Jugoslovenska Ratno Vazduhoplovstyo (Yugoslav Air Force)
AFS	Advanced Flying School		
AHU	Aircraft Holding Unit	LNSF	Light Night Striking Force
AI	Airborne Interception	MAAF	Mediterranean Allied Air Forces
AID	Aeronautical Inspection Directorate	MU	Maintenance Unit
APS	Armament Practice Station	OAPU	Overseas Aircraft Preparation Unit
ARF	Aircraft Reception Flight	OCU	Operational Conversion Unit
ARI	Airborne Radio Installation	OFU	Overseas Ferry Unit
ASH	Air-to-Surface Home	OTU	Operational Training Unit
ASI	Air Speed Indicated	PFF	Pathfinder Force
ARB	Air Registration Board	PNTU	Pathfinder Navigation Training Unit
BAFO	British Air Forces of Occupation	PRU	Photographic Reconnaissance Unit
BCBS	Bomber Command Bombing School	RAE	Royal Aircraft Establishment
BEA	British European Airways	RAF	Royal Air Force
BG	Bombardment Group	RATOG	Rocket Assisted Take-Off Gear
BOAC	British Overseas Airways Corporation	RAAF	Royal Australian Air Force
BS	Bombardment Squadron	RCAF	Royal Canadian Air Force
CAACU	Civilian Anti-Aircraft Co-operation Unit	RDU	Receipt & Despatch Unit
CBE	Central Bomber Establishment	RIDS	Radar Interception Development Squadron
CGS	Central Gunnery School		
CMU	Civilian Maintenance Unit	RNAS	Royal Naval Air Station
CRD	Controller of Reasearch and Development	RNZAF	Royal New Zealand Air Force
		SAC	Senior Aircraftsman
CSBS	Course Setting Bomb Sight	SAG	Second Aircraft Group
DTD	Directorate of Technical Development	SBAC	Society of British Aircraft Constructors
FAA	Fleet Air Arm	SCI	Smoke Curtain Installation
FAERA	Fuerza Aerea del Ejertico de la Revolucion Americana	SEAC	South East Asia Command
		SOC	Struck Off Charge
FCCS	Fighter Command Communications Squadron	TAF	Tactical Air Force
		TFU	Telecommunications Flying Unit
FEAF	Far East Air Force	THUM	Temperature and Humidity
FETS	Far East Training Squadron	TRE	Telecommunications Research Establishment
FIU	Fighter Interception Unit		
Flygvapnet	Swedish Air Force	TTO	Target Towing Operator
FRU	Fleet Requirements Unit	USAAF	United States Army Air Force

Acknowledgements

This book would have been impossible without the help of a great many people, all of whom gave so freely and enthusiastically of their time. However, very special mention must go to Mike Packham for providing invaluable information on aircraft histories in addition to scanning hundreds of photographs; Matt George for countless weekends breathing new life into faded and damaged images; Bob Glasby for patiently scanning and cleaning more than 1,000 copy negatives; and Ralph Hare for contributing the Foreword in addition to answering a multitude of questions. I am also indebted to Dr Michael Fopp, Director General of the RAF Museum, for his valuable advice at the start of the project, and the RAF Museum Department of Research and Information Services, particularly Peter Elliott, Stuart Hadaway, Gordon Leith and Peter Devitt, together with Andrew Renwick of the RAF Museum Photographic Department.

Extremely grateful thanks are also due to Mike Gray, Brian Wright, Ted Wilkins, Brian Rose, Peter Verney, Barry Guess and Mike Fielding of BAe Systems at Farnborough, Terry Holloway of The Marshall Group of Companies, The National Archives at Kew, Alan Brackley, Iain Duncan, Bruce Gordon, Neil Hutchinson, Dr Andy Dawson, David Coeshall, John Stride, Ralph Steiner, Philip Birtles, John Gerrish, Ross Shepherd and Mike Nelmes of the Narromine Aviation Museum, Simon Baker, Keith Saunders, Jonathan Falconer, Richard Riding, Francois Prins, Ken Ellis (*Flypast* magazine), David Oliver, Nick Stroud and Michael Oakey (*Aeroplane Monthly* magazine), Dick Whittingham, Brian Rose, Alan Johnson, Bill Cotterell of the Alberta Aviation Museum, Noel Sparrow, Stuart Redfern, Geoffrey Perks, Mike Levy, David Fuller, Roger Topp, Harold Stillwell, Patrick Fell, Ken Bowman, Richard Livermore, Charbel Perez Caram, Bob Tatum, F. R. Gordon of the Berkshire Aviation Museum, George Stewart, Roy Quantick, Archiv Flieger Flab Museum, Dubendorf, Mrs Myrna Jewell, Howard Sandall, George Mahony, 613 (City of Manchester) Squadron Association, Don Chapman, George Kilcoyne, DHAMT Ltd, Alan Harwin, Alan Copas, Cyril Howe, H. O. Baker, Ted Lovatt, Tommy Adamson, Jack and Sylvia Page, R. A. Scholefield, *Flight International* magazine, Public Archives of Canada, Canadian National Museum of Science and Technology, Marshall Group, Howard Lees, Roley Manning, James Earnshaw, Bob Jacobs, Dave Cooke, Peter Arnold, Steve Bond, Colin Thirsk, Neil Thirsk, Imperial War Museum, E. G. Hayes and Ken Allen.

For information relating to Norwegian Mosquitoes I would like to thank Bjorn Olsen, Bjorn Hafsten and Sverre Thuve.

On behalf of Stuart Howe I would also like to thank to Brian Harris, Jake Jacobs, Peter Cook, Ken Lambert, Basil Nash, J. B. Coll, Gus Weedon, Betty Aherne, R. Bimmemans, Milan Micevski, Bill Simpson, Frank Joliffe, Don Aris, J. M. Petit, Hillel Neuman, J. M. G. Gradidge, Bill Holdridge, Ken Bernau, A. J. Jones, M. R. S. Cunningham, David Hughes, Bernard B. Deatrick, Gary Brown, Patrick Fell, Peter Kempe, David Hughes, Alan Shufflebottom, Wally Froud, H. C. Randell, Bill Britain, Doug Mount, Keith Rimmer, Vic Hewes, J. D. Oughton, Bill Binnie, Frank Smith, R. Neep, Chris Buck, Dick Hin and Ken Dunbar. Last but by no means least, Barbara Howe, for all her encouragement and support throughout the project.

Ian Thirsk

Introduction

This book is not only a tribute to all who designed, built, flew and maintained the Mosquito, but also to one particular individual, Mr Stuart Howe.

To aviation historians worldwide the name Stuart Howe is synonymous with the Mosquito. Through his voluntary work at the Mosquito Museum, Stuart made an invaluable contribution to Mosquito preservation and inspired a whole new generation of Mosquito enthusiasts. Sadly, at the age of just fifty-eight, Stuart died in April 2004 following a brave battle against illness.

Stuart wrote prolifically on the Mosquito, and this was scheduled to be his fifth book on the type. He was extremely enthusiastic about this project, for which he had been gathering material for several years. Shortly after his death Stuart's widow Barbara, together with myself, decided that it would make a fitting tribute to Stuart if this, his final work, could be completed. Although new to book compilation, I decided to take up the mantle and began work in September 2004. I too have had a lifelong interest in the Mosquito and first met Stuart when I joined the Mosquito Museum as a teenage volunteer back in 1975. Over the years Stuart and I became good friends and worked together on the restoration of the Mosquito Museum's TT.35 TA634 during the 1980s. It has therefore been a tremendous challenge, and privilege, to finish this work on Stuart's behalf.

I have tried as closely as possible to keep the book within Stuart's proposed format. These are the photographs Stuart wanted everyone to see, so I hope my caption attempts approach something resembling his previous standards. I've done my utmost to contact everyone who originally supplied Stuart with material and apologise if I have missed anyone out during this process.

A charismatic aeroplane with a unique aura, there is nothing quite like the sight and sound of a Mosquito in flight. Growing up close to Hatfield aerodrome during the 1960s and 1970s, my interest in the Mosquito was inspired by T.3 RR299 regularly passing overhead during the summer air display seasons. RR299, and the crews who gave up their time to maintain and fly it, helped increase public awareness of the Mosquito for more than thirty years. In this regard I would like, finally, to make special mention of Kevin Moorhouse and Steve Watson, who were so tragically killed in the aeroplane on 21 July 1996.

Once seen, never forgotten, admiration for the Mosquito continues to grow; I only hope this book will play a part in keeping the legend alive.

Ian Thirsk
Hatfield
June 2006

Stuart Howe: a Dedication

by
Barbara Howe

This book is dedicated to the memory of Stuart Howe,
who passed away on 14 April 2004, aged 58 – 'Mr Mosquito Man'

This has to be one of the hardest things I've ever had to write, as Stuart was dedicating his book to me, and instead I'm having to write the dedication to my late wonderful, beloved husband who was so passionate about the 'Mossie'. Those of you who were fortunate to know him well, know that his interest and enthusiasm always was for old aircraft, antiques and Art Deco china. He always enjoyed telling his pals that he loved old things and that was why he married me!

The meaning of 'Stuart' as a name comes from an old English word 'Stigweard', and suggests someone that is strong, gallant and will always rise to the challenge whatever it may be. He will not be defeated. This sums up Stuart so well, and the only thing missing was his never-ending sense of humour!

Looking back to his short sudden illness I believe that doing the research for this book kept his mind very firmly focused, and he would sit typing all day and manage to forget his illness briefly. Always the optimist, he never gave up planning ahead, and although he fought so terribly hard, cancer did defeat him in the end. With Ian carrying on with Stuart's project, we hope to overcome defeat as we both felt so very, very strongly that this was the right thing to do.

Ian feels that Stuart is guiding him and, judging by the incredible amount of help we have received, we are both one hundred percent sure that it was the right and proper thing to do.

I will never be able to say a big enough 'Thank you' to Ian for all the hard work and effort that he put into the book, and of course everyone else involved too. Also, I cannot thank enough all the people who kindly lent us photographs, many of which have never been published before.

Ian has done his very best to make this a fitting tribute to Stuart and I hope that all of you who purchase the book will agree with us. Thank you Stuart for so many, many wonderful memories, until we fly once again in formation.

Babs Howe

W4050, The Mosquito Prototype

In contrast to many other first prototypes of Second World War combat aircraft, the Mosquito prototype, W4050, played a significant role well into the development of much later variants of the basic design. Unique in many ways, this aircraft had a long and varied career, made even more remarkable through its continued existence to this day.

W4050 was the principal experimental Mosquito to evaluate the basic design, and was not representative of a Bomber or Photographic Reconnaissance version, although externally this may have seemed so. This first prototype was constructed in a special hangar, disguised as a barn, within the grounds of Salisbury Hall, a seventeenth-century manor house sited close to St Albans. de Havilland's chose Salisbury Hall for purely practical reasons, the location offering security from the danger of bombing, together with peace from inevitable disturbances at the company's nearby Hatfield headquarters.

Constructed using initial schemes prior to the completion of production drawings, the prototype was subsequently built in the relatively short period of eleven months. Transported to Hatfield on 3 November 1940, the aircraft was re-assembled and prepared for flight testing. Finished in an overall Trainer Yellow colour scheme with black spinners, the machine initially wore the de Havilland Company 'B Condition' markings of E0234.

On 25 November 1940 de Havilland Chief Test Pilot Geoffrey de Havilland Junior, accompanied by engine installation designer John E. Walker as observer, piloted E0234 on its maiden flight. Over the next three months the prototype continued its test flight programme, the 'B Condition' markings being replaced by the official Air Ministry registration W4050 in either December 1940 or early January 1941 (although the de Havilland 'Experimental Aircraft Pilot's Test Record' continues to list 'E0234' as late as July 1941).

The initial test flight programme confirmed the aircraft's great potential and began to win over official opposition to the Mosquito project. Among the problems encountered during these early tests were castoring difficulties with the tailwheel, tail 'buffeting' caused by disturbed airflow off the inner engine nacelles and inner wing under surfaces, together with opening of the undercarriage doors in flight. The tail 'buffeting' took several weeks to overcome, initial countering attempts consisting of aerodynamic 'slots' (also referred to as 'air straighteners' and similar to those featured on the DH.95 Flamingo airliner) affixed to the inner nacelles and inboard underwing surfaces, designed to 'smooth out' the disturbed airflow before it struck the tailplane. Many 'slot' configurations were evaluated, but the 'buffeting' was eventually cured by temporarily (until a production modification could be introduced) extending the engine nacelle rear sections beyond the wing trailing edge.

In early February 1941 W4050 received a coat of Dark Earth and Dark Green camouflage on its upper surfaces in readiness for service acceptance trials at the A&AEE Boscombe Down (large 'Circle P' markings also being applied to the fuselage sides aft of the roundel). Delivered to the Performance Testing Squadron at Boscombe Down on 19 February, W4050 greatly impressed the A&AEE test pilots, but on 24 February, while being taxied by Flt Lt Slee, W4050's fuselage fractured after the tailwheel jammed (due to the castoring problems) on Boscombe's rough aerodrome surface. The late Air Commodore Allen Wheeler was in charge of the Performance Testing Squadron at this time and recalled that Flt Lt Slee was initially unaware of the problem until all of W4050's controls tightened up. Airmen were called over to check through the control lines, one of them eventually shouting out from beneath the Mosquito: 'It's all right, sir, there's nothing wrong with the controls but she's broken her bleedin' back.' The fuselage had fractured around the access hatch cut out on the starboard side, damage being extensive enough for the decision to be taken to change the fuselage with that destined for W4051, the Photo Reconnaissance prototype. A small working party was despatched to Boscombe Down to fit this new fuselage, W4050 returning to Hatfield on 14 March (an externally mounted longitudinal stiffening strake was subsequently mounted above the hatch cut-out, this later becoming a standard feature of production aircraft).

During level speed trials from Boscombe Down, A&AEE pilots recorded a maximum speed of 388mph at 22,000 feet with W4050, a figure exceeding that measured by de Havilland. After the re-fitting of the nacelle extensions, W4050 returned to Boscombe Down on 18 March, the A&AEE pilots being duly impressed with the machine's smoother handling qualities. W4050 returned to Boscombe Down in May for further trials during which the fuselage was damaged once more, this time after a heavy landing. The damage occurred to the port side of the fuselage, just aft of the wing trailing edge, and was repaired with a large wooden patch that is still visible to this day.

From July until October 1941 W4050 was engaged on a variety of tests, which included handling and speed trials with a mock-up turret located aft of the cockpit, evaluation of a redesigned tailwheel unit (culminating in the elimination of the earlier castoring troubles), diving trials with the bomb doors open, together with handling and level speed tests with 250lb bomb-carriers mounted beneath the outer wings.

In October 1941 the aircraft was dismantled and the wing returned to Salisbury Hall in preparation for the installation of two-speed, two-stage supercharged Merlin 61 engines. Flight tests began the following June, speed and altitude performance being markedly improved. Climb and level speed test comparisons were made with three- and four-bladed propellers, W4050 attaining a maximum level speed of 437mph during the course of these trials (the highest speed measured on any Mosquito up to that time). In November 1942 W4050's Merlin 61s were replaced by Merlin 70 series engines equipped with Bendix Stromberg carburettors. Concurrently and in connection with development work for the Mosquito NF.XV, W4050's wingspan was extended to 59ft 2in before the aircraft made its first flight with the Merlin 70 engines in December 1942. Climb and level speed tests followed, the aircraft then reverting to its normal 52ft 5in wingspan before the tests were repeated for comparative purposes. Climb and level speed trials continued into 1943, endurance tests also being conducted on various exhaust stub designs.

By the close of 1943 the prototype had ended its flying career and had been officially grounded by January 1944. The aircraft remained at Hatfield, its existence noted by Bill Baird, assistant to the Public Relations Manager, C. Martin Sharp. Towards the end of 1945 plans were in hand to turn one of the Hatfield hangars into a reception area housing significant aircraft from the de Havilland Company's history. Bill Baird included W4050 in this scheme and arranged for the company to purchase the aircraft from the Air Ministry. However, the reception area plans came to naught, W4050 instead being transferred to the de Havilland Technical College hangar at Salisbury Hall where it served as an instructional airframe. It made static appearances at the 1946 and 1947 SBAC displays at Radlett before the de Havilland Technical

College vacated Salisbury Hall and Bill Baird was told to move the aircraft. Despite being instructed to burn W4050, Bill Baird's ingenuity had the aircraft moved to several locations including Hatfield, Panshangar and Chester before it eventually ended up in the 'Fiddle Bridge Stores' (located in Fiddle Bridge Lane) outside the aerodrome perimeter at Hatfield.

During the late 1950s Walter and Audrey Goldsmith purchased Salisbury Hall and set about restoring the property to its former glory. During the course of this work they discovered evidence of the house's former occupation by de Havilland. As they were restoring the property under an arrangement with the Ministry of Works & Buildings, the house would have to open to the public each year. Learning that the Mosquito had been designed and built there, Walter Goldsmith contacted de Havilland to enquire as to the availability of Mosquito memorabilia that he could place on display. In due course he was put in touch with Bill Baird, and the idea of returning W4050 to Salisbury Hall was agreed in principle. However, before this could proceed funds had to be raised for the purchase of a hangar to house the aircraft. Funds were not forthcoming from the de Havilland Company itself, but eventually £1,800 was raised from various sub-contractors formerly engaged on Mosquito production. This figure was sufficient to obtain a Robin hangar, which was erected at the back of the house just over the moat. Following concreting of the hangar floor, W4050 was transported back to Salisbury Hall in September 1958 and re-assembled the following month.

In the early 1970s Walter Goldsmith and Stuart Howe repainted W4050 in a scheme resembling its initial overall yellow finish. Although an incorrect scheme for the aircraft's configuration, this was carried out using marine paint, which protected the aircraft for more than thirty years. W4050 remains on display at Salisbury Hall to this day and forms the centrepiece of the de Havilland Aircraft Museum Trust (formerly the Mosquito Aircraft Museum) collection, which has been established on the site for more than thirty years. W4050 is currently undergoing a protracted but detailed restoration programme that will see it returned to the condition in which it appeared at the postwar SBAC displays.

The historic seventeenth-century moated manor house of
Salisbury Hall near St Albans will be forever linked with the
Mosquito. Listed in the Domesday Book as the Saxon
Manor of Shenley, three buildings are known to have
occupied this site. The first was a moated stronghold
known as 'Salisburies' from where (in 1471) the Earl of
Warwick and Salisbury led the Lancastrian army to death
and defeat at the Battle of Barnet. In Tudor times Sir John
Cutte, Treasurer to Henry VIII, constructed a large
mansion on the site, but little of this now remains. The
house's current appearance is the work of Sir Jeremy Snow,
who purchased the property in 1668 on behalf of Charles II,
the latter making frequent visits accompanied by his
mistress Nell Gwynne. At the beginning of the last century
Jenny Churchill (mother of Sir Winston) occupied the
property, and during the 1930s it became the residence of
celebrated locomotive engineer Sir Nigel Gresley.

Sited close to its main Hatfield factory, de Havilland
selected Salisbury Hall as a secret design centre for the
Mosquito, its detached location reducing the bombing risk
in addition to freeing the design and production teams
from the inevitable disturbances of the Hatfield plant. Led
by Chief Designer Ronald Bishop, the core of the
Mosquito design team moved into Salisbury Hall on 5
October 1939. This group comprised Richard Clarkson,
Tim Wilkins, W. A. Tamblin, D. R. Adams, M. Herrod-
Hempsall, Jim Crowe, Ralph Hare and R. Hutchinson,
together with secretary Mrs D. Ledeboer.

Senior Draughtsman 'H. O.' Henry Baker later became
a member of the Salisbury Hall design staff, and recalls the
atmosphere as 'completely informal – at Hatfield a man
employed as a draughtsman, senior draughtsman or design
draughtsman would normally do a particular kind of job, be
it wing structure, fuselage structure, engines or hydraulics.
At Salisbury Hall you were asked to do the next job that
came along, even if it was something you wouldn't normally
work on. The simple explanation was that there were jobs
to be done and everybody was asked to do them and
everyone got on with it.' *(BAE SYSTEMS)*

While design work went on in Salisbury Hall, construction
of the first Mosquito prototype took place in this single-bay
hangar (disguised as a barn) located across the moat in the
grounds of the house. This picture was taken in the
summer of 1940 while production of the first aircraft was
still under way. Note the gantries at the hangar mouth,
together with the workers' cars parked on the left-hand
side. An additional bay was later added in order to conduct
detail assembly of the initial Mosquito Fighter prototypes
(W4052, W4053 and W4073); these aircraft were later
flown to Hatfield from fields bordering the house. Both
hangars no longer exist, but the door track to this building
is still visible. Part of the brick structure to the rear of the
hangar today acts as an admissions/shop building for the de
Havilland Aircraft Museum Trust. *(BAE SYSTEMS)*

The Mosquito detailed mock-up pictured within the original hangar at Salisbury Hall on 16 June 1940. Rudimentary mock-ups were previously assembled at Hatfield and Salisbury Hall; at the latter location they were housed in a small building known as 'Nell Gwynne's Cottage' located next to the moat (this building also serving as a material store). Alan Copas was a member of the Mosquito prototype construction team at Salisbury Hall and worked as an assistant to Ted Lovatt, the charge-hand responsible for installation of all hydraulic and pneumatic systems on the aeroplane. Alan recalled that the Hatfield mock-up originally featured smooth nose contours (very similar to the Blenheim Mk 1) and remembers Chief Designer Ronald Bishop inspecting this one day before exclaiming, 'How on earth can we expect people to fight in a thing like this? It's absolutely no good – we'll have to put a cockpit blister on the top!'

The office behind the mock-up was occupied by Fred Plumb, foreman in charge of Mosquito prototype construction at Salisbury Hall, together with his secretary, Sylvia Page. Wilf Joyce is descending the steps by the nose while work on the first aircraft goes on in the foreground. Note the original nose design with its wrap-around framing. Much of this mock-up was created by woodworker Claude Brooks. *(BAE SYSTEMS)*

Taken in the Salisbury Hall hangar during June 1940, this rare photograph illustrates the Mosquito prototype's fuselage shells supported in vertical cradles prior to fitting-out. The first prototypes were literally hand-built aeroplanes; workers engaged on their construction included woodworkers Cyril Howe, Jack English and Ronnie Dunn (together with their foreman Jimmie Rigglesworth); Percy Grigsby, foreman of the sheet metal shop; Sam Porter, foreman of the fitting and machine shop; fitters Ralph Blakey and George Phillips (the latter both Snr and Jnr); and welders Tom Faithful and Ronnie Rodford. An undercarriage mudguard is visible propped up on a shelf directly above the rear section of the fuselage canopy frame cut-out. As recounted in the introduction to this section, the fuselage illustrated here was destined for a short lifespan. Note the canopy frame jig in the left foreground. *(BAE SYSTEMS)*

The prototype is seen assembled in the Salisbury Hall hangar during October 1940. The workers featured in this composite picture are believed to include Claude Brooks (working on the tailplane) and Jack English (holding the sling beneath the rear fuselage). The hangar was initially occupied only by woodworkers who built the jigs and manufactured the airframe. Prior to assembling the aircraft, sheet metal workers, engine fitters, electricians and hydraulics engineers arrived from Hatfield. Woodworker Cyril Howe recalled the early days at Salisbury Hall: 'Hatfield was lovely and warm but when we got to Salisbury Hall there wasn't any heat. Part of the hangar was hot and the other part was cold, and when it got hot the earwigs used to fall down your neck!'

The drawing office and construction teams worked long hours (twelve-hour days being a regular occurrence) and completed the prototype in only eleven months following commencement of detail design. This picture was taken from a balcony running along the hangar's right-hand side (erected during the later stages of the prototype's construction) and shows the detailed mock-up in the right-hand corner. Together with the original short engine nacelle and one-piece flap design, the cockpit 'tear drop'-shaped observation blisters are very evident. Note that the fabric-covered elevators (together with the rudder) appear to be at the red dope finish stage. *(BAE SYSTEMS)*

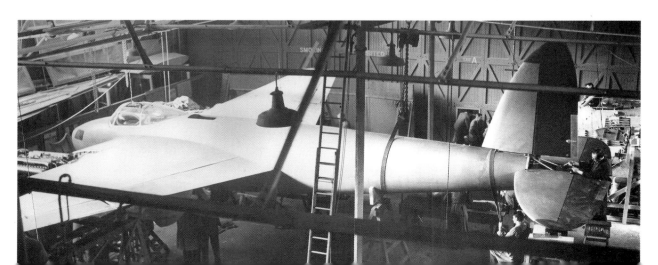

Another October 1940 shot shows the prototype assembled at Salisbury Hall with the wings and fuselage trestled in the neutral incidence position (a sling is positioned around fuselage bulkhead number five). The first prototype has a wingspan of 52ft 5in, culminating in gently rounded-off wingtips of almost 'stub' appearance. For a very short period in its later career the aircraft would be fitted with extended wingtips, increasing the overall wingspan to 59ft 2in, but it never received the slightly larger wingtips fitted to the remaining prototypes and all the standard production aircraft. The 'stub' port wingtip is shown here, as are the fabric-covered elevators.

Alan Copas recalled the rapid rate of construction progress with the prototype: 'To be perfectly honest, it was such an astonishing programme that to my knowledge there were few problems that held it back. It was almost unbelievable that even such radical things as the split fuselage were all put together so quickly. In those days we used to make everything internally including all the specialist stuff such as selectors and jacks – even the undercarriage legs were made in the hangar.'

The inboard trailing edge shroud box on the starboard wing has yet to receive its top skin and a group discussion is in progress beneath the tailplane centre section. Note the smooth surface finish of the fuselage. *(BAE SYSTEMS)*

Trial fitting of the prototype's tail fairing cone being undertaken at Salisbury Hall in late 1940. The gentleman on the right is holding on to one of the four tubes connecting the tailplane rear spar to the fuselage rear bulkhead (bulkhead number seven, or 'G' as it was later referred to on the Hatfield production line). These tubes were adjustable in order to alter tailplane incidence, the tailplane forward spar being attached to bulkhead number seven at three points (one in the centre and two outboard). The tail fairing cone has yet to receive longitudinal fillet fairings along its aft section (to blend in with the elevator line), and initially did not feature a navigation lamp on its aft section. The gap between the lower fuselage and tail fairing cone would be closed by a detachable aluminium under fairing retained in place largely by Dzus fasteners. Fuselage bulkhead number seven bore tremendous loads, and it was essential to ensure a good close-matching glued joint (with no voids around the periphery) between this bulkhead and the rear fuselage structure. Note the metal trim tabs on the elevators and rudder. *(BAE SYSTEMS)*

In late October 1940 the prototype was dismantled at Salisbury Hall in preparation for road transport to Hatfield. In this rare composite picture the wing is seen (complete with engines) mounted on a flat platform trailer positioned within the Salisbury Hall hangar. Note that the undercarriage has been retracted and the flaps removed. *(BAE SYSTEMS)*

On 3 November 1940 the prototype was transported from Salisbury Hall to Hatfield for re-assembly and flight testing. The fuselage and wing were transported separately using flat-bed trailers, Hatfield Transport Department staff Ron Vernall and Ted Livett being involved in this operation. Here the wing is pictured shortly after its arrival at Hatfield. *(BAE SYSTEMS)*

The prototype's fuselage has been hoisted from its flat-bed trailer following transport from Salisbury Hall to Hatfield. Salisbury Hall works foreman Fred Plumb (second from the left) looks on. Note the jury strut bridging the ventral bay wing 'gap', vital to maintain fuselage structural integrity in addition to preventing distortion. The fuselage is trestled at bulkheads two and five and would appear to have arrived from Salisbury Hall in a silver dope finish. The circular port in the rear fuselage access hatch would provide a useful means of observation during the prototype's initial flight testing. *(BAE SYSTEMS)*

The prototype being prepared for engine runs and fuel flow tests at Hatfield on 19 November 1940. Following re-assembly in a building located close to the St Albans end of Hatfield aerodrome, the prototype was finished Trainer Yellow overall with the spinners in black. This distinctive scheme was applied to alert the home defences that this unfamiliar design was a 'friendly' aircraft on test. The prototype also received the manufacturer's 'B Condition' marking 'E0234', which was applied to both sides of the rear fuselage just forward of the tailplane. This shot provides a good illustration of the original exhaust manifold ducting system with its outlet positioned on the side cowling rear section. Rex King, experimental shop superintendent, is believed to be standing immediately forward of the port propeller. The building used for E0234's re-assembly is on the right. *(BAE SYSTEMS)*

In this second view of E0234 outside its assembly building on 19 November 1940, the new aircraft's sleek form is readily apparent beneath the tarpaulin coverings, the latter applied to guard against aerial observation. Note that the starboard undercarriage doors have yet to be installed. *(BAE SYSTEMS)*

This pre-first-flight shot of E0234 was taken at Hatfield between engine runs. The group on the right have just removed the port outer side cowling and Rex King (standing on the steps) is inspecting the engine. Woodworkers Jack Page (husband of Sylvia, Fred Plumb's secretary) and Tommy Adamson were chosen for fire duties during E0234's initial engine runs, as Jack recalls:

'Well, I can remember one of the engine runs particularly. There was Tommy Adamson on one side with the fire extinguisher and me on the other. Both engines were running and of course it would be mine that caught fire! I ran up with the fire extinguisher and directed the nozzle at the exhaust outlet. Well, Fred Plumb ran up

behind, practically fighting me for control of the extinguisher, which directed its contents on to the side cowling before splashing back all over him – he retired then! The engine was shut down and I finished putting out the fire.' The damage was not serious.

Note E0234's Handley Page leading edge slots together with the Type A underwing roundels. Second and third from the right are Alan S. Butler and Frank Hearle, de Havilland Company Chairman and Managing Director respectively. The new aeroplane's beautiful lines and low frontal area are readily apparent and provide a marked contrast to the Lysander parked beyond. E0234's undercarriage doors have still to be fitted. (BAE SYSTEMS)

E0234's tail is being held down during engine runs, probably on 24 November 1940, the eve of the aircraft's maiden flight. Fire extinguishers are to hand on both sides of the aeroplane, which sports Type A roundels on the fuselage sides. Note that the undercarriage doors have now been installed. (BAE SYSTEMS)

With Geoffrey de Havilland Junior at the controls, E0234 commenced taxying trials at 1500hrs on the afternoon of 24 November 1940. The aircraft was at an all-up weight of 14,150lb and aerodrome surface conditions were soft, muddy and skiddy with a 5mph SW wind. In the absence of a Rolls Royce representative, engine boosts were limited to plus-11lb per sq in by means of a throttle stop in the cockpit. Engine rpm tick-overs were recorded as 450 on the starboard engine and 750 on the port, the latter being much too high.

As E0234 began taxying there was a general tendency for the aircraft to swing to starboard. At first it was thought that this was due to a binding starboard brake or the high tick-over speed of the port engine, but it later transpired that the tailwheel was not castoring correctly. Due to the latter problem, turning on the skiddy aerodrome surface was not easy, but the main undercarriage felt good at all speeds.

Geoffrey de Havilland Junior carried out several high-speed runs, momentarily opening the engines up to plus-11lb boost and afterwards reporting that 'the machine shows great acceleration power, the tail comes up readily and directional control is good right from the start … the machine actually became airborne for a short while on the last run, but ASI readings were not observed on account of the amount of traffic on the aerodrome.'

Runs were carried out with 0 degrees and 10 degrees of flap, but it was felt unwise to comment on ground looping due to the tailwheel castoring problems. E0234's radiator flaps were in the open position, coolant temperatures being recorded as around 100°C. Following these trials it was recommended 'that a cover be placed over the emergency chassis operating plunger for fear of the crew's feet inadvertently operating it'. Note the No 1 EFTS Tiger Moths visible in the background beneath E0234's port wing. *(BAE SYSTEMS)*

Taken on the afternoon of Tuesday 25 November 1940, this historic photo shows E0234 taking off from Hatfield on its maiden flight. Piloted by Geoffrey de Havilland Junior with engine installation designer John E. Walker as observer, E0234 was at an all-up weight of 14,150lb as per the previous day's taxying tests. The flight was preceded by a short 'hop' to ensure that the flaps were not changing position in relation to each other (there had been fears that this could occur). Set at 15 degrees, the flaps were examined after the 'hop' and found to be still in the same position.

Take-off took place at 1545hrs and was reported by Geoffrey de Havilland Junior as 'straightforward and easy'. E0234's undercarriage was only retracted after considerable height had been gained, this operation being observed through the nose windows by John E. Walker. The chief objective of this flight was to check engine installation and operation, which was regarded as 'quite satisfactory', though it was recommended that starboard engine rpm be increased by 100. There appeared to be little change of trim with operation of the undercarriage, flaps or radiator cooling flaps, and all controls seemed promising. However, E0234 was flying rather 'left wing low' (a rigging adjustment was required), so it was more or less impossible to assess stability at this stage. John E. Walker observed that the undercarriage doors remained open by some 4 inches when the undercarriage was raised, this gap increasing to 12 inches when E0234 reached 220mph, the highest speed attained on this flight. The canopy direct vision quarter windows 'showed great promise as no draught enters the machine, even at 150 ASI', but it was recommended that they be made to 'fold back along the blister, making the view straight forward much better' (the latter modification was introduced on production aircraft).

E0234 was brought very close to the stall with undercarriage lowered and flaps at 25 degrees, aileron control being reported good at this end of the speed range. E0234's landing approach speed was 120mph (with flaps set at 25 degrees) and although the aircraft was held off rather too high 'there was NO indication of lateral instability and the action of the chassis was such that the machine touched the ground with the minimum of shock'. E0234 landed at 1615hrs, having been airborne for thirty minutes. *(BAE SYSTEMS)*

Geoffrey de Havilland Junior lands E0234 at Hatfield on 29 November 1940 following the aircraft's second flight. Two flights took place that day, the first between 11.40 and 12.00, the second between 12.30 and 13.10. Following the maiden flight four days earlier, adjustments had been made to E0234's aileron tabs (to cure the 'left wing low' trim tendency previously reported), and stronger bungee chord was fitted to the undercarriage doors. In an attempt to overcome its castoring problems, the tailwheel's self-centring gear had been removed and a length of bungee installed. E0234's all-up weight had been increased to 15,187lb and a 13mph W wind was recorded over the aerodrome.

The 'Experimental Aircraft Pilot's Test Record' lists the objective of the day's flights as 'Check petrol system cooling, chassis doors and general flight'. John E. Walker accompanied Geoffrey de Havilland Junior as observer for the first flight, but his report on petrol system cooling has (unfortunately) not survived. Chief Designer Ronald Bishop flew as observer on the second flight, during which it was noted that the undercarriage doors 'do not close correctly and open wider as speed is increased'. The latter problem restricted any assessment of handling, but Geoffrey de Havilland Junior reported that 'it does look as if directional stability and probably lateral stability will be satisfactory'. The adjustments to E0234's aileron tabs had overcome the tendency to fly 'left wing low', but functioning of the propellers was regarded as unsatisfactory (they were later cropped by 3 inches to cure cockpit instrument vibration). Stall investigations were carried out with the flaps set at 50 degrees, E0234 exhibiting only slight starboard wing drop, but 'thorough investigation will come later with further aft c.g. and increased load'.

Ronald Bishop spent most of the second flight pumping the undercarriage down by hand, and (as it later transpired) by compressed air, as the main oil return pipe had failed and the emergency suction line was incorrectly connected up. The undercarriage warning lights were regarded as unsatisfactory, and the tailwheel was still not castoring correctly. Note the Hurricane on the far side of the aerodrome, and the bombed-out shell of the 94 Shop directly behind E0234's tail. (BAE SYSTEMS)

E0234 photographed at Hatfield on 10 December 1940 with an experimental fillet attached to the nacelle rear section (precluding use of the flaps), together with wool tufts on the nacelle and wing. Five days earlier, during the course of E0234's fourth test flight, the aircraft had been allowed to settle down to fairly steady cruising conditions for the first time. With engines set at plus-7lb boost and 2,650rpm, E0234 was travelling at between 240 and 250mph when a general 'shake' could be felt throughout the aircraft, this being particularly noticeable on the control column. The prototype had made its first encounter with tail buffeting, a problem that was to plague the machine for much of its early testing. In order to investigate this phenomenon, wool tufts were affixed (using 'Bostik' glue) to both sides of the engine nacelles, the lower surface of the inner wing and flaps, and the flap top surfaces immediately above the nacelle. The tufts would provide an indication of air flow movement and were supplemented by fillets attached to the exhaust outlet/inner wing under surface (see next picture), together with the nacelle rear sections. Members of the design team are seen inspecting this configuration prior to flight testing, the results of which are described in the following picture caption. This view was taken in the building used for the aircraft's assembly following its arrival from Salisbury Hall. (BAE SYSTEMS)

E0234 pictured with de Havilland aerodynamicist David Newman on 10 December 1940; he is checking the installation of an aerodynamic fillet positioned between the exhaust outlet and inner port wing under surface. The fillet was designed to smooth out the airflow between the nacelle and tailplane in an attempt to eliminate the tail buffeting problem. Note the wool tufts attached to the cowling and wing surface. On this day E0234 made two flights (totalling 4hrs 50mins) in this configuration, the first with aerodynamicist Richard Clarkson as observer, the second with assistant chief designer Tim Wilkins (both had been seated in the rear fuselage to observe the tufts from the rear access door window). For these tests E0234 was also fitted with fillets and wool tufts on the aft section of both nacelles (see the previous photograph). Neither the exhaust nor nacelle fillets decreased the tail buffeting, Geoffrey de Havilland Junior reporting that 'no difference could be detected or felt on the control column'. The wool tufts were observed by de Havilland test pilot Pat Fillingham (from Hurricane 1 P3090), who flew alongside and beneath E0234 at speeds of 240 to 250mph ASI. Clarkson and Wilkins ascertained that severe stalling was taking place along the rear section of the inner nacelles, but Fillingham reported that the outer nacelle tufts 'remained nicely streamlined'. *(BAE SYSTEMS)*

In a further attempt to cure the tail buffeting, aerodynamic 'slots' (similar to those featured on the de Havilland DH.95 Flamingo airliner) were fitted to the inner nacelles of the prototype and tested on 11 December 1940. These replaced the exhaust and nacelle fillets tried the previous day and made a slight improvement, although tail buffeting was still very evident. Two test flights were carried out, Geoffrey de Havilland Junior climbing to 10,000 feet on both occasions in order to obtain calm conditions for the tests. Aerodynamicist Richard Clarkson and experimental shop foreman Fred Plumb flew as observers on the first flight, Clarkson noting from the rear fuselage that 'stalling of nacelles was okay but that stalling was still taking place along under surfaces of the wings'. On the day's second test flight, Mr Cross and Mr Gardiner flew as observers, but the aircraft had barely settled down to cruising conditions (around 265mph) when there was a smell of burning. The starboard engine cowling was blistering badly, so Geoffrey de Havilland Junior shut the engine down and returned to Hatfield. Upon examination the left exhaust of the starboard engine was discovered adrift inside the cowling – an early example of the problems that would be encountered with this initial exhaust layout. Additionally, the tailwheel was reported as still not castoring correctly. This photo depicts the 'slot' and wool tufts fitted to the inboard section of the port nacelle. A total of forty-five minutes were flown by the prototype on this day. *(BAE SYSTEMS)*

On 13 January 1941 the prototype (by now wearing its official Air Ministry serial 'W4050') made a short ten-minute flight with these aerodynamic 'slots' attached to the outboard section of the tailplane leading edge (both port and starboard). Wool tufts (illustrated here) were fixed to 'stalks' mounted on the inboard and outboard sections of the upper 'slot'. These slightly diminished the tail buffet, but the 'Experimental Aircraft Pilot's Test Record' states that 'observation of No 2 wool tuft (from outboard of tailplane) shows very considerable turbulence however'. W4050 made three flights that day and encountered problems with the port propeller, which began to function as a fixed-pitch type once the aircraft had reached cruising speed. The propeller could not be shifted into the coarse pitch position, this problem subsequently being referred to the de Havilland Airscrew Division. Former de Havilland test pilot John Cunningham (then a serving RAF Beaufighter pilot) flew as observer in W4050 during the day's test flying. Regarding the tail

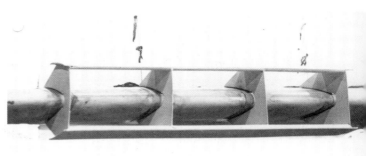

buffeting Cunningham observed: 'General "feel" just about the same as a Beaufighter, but rather a quicker stick movement period. Identical nodding up and down of the nose … on a prolonged flight this buffet and vibration constitute a very fatiguing element, the pilot being subconsciously aware of it the entire time.' *(BAE SYSTEMS)*

This side view of W4050's port undercarriage nacelle shows the original 'short' configuration with provision for the flaps to retract into the nacelle's rear lower section. The original short nacelle lower sections remain on W4050 to this day, visible beneath the flap jack inspection covers on the wing top surface. Note the Trainer Yellow colour scheme and Type A fuselage roundel. *(BAE SYSTEMS)*

Aerodynamic 'slots' fixed to W4050's starboard inner nacelle and underwing. In yet another attempt to overcome the tail buffeting problem, several 'slot' configurations were tested on W4050, the most effective consisting of 'slots' fixed spanwise on the under surface of the wing (in addition to those on the inner nacelles) between nacelle and fuselage. The latter were first evaluated on 15 December 1940 (during the aircraft's seventeenth test flight) and provided a marked improvement up to 300mph. The spanwise 'slot' pictured here was located around 2 feet further forward than previous examples, this particular arrangement being test flown on 10 January 1941. Despite this alteration the tail buffeting was more pronounced, the 'Experimental Aircraft Pilot's Test Record' reporting that the wool tufts 'displayed considerable turbulence, in fact, the tufts are described as being "as bad as ever"'. (BAE SYSTEMS)

Despite exhaustive tests with aerodynamic 'slots' fitted to W4050's engine nacelles and inboard underwing surfaces, the tail buffeting problem could not be completely eradicated. In an attempt to improve air separation from the nacelle's rear section, de Havilland's contacted the Aerodynamics Department of RAE Farnborough for advice, forwarding a report on its findings to the RAE Chief Superintendent on 7 January 1941. RAE developed a wind tunnel model and suggested that extending the nacelle would solve the buffeting. W4050's nacelles were subsequently lengthened in three stages, this photograph portraying the initial modification, which consisted of triangular plates extending the nacelle line rearwards (and faired in on their aft sections). Test-flown on 3 February 1941, the plates made no difference to the aircraft's handling but wool tufts showed an improvement in turbulence away from the nacelles. Geoffrey de Havilland Junior reported that 'the general feel of the machine is still unpleasantly bad, especially in the neighbourhood of 300mph ASI. The usual "thumping" in the pilot's seat is most noticeable.' The nacelle extensions once again precluded use of the flaps, it being noted that 'ground effect is very marked when landing with flaps not in operation'. *(BAE SYSTEMS)*

This aft view of the initial nacelle extension modification shows the faired-in triangular plates. The cables attached to the undercarriage door rear sections were secured by eyebolt anchorages and connected to tension springs fixed at the top of the rear nacelle. Access to the flap jack was provided via the square panel located on the wing upper surface trailing edge. Note the flap hinge protruding beneath the outboard port wing. All of the nacelle extension modifications applied to W4050 obviated use of the flaps. *(BAE SYSTEMS)*

On 5 February 1941 W4050 flew with this exhaust fairing fitted to the starboard inner engine cowling together with spanwise aerodynamic 'slots' on the inboard wing under surface. The spanwise 'slots' featured two vertical 'air straighteners' close to the nacelle, but this configuration made no difference to the tail buffeting. Note the manifold cooling intake located on the side cowling's forward section. First flown on W4050 during 22 January, the intake was added to alleviate exhaust manifold cooling problems and initially featured on this cowling only. Manifold cooling intakes (one on each cowling side panel) later became a standard feature of all production PR.1 and B.IV Series 1 aircraft. The compact leading edge ducted radiator installation (together with its underwing cooling flap) is well illustrated here, and contributed some 9mph in thrust to the Mosquito's top speed. The Mosquito radiator intake design was reportedly based upon data obtained from a Westland Whirlwind wind tunnel model tested at RAE Farnborough. *(BAE SYSTEMS)*

This very rare photograph illustrates a wing root fairing fitted to the starboard radiator entry on W4050. Also designed to reduce tail buffeting, these fairings (fitted on both port and starboard sides) were first flown on W4050 during a thirty-five-minute test sortie on 5 February 1941. On this occasion weather conditions cancelled any possibility of evaluating the fairing's effectiveness, so further flights were carried out the next day. The wing root fairings were tested in conjunction with inboard exhaust fillets and spanwise aerodynamic 'slots' (the latter on the inboard wing under surfaces), but Geoffrey de Havilland Junior reported, 'Although the machine feels generally smoother on account of decrease in vibration, the actual buffet is considered as being about the same, with the usual "thumping" felt in the pilot's seat.' A 'speed course' was also flown on this day, but results were not good, partly because of the weather conditions but also due to the radiator flaps being inadvertently left open after taxying out for take off. Note that the starboard direct vision quarter window (on the cockpit canopy) hinges forward towards the windscreen, later being hinged rearwards so as not to impede forward visibility. *(BAE SYSTEMS)*

W4050 lands at Hatfield on the afternoon of 10 January 1941. The prototype made four flights that day (officially recorded as 'Tests 33 to 36'), these taking place between 1445 and 1720hrs. Among the items evaluated were modifications to the closing mechanism for the undercarriage doors, a new arrangement of anti-buffet 'slots' on the engine nacelles and underwing (see the picture on page 27), and operation of the radiator cooling flaps and undercarriage retraction system. The undercarriage door bungee cables had been tensioned up prior to the day's flying and only opened by ¼ to ⅜in at 300mph (a marked improvement over the initial test flights the previous November). The radiator cooling flaps were noted as 'commencing to shift down a little at 150mph IAS and are down by about 1.25in (measured at trailing end) at 300mph IAS at nacelle end.'

In order to carry out adjustments to hydraulic pressure, a representative from the Lockheed (Hydraulics) Company flew in W4050 during 'Test 34', this gentleman becoming the first non-de Havilland man to fly in a Mosquito. All anti-buffet 'slots' were removed for the day's last test flight, but the port undercarriage failed to retract and fell down when nearly up. To quote the 'Experimental Aircraft Pilot's Test Record': 'As the port undercarriage red light had failed during the previous flight, the fact of the chassis not being retracted was not known, and the machine was flown for some time with this leg swinging about.' As a result it was not possible to give a fair report on the tail buffeting.

Beside the Lockheed representative, other observers who flew with Geoffrey de Havilland on this day were Richard Clarkson, Brian Cross, Mr Fitch and Mervyn Waghorn. During tests to establish the cause of W4050's tail buffeting, the observation port in the rear fuselage access door provided a prime vantage point for viewing movement of the wool tufts affixed to the starboard inner nacelle. Note the starboard flap retracting into the nacelle rear section. *(BAE SYSTEMS)*

This photograph of W4050's port engine nacelle shows the second and third extension modifications designed to eliminate tail buffeting. The second modification is the pointed fillet extending backwards from the nacelle's top section, the third consisting of the deeper-profiled fairing running from the lower nacelle before curving up to meet the fillet. As 'Test 69', these nacelle extensions (with all anti-buffet 'slots' removed from the aircraft) were evaluated on 9 February 1941, the 'Experimental Aircraft Pilot's Test Record' stating: 'There is no doubt that this modification has had the greatest curative effect of tail buffet to date, and could be regarded as "acceptable". However, an even smoother flow is really desirable. Observation of wool tufts also indicates a far less turbulent flow away from the nacelles. The "thumping" referred to in previous tests is still discernable throughout the machine, but to greatly reduced degree.' On later production Mosquitoes the lower fairing profile was extended out even further (meeting the point of the fillet), this final form of nacelle extension initially being fitted to Fighter prototype W4052. Note the mudguard protruding from the undercarriage bay. *(BAE SYSTEMS)*

This rear view shows the second and third nacelle extension modifications made to W4050. The production form of extended nacelle necessitated splitting the flap on either side of the extension, the two halves being joined together with torque tubes (design work for this modification was overseen by Henry 'H. O.' Baker). On the same day that these nacelle extensions were flight-tested (9 February 1941) John Cunningham became the second pilot to fly W4050. The 'Experimental Aircraft Pilot's Test Record' states his impressions thus: 'On test No 70, John Cunningham piloted the machine and was very greatly impressed with lightness of the controls, especially ailerons, and general pleasant handling characteristics. He adversely criticised the closing of the throttles on take off, unless the damper is tightened up to an excessive degree. He also did not like the big change of trim with flap operation.' Earlier that day the starboard 'tear drop' observation blister was torn away in a shallow dive; no air subsequently entered the cockpit, but a definite suction out was recorded. Note the port radiator cover lying on top of the wing. *(BAE SYSTEMS)*

In April 1941 the Air Ministry instructed de Havilland's to equip two Fighter Mosquitoes with four-gun Bristol turrets, prototypes W4053 and W4073 (then under construction at Salisbury Hall) being selected for this installation. To assess the effect of the turret on handling and level speed, W4050 received this mock-up unit, which was test-flown on 24 and 25 July 1941. Over these two days seven flights were made ('Tests 162 to 168'), piloting being shared between Geoffrey de Havilland Junior and George Gibbins, with Mervyn Waghorn and Brian Cross as observers. Aside from reduced level speed, restricted rear view and slightly increased tail buffet at the stall, the turret appeared to have very little effect on W4050's general flying qualities. The dummy guns were located forwards and upwards, aft and sideways (observe the attachment holes in the 'turret' side), the whole installation cutting maximum level speed by around 20mph. Note the camouflage finish on W4050's upper surfaces, this Dark Earth and Dark Green scheme originally being applied prior to A&AEE trials the previous February.

During the dummy gun turret tests, de Havilland Flight Test records describe W4050's general condition as follows: 'The aircraft is in an extremely bad external condition, being hand camouflaged and having all fillered surfaces cracked and peeling off.' Note that the starboard flap and aileron have been removed. Originally equipped with fabric-covered ailerons, W4050 first flew with metal-skinned units on 3 February 1941, Geoffrey de Havilland Junior reporting them as '…an improvement on the fabric-covered type. They feel lighter at speed (although not very much lighter), do not have the "spongy" feeling of fabric-covered ailerons and do not snatch near the stall.' W4050's original fabric-covered ailerons required 30 inches of cane on the under surface of the starboard unit before satisfactory lateral trim could be attained. Metal ailerons required no cane and exhibited superior lateral trim characteristics, this count alone leading to their eventual adoption on production Mosquitoes. The canopy 'tear drop' observation blisters have been replaced by flat Perspex panels, the blisters having shown a tendency to shatter during dive tests. *(BAE SYSTEMS)*

Photographs of W4050 airborne are extremely scarce, but within weeks of the manuscript being completed this rare image came to light. W4050's short engine nacelles, single-stage supercharged engines and original exhaust outlet/ manifold cooling intake layout on the engine side cowlings positively date this picture as 1941, probably between June and July. Note the Dark Earth and Dark Green camouflaged upper surfaces and Trainer Yellow under surfaces. The aircraft's serial number is applied in yellow. *(Source unknown)*

In connection with development work for the Mosquito Fighter-Bomber variant, 250lb bomb-carriers and fairings were fitted beneath W4050's outboard wings during October 1941. On 20 October Geoffrey de Havilland Junior flight-tested W4050 to evaluate the effect of the carriers (with and without bombs) on W4050's handling and level speed. He reported: 'Tests done on W4050 indicate that the fitting of two 250lb bombs to the wings of this machine has no effect on the general handling characteristics. The carriers alone cause a loss of approximately 5mph, and the carriers with their bombs some 9mph at 22,000ft. These losses are less at lower altitudes.' Note the Handley Page leading edge slot, locked in position with metal bands. W4050 was the only Mosquito fitted with Handley Page slots, but the aircraft's stall behaviour deemed them unnecessary – look at W4050 today and you can still see them (complete with original locking bands) beneath the leading edge fabric. Note the 'Circle P' (for 'Prototype') marking on W4050's rear fuselage. In this picture the aircraft retains its original short engine nacelle configuration, the production extended shape being permanently installed the following year. *(BAE SYSTEMS)*

This well-known photograph of W4050 equipped with two-speed, two-stage supercharged Merlin 61s was taken at Hatfield in September 1942. Standing forward of the nose is John de Havilland with 'Johnnie', the Experimental Flight Test Department 'shop boy', to his left. W4050 pioneered the Mosquito's two-speed, two-stage supercharged Merlin installation, making its first flight with Merlin 61s on 20 June 1942. These Merlins significantly increased altitude and maximum level speed performance, W4050 readily attaining heights in excess of 38,000 feet during the first month of testing. For the initial Merlin 61 flights (carried out by Geoffrey de Havilland Junior, John de Havilland and Pat Fillingham) W4050 retained its short engine nacelles and short-span (19ft 5½in) 'No 1' tailplane, these having been required for A&AEE trials the previous month; however, production-shape nacelle extensions and a long-span (20ft 9in) 'No 2' tailplane were installed shortly afterwards.

During July 1942 comparison trials were made between three- and four-bladed propellers, these including position error tests followed by climb and level speed trials with and without tropical intakes and snow guards (the latter two items fitted to the carburettor air intakes on the lower engine cowlings). Equipped with Merlin 61s (and at an all-up weight of 18,000lb) W4050 recorded some exceptionally high level speeds including 428mph at 28,500 feet (with straight-through intakes plus snowguards and with engines in full supercharger gear), and 437mph at 29,200 feet (with straight-through intakes less snowguards and with engines in full supercharger gear). These were the highest level speeds attained by any Mosquito up to that time, but even greater things were to follow.

The two-speed, two-stage supercharged Merlin required an intercooler between the supercharger and the cylinders. This had its own coolant circulating system, so an additional radiator had to be provided to cater for this. On the Mosquito this was located under the forward section of the engine and featured a cooling intake immediately beneath the spinner. The additional supercharger extended the length of the engine, bringing the Mosquito's spinners forward of the nose line. In this picture W4050 is equipped with three-bladed propellers and snowguards, and the intake 'lips' for the intercooler radiators are clearly visible on the forward lower cowlings. The aircraft's 'short' 52½-foot wingspan is evident here. *(BAE SYSTEMS)*

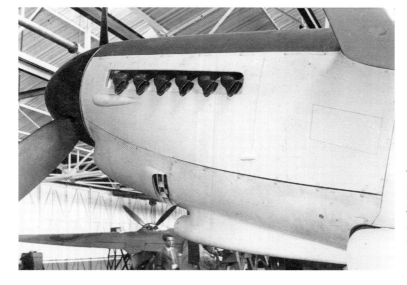

Taken at Hatfield in August 1942, this view predominantly features an experimental Merlin 72 installation on Bomber prototype W4057. However, the background is certainly worth noting for it appears to illustrate W4050 while equipped with four-bladed propellers. *(BAE SYSTEMS)*

A well-used W4050 photographed towards the close of its operational career. Following trials with Merlin 61s, W4050 was grounded in October 1942 in readiness for installing Merlin 70 series engines (a 72 on the port side and a 77 on the starboard) equipped with Bendix Stromberg carburettors. During this process, and in connection with development work on the NF.XV, W4050 received extended wingtips, increasing the overall wing span to 59ft 2in. The aircraft was first flown in this configuration (by John de Havilland) on 8 December 1942, the second flight taking place two days later when the value of 'Worth' oil dilution valves in the fuel pressure line to the carburettor was assessed. Between 12 and 29 December W4050 underwent tests to determine the effect on ceiling and rate of climb of the increase in span. W4050 was initially flown with the 59ft 2in wingspan, then with its original 52ft 5in span. Since W4050 was not equipped with a pressure cabin, partial ceiling climbs were carried out at 2,650rpm and in medium supercharger gear, for crew comfort. Results indicated a maximum rate of climb with the 52ft 5in span of 145mph, this dropping to 140mph with the 59ft 2in span. The greatest altitude reached on test with the 52ft 5in span was 35,800 feet, 36,300 feet being attained with the 59ft 2in span.

The official de Havilland report on these trials summarised the results thus: 'It seems reasonable, therefore, having regard to the experimental errors involved in the measurement, to say that the value of span stretching for ceiling and rate of climb near the ceiling on the Mosquito is perhaps 70 percent of the calculated theoretical effect. This may be summarised by saying that on the Mosquito an increase of absolute ceiling of about 200 feet per 1 foot increase in span may be expected.'

Between January and July 1943 W4050 conducted a variety of tests including full-throttle climb, partial climb and level speed trials with four-bladed propellers, together with comparison trials with three-bladed propellers of both British and American manufacture. During climbs to 40,000 feet, the port and starboard main coolant temperatures remained consistently equal up to 35,000 feet, but during the remainder of the climb the starboard temperature gradually rose above the port to a difference of 15°C. This was thought to be due to the fact that at high angles of incidence, heat from the exhaust stubs was directed into the radiator inlet duct by the upgoing propeller blade. Records indicate that during level speed trials with Merlin 70 series engines W4050 attained 439mph at 28,400 feet. Note the reinforcement band on the nose (covered with red doped fabric) and the later style of fin flash and fuselage roundel. *(Michael J. F. Bowyer collection)*

W4050 receives attention to its starboard Merlin 77 at Hatfield on 11 November 1943. Experimental Flight Test Department Inspector Dick Whittingham looked after W4050 for the majority of 1943 and regularly flew in the aircraft with Geoffrey de Havilland Junior. Dick recalls one particular test flight with Geoffrey when they raced a new Mark of Spitfire (type unknown and flown by a pilot from the de Havilland Engine Company) across Hertfordshire. At full throttle W4050 and the Spitfire were absolutely level, so Geoffrey pulled the emergency boost control (referred to as the 'tit' and used only if absolutely necessary) and W4050 immediately pulled ahead, leaving the Spitfire in its wake. Back on the ground at Hatfield the Spitfire pilot said to Geoffrey, 'I know what you did, you pulled the "tit" didn't you?', to which Geoffrey replied, 'What, with an Inspector sitting next to me?'

Following the climb and level speed trials during the early part of the year, W4050 spent the majority of 1943 testing experimental exhaust stubs and shrouds, encountering engine starting and surge problems along the way (the latter resolved by Rolls Royce at Hucknall). This picture was taken almost at the end of W4050's active career, for evidence would suggest the aircraft was grounded in early December 1943. The exhaust shroud on the port outer side cowling was probably being tested in connection with development work on the Mosquito NF.30. A new FB.VI is visible on the left. *(BAE SYSTEMS)*

de Havilland apprentices are pictured with W4050 at Hatfield on 12 February 1944. Just over a month earlier (on 7 January), Experimental Flight Test Department Inspector Dick Whittingham conducted a general survey of W4050, compiling a list of the non-standard parts as the aircraft was scheduled to be scrapped. Luckily, of course, this never happened, W4050 remaining at Hatfield in use (it is believed) as an instructional airframe. The Merlin 70 series engines were replaced by Merlin 25s, the machine later 'starring' (playing itself) in the Merton Park Studios production *de Havilland Presents The Mosquito*. During the latter, W4050 is featured 'undergoing completion' in addition to appearing on the aerodrome at Hatfield for 'pre and post first flight' scenes (with Geoffrey de Havilland Junior). In this photograph W4050 retains its port Merlin 72 but the starboard propeller (and probably the starboard engine) has been removed. The large patch on the fuselage side (visible immediately adjacent to the port inboard flap) was applied following a heavy landing at Boscombe Down in May 1941. W4050 was later purchased (for £25!) from the Air Ministry and returned to Salisbury Hall for use by the de Havilland Technical College, this move taking place in either late 1945 or early 1946. Note the PR.XVI parked to W4050's right. *(BAE SYSTEMS)*

The prototype was displayed as a static exhibit during the 1946 SBAC show at Radlett. W4050's appearance at this venue was arranged by Bill Baird, assistant to de Havilland Public Relations Manager C. Martin Sharp. To demonstrate the Mosquito's great versatility, Bill arranged for W4050 to be displayed with an example of virtually every piece of armament and equipment ever carried by the design. In early 1984 Bill Baird recalled events leading up to the show: 'The Mosquito was reckoned to be able to carry "everything but the kitchen stove" so my chief, C. Martin Sharp, asked me to locate such a kitchen stove and place it with the armament and equipment on display with W4050 at the SBAC show. This I did, and found a suitable example in a builder's yard in Potters Bar, which I then hired for the duration of the show – there is no record of it having flown in a Mosquito though…' Note the range of drop tanks displayed in the foreground (running from left to right, these are 50, 100 and 200 gallon types), and the fighter-style canopy and 57mm cannon beneath W4050's starboard engine. The kitchen stove was placed next to the port side of W4050's rear fuselage, its base clearly visible in this shot. *(Jim D. Oughton, via Stuart Howe)*

Following W4050's successful appearance at the 1946 SBAC show, Bill Baird arranged for it to be displayed at the 1947 show, also held at Radlett. Seen on 12 September, W4050 was once again surrounded by a multitude of loads capable of being carried by different variants of the design. Note that 'paddle'-blade propellers have replaced the 'needle'-blade units installed on W4050 the previous year. W4050's current restoration will result in the aircraft being returned to this appearance and configuration. *(BAE SYSTEMS)*

In September 1958 W4050 returned 'home' to Salisbury Hall for the very last time. The wings and fuselage were transported from the 'Fiddle Bridge Stores' (located in Fiddle Bridge Lane just outside Hatfield aerodrome) on two 'Queen Mary' trailers specially loaned by the RAF. The move was co-ordinated by the de Havilland Transport & Services Department at Hatfield. Note the Robin hangar in the background, which was to become the aircraft's new home and where it is still kept to this day. The crane in the background (supplied by the Hatfield factory) was used to lift W4050 off the trailers. The concrete hardstand in the foreground was formerly the base of the old Airspeed hangar, where the Horsa glider prototype was constructed and which housed W4050 during the late 1940s when in use by the de Havilland Technical School. Prior to its departure from Hatfield W4050 had been 'spruced up' in readiness for its new career as a museum exhibit. *(BAE SYSTEMS)*

Following arrival from Hatfield in September 1958, W4050 was assembled in its new hangar at Salisbury Hall the following month. This work was carried out by volunteers from the Hatfield factory, most of whom had previously worked on Mosquitoes and were more than happy to lend a hand. Major Walter Goldsmith, the new owner of Salisbury Hall (and the man responsible for the plan to bring W4050 back 'home'), is standing by the port wing's leading edge while his children sit on top of the fuselage. *(BAE SYSTEMS)*

W4050 is seen on display at Salisbury Hall during the early 1970s, resplendent in its freshly painted yellow scheme. Note the Molins 57mm cannon exhibited beneath the aircraft. *(Stuart Howe)*

Mosquito Construction

The Mosquito's wooden airframe was an anachronism in the age of the metal monoplane, yet this 'throwback' to a bygone age outperformed nearly all of its contemporaries and is today regarded as a benchmark in aeronautical design and construction.

Pre-war the de Havilland Company was well versed in the construction of high-performance wooden aircraft, having produced the record-breaking Comet racer and the four-engined Albatross airliner. Both designs achieved high efficiency through aerodynamic cleanliness and low skin area. With the imminence of war de Havilland's turned its attentions to the design of a wooden high-speed unarmed bomber, which eventually emerged as the Mosquito. Despite official disinterest in both the concept and the manufacturing medium, de Havilland's pressed its case, which was eventually accepted by the Air Ministry, thanks largely to the intervention of Sir Wilfred Freeman, Air Member for Design and Development.

On the construction side de Havilland's advocated that wood offered great advantages through strength, lightness and ease of manufacture. Timber construction would speed up prototype development and make use of a vast untapped woodworking industry at a time when metal industries were under great pressure. Stressed wooden skins obviated the necessity for internal strengthening, providing installation space for equipment, fuel tanks and armament. Ducted radiators and exhaust thrust, together with wood's smooth external finish, were all factors in the attainment of high speed. Of course all this proved to be, production initially taking place at de Havilland's Hatfield factory but later widely sub-contracted to reduce loss of output should production plants be bombed.

The plywood and balsa sandwich monocoque fuselage was produced in two halves over wooden or concrete moulds, the completed halves greatly easing the installation of internal equipment in addition to keeping workers out of each other's way. For lightness, strength and simplicity, the Mosquito wing was built in one piece, comprising laminated spruce forward and rear spars with a double top skin and single lower skin of birch plywood. The tailplane and fin were similar in construction to the wing, consisting of spruce spars but with half-box interspar and nose ribs. The rudder was metal-framed and covered in fabric, ailerons and elevators eventually being of all-metal construction (early aircraft featured fabric-covered elevators).

Mosquito production rapidly accelerated the development of wood-bonding cements, early casein glues being replaced by more durable formaldehyde-based resins. With its closely cowled Rolls Royce Merlin engines and radiators built into the wing leading edge, the Mosquito design presented a very low frontal area, which (combined with its smooth external skin surface) greatly contributed to its extremely high performance.

As the demand for production increased, mass production techniques were imported from the motor industry, and additional assembly lines were set up at Standard Motors in Coventry, Airspeed at Portsmouth, and Percival Aircraft at Luton. More than 400 subcontractors were turned over to building Mosquito components in the UK, ranging from coachbuilders and furniture manufacturers to small engineering companies and cottage industries. The de Havilland Second Aircraft Group (SAG) shadow factory at Leavesden (planned well in advance) specialised in the manufacture of Night-Fighter and Trainer variants. Mosquito production also took place in the Canadian and Australian de Havilland factories, the former regarded as a vital source of supply should the war situation deteriorate in Britain. Canadian production totalled more than 1,000, largely focused on Bomber variants but also including Fighter-Bombers and Trainers. More than 200 Australian aircraft were produced at Bankstown near Sydney, all based on the Fighter-Bomber airframe. Both Canadian and Australian production incorporated American-built Packard Merlin engines. Mosquito production terminated in 1950 when the final batch of NF.38s left the de Havilland Chester factory in the UK.

To use a modern term, the Mosquito was, in many ways, one of the first high-performance military aircraft constructed from 'composite' materials.

Mahogany moulds for the construction of Mosquito fuselage half shells are seen at the Aldenham bus depot works. Plywood double-curvature limitations dictated the production of the monocoque fuselage in two separate halves. This offered considerable production advantages as it simplified the installation of equipment and services before the halves were joined along the centre-line. Each half was built horizontally (with its joint line face down) on a male mould shaped to the interior form of the fuselage. The first stage of manufacture began with the installation of fuselage bulkheads one to six within transverse slots on the mould. The slots located the bulkheads longitudinally, lateral retention being provided by stops pressing the bulkheads inwards following skin application. The fuselage side panels and bomb doors were produced as an integral part of the half shell and were later detached as separate units. The main attachments for the wing, together with their support member, were also moulded into each half shell, their fittings located on the mould via pins running through the fuselage pick-up lug.

Next, the inner plywood skin (a three-ply birch 1.5 and 2mm thick) was applied across the structural members, vertical joints between skin panels designed to occur between and no less than 6 inches from the bulkheads. Longitudinal joints were made on spruce stringers, which formed part of the between-skin stiffening structure. Scarfed and glued narrower strips of skin were used for the enhanced double curvatures of the nose. Once the inner skin had been glued and applied, flexible steel band cramps were employed to hold it in position. The cramps were tightened by turnbuckles (rotated by a tommy-bar), which drew the bands hard over the skin surface, applying great pressure during the bonding process. The cramps were positioned closely to ensure pressure was applied across the whole skin surface. The skin was pierced during bonding (via holes in the cramps), allowing excess glue to escape.

A stiffening structure of laminated spruce was applied between the inner and outer skins, providing extra strength at bulkhead stations, where they were screwed through the inner skin. The next stage was to attach the balsa-wood centre filling, which acted as a stabilising core between the extremely thin inner and outer fuselage skins. Around 3/8 inch thick, the balsa was glued in strips across the whole area of between-skin members and held in position by cramps. Afterwards the balsa was smoothed to the fuselage contours before the three-ply birch outer skin was glued in position and the cramps applied once more.

As complete units the half shells were later lifted off the moulds and despatched to the assembly department. The mould seen in the immediate foreground has been fitted with bulkheads and internal structure plus the first sections of rear fuselage inner skin, the latter cramped in position. The Aldenham bus depot formed part of the de Havilland Second Aircraft Group (SAG) shadow factory organisation, planned as early as 1940 to cope with wartime demands on aircraft production. Note the steel band cramps hanging along the far wall. Mosquito fuselage moulds were later constructed of concrete. *(BAE SYSTEMS)*

Fighter fuselage half shells are seen in the Hatfield assembly shop prior to equipment installation and 'boxing-up'. The shells are supported within simple vertical cradles positioned over their forward, rear and mid sections. The first task for the assembly shop staff was the installation of 'ferrules' on the half shell interior skins; these were designed for attaching interior fittings to the fuselage and comprised a plywood disc mounted on an ebonite or wood plug. Within the plug a threaded brass ferrule was set with its open end in the disc centre. Holes for installing the ferrules were drilled in the fuselage skin from the inside, a large wooden template ensuring that the holes did not break through the outer fuselage skin. The plugs were glued into the holes and the ferrules affixed by tacks through the plywood disc. In this photograph ferrules have been installed in the nose and cockpit areas of the half shell on the right. At this stage most of the interior equipment was installed, the separate fuselage halves facilitating ease of access in addition to keeping production workers out of each other's way.

The fuselage shell interiors were sprayed with water-resistant paint, after which the fuselage metal fittings were electrically bonded. The control cable runs were fitted to the fuselage port side, with the majority of hydraulic piping on the starboard side; this greatly simplified the assembly process. Before joining the fuselage halves the rudder and elevator linkages were installed, together with the control column.

The number '837' chalked on the forward (right-hand) vertical cradle may well refer to the construction number '98837', which was assigned to Hatfield-built FB.VI HJ791. This aircraft served with 605 Squadron from 23 June 1943, passing to 60 OTU in April the following year. Allocated to 13 OTU on 15 March 1945, HJ791 crashed into the sea off Filey during a night cross-country exercise on 4 August 1945. *(BAE SYSTEMS)*

Conducted on a purpose-built fixture, the process of joining the fuselage half shells was known as 'boxing-up'. Both half shells were located (by the forward and rear wing spar fittings) on trunnion-mounted pick-up arms affixed to a pedestal. Levelling pads were built into the pick-up arms, these acting as datum faces for placing the fuselage level both longitudinally and

transversely. The rear fuselage was supported in a cradle (divided in half on its centre-line), which could be drawn apart to ease the mounting of the fuselage for mating the two shells. The fuselage nose section was supported by cradles mounted on screw-jacks, allowing vertical adjustments for levelling (through clinometer readings using nose datum points for reference). Checks on the fuselage centre-line position were carried out via plumb lines (suspended from mid-points on the bulkheads) aligned with floor datum markings. Due to the removal of the fuselage side panels and the subsequent wing 'gap', a jury strut was fitted across the 'gap' to maintain structural integrity and prevent distortion during assembly. The fuselage half shells were edged

with male to female laminated spruce wedge joints, which were glued and screwed. The inter-skin member on the free edge of the starboard shell was shaped into a 'V' section, which located into a 'V'-shaped recess on the corresponding section of the port shell. Inside and out, the skin was recessed on each side of the centre-line to accommodate a plywood strip fitted flush with the skin (a second strip, double the width of the first, was applied to the inside of the fuselage).

In this picture former cabinetmaker Herbert Holgate is attaching the lower external centre-line plywood strip prior to the rear fuselage being lowered into the boxing-up fixture. Once glued together, the half shells were cramped together with wooden bands drawn together using turnbuckle fasteners, rear fuselage bulkhead seven (seen here) being glued in position afterwards Note the diagonally applied plywood skins on the rear fuselage, designed to increase strength and reduce twist in this high-stress area. The separate (trestle-shaped) halves of the rear 'boxing-up' fixture are clearly evident here. *(Crown Copyright)*

This production line scene at Hatfield in 1945 shows Miss Eva Doe (left) and a colleague of the Mosquito Dope Shop attaching fabric to a Mosquito fuselage. For waterproofing and strengthening purposes, the Mosquito airframe was covered in Madapolam and Irish Linen fabric (the latter employed on the leading edge and the top surfaces of the wing), attached using either red or clear cellulose tautening dope. Prior to fabric application, all screw and brad holes on the external skin surface were filled with 'Titanine' white stopper and rubbed down flush. Next, two coats of either clear or red dope were brushed on to the skin in preparation for receiving the fabric. Once in position, dope was brushed on and the fabric stretched and smoothed down until it firmly adhered to the skin surface. Fabric tapes were then doped on all edges and openings and drain eyelets fixed where necessary. Finally, as protection against the ultraviolet

rays of the sun, four coats of aluminium dope were sprayed on in preparation for the external paint finish. In this picture Eva Doe is applying the initial coat of red dope while her colleague fixes a fabric tape to the edge of the rear fuselage. The rudder mounting post is visible at the top of the rear fuselage bulkhead (bulkhead number seven) with the rudder trim tab jack directly beneath it. The tailplane-to-fuselage pick-up joints are located on the centre outboard sections of bulkhead seven. The lack of face masks on these two ladies (in the proximity of such noxious cellulose fumes) would alarm today's Health & Safety inspectors! To ensure a smooth surface finish (particularly over double curvature sections on the nose) with no creases or air bubbles, this extremely messy job required great skill and dexterity. Note the tailwheel jack protruding from the lower section of the fuselage. *(BAE SYSTEMS)*

Wing rear main spars are being manufactured at one of the many sub-contractors employed on Mosquito production during the war. The Mosquito wing was a two-spar structure built in one piece. Both spars were of box construction and featured laminated spruce booms with plywood webs. The front spar was straight but the rear spar incorporated forward sweep and dihedral, which gave the wing its distinctive shape. Initially, front spar booms were made of three horizontal laminations and rear spars of three vertical laminations. Laminations permitted ease of manufacture and were a more efficient use of spruce supplies. However, on later production aircraft the three laminations were altered to ten in an effort to conserve wood. The rear spar booms were built up from a centre section and comprised two outer sections and two tip extensions, all spliced at 1 in 15. On the extreme right of this photograph rear spar booms have been placed in a bonding fixture shaped to the required angle of forward sweep, and screw clamps are being used to force the glued laminations hard down over the formed base of the fixture. During the drying process the laminations would permanently set to the required shape. Casein glue was initially used for Mosquito construction, but this was later replaced by more durable formaldehyde resins. Spar accuracy over a 50-foot length amounted to 0.04in, an astoundingly precise figure for such a high wartime production rate. The sign hanging from the roof reads: 'Never hide up an error or mistake – report at once to works manager. An error is no sin but failure to report is'. (DHAMT Ltd)

A starboard upper wing outer surface skin panel being offered up to the wing itself. The upper surface of the Mosquito wing featured two skins separated by a 'sandwich' of Douglas fir stringers. On the outboard lower surface panels and the inner top skin, the stringers were assembled with the wing as single units. The inner top skin (referred to as the 'inner shell') was constructed in three sections: a centre portion with stringers projecting from each side, and two outboard sections, the stringers of which were scarf-jointed to those of the centre portion. The stringers were composed of scarf-jointed shorter lengths, the taper of the scarfing being saw-cut. The skins were assembled from scarf-jointed sections and drilled through wooden templates. During assembly with the inner skin, the stringers were located with metal-faced slots on a horizontally mounted table. Glue was then applied to the top surface of the stringers and the skin underside, before the skin was laid over the table and located by metal stops. The skin was then screwed down using pump screwdrivers, which supplied the pressure necessary to ensure a good joint. Following assembly of reinforcing plies and the cutting out of inspection and access panels, the outer skins were sprayed with red dope and the stringers coated with white (water-resistant) paint.

The upper wing surface outer skin panels were made from smaller sections, scarfed and glued. These were first offered up to the inner shell (as shown here) and adjusted to align the pre-drilled attachment holes with the spar booms and stringers of the inner shell. Before attachment, the skin's inner surface was completely coated in glue, which, in addition to acting as the adhesive, also waterproofing the plywood. A gang of men were needed to apply the wing skin, which was then screwed to the spar booms and the stringers of the inner shell (some 28 gross of brass screws were used to attach the upper wing skin alone). The inner shell stringers are clearly visible here. *(BAE SYSTEMS)*

This rare shot shows PR.1 or B.IV Series 1 wings under construction at Hatfield in 1941. Note the single-piece flaps on the wing in the foreground (the starboard unit has yet to be fitted), a characteristic feature of these early production Mosquitoes. The fabric covering on this particular wing has yet to be brought up to silver dope status.
(BAE SYSTEMS)

This is the interior of an engine cowling side panel as fitted to the PR.1 and B.IV Series 1. Of all-metal construction, the Mosquito engine cowlings were manufactured on jigs, individual units being 'handed' for installation on the engine inboard and outboard sides. Note the recess for the exhaust manifold cooling intake (forward) and the opening for the exhaust manifold exit duct (rear). This is a starboard engine outer side cowling. *(BAE SYSTEMS)*

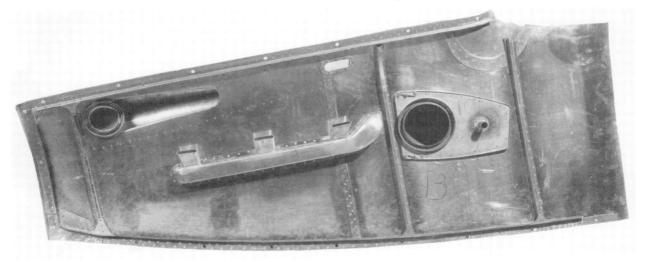

Fabric tapes being doped to newly constructed Mosquito tailplanes at Hoopers Coachbuilders, Park Royal, West London. Structurally (and in appearance) the tailplane resembled a reversed version of the wing and featured pronounced sweep-back on its leading edge. Like the wing, the tailplane was manufactured in one piece and comprised laminated spruce forward and rear box spars, with half-box interspar and nose ribs.

The tailplane was assembled in two distinct stages within vertical fixtures, the leading edge and front spar being treated as a separate assembly. The front spar was pre-drilled and the fuselage pick-up fittings initially assembled by bolting them up to the existing holes. The front spar was located to datum centre-lines on the forward web, locations being provided (on the fixture) for the outboard end ribs in order to dictate overall length. The latter was vital as proper clearance for the elevator horn balances (which overlapped the tailplane tips) was required. Rib posts were pre-positioned on the spar faces, so nose ribs were placed from these as well as slot locations on the fixture. Final setting and gluing of the nose ribs was carried out using datum centre-lines on the ribs and spar.

The leading-edge curve was similarly set to a datum line before being glued and screwed in position. Shaping of the leading edge was carried out by hand, after which the leading edge structure was ready for transfer to the main assembly fixture. As on the front spar, the rear spar fittings were initially mounted out of fixture. The centre hinge fittings were first mounted to the holes pre-drilled in the spar together with the outer tailplane hinge brackets. Within the main assembly fixture, the rear spar was located on the hinge fittings while the leading edge was once again located from the fuselage attachment fittings on the front spar. The box-type interspar ribs were attached by sliding them in over the rib posts (located on the inner web of each spar) before gluing and pinning them in position. The plywood skin covering on each side was attached as a single panel (scarfed from smaller sections), and glued, screwed and pinned to the structure. Following application of the first skin, the tailplane was removed from the fixture for bonding of its metal fittings and internal spraying with water-resistant white paint. The complete unit was then returned to the fixture to receive its second skin and a covering of Madapolam. In this photograph workers are clear-doping 12- and 10-inch-wide serrated edge fabric tapes (the 10-inch one on top of the 12-inch) to the tailplane leading edges to protect the latter from stones and dirt thrown up during landing and take-off. In addition to tailplanes, Hoopers Coachbuilders also manufactured Mosquito wings and drop tanks. *(BAE SYSTEMS)*

B.IV Series ii DZ606 pictured on the final assembly line at Hatfield in May 1943. The Hatfield assembly line consisted of a track system laid out in 'U' form; aircraft moved down one side of the 'U' before traversing the end to return down the other side. A notable feature of this layout was the low working level (and subsequent excellent accessibility) at which aircraft were supported throughout the various assembly operations. At the beginning of the assembly line, the wing was positioned on cradles located outboard of each engine nacelle, screw jacks (on the cradles) being used to provide vertical adjustments. The entire system of supports rested on a wheeled bogie, which ran along the assembly line tracks, step-ladders also being fitted (visible between DZ606's nose and port engine) to provide access to the wing top surface.

Once the wing was levelled in position, the fuselage was lowered on to it (via an overhead crane) before the tail assembly and tailwheel were fitted. These were followed by the radiators, fuel and oil tanks, radio equipment and bomb racks. At the engine installation stage, branch tracks from the overhead conveyor system were employed to offer the engines up to their mounting points, both engines being fitted (with their bearers) as complete units. The engine nacelles and undercarriage doors were then added before the aircraft crossed to the return section of the assembly line track. DZ606 is pictured shortly after the latter operation (travelling from left to right), and will shortly undergo undercarriage retraction tests (using pits sunk into the floor) before receiving its propellers, spinners and engine cowlings. Following AID inspection, the newly assembled Mosquito would then be wheeled away to the paint shop for final finishing.

On 3 June 1943 DZ606 was delivered to Vickers at Weybridge for conversion to carry the 4,000lb bomb. Just over two months later it was delivered to 10 MU, but returned to de Havilland's for modifications on 12 December. Allocated to 692 Squadron on 20 February 1944, DZ606 passed to 627 Squadron on 12 March (receiving the unit code letters 'AZ-M') and operated to Frankfurt the following night. By 12 April the aircraft had completed nineteen operational sorties with 627 Squadron and passed to 139 Squadron later that month. A brief spell at 1655 MTU (in April 1944) was followed by a return to operations with 139 Squadron, and by 7 June DZ606 had flown a further twenty-nine sorties. Later returning to 1655 MTU, this Mosquito rejoined 627 Squadron in November 1944 (this time being coded 'AZ-H') and completed thirty-seven more operations by the war's end. Delivered to 109 Squadron in October 1945, DZ606 was damaged on 17 October and Struck Off Charge later that month.

The workers in the foreground are checking the engine installation, while the female worker on the right attaches the external band for the Perspex nose mounting. Note DZ606's construction number (98622) chalked on the starboard side of the nose. *(Central Press)*

Fuselage bulkhead construction under way at W. L. Thurgood Coachworks in Ware, Hertfordshire. The Mosquito fuselage consisted of seven bulkheads, each comprising two plywood skins separated by spruce blocks and all manufactured on separate jigs. Note the completed number seven bulkheads on the table in the foreground, and the newly manufactured bulkhead assemblies stacked up on the extreme right. Number seven bulkhead carried the tailplane and fin (rear) attachment fittings, all assembled to jig and placed in position by the time the bulkhead arrived at the fuselage for assembly. Spruce rings replaced the balsa core at points where the fuselage bulkheads were attached to the fuselage. In addition to tailplanes, W. L. Thurgood also produced Mosquito underwing drop tanks. *(BAE SYSTEMS)*

Ailerons are under construction in the sheet metal department of a Watford-based sub-contractor (believed to be 'Greycaines' Garage) during the war. Mosquito ailerons were 12ft 5½in long and extended inboard from the wingtip to the edge of the outboard flap. Of all-metal construction, they featured a flanged alcad spar to which were riveted flanged ribs and nose formers, with an alcad sheet covering. Mass balance weights were attached to the forward end of the nose formers and metal balance tabs to their inboard ends (the latter secured by piano-type hinges). Each aileron was attached to the wing by bolts passing through forked lugs at three hinge brackets. Adjustments to hinge alignment were made by installing washers behind the hinge brackets and shims on each side of the forked lugs. The balance tabs were linked by connecting rods to levers on the inner hinge ribs. The port balance lever was adjustable from the cockpit for aileron trim, the starboard unit being adjusted manually while the aircraft was on the ground. The ailerons (both port units) in this photograph are undergoing final completion; the one on the left is soon to receive its alcad lower surface covering. The balance tab is clearly visible on the aileron to the right. *(BAE SYSTEMS)*

Taken in the 'Detail Dope Room' at the Standard Motors factory at Ansty, near Coventry, this photograph illustrates fabric being red-doped to a newly completed Mosquito rudder. With the exception of its fabric covering, construction of the rudder was very similar to the elevators. A spar torque tube carried the bottom hinge and rudder operating lever lugs and was bolted to the two lower ribs. Mass balance weights were fitted to the rudder horn and secured in position by a bolt running through the horn's bottom rib. The rudder featured an adjustable servo trimming tab, its connecting rod operated by a torque shaft turned on ball bearings within the spar torque tube. The torque tube's lower lever was connected to the trim jack links. This rudder trim tab system was initially developed on the pre-war Flamingo airliner, any load on the rudder (caused by yaw from one engine) being corrected and the rudder forced over by the tab to offset the load. In the event of an engine failure the pilot was therefore relieved of exerting continuous (and fatiguing) pressure on the rudder pedals in order to fly straight and level.

During the fabric covering process all rib flanges, rivet heads and sharp corners were covered with acid-free adhesive tape, fabric attachment to metal surfaces being carried out using Cellon special thermolastic adhesive. Serrated fabric strips were applied overall (Egyptian tape and No 40 thread being specified), the fabric being strung to the ribs using 17lb strength No 1 braided chord. In this photograph the first of three coats of red tautening dope is being brushed on to the rudder fabric. Once the red dope has dried, two coats of aluminium dope will be sprayed on before a finishing coat of matt cellulose white is applied. The rudder would later receive its external paint finish, in this case Medium Sea Grey. *(Standard Motor Company)*

Taken in October 1944, this photograph shows an NF.30 fuselage at the de Havilland Second Aircraft Group Leavesden factory prior to being mated with its wing. With ventral doors attached, the fuselage has probably just been lifted off the transport cradle in the background following delivery from a sub-contractor. This aircraft has yet to receive its serial number but is likely to originate from the batch MV521 to MV570, which were built at Leavesden between September and October 1944. Note the lifting straps positioned over bulkheads two and five, both linked by a spreader bar suspended over the top of the fuselage. Newly assembled NF.30s are parked to the right and left, including MV547 (background left), which was flown direct from Leavesden to 218 MU on 1 November 1944. Six days later it passed to 307 Squadron at Church Fenton, remaining with that unit until it disbanded at Horsham St Faith in January 1947. Stored at 37 MU from 17 January 1947, MV547 was sold as scrap to John Dale on 11 August 1948.

These aircraft are finished in the standard Night-Fighter scheme of Medium Sea Grey overall with Dark Green camouflaged upper surfaces (note the high position of the fuselage camouflage demarcation line). Fuselage side panels, an engine top cowling and a tail fairing cone are lying on the floor. *(P. J. Joynor)*

This production line scene shows Inspector Mrs M. Drummond carrying out resistance checks (probably a bonding or circuit function test) in the cannon bay of a new FB.VI. The photograph provides a good illustration of the two separate sets of ventral doors fitted to Mosquito Fighter-Bomber variants, the forward pair providing access to the cannon bay, the rear pair functioning as doors for the bomb compartment. The 'dished' sections on the bomb doors provided clearance for the carriage of 500lb bombs. Note the bomb door jack rams, clearly visible on the door front and rear sections. Typical of the factory workers (from all walks of life) engaged on wartime aircraft production, Mrs Drummond formerly worked as a nurse in a mental hospital. *(Crown Copyright)*

Using a specially designed rig, an NF.30's port radiator unit is lowered into position on the Leavesden production line. Prior to this operation a triangulated tubular jig was installed on the main spar radiator pick-up points. The jig's inboard end featured a profile plate with holes representing the radiator end rib pick-up points on the fuselage side. The end rib was set to the jig to provide complete interchangeability of assembly when the radiator unit was installed. A combined block assembly, the radiator unit sat on a tray secured to leading edge mounting ribs (on the main spar pick-up points) by pillar bolts. In addition to a coolant radiator, the unit consisted of a cabin heater and oil cooler located on the inboard and rear sections respectively. A circulating pump (mounted beneath the engine crankcase) drew fluid from the coolant header tank and passed it through a thermostatic by-pass valve. At temperatures of up to 85°C the fluid by-passed directly to the cylinder jackets, but as the temperature increased the by-pass valve progressively closed until (at temperatures of 105°C and over) all the coolant entering the thermostat passed through the radiator. Note the transparent plastic 'bull-nose' radome, which would normally be painted once the aircraft entered service. *(P. J. Joynor)*

Using pits sunk into the factory floor, undercarriage lowering and retraction tests (controlled from a portable rig) are carried out on a new NF.30 at the Leavesden factory in October 1944. The Mosquito undercarriage was extremely unconventional for an aircraft of its size and consisted of compressed rubber blocks enclosed in a metal casing. This simplistic approach eliminated the high degree of precision machining required by an oleo-pneumatic unit and entirely removed any necessity for maintaining leakproof joints under high air pressure. The casing consisted of two semi-elliptical pressings of 16swg steel joined down the centre-line. The undercarriage operating mechanism comprised of a piston tube connected to the wheel axle and (mounted at the top end) an elliptical piston composed of laminated Bakelite material that functioned within the casing. A Bakelite guide block was screwed into the casing's lower end and served as a bearing and guide for the piston tube during its travel. The leg's rubber compression feature consisted of ten full rubber blocks and one half block. Each block was moulded with locating dowels on its upper section (and two corresponding recesses on its lower face) in order for the whole pack to self-align upon assembly. Duralumin spacer plates were fitted between each block, their edges flanged to locate within the casing interior. The spacer plates were holed for each block's dowel lobes, these protruding into the recesses of the block above. Finally, a rebound rubber block was mounted on the piston tube between the piston tube and guide block. Each undercarriage assembly consisted of two casings connected by cross-bracing tubes and jointed radius rods.

NF.30s were powered by either Merlin 72s or 76s, the latter differing from the former through provision of Bendix carburettors and their attendant controls. This aircraft's exhaust stubs, engine cowlings, starboard propeller dome and spinner have yet to be fitted. Note the wheeled bogie (carrying the starboard wing support cradle) located on the assembly line tracks. *(P. J. Joynor)*

Bomber fuselages undergo fitting out at the de Havilland Canada Downsview factory. Canadian-built Mosquito fuselages were manufactured at Dupont Street in Toronto with production later being sub-contracted to General Motors at Oshawa. Wings were constructed by Massey Harris in Weston, Ontario, and tailplanes by Boeing Vancouver. Mosquito production represented quite a technological leap for the Canadian de Havilland Company, which had previously constructed nothing more sophisticated than the Avro Anson. The initial batch of Canadian Mosquitoes incorporated components shipped from the UK, but subsequent aircraft comprised parts constructed wholly in North America. As with all new aircraft projects, production was initially slow, but Canadian resourcefulness overcame many problems and engineered several new production innovations. Between September 1942 and October 1945, 1,133 Canadian Mosquitoes are believed to have been constructed, a figure representing one-seventh of the total production. The fuselage on the right features an external capping strip on its Perspex nose upper section, a feature also seen on British-built PR.1s and B.IV Series 1s. *(National Museum of Science and Technology)*

B.XXs fill Bay 3 of the de Havilland Canada Downsview production line. In June 1944 a fully mechanised production facility opened in Plant 2 of the Downsview factory, by which time it had essentially become an assembly plant for the various sub-contracted components that were being delivered at a vast rate. The new facility featured two link-belt conveyorised 'U' circuit assembly lines with a combined length of around 2,400 feet. Fuselages and wings were transported to Bay 2 of Plant 2 and joined together on carriages (referred to as 'corvettes') equipped with fixed platforms, electrical and compressed air outlets, and provision for large components and parts kits. Thirty-nine such 'corvettes' were incorporated in the line, each one transporting aircraft through various stations for assembly, installation, functional tests and inspections. Aircraft initially travelled backwards up one side of the inverted 'U' before returning nose first down the other side. After completing its journey through Bay 2, the Mosquito proceeded out of the building to be winched up an incline and into the entrance of Bay 3. Having travelled along Bay 3's 'U' circuit, the aircraft emerged as a complete Mosquito. The sign on the far wall reads: 'Bay 3 Weekly Production of Mosquitoes: This Week's Objective – 10; Production to Date – 4'. Note the radiator cover lying on the port wing upper surface of the aircraft in the foreground. (BAE SYSTEMS)

The Mosquito fuselage accommodated an inflatable dinghy stowed in a blow-out-type box above the wing centre section (forward of bulkhead number three). In the event of ditching, two immersion switches automatically controlled dinghy inflation, but the unit could also be inflated manually by pulling a cable located in the cockpit roof behind the pilot's seat. This photograph was taken at an unidentified sub-contractor's production facility and shows a dinghy box being assembled in its jig. The worker on the left is about to install the metal external outer rim, which located flush with the fuselage top section. The hole at the rear of the box is for the manual release cable running from the cockpit roof. Inflated by a CO_2 bottle, the dinghy was packed with survival equipment including paddles, sea markers, two tins of rations, a signal pistol and leak stoppers. Note the completed boxes piled on top of each other in the background. *(DHAMT Ltd)*

Perfecta Motor Equipment in Birmingham produced Mosquito cockpit canopies and windscreens. This photograph was taken in 1943 and shows a batch of new canopies mounted on their construction jigs while glazing is installed. The cockpit canopy frame was a welded steel tube structure bolted and screwed to the fuselage. With the exception of the armoured glass windscreen, the canopy frame was completely covered with Perspex panels including sliding direct vision windows and a roof-mounted escape hatch. Note the newly finished canopies wrapped up and lined against the far wall. *(BAE SYSTEMS)*

This interior view of the 'Fuselage Dope Room' at the Standard Motors factory shows new FB.VI fuselages being sprayed in silver dope. Standard Motors made a significant contribution to FB.VI production, constructing 1,066 aircraft at its Ansty plant near Coventry. The first Standard Motors-built FB.VI (HP848) flew in May 1943 and production ceased in 1945; many were allocated for service in the Far East. Note that the fuselage roundels have already been applied.
(Standard Motor Company)

Mr P. W. Stanfield, foreman of the Mosquito running sheds at Hatfield, adjusts the port spinner backplate of a new FB.VI in March 1945. The running sheds were open-ended corrugated structures located close to the factory erecting shop. Newly assembled Mosquitoes were wheeled directly into the running sheds for engine tests before despatch for flight-testing. Note the 'saxophone' exhaust manifold and the 50-gallon underwing drop tank. P. W. Stanfield (known as 'Stan') remained at Hatfield after the war, later working in the Flight Test Department. The worker beneath the engine appears to making adjustments to the hydraulic pump. *(BAE SYSTEMS)*

Sky Blue under surface finish is being applied to the fuselage of FB.40 A52-46 at the Beale Piano Factory, Annandale. Requisitioned by the Australian de Havilland Company, the factory produced Mosquito fuselages, tailplanes, flaps, wing leading edges and ailerons, these components being transported to Bankstown for final assembly. Australian Mosquito wing production took place at the General Motors-Holdens Ltd Pagewood plant. A52-46 went on to serve with 5 OTU RAAF at Williamtown, where it was written off following a ground loop on 6 February 1945. Note the jury strut fitted across the ventral bay wing 'gap'. *(Milton Kent/ Hawker de Havilland)*

This panoramic shot was taken at the de Havilland Canada Downsview factory during 'Million-Dollar-Day' ceremonies on 14 May 1944. Company employees are gathered to witness Hollywood star Joan Fontaine (cousin of Geoffrey de Havilland Junior) unveil B.XX KB273, specially named 'Joan' in her honour. Following the unveiling, Miss Fontaine toured the factory for five hours, visiting every plant and office division. 'Joan' was painted on the side of KB273's nose, seen here covered by the Union Jack flag used for the unveiling. KB273 was assigned to the RAF and flown to the UK, arriving at Prestwick on 9 June 1944. Following modifications at 13 MU Henlow, KB273 was allocated to 139 Squadron on 3 August 1944. On 12 August it passed to 608 Squadron (receiving the unit code letters '6T-E') and operated to Frankfurt the same night. By 20 November 1944 KB273 had flown a total of twenty-three operational sorties, but underwent repairs from 25 November, returning to service with 139 Squadron on 9 December. Three days later the aircraft resumed service with 608 Squadron (still coded '6T-E'), operating to Munster on Christmas Eve. It completed a further fourteen operational sorties until the night of 28 February 1945 when it failed to return from a raid on Berlin, the crew (Fg Off H. W. Tyrrel and Sgt H. J. Erben) becoming prisoners-of-war. *(BAE SYSTEMS)*

Newly completed FB.40s are pictured in the Flight Shed at Bankstown. The two aircraft in the centre of each row are finished in Foliage Green overall, the remainder bearing the RAAF's initial 'Mosquito Attack' colour scheme of Foliage Green and Earth Brown camouflaged upper surfaces and Sky Blue under surfaces. From late 1944 Foliage Green became the standard finish for Australian-built Mosquitoes, this later giving way to aluminium dope. The aircraft in the foreground appears to be receiving attention to its starboard flap jack. The Bankstown Assembly Hangar and Flight Shed was specially erected for Mosquito production and occupied 115,000sq ft. Note the 'needle'-blade propellers, a feature of the first 100 Australian-built Mosquitoes. The aircraft in the far corner is likely to be A52-35, which went on to serve with 5 OTU before being destroyed in a crash during February 1945. Both aircraft on the extreme left have been trestled in the 'rigging' (neutral incidence) position. *(Milton Kent/Hawker de Havilland)*

Bert Gray, foreman of the Hatfield factory 'Mosquito Flight Test and Delivery Service' photographed on 21 March 1945. He took over this job from Godfrey Carter, who was tragically killed in a mid-air collision between FB.VIs HJ734 and HX897 during test flying on Monday 23 August 1943. Godfrey Carter was flying as observer in HX897 (piloted by George Gibbins) when it collided with HJ734 at 1615hrs 2 miles south-west of Hatfield. HJ734 was being flown by John de Havilland with Technical Assistant Aerodynamicist John Scrope as observer. HJ734 had taken off to conduct level speed trials, HX897 to carry out a hydraulic pressure test prior to being signed off for delivery. Dick Whittingham, an Inspector with the Hatfield Experimental Flight Test Department, regularly flew with the Hatfield-based test pilots, including both John and Geoffrey de Havilland Junior. Dick recalls that the pilots would often engage in 'dog fighting' once they'd completed their tasks, and it is likely that this activity may have contributed to the accident involving HJ734 and HX897. All four men were killed in the collision, the wreckage of both aircraft landing in the grounds of Hill End Hospital.

Bert Gray is pictured checking the port engine of a new FB.VI. The 'tear drop' bulge on the engine lower cowling's forward section provided space for the coolant pipe linking the header tank to the circulating pump. Note the Dzus fastener locking alignment lines painted on the top edge of the lower engine cowling. This aircraft was equipped with shrouded exhausts. *(BAE SYSTEMS)*

Mosquito Bombers

Although celebrated as the original multi-role combat aircraft, it should not be forgotten that the Mosquito was designed as a high-speed unarmed bomber relying on sheer performance to escape defending fighters. The story of initial Air Ministry opposition to the Mosquito concept has been told many times before, but it is worth noting that the role that kept the project alive was Photographic Reconnaissance. The initial contract for fifty Mosquitoes was altered several times but led eventually to the first Bomber version of the design, the B.IV Series 1. This was a conversion of the PR.1 airframe and could be readily identified by its short engine nacelles, distinctive air intake and exhaust duct layout on the engine side cowlings, together with a short-span 'No 1' tailplane. A total of nine B.IV Series 1 Mosquitoes were produced, all with provision for a 2000lb bomb load and 690 gallons of fuel. They carried out the first Mosquito bombing raid of the war, and one example, W4071, was still flying operationally in January 1945.

The first Mosquito version produced as a bomber from the outset was the B.IV Series ii, which first flew in March 1942. This differed from the earlier B.IV Series 1 through the fitment of extended engine nacelles, a 20ft 9in-span 'No 2' tailplane and a revised engine exhaust system. Equipping 105 and 139 Squadrons of 2 Group, they carried out many precision daylight bombing raids between March 1942 and June 1943, attacking targets such as the Gestapo Headquarters in Oslo and the Schott glassworks at Jena. The margins in performance between the B.IV Series ii and the Fw.190 were small, and losses proved relatively high on these daylight missions. A subsequent change of tactics led to the Mosquito bomber force being transferred to 8 Group Pathfinder Force for night-time target-marking and high-level nuisance raid activities. B.IV Series iis were the first Mosquito Bombers equipped with OBOE, a radar bombing aid whereby aircraft followed signals transmitted by two ground stations, enabling the bombing point to be reached with great accuracy and without reference to the ground.

The next Bomber version was the B.IX, the first aircraft, LR495, making its maiden flight in March 1943. The B.IX introduced two-speed, two-stage supercharged Merlin engines to the Bomber airframe, increasing altitude performance and immunity from interception. The two-stage Merlin installation led to a slight alteration in the Mosquito profile, the additional supercharger increasing the length of the engine and thus extending the spinner line forward of the nose. The new engine installation also featured an air intake on the forward lower cowling, directly beneath the spinner. This intake was ducted to the additional supercharger's intercooler radiator and is a recognition feature of all production two-speed, two-stage Merlin Mosquitoes. The B.IX also increased the Mosquito bomb load capacity to 3,000lb, made possible through the carriage of two 500lb bombs on underwing hardpoints. B.IXs of 139 Squadron pioneered the use of G-H, a radar bombing aid similar to OBOE but relying on position plotting in the aircraft. Several B.IXs led charmed lives, and one example, LR503, flew more operational sorties than any other Allied bomber during the Second World War.

The B.XVI succeeded the B.IX and represented a great stride in Mosquito Bomber development, being equipped with a pressurised cockpit and (aside from the first twelve production aircraft) enlarged or 'bulged' bomb bay doors to accommodate a 4,000lb 'Cookie' blockbuster bomb. Equipped with Merlin 70 series engines, the B.XVI had a maximum speed of 419mph at 28,500 feet and a still-air range of 1,470 miles. Several B.XVIs (together with a number of B.IV Series iis and B.IXs) were fitted with H2S, an extremely accurate radar bombing aid, which, unlike OBOE and G-H, was wholly independent of ground stations.

The de Havilland Canada factory also produced Mosquito bombers, its first aircraft, KB300, flying in September 1942. The first twenty-five Canadian bombers, designated B.VII, were based on the projected British B.V but powered by American-manufactured Packard Merlin 31 engines. The B.VII was followed by the B.XX and B.XXV, similar to the B.IV but powered by Packard Merlin 31/33 and 225 engines respectively. These aircraft gave great service to 8 and 5 Groups RAF, and many B.XXVs were taken on charge by the postwar Fleet Air Arm.

Mosquito bombers flew a total of 39,795 sorties during the Second World War, delivering 26,867 tons of bombs. Losses amounted to 254 aircraft, representing a loss rate of 0.63 percent, the lowest of any aircraft type in Bomber Command.

The ultimate Mosquito Bomber version, the B.35, made its maiden flight in March 1945, but arrived too late for wartime operational service. It was basically an updated version of the B.XVI, being equipped with fuel-injected Merlin 113 and 114 engines of 1,690hp, providing this variant with a maximum speed of 422mph. B.35s equipped the postwar RAF, serving in Germany with the British Air Forces of Occupation (BAFO) and with two Squadrons, 109 and 139, in the UK. The B.35 was finally replaced by the Canberra jet in 1953, another unarmed bomber following the original Mosquito concept of speed for defence.

W4057, the Mosquito Bomber prototype, seen at Hatfield on 5 September 1941, three days prior to its maiden flight. W4057 served as a prototype for the Mosquito B.IV Series 1, at the same time acting as a trials installation aircraft for the strengthened or 'basic' wing of the projected B.V. The 'basic' wing incorporated underwing hardpoints for drop tanks or bombs and was introduced on the Mosquito bomber production line from the B.IX onwards. The B.V also provided the basis for the initial Canadian-built Mosquito bomber version, the B.VII.

W4057 wears the standard Service Prototype colour scheme of Dark Earth and Dark Green camouflaged upper surfaces, Trainer Yellow under surfaces and a 'Circle P' (for 'Prototype') marking on the fuselage sides. Other points of interest are the small-span (19ft 5½in) 'No 1' tailplane, the short engine nacelles and the one-piece flaps. W4057 made its maiden flight on 8 September 1941 in the hands of Geoffrey de Havilland Junior. Following A&AEE trials it returned to Hatfield, being retained by de Havilland's for development work including the carriage of four 500lb bombs in the bomb bay (twice the original design load), made possible by cropping the bomb vanes. The latter trials were very successful, the cropped vanes being adopted as standard, thus doubling the Mosquito Bomber's offensive load before it commenced operational service. W4057 was also used for fuselage distortion (in relation to tailplane incidence) investigations, as well as trials of the two-speed, two-stage supercharged Merlin engine installation. W4057 was damaged on 26 September 1943 and Struck Off Charge shortly afterwards. *(BAE SYSTEMS)*

A crowd of de Havilland workers surrounds a brand new B.IV Series 1 Mosquito, probably W4064, at Hatfield in November 1941. This aircraft had just been demonstrated to the de Havilland workforce by Company Chief Test Pilot Geoffrey de Havilland Junior. Nine B.IV Series 1 Mosquitoes were constructed (serialled W4064 to W4072), all converted on the production line from PR.1 airframes. Note the exhaust exit duct fairings on the side cowling rear sections; these, together with the manifold cooling intakes on the side cowling forward sections, were characteristic features of all PR.1 and B.IV Series 1 Mosquitoes. B.IV Series 1 aircraft were powered by 1,280hp Merlin 21 engines, featured a maximum fuel capacity of 690 gallons and could accommodate a 2,000lb bomb load. Of the nine examples produced, only W4071 survived the war. *(Both BAE SYSTEMS)*

Taken on the same occasion as the previous two photos, Geoffrey de Havilland Junior (second from the left) chats to the crowd following his demonstration of the Mosquito B.IV Series 1. This picture clearly illustrates the short engine nacelle, hinged at the rear to facilitate operation of the one-piece flap. The aircraft is finished in the Temperate Land Scheme finish of Dark Green and Dark Earth camouflaged upper surfaces with Sky under surfaces. Geoffrey de Havilland Junior delivered the first production Mosquito bomber (W4064) to 105 Squadron at Swanton Morley on 15 November 1941. As de Havilland's Chief Test Pilot, he was responsible for the Mosquito prototype flight-test programme and was tragically killed during trials of the DH.108 research aircraft in September 1946. *(BAE SYSTEMS)*

Here is an excellent illustration of the exhaust duct and air intake layout featured on the engine side cowlings of PR.1 and B.IV Series 1 aircraft. On the inboard and outboard sides of each engine, all six exhaust ports were amalgamated into a single manifold exiting through the duct at the rear centre of the cowling. The air intake located at the top of the side cowling provided cooling air for the exhaust manifold and was introduced as a result of initial trials with W4050. This exhaust installation proved troublesome in service, often leading to overheating and blistered cowlings, and was replaced by a simpler system of combined 'saxophone' exhausts (within a flame-damping shroud) or individual exhaust stubs from the B.IV Series ii and F.II onwards. Note the modification to the carburettor air intake on the lower cowling, probably applied for airflow investigation purposes. Taken at Hatfield on 21 January 1942, this is probably the Bomber prototype W4057. *(BAE SYSTEMS)*

This rare photograph of B.IV Series 1 W4067 was taken at Hatfield in late 1941. Note the short engine nacelles, one-piece flaps and fabric-covered elevators. This aircraft was delivered to the CRD at Farnborough on 20 November 1941 before returning to Hatfield the following January. A month later it was assigned to the Handling Squadron at Boscombe Down before cameras were installed and the aircraft diverted to No 1 PRU at Benson in April 1942. Aside from a short stint at Rolls Royce Hucknall in early June, W4067 remained with No 1 PRU, flying from Benson and Leuchars, until it failed to return from an operational flight on 27 July 1942. *(BAE SYSTEMS)*

With its starboard undercarriage collapsed, 105 Squadron B.IV Series 1 W4072 ('GB-D') lies in a field beyond the Horsham St Faith runway on 26 June 1942. Loaned to 139 Squadron and piloted by Flt Lt Bagguley, W4072 had taken off at 1930hrs the previous evening for a low-level dusk raid on Stade aerodrome near Hamburg. However, instead of attacking Stade, Flt Lt Bagguley bombed the town of Dorum, to the north of Bremerhaven. During the run away from the target and while travelling at 385mph, Flt Lt Bagguley mistakenly lowered the flaps instead of closing the bomb doors, most of the flap structure subsequently being torn away in the slipstream. On arrival back at Horsham St Faith W4072 overshot the runway, its starboard undercarriage collapsing after running into a trench.

The final production B.IV Series 1, W4072 made its maiden flight on 11 December 1941 in the hands of de Havilland test pilot George Gibbins. Following an engine change and adjustments to the ailerons, the aircraft was declared ready for collection on 14 February 1942. Thirteen days later it was delivered to 105 Squadron at Horsham St Faith, where it was allocated the unit code letters 'GB-D'. On 31 May 1942, immediately following the 'Thousand Bomber Raid' on Cologne, W4072 (flown by Sqn Ldr Oakeshott and navigated by Fg Off Hayden) carried out the first bombing operation by a Mosquito when it attacked the city during the early morning. It flew a daylight operation to Bremen on 18 June, but a week later suffered the accident depicted here.

Repairs were carried out at Hatfield and took three months to complete. W4072 was then assigned to 1655 MTU on 1 October 1942 before passing to 105 Squadron the same day. On 13 and 14 October operations were flown against targets on the Dutch coast, but the aircraft transferred to 1655 MTU a month later. Damaged in March 1943, W4072 was repaired by Martin Hearn

before delivery to 10 MU on 8 November. 627 Squadron received this veteran aircraft in December 1943 (assigning it the unit code letters 'AZ-Q'), but on 8 January 1944 it crashed into the sea off East Mersea while returning from a night raid on Frankfurt (having accumulated a total of 286hrs 45mins flying time). In the first picture note the exhaust manifold cooling intake on the starboard outer side cowling, the crushed rear section of the starboard engine nacelle and the missing flaps. A section of torn-off starboard flap caused the fuselage damage immediately above the code letter 'D'.

The second picture shows the remaining section of port flap and provides a good illustration of the short nacelle rear structure. W4072 appears to be finished in the Temperate Land Scheme of Dark Green and Dark Earth camouflaged upper surfaces with Sky under surfaces. The 105 Squadron unit code letters 'GB-N' seem to be applied in Sky with their lower sections outlined in black. Photographs of operational B.IV Series 1 Mosquitoes are comparatively rare. *(Both Crown Copyright)*

105 Squadron B.IV Series ii DZ379 'GB-H' photographed at Marham by Charles E. Brown in December 1942. Unlike the earlier B.IV Series 1, which was a conversion of the PR.1 airframe, the B.IV Series ii was the first production Mosquito built specifically as a bomber from the outset. B.IV Series iis differed principally from the earlier variant through the fitment of extended engine nacelles, a revised engine exhaust system and a 20ft 9in-span 'No 2' tailplane, the latter necessary to improve longitudinal stability. Constructed at Hatfield, DZ379 was delivered to 105 Squadron on 30 November 1942, receiving the unit code letters 'GB-H'. It took part in many of 105 Squadron's daylight bombing raids and was transferred to 139 Squadron on 25 June 1943. At 2052hrs on 17 August 1943, DZ379 (flown by Fg Off A. S. Cooke and navigated by Sgt D. A. H. Dixon) failed to return from a raid on Berlin, this being the aircraft's eleventh operational sortie. Note the fabric-covered elevators, a feature of early production Mosquitoes and one that later gave way to metal-skinned units. DZ379 has yet to be fitted with a longitudinal stiffening strake above the rear fuselage access hatch.
(RAF Museum, Charles E. Brown)

B.IV Series ii DK290/G seen during a test flight from Boscombe Down in 1943. Hatfield-built DK290 made its maiden flight on 23 May 1942 in the hands of John de Havilland, and was retained by de Havilland's for development work in connection with the Mosquito B.V. This involved investigations into stability with a 2,000lb bomb load (four 500lb bombs) including trials with a modified tailplane of 10 degrees dihedral. Subsequent tests at the A&AEE at Boscombe Down revealed the dihedral tailplane to offer no improvement over the standard unit and the latter was cleared for full bomb loads. In an attempt to improve the Mosquito Bomber's maximum level speed, DK290's surface finish was highly polished, but performance increase was negligible so this practice was not adopted as standard. February 1943 saw DK290 back at the A&AEE, this time to evaluate the flame-damping qualities of 'fish tail' ejector exhaust stubs of de Havilland design.

On 24 March 1943 DK290 was assigned to Heston Aircraft for trial installation of the Vickers 'Highball' bouncing bomb, the 'G' suffix to the serial number signifying that, as the carrier of secret equipment, the aircraft should be guarded at all times. DK290/G returned to Boscombe Down on 3 April 1943 for further trials including fuel flow tests and comparative level speeds with various exhaust stub designs. Heston Aircraft removed DK290/G's 'Highball' equipment in August 1943, after which the Mosquito passed to 27 MU Shawbury. On 3 December 1943 DK290 was allocated to No 10 School of Technical Training at Kirkham as instructional airframe 4411M.

Note the six exhaust stubs on the outboard side of the port engine (a non-standard practice on the engine outboard side of British-built single-stage Merlin Mosquitoes), and the continuation of the upper surface camouflage down the engine side cowlings. An early production B.IV Series ii, DK290/G sports the Fighter Command Special Recognition Markings of a Sky rear fuselage band, Sky spinners and yellow-striped wing leading edges. These were applied to confuse German fighters as to the unarmed status of RAF Mosquito Bombers, but were only a short-term feature. *(Richard Riding collection)*

An underside view of DK290/G clearly shows two 'Highball' bouncing bombs mounted in the bomb bay. This aircraft pioneered the Mosquito 'Highball' installation, the initial fitment being carried out by Heston Aircraft in early 1943. To enhance weapon stability and accuracy, 'Highball' was spun before release, motive power being provided by a ram air turbine fed via an extendable air scoop mounted in the bomb bay's mid section. *(Flypast collection)*

Following a daylight raid to Ijmuiden on 22 September 1942, 105 Squadron B.IV Series ii DK337 'GB-N' suffered light flak damage to the fuselage and flaps. DK337 was built at Hatfield during the summer of 1942 and delivered to 105 Squadron on 10 September. Four days later it operated to Emden and received the damage shown here during its third sortie. Repairs were complete by 28 December, following which it flew to Oldenburg in the hands of a 139 Squadron crew on 23 January 1943, and was damaged by flak over Jena on 27 May 1943 (during the course of its twenty-third sortie). DK337 later passed to 139 Squadron, and on 30 August 1943 took off for Duisberg on its tenth sortie with that Squadron but failed to return, being Struck Off Charge the following day with a total of 190hrs 15mins flying time. These pictures were taken at Horsham St Faith. *(Both Crown Copyright)*

Groundcrew plug in the trolley accumulator as B.IV Series ii DZ367 'GB-J' prepares to start its engines at Marham on 10 December 1942. Note 139 Squadron T.3 'XD-Z' to the right, an early example of the trainer version of the Mosquito, which sports a Sky-painted rear fuselage band and spinners. *(Aeroplane Monthly)*

FASTEST BOMBER IN THE WORLD

The de Havilland MOSQUITO *Rolls Royce engines and de Havilland variable pitch propellers*

DE HAVILLAND

Clearing the skies for commerce

GREAT BRITAIN   CANADA   AUSTRALIA   NEW ZEALAND   INDIA   SOUTH AFRICA

(BAE SYSTEMS)

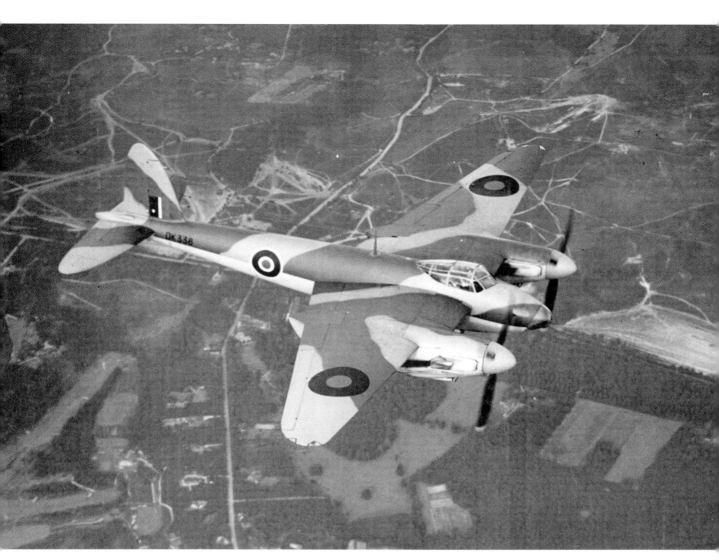

B.IV Series ii DK338 seen during a test flight from
Hatfield. This aircraft made its maiden flight on 31 August
1942 and was cleared for service the following day. Two
weeks later it was allocated to 105 Squadron with the unit
code letters 'GB-O'. Following the installation of film
equipment, DK338's first operation was to Wiesbaden on
16 September 1942. The aircraft's sixteenth sortie took
place on 27 January 1943 against the Burmeister & Wain
diesel works in Copenhagen, and despite colliding with
telephone cables north of Grimstrup, it successfully
bombed the target and returned home safely. Following
repairs it operated to Tours on 15 February and to Rennes
on the 26th, receiving damage on the latter sortie that was
repaired at its Marham home base. DK338's twenty-sixth
and final operation took place on 5 May 1943 when 105
Squadron's target was Eindhoven. Following an engine
failure the aircraft abandoned the operation, but crashed on
return to Marham and was Struck Off Charge the following
day with a total of 167hrs 35mins flying time.
(RAF Museum, Charles E. Brown)

This is the Mark IXA3 Course Setting Bomb Sight (CSBS) installed in the nose of a B.IV Series 1 at Hatfield in late 1941. At the start of the Second World War the Mark IXA CSBS was RAF Bomber Command's standard bomb sight; it was manufactured in three versions (A, B and C) for use by Bomber Command, the Fleet Air Arm and Coastal Command respectively. The B and C versions were calibrated in knots with height bars configured for operations at a lower altitude than the A version. The Mark IXA and C were pre-set vector bomb sights, the functions of which were dependent on prior determination of data for solving the triangles of velocities. Data was set on the sight prior to a bombing attack, the final course being a straight line indicated by the sight's drift wires. The cylindrical object in the foreground is the Type D Bomb Sight Compass with the height bar mounted vertically and directly ahead of it. Of rectangular section, the height bar was capable of pivoting (around a wind gauge bar bolt) from the vertical to horizontal position for storage purposes. The starboard side face of the height bar featured an inset timing scale graduated from 600 to 1,400 feet in 100-foot divisions. The index for this scale was on a height slider with an engraved orange arrow. Mid-way up the height bar is the adjustable back sight with the drift scale located immediately forward and slightly above the front section of the bomb aimer's flat glass panel.

Note the curved frame running up the middle section of the Perspex nose. On early Bomber and PR versions the Perspex nose was fitted with external capping strips running along the centre-line top and bottom. On later production aircraft the Perspex nose was slightly more bulbous in its forward section and did not feature these capping strips. (Look at W4050 today and you can still see the initial configuration.) The oval-shaped fitting (located at the lower end of the vertical frame) housed the forward navigation lamp. The Mark IX CSBS was replaced by the Mark XIV bomb sight and the TIB bomb sight in later Bomber versions of the Mosquito. *(BAE SYSTEMS)*

Note that this 105 Squadron B.IV Series ii (probably DK336), photographed in December 1942, is equipped with exhaust stubs in place of the more usual 'saxophone' exhausts enclosed within flame-damping shrouds. It was realised early on that the use of stub exhausts would create enough propulsion effect to boost maximum speed. Stub ends of oval section were most efficient, leading to a speed increase of between 10 and 13mph (dependant on altitude). Open stubs obviously produced more glare than flame-damping shrouds, so 105 Squadron requested fifteen aircraft with shrouds and three with stubs (as the Squadron operated between dawn and dusk). Note that this B.IV Series ii is fitted with six stubs on the outboard side of the engine (the inboard side would have featured five stubs – see page 71) in order to maximise the propulsion effect. DK336 was constructed at Hatfield in September 1942 and assigned to 105 Squadron on 6 September. As 'GB-P' it flew seventeen sorties with 105 before transfer to 139 Squadron on 27 January 1943, operating against the Burmeister & Wain diesel works in Copenhagen the same day. DK336 was badly damaged during the latter sortie and crashed during the return flight after hitting a balloon cable at Shipdham; the pilot, Sgt R. F. Clare, and navigator, Fg Off E. Doyle, were both killed. Note the modifications to the exhaust stub 'slot' on the cowling side panel (to provide space for the rear stub). *(Aeroplane Monthly)*

No book on the Mosquito would be complete without at least one photograph of 105 Squadron's B.IV Series ii aircraft at RAF Marham. This *Flight* picture was taken during the famous Press Day on 10 December 1942 and shows the Squadron's aircraft preparing for take-off. Nearest the camera is the renowned DZ353 'GB-E', arguably the most famous B.IV Series ii ever produced and the subject of countless photographs, models and pictures. Beyond it is DZ367 'GB-J'. Following the introduction of the B.IV Series ii into RAF service, the de Havilland technical representative attached to 105 Squadron reported: 'The general opinion of pilots is that the "2nd series" bombers, with flame-damped exhaust and long nacelles, are considerably slower than the 1st series.' *(Flight International)*

This classic Charles E. Brown study was taken in December 1942, depicting 105 Squadron's B.IV Series ii DZ367 'GB-J'. Hatfield-built DZ367 was delivered to 105 Squadron on 6 November 1942 and flew a total of ten operations with 105 before transfer to 139 Squadron. On 30 January 1943 105 and 139 Squadrons bombed Berlin in daylight with the intention of interrupting radio broadcasts by Goering and Goebbels. DZ367, flown by Sqn Ldr D. F. W. Darling DFC and navigated by Fg Off W. Wright, was the last of three 139 Squadron Mosquitoes to attack, and was shot down by flak over the city. The aircraft was Struck Off Charge on 2 February 1943 with a total of 62hrs 35mins flying time. Note the partially retracted tailwheel. *(RAF Museum, Charles E. Brown)*

This close-up shot of the port engine outer side cowling on B.IV Series ii DK290/G was taken at the A&AEE, Boscombe Down, in 1943 during trials of flame-damping 'fish tail' exhaust stubs. It was unusual to see six exhaust stubs on the engine outboard side of British-built two-speed, single-stage supercharged Merlin Mosquitoes as normally the rear two cylinders were combined into a single stub, creating the appearance of five stubs per side. Much has been proclaimed regarding the reason for this, the most common explanation citing that a sixth individual stub would have caused scorch damage to the wing leading edge. While understandable, this deduction appears incorrect, the real reason being probably to do with the exhaust layout on the inboard side of the engine. In the latter case the radiator structure physically prohibited the installation of a separate exhaust stub on the rearmost cylinder (as the radiator structure extended forward of the wing leading edge), so the exhaust for this cylinder and the previous one (number five) were combined into one stub. It would seem that to balance exhaust thrust and standardise production of exhaust inner shrouds (as well as the size of exhaust 'slots' within cowling side panel jigs), the last two cylinders on the outboard side of the engine were also combined into a single stub. In this picture, number six cylinder has been fitted with its own stub in order to evaluate exhaust propulsion and flame-damping properties. The 'wing scorching' argument is further negated by the fact that several B.IV Series iis, PR.IVs and F.IIs, as well as all Australian-built single-stage supercharged Merlin Mosquitoes (FB.40s, PR.40s and T.43s) were equipped with six exhaust stubs on the outboard side. *(Crown Copyright)*

DZ313, a brand new B.IV Series ii, is being prepared for a test flight from Hatfield in the summer of 1942. DZ313 was allocated to 105 Squadron on 16 September 1942, receiving the unit codes 'GB-E'. It operated to Berlin on 19 September in the hands of a 139 Squadron crew, and to Ijmuiden on 27 September, although Haarlem was actually bombed during the latter sortie. On 20 October 1942 DZ313, piloted by Fg Off S. Johnson and navigated by Sgt E. C. Draper, took off to bomb Hanover but failed to return. Note the rather spindly cockpit entrance ladder, which folded telescopically for stowage beneath the floor of the nose compartment. Also noteworthy are the shrouded exhausts and 'needle'-blade propellers. *(BAE SYSTEMS)*

In another view of B.IV Series ii DZ313 at Hatfield in the summer of 1942, note the 'tear drop'-shaped observation blisters on the cockpit canopy side panel glazing. The blisters were a feature of the Mosquito PR.1, B.IV, PR.IV, PR.VIII, B.IX and PR.IX (as well as the Canadian B.XX and B.XXV) and were replaced by bulged Perspex sandwich panels on the pressurised cockpit of Photographic Reconnaissance and Bomber versions from the PR.XVI and B.XVI onwards. The latter variants introduced a slightly redesigned cockpit canopy structure as a result of the pressurisation modifications, featuring slightly smaller direct vision quarter windows and revised external framing. The new canopy also featured on the PR.32, PR.34 and B.35. *(BAE SYSTEMS)*

Three of the original Mosquito design and development team pose in front of a B.IV Series ii at Hatfield on 15 May 1943. From left to right, these gentleman are Arthur W. Fawcett (design office draughtsman), Cyril C. Jackson (electrical installation designer) and John E. Walker (engine installation designer). The latter accompanied Geoffrey de Havilland Junior during the maiden flight of the Mosquito prototype on 25 November 1940. *(BAE SYSTEMS)*

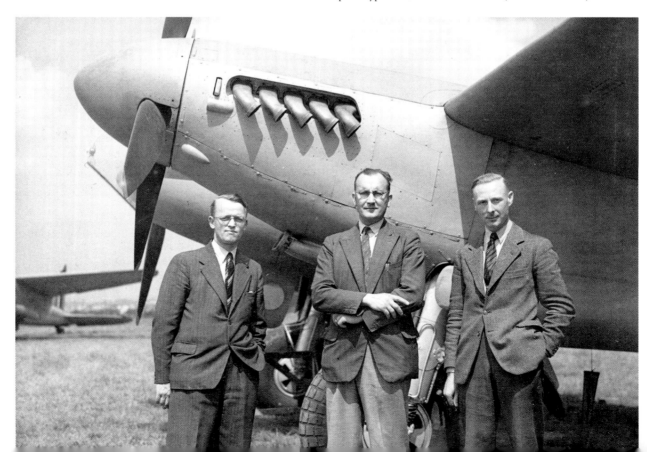

On 3 October 1943 the RAF Film Production Unit's celebrated B.IV Series ii DZ414 ('O for Orange') accompanied the first operational flight by 2 Group FB.VIs of 464 and 487 Squadrons. The targets on this occasion were the power stations at Pont-Chateau and Guerleden, which were bombed in low-level and shallow-dive attacks. Flown by Flt Lt Charles Patterson, DZ414 suffered flak damage to the canopy and dinghy box area. Following repairs by a de Havilland working party, DZ414 was serviceable again just over two weeks later. *(John Stride collection)*

The lower picture shows the damaged rudder of 139 Squadron B.IV Series ii DZ597 'XD-L' following a mid-air collision with B.IV Series ii DZ423 'XD-K', seen in the other photograph, during the early hours of 8 October 1943. Hatfield-built DZ597 was delivered to 139 Squadron on 15 May 1943 and flew its first operational sortie (to Berlin) four days later. DZ597's second operation was to Orleans on 21 May, during which it was hit by flak, the subsequent damage leading to a crash-landing at Coltishall. After repairs, DZ597 continued to

operate with 139 Squadron and received further flak damage on 24 August 1943 during its thirtieth sortie, the target on that occasion being Berlin. On 7 October 1943 DZ597 bombed Munich, but collided with DZ423 during the return flight, leading to the latter's rudder damage shown here (despite the aircraft's condition the pilot effected a very skilful landing). Repairs were quickly carried out, and DZ597 operated to Berlin two nights later. At 1839hrs on 20 October 1943 DZ597 (flown by Flt Sgt T. K. Forsyth and navigated by Sgt L. C. James) took off for Berlin on its forty-sixth operational sortie but was hit by flak over Bremen Oldenberg and failed to return. It was Struck Off Charge on 31 October 1943 with a recorded total of 200hrs 15mins flying time.

The above picture shows DZ423's shattered starboard nose window and torn fabric following the collision. This aircraft entered service with 139 Squadron as 'XD-T' in January 1943, but transferred to 618 Squadron the following April. Returning to 139 Squadron in July, DZ423 was re-coded 'XD-K' and remained with 139 until November 1944 when it passed to 27 MU. The PNTU received DZ423 in May 1945 and flew the aircraft until August 1945, when it was delivered into storage with 44 MU. It was eventually Struck Off Charge on 21 September 1945. The pyramid-shaped bump forward of the cockpit is the windscreen de-icing jet fairing. *(Both Crown Copyright)*

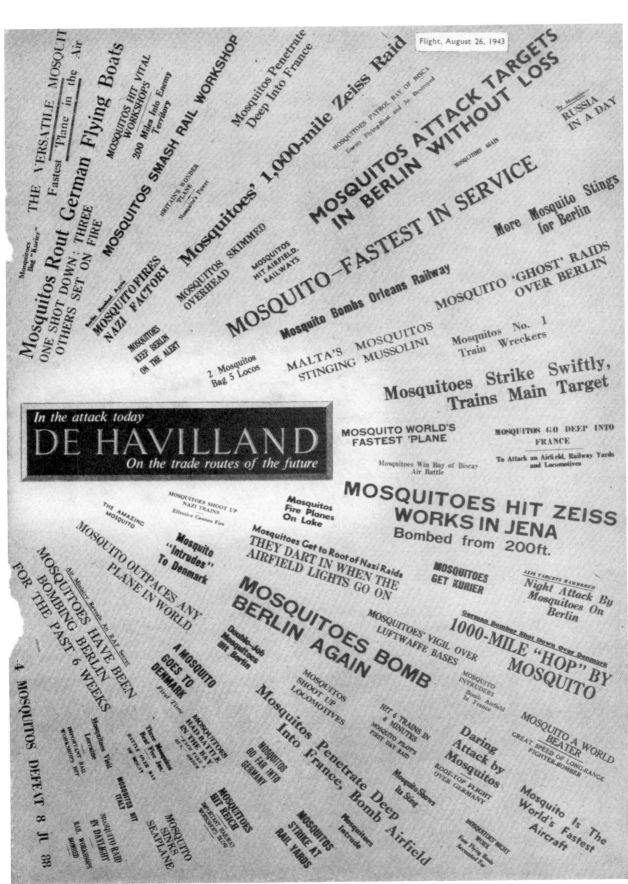

B.IV Series ii DZ534 'AZ-H' of 627 Squadron is pictured at Woodhall Spa during the summer of 1944. Note the Night under surface finish extending to the top of the fuselage sides (applied as per DTD Technical Circular Pattern No 2), and the thirty-three-mission tally on the nose, although this Mosquito had actually flown more than forty operations by the time of this photograph.

DZ534 was built at Hatfield in March 1943 and issued to Vickers at Weybridge for development work on the 'Highball' bouncing bomb. It returned to Hatfield for modifications on 21 May 1943 before passing to 618 Squadron at Skitten on 18 September. In November 1943 DZ534 flew to Hatfield for further modifications (reportedly to have included conversion to carry the 4,000lb bomb, but this was never undertaken) before transfer to 627 Squadron of 8 Group (Pathfinder Force) on 31 January 1944. Four days later DZ534 passed to 692 Squadron of 8 Group's Light Night Striking Force (LNSF), receiving the unit codes 'P3-M'. This aircraft flew forty-one operations with 692 Squadron before re-allocation to 627 Squadron (by now transferred to 5 Group), where it was re-coded 'AZ-H'. On 26 July 1944 DZ534 took off for the Givors marshalling yards on its sixth sortie with 627 Squadron, but turned back with both the compass and Gee set unserviceable. After calling Biggin Hill for a fix and sending an SOS to Exeter, DZ534 ditched 12 miles off Cherbourg. Pilot and navigator (Flg Off M. D. Gribbin and Flt Lt R. W. Griffiths RCAF) were picked up by a US Navy destroyer and taken to No 12 Field Hospital at Cherbourg, returning to 627 Squadron shortly afterwards. *(B. E. B. Harris)*

This is the view from the navigator's seat of a 627 Squadron B.IV Series ii as it passes low over the Lincolnshire countryside. From June 1944 627 Squadron flew many day-bombing sorties marking V1 Flying Bomb sites in Northern France. The Squadron continued to provide precise target-marking, day and night, for the heavy bombers of 5 Group until the war's end. Note the close proximity of the exhaust stubs relative to the cockpit, the resultant noise factor proving quite fatiguing on long flights. This unidentified Mosquito wears a Night under surface finish, evident from the starboard engine's inner side cowling and the starboard spinner. *(B. E. B. Harris)*

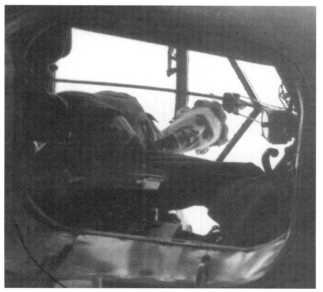

'Okay, get in!' shouts Fg Off J. F. Thompson DFC (RNZAF) to navigator Fg Off B. E. B. Harris DFC at Woodhall Spa during the summer of 1944. The aircraft is 627 Squadron B.IV Series ii DZ601 'AZ-A', which joined 627 direct from 139 Squadron on 25 May 1944. It led the famous Jena daylight raid (against the Schott glassworks) on 27 May 1943, receiving flak damage that injured the pilot, Wg Cdr Reynolds DSO DFC. DZ601 flew a total of fifty-five operations with 139 Squadron (both day and night sorties) and made its last sortie on 1 June 1944 when 627 Squadron's target was Saumur. On return to Woodhall Spa, DZ601's port engine failed after the propeller thrust race bearing seized, causing shearing of the propeller distribution valve. Unable to maintain height on one engine DZ601 was forced to make a belly-landing, suffering Category B damage in the process. Repairs were not completed until 1 January 1945, but the aircraft again suffered damage, this time during transit to 44 MU on 11 January 1945. Following repairs by 58 MU, DZ601 eventually reached 44 MU in March 1945 and was Struck Off Charge on 16 October 1946. *(B. E. B. Harris)*

At Graveley in 1944, aircrew of 692 Squadron hitch a lift aboard a 4,000 lb bomb destined for one of the unit's Mosquitoes. The aircraft behind them is B.IV Series ii DZ637 'P3-C', which had been converted to carry the 4,000lb bomb. This Hatfield-built Mosquito was assigned to Vickers on 24 June 1943 for the 4000lb bomb load modifications, the work being complete by 2 September 1943, after which DZ637 entered storage with 27 MU. On 3 February 1944 the aircraft was assigned to 627 Squadron, but passed to 692 Squadron two weeks later, receiving the unit codes 'P3-C'. DZ637 completed forty-six sorties with 692 before re-allocation to 627 Squadron at Woodhall Spa in July 1944 (where it was re-coded 'AZ-O'). Damage repairs were carried out between 29 August and 12 December 1944, by which time it had been re-coded 'AZ-X'. At 1714hrs on 1 February 1945 DZ637 took off for Steigen on its eleventh sortie with 627 Squadron, but was shot down over the target. The crew (pilot Flt Lt R. Baker and navigator Sgt D. G. Betts) were killed and are buried in the Reichswald War Cemetery. Note the Night under surface finish (applied as per DTD Technical Circular Pattern No 2), which extends to the top of the fuselage sides and completely covers the fin and rudder. The upper surfaces are finished in Ocean Grey and Dark Green camouflage and the Squadron code letters are in red. *(Key)*

B.IV Series ii DZ599 pictured at Hatfield in May 1943. DZ599 was also selected for conversion to carry the 4,000lb bomb, being delivered to Vickers at Weybridge for the necessary modifications on 28 May 1943. Following storage at 10 MU it was delivered to Marshalls on 5 February 1944 before allocation to 692 Squadron two months later. DZ599's first operational sortie was to Essen on 26 April 1944, thirty-seven further operations being flown before the aircraft passed to 627 Squadron on 28 June 1944. As 'AZ-F', it carried out thirty-five operations with 627 Squadron, the final one being to the Elbe River on the night of 27 March 1945, during which it ditched off the East Frisian Islands. The pilot, Fg Off W. A. Barnett (RNZAF) and navigator, Flt Sgt J. A. Day (RAAF) were both killed. DZ599 was the last 627 Squadron loss of the war. *(Central Press)*

These 618 Squadron B.IV Series iis are in storage at RAAF Narromine in 1946. The aircraft in the background is DZ546 ('G'), which was built at the de Havilland Hatfield factory in early 1943. On 28 March of that year it was delivered to Vickers at Weybridge for the installation of 'Highball' equipment before allocation to 618 Squadron on 7 May 1943. On 5 July 1944 it passed to Airspeed for more 'Highball' modifications, this time in connection with 618 Squadron's intended anti-shipping role (code-named 'Oxtail') in the Pacific Theatre. DZ546 returned to 618 Squadron on 6 September 1944 (by now wearing the unit code letter 'G') before shipment to Australia with the rest of the Squadron's B.IVs and PR.XVIs on 31 October 1944. 'Highball' became the subject of politico-strategic debate between the British Pacific Fleet and US military and naval commanders, and no satisfactory role was ever found for the weapon. Consequently, 618 Squadron disbanded at RAAF Narromine in July 1945, its Mosquitoes remaining in storage until Struck Off Charge in April 1946, later being disposed of by public auction (DZ546 being sold to Ken and Rob Bowman of Dunedoo). Note the rear fuselage arrestor hook fittings, the engine covers and four-bladed propellers. The upper surfaces are finished in Medium Sea Grey and Dark Green with the under surfaces in Azure Blue. The fuselage roundels (36-inch Type C), upper wing roundels (54-inch Type B) and fin flashes (2 x 24 inches) were White and Blue in accordance with Australian-style national markings, while the serial numbers were applied in Night. *(Roley Manning)*

This rare shot of an unidentified 618 Squadron B.IV Series ii was taken at RAAF Narromine in 1945. The four Squadron members standing in front of the Mosquito are (left to right) John Boyd (Squadron Doctor), Don Maynard, Jackie Price and Bertie Umbers. 618 Squadron formed at Skitten on 1 April 1943 for the purpose of using 'Highball' bouncing bombs against German shipping targets, specifically the battleship *Tirpitz*. For various reasons (which included a lack of aircraft, weapons and training) 618 Squadron never attacked the *Tirpitz* and was selected instead for carrier-borne operations in the Pacific Theatre. Twenty-five of the Squadron's specially modified B.IV Series iis, together with three PR.XVIs for reconnaissance duties, were transported to Australia aboard the light fleet carriers *Fencer* and *Striker*, arriving in Melbourne on 23 December 1944.

The B.IVs were modified by Vickers, Airspeed and Marshalls, each aircraft equipped with Merlin 25s and four-bladed propellers. This work involved the fitment of appropriate Constant Speed Units (CSUs) and spinners, as well as corresponding alterations in the cockpit including new boost gauges and engine data plate, and the deletion of the boost cut-out control. The main undercarriage featured heavier-gauge leg casings and the wheels were equipped with twin brake units. Tropical filters, armoured windscreens and hydraulic windscreen wipers were also installed and provision made for two 'Highballs' in the converted bomb bay, the latter no longer retaining its doors and hinges. Special slinging gear was required to allow both the B.IV and PR.XVI aircraft to be lifted complete, de Havilland's supplying basic design parameters to the MAP, which arranged detail design and manufacture by a sub-contractor.

By February 1945 618 Squadron had been transferred to RAAF Narromine, remaining there until disbandment in July 1945, never having flown a single operation. The B.IVs were Struck Off Charge in 1947 together with several FB.VIs, which had been shipped from the UK for training purposes. Aside from some later production B.XXVs (operated by the postwar RAF and Fleet Air Arm), it was unusual to see tropical air intakes on Mosquito bombers powered by single-stage supercharged Merlin engines. The de Havilland project number for the 'Highball' Mosquito conversion was 23691. *(Narromine Aviation Museum)*

An unidentified 618 Squadron B.IV Series ii undergoes engine runs at Narromine, probably in August 1945. 618 Squadrons B.IVs and PR.XVIs were fitted with four-bladed propellers to enhance their take-off performance from aircraft carriers. The blades were narrower in width than those of the more usual three-blade units and consequently revved up much faster and were quicker to respond to throttle movements. This was vital during carrier operations, as maximum revs were required almost from the beginning of the (limited) take-off run. Note the modified bomb bay, which did not feature doors and was adapted to accommodate two 'Highball' bouncing bombs. *(Roley Manning)*

Former 618 Squadron B.IV Series ii DZ559 'W' is parked on farmer Roland Shepherd's 'Baroona' homestead in Australia. For their carrier-borne role, 618 Squadron's B.IVs received a number of fuselage modifications including the installation of an arrestor hook, the mountings for which are clearly visible beneath the letter 'W' on DZ559's rear fuselage. To accept the arrestor hook, structural modifications were made to the fuselage, bulkheads four and five being altered to allow for the fitting of a special internal longeron, while bulkhead six was modified to house the hook snap gear. To withstand the extra loads imposed by carrier deck landings, additional strengthening was incorporated, including a longitudinal stiffening strake fitted externally to the fuselage port side. This strake was a mirror image of that fitted to the starboard side of production Mosquitoes and ran from just forward of bulkhead four to immediately aft of bulkhead five (this feature was also incorporated in the Mosquito PR.40 and PR.41 as well as the Sea Mosquito and several Royal Navy PR.XVIs). The rear fuselage access hatch was deleted and repositioned on the under fuselage (immediately aft of bulkhead four), and an additional fuselage bulkhead (No 5A) inserted 64 inches forward of bulkhead six. Externally fitted on the lower fuselage (from just forward of bulkhead five to just aft of bulkhead three) were packing blocks, mounted to which was an assembly forming the arrestor hook pivot joint. On the bottom

centre-line aft of bulkhead 5A were three 4.9-inch holes for downward identification lamps. The arrestor hook was a simple 'Vee' frame of Fairey design with a hook (supplied by the RAE) bolted to its rear end. A striker, installed on the port tube adjacent to the pivot lug, operated a microswitch on the fuselage next to bulkhead 5A. The arrestor hook release lever was mounted on the cockpit port side and operated the snap gear via a Bowden cable. Finally, the tailwheel fork pivot incorporated end plates to prevent it being caught by deck wires.

DZ559 was built at the de Havilland Hatfield factory in April 1943, passing to Vickers for 'Highball' equipment installation later the same month. It returned to Hatfield on 21 May before allocation to 618 Squadron on 9 June. DZ559 was due for transfer to 627 Squadron but was retained by 618 and shipped to Australia in October 1944. The aircraft was Struck Off Charge at Narromine on 5 April 1946 and sold to local farmer Quentin Shepherd (for $70!) in 1947. His son Roland fondly recalls DZ559 as 'the best toy I ever had!' Over the next twenty years DZ559, together with the other 618 Squadron Mosquitoes purchased by local farmers, gradually rotted away, their remains being either burned or buried. DZ559's arrestor hook retaining catch is now owned by the Narromine Aviation Museum. *(Eileen Shepherd, via Ross Shepherd)*

This second view of B.IV Series ii DZ559 was taken in 1947 and shows the aircraft crossing the old Brummagen Bridge during the journey from Narromine to farmer Roland Shepherd's 'Baroona' homestead. Roland's brother Quentin is standing on the starboard wing. (via Ross Shepherd)

This unidentified former 618 Squadron B.IV Series ii was bought at the Narromine auction by a Mr Woods. Pictured with their father's new acquisition during the summer of 1947 are (top to bottom) Roger, Brian, Diane and Nic. Note the hub for the four-bladed propeller and the lower cowling's extended carburettor air intake (the latter housing tropical filters). Fourteen of the 618 Squadron Mosquitoes auctioned at Narromine came complete with engines and were priced at $70 each (or $30 without engines). Diane Woods is today married to Col Pay, the well-known Australian collector and restorer of vintage military aircraft.
(Dulcie Woods, via Ross Shepherd)

This series of photographs depicts former 618 Squadron B.IV Series ii DZ546 (see page 78) in the process of being 'dismantled' at 'Baroona' in 1947. The aircraft was purchased at the Narromine auction by farmer brothers Rob and Ken Bowman. Supported on 44-gallon drums, DZ546 was dismembered by chain-saw before transport to the Bowman's property at Dunedoo. The remains of the aircraft are now being incorporated in a Mosquito restoration project at Narromine. The stencilling 'ESA 199' on the starboard main spar web signifies that DZ546's wing was constructed by the 'Educational Supplies Association' of Stevenage.
(All Ken Bowman)

The beautiful B.VII KB300, the first Canadian-built Mosquito, undergoes engine runs at the de Havilland Canada Downsview plant in September 1942. The B.VII was based on the projected British B.V but powered by American-built Packard Merlin 31 engines. *(National Museum of Science and Technology)*

This historic picture was taken at Downsview on 24 September 1942 during KB300's maiden flight by de Havilland Canada Chief Test Pilot Ralph Spradbrow accompanied by Hatfield prototype flight shed engineer Pepe Burrell. The flight was a great success and took place just over a year from receipt of the first batch of drawings from Hatfield. *(BAE SYSTEMS)*

Geoffrey de Havilland Junior sits in the cockpit of B.VII KB300, the first Canadian-built Mosquito, at Downsview in October 1942. He was originally scheduled to make KB300's maiden flight, but his journey from the UK was delayed due to bad weather. As a result, Ralph Spradrow carried out the first flight, Geoffrey arriving in Toronto from Hatfield on 27 September, three days later. Geoffrey first flew the aircraft on 2 October and remained in Canada for the next two months, demonstrating KB300 to senior officials in Canada and the USA before returning to England. KB300 wears an overall silver dope scheme with the spinners finished in black. *(BAE SYSTEMS)*

This striking shot shows a B.VII (probably KB300) being put through its paces at Downsview. A total of twenty-five B.VIIs were produced, the majority being retained in Canada for use by the RCAF, the remainder passing to the USAAF as F-8-DH photographic reconnaissance aircraft. This example is finished in overall silver with black spinners, a scheme that highlights the extremely clean lines of the Mosquito design. *(National Museum of Science and Technology)*

These two views of early production B.XX KB125 were taken at Hatfield on 18 March 1944. Note that the starboard engine has suffered a major oil leak, evident from the stains on the lower cowling, wing under surface and rear fuselage. KB125 went on to serve with 139 Squadron and 16 OTU, ending its days on 20 March 1945 when the undercarriage collapsed on landing at Barford St John. *(Both BAE SYSTEMS)*

In a wintry scene B.XX KB112 'EI' of 36 OTU stands at the unit's Greenwood, Nova Scotia, base in around February 1944. KB112 was the thirteenth B.XX to come off the Downsview production line and remained in Canada for the training of Mosquito aircrews. More than 500 B.XXs were produced between August 1943 and April 1945; a small number passed to the USAAF as F-8-DH photographic reconnaissance aircraft, some remaining in Canada for training purposes with the remainder being assigned to the RAF in the UK. The B.XX had a loaded weight of 21,980lb and a maximum fuel capacity of 539 gallons with useful load. *(Bell Aircraft Corporation, via Robert Dorr and Stuart Howe)*

36 OTU B.XX KB129 'LI' shares the ramp with a Douglas B.18 at Greenwood, Nova Scotia. KB129 was the thirtieth aircraft in the initial batch of 80 B.XXs (serial range KB100-KB179), which superseded the first Canadian bomber variant, the B.VII, on the de Havilland Canada production lines. Powered by Packard Merlin 31s or 33s, the B.XX was, in essence, the Canadian equivalent of the British B.IV Series ii with a performance similar to the latter marque and internal equipment of North American manufacture. KB129 is finished in the standard RAF day bomber camouflage scheme of Medium Sea Grey under surfaces with Ocean Grey and Dark Green camouflaged upper surfaces. Additionally, the aircraft wears the Fighter Command Special Recognition Markings of an 18-inch-wide Sky rear fuselage band, Sky spinners and Yellow striped wing leading edges. *(The Public Archives of Canada)*

'Z', an unidentified B.VII or B.XX of 36 OTU, is photographed following a force-landing (believed to have taken place at Lawrencetown, Nova Scotia, in December 1943). 36 OTU left the UK on 24 February 1943 bound for RCAF Greenwood, Nova Scotia, where it began training General Reconnaissance crews for Ansons and Hudsons on 9 March. In April 1943 36 OTU switched to training Mosquito aircrews and continued in this role until 30 June 1944, when it was re-designated 8 OTU RCAF. *(Stuart Howe collection)*

(BAE SYSTEMS)

B.XX KB329 seen in the UK during December 1943. In September of that year KB329 had been delivered to de Havilland's at Hatfield before allocation to 627 Squadron on 5 January 1944. Two days later it was assigned to 139 Squadron at Wyton, remaining with 627 when the Squadron moved to Upwood in February 1944. At 0345hrs on 25 June 1944 KB329, crewed by Flt Lt W. W. Boylson DFC & Bar (RAAF) and Sqn Ldr G. H. Wilson DSO DFC, took off from Upwood for a raid on Berlin, but was shot by a night-fighter and crashed 4 miles north of Flatow. *(Richard Riding collection)*

Navigator Flt Lt Pete Hobbs DFC (left) and pilot Flt Lt 'Jake' Jacobs pictured with 608 Squadron B.XX KB358 '6T-J' at Downham Market on 20 February 1945 following the last operation of Flt Lt Jacob's second tour (the target on this occasion being the railway yard at Erfurt). Note the bundles of 'Window' stacked beneath the starboard propeller, a regular payload for 608 Squadron's Mosquitoes. KB358 was built at the de Havilland Canada Downsview factory in August 1944 and flown to the UK, arriving at Prestwick on 29 September. Following modifications at 13 MU Henlow (the reception point for Canadian-built Mosquitoes despatched to the UK), KB358 was issued to 139 Squadron at Upwood on 29 October 1944. Three weeks later it was transferred to

608 Squadron at Downham Market and assigned the unit codes '6T-L'. KB358 flew its first operation (target Berlin) on 27 November 1944 and its twentieth on 14 January 1945, by which time it had been re-coded '6T-B'. It was later recoded '6T-J' and in all flew a total of forty-nine operations with 608 Squadron, the last on 30 March 1945. Damaged during the latter sortie, KB358 was later declared a write-off and Struck Off Charge on 3 May 1945. Note the 'paddle'-blade propellers and 'fish tail' exhaust stubs. *(Jake Jacobs)*

In this atmospheric shot featuring brand new B.XXVs at Toronto airport awaiting delivery, the Mosquito in the background is KB660, which arrived in the UK during early 1945, passing to the Admiralty on 3 August that same year. In January 1946 it was allocated to 733 Squadron Fleet Air Arm at Trincomalee, Ceylon. Note the 'paddle'-blade propellers and 100-gallon drop tanks on the Mosquito in the foreground. By the end of May 1945 489 Canadian-built Mosquitoes had been flown across the Atlantic to Britain, several record-breaking flights being made in the process. In May 1944 a Canadian-built Mosquito Bomber flew (coast to coast) from Labrador to Prestwick in 5hrs 39mins. de Havilland representatives in the UK reported that 'Canadian-built Mosquitoes are popular, and reported to be "considerably faster" than English-built, swing less and have more stability at height; the last two points are probably incorrect.' *(BAE SYSTEMS)*

These three pictures are of a unique Mosquito, in this case Canadian-built B.XXV KB471 photographed at Marshalls of Cambridge in late 1944. Close inspection of the first photograph reveals that KB471 is equipped with two-speed, two-stage supercharged Merlin engines but retains the five stub exhausts of the B.XXV's single-stage supercharged Merlin 225 installation. This conversion resulted from a requirement by 8 Group concerning the load-carrying capabilities of Mosquito B.XXs and B.XXVs. A need existed for bulged bomb bay doors on these aircraft to permit carriage of the 4,000lb bomb (as featured on the B.XVI and some converted B.IV Series iis and B.IXs). In order to bring the centre of gravity within safe limits it was deemed necessary to install two-speed, two-stage supercharged Merlin engines, as seen in the second photograph, as well as enlarged elevator horn balances, the latter to improve handling characteristics. Canadian-built Mosquito bombers were not produced with two-speed, two-stage supercharged engines (although a 'B.23' with Merlin 69s had been projected), so B.XXV KB471 was chosen for the first conversion, which was begun by Marshalls in October 1944.

In addition to bulged bomb bay doors, as seen in the third photograph, Packard Merlin 69s were installed, but KB471's original Merlin 225 radiators, oil coolers and cabin heaters were retained. The original starboard engine outer side cowling was lengthened and Merlin 72/73 lower cowlings fitted. As depicted, KB471's starboard outer side cowling retained provision for the B.XXV's original five-stub exhaust layout, although the port outer cowling was a standard unit for the Merlin 70 series installation.

KB471 was successfully flight-tested in this configuration during January 1945, but no further conversions were undertaken as the war was drawing to an end (although at least five of the RAF's B.XXVs were modified with bulged bomb bay doors). Note the sheet metal inserts and the original dark green camouflage on KB471's modified side cowling. Similar installations of two-speed, two-stage supercharged Packard Merlins were made on two postwar US civilian-operated Mosquito racers, although neither machine featured production two-stage Merlin Mosquito lower cowlings. *(All Marshall Group)*

Two further views of B.XXV KB471 taken following the installation of two-speed, two-stage supercharged Merlin 69s by Marshalls of Cambridge. Note the bulged bomb bay doors, 'paddle'-blade propellers, canopy 'tear drop' observation blisters, and the enlarged elevator horn balances. KB471's original engine inner side cowlings were replaced with Merlin 70 series units (as this was simpler than modifying the existing single-stage Merlin ones), evident from the spark plug cooling intake on the port cowling's forward section, and the six exhaust stubs normally associated with the two-stage Merlin installation. The latter contrasts markedly with the five stubs exiting

KB471's (original) modified starboard outer cowling. Although not equipped with a pressurised cockpit, in this configuration KB471 approximated the British-built B.XVI. KB471 had been allocated to 608 Squadron prior to this conversion and was delivered to Boscombe Down for trials work in February 1945.

In the second picture note the tailcone-mounted aerial for the TRE Type 338 rearward-looking Boozer III radar. The latter was used to detect German Wurzburg or FuG 202/212 night-fighter radar transmissions. This unique aeroplane was Struck Off Charge in January 1947.
(Richard Riding collection/Alan Brackley collection)

B.XXV KA993 of 8 OTU RCAF seen from another Mosquito during a training flight from Greenwood, Nova Scotia, in June 1945. KA993 was flown on this occasion by newly qualified Mosquito pilot Alan Johnson, with Plt Off Jacobs as navigator. The B.XXV was developed from the B.XX and differed principally from the earlier variant through the installation of more powerful engines, namely Packard Merlin 225s of 1,620hp each. While the majority of B.XXVs were despatched to the UK, KA993 remained in Canada for the training of Mosquito aircrews. Note the Sky-painted spinners and the extension of the upper surface camouflage down the engine side cowlings. *(Alan Johnson)*

'I was already familiar with the features of the Mossie, but to stand beside one, to marvel at its beautiful yet purposeful lines, was an ambition realised,' recalls pilot Alan Johnson as he remembers his introduction to the Mosquito at 8 OTU, RCAF Greenwood. Alan photographed this B.XXV (KA991) at Greenwood during his ten-week Mosquito training course, which ended on 8 July 1945. Following initial training on the Airspeed Oxford, he went on to complete six dual flights in Mosquitoes (three in T.27s, two in T.IIIs and one in a B.XX) before making his first solo in a B.XX on 14 June 1945. He also made fifteen training sorties in B.XXVs, including this example as well as KA992 and KA993. Alan Johnson later flew FB.VIs with 84 Squadron in Java. *(Alan Johnson)*

The flight-line and control tower at 8 OTU, RCAF Greenwood, in June 1945. 8 OTU operated various marks of Mosquito including the T.3, T.27, B.XX and B.XXV. *(Alan Johnson)*

162 Squadron B.XXV KB534 'Z' following an argument with a Nissen hut at Blackbushe on 14 March 1946. During this period 162 Squadron was operating a high-speed courier service known as the 'Air Delivery Letter Service' (ADLS) to the capitals of Central and Northern Europe. This service included the carriage of mail and newspapers in special containers within the bomb bay. To maximise the Mosquitoes' speed advantage and provide the fastest possible service, the containers were dropped from the aircraft. During early operations the containers occasionally split, and during one drop at Fornebu the pilot reported flying down the fjord in a storm of newspapers! The problem was eventually solved by using airmen's kit-bags, which could accommodate 800 newspapers. On long flights pilots normally flew above 20,000 feet to avoid bad weather, often using favourable winds to achieve ground speeds of 400mph.

Canadian-built KB534 arrived in the UK on 29 November 1944, passing to 13 MU Henlow for modifications on 2 December. Allocated to 162 Squadron on 2 January 1945, KB534 suffered an undercarriage collapse during a landing accident at Woodbridge on 27 March. After repairs it returned to service in May 1945, but was written off following the incident depicted here. *(Geoffrey Perks)*

This is the end of 162 Squadron B.XXV KB677 at Ciampino, Rome, on 17 January 1946. KB677 was built by de Havilland Canada and arrived in the UK on 30 March 1945. Delivered to 13 MU Henlow for modifications on 6 April 1945, it entered storage with 27 MU Shawbury two months later. On 4 January 1946 it was issued to 162 Squadron for its high-speed mail flights from Blackbushe. KB677's career was very brief: While taking off from Ciampino during the morning of 17 January 1946 in the hands of Flt Lt Geoffrey Perks, it suffered a burst port main wheel tyre, causing the aircraft to swing to port and the undercarriage to collapse. The fuel tanks subsequently ignited and KB677 was very quickly consumed by fire. Both crew members escaped unhurt, investigation later revealing that the port main wheel tyre had been punctured by a section of the PSP runway surface. *(Geoffrey Perks)*

162 Squadron B.XXV KB643 photographed during recovery at Buckeburg following a landing accident on 28 April 1946. Built by de Havilland Canada in March 1945, KB643 was delivered to 13 MU Henlow for modifications on 30 March 1945, remaining there until 8 August, when it entered storage at 27 MU Shawbury. On 9 February 1946 it entered service with 162 Squadron at Blackbushe, receiving the unit codes 'CR-L'. During the course of high-speed mail flights KB643 was involved in two accidents. The first took place at Istres on 19 April 1946, but damage was not serious and KB643 was repaired on site. The second incident occurred nine days later when KB643 undershot on landing at Buckeburg, a burst tyre leading to collapse of the undercarriage. Note the damaged fuselage, severed at number three bulkhead, and the bent 'paddle'-blade propellers. KB643 was subsequently written off. *(Dave Welch)*

KA965, a rather forlorn-looking B.XXV, photographed at Royal Naval Air Station Stretton during the late 1940s. KA965 was built at the de Havilland Canada Downsview factory and flown to the United Kingdom, where it was received at 13 MU Henlow. On 21 June 1945 it was transferred to the Admiralty and flown to RNAS Middle Wallop, eventually making its way to the Aircraft Holding Unit at Stretton in 1946. KA965 appears to be in the process of being scrapped, as the engines have been removed and the outer wings crudely chopped off. *(Peter Cook)*

B.XXV KB428 running up next to Halifax RG184 at the RCAF Winter Experimental Establishment (WEE) at Edmonton in 1945. Two Mosquito Bombers were assigned to the WEE for cold weather testing, the other being KB642, also a B.XXV. KB428 was delivered to the RCAF in September 1944 and assigned to the Winter Experimental & Training Flight at Gimli, Manitoba, later the same month. In September 1945 the WE&TF was retitled the Winter Experimental Establishment and transferred to RCAF Edmonton. On 9 October KB428 moved to RCAF Camp Borden, where it became an instructional airframe, remaining there until 27 February 1950 when it passed to the War Assets Corporation for public disposal. In connection with WEE trials work, KB428's wing and tailplane under surfaces have been finished in high-visibility yellow. The cockpit entrance door is noticeably absent. *(W. Cottrell, Alberta Aviation Museum collection)*

LR495, the first Mosquito B.IX, banks away from the camera aircraft during a test flight from the A&AEE at Boscombe Down in 1943. Based on the PR.IX, the B.IX introduced two-speed, two-stage supercharged Merlin engines to the Bomber airframe, increasing altitude performance and maximum level speed. Early B.IXs were equipped with 1,680hp Merlin 72/73s, but later production aircraft featured Merlin 76/77s of 1,710hp. The Merlin 70 series featured a cabin blower drive but a cockpit pressurisation system had not been developed in time for the PR and B.IX, being introduced instead on the PR and B. XVI. LR495 made its maiden flight on 23 March 1943 and the first production B.IXs were delivered to 109 Squadron in April 1943. This photograph was taken during trials of experimental Smoke Curtain Installation (SCI) equipment, the containers for which can be seen mounted beneath LR495's wings. *(Richard Riding collection)*

B.IX LR495 is seen again equipped with SCI canisters on the underwing hardpoints. The B.IX was the first Bomber version to incorporate the strengthened or 'basic' wing originally intended for the projected B.V. This 'basic' wing featured underwing hardpoints (at Rib 8) for drop tanks or two 500lb bombs, the latter increasing the Mosquito Bomber's offensive load to 3,000lb.

LR495 was employed on experimental work at Farnborough and Boscombe Down, including level speed trials with and without external loads, and overload performance tests up to 23,000lb all-up weight. Performance trials without external bombs or fuel tanks were conducted at a take-off weight of 21,910lb, corresponding to a 2,000lb internal bomb load plus full fuel and oil tanks. In this condition LR495 recorded a maximum speed (in full supercharger gear) of 405mph at 25,700 feet. Later tests with the external bombs in position (corresponding to A&AEE calculations for a maximum permissible take-off weight of 22,850lb) recorded a maximum speed of 388mph at 23,000 feet. LR495 was lost on 29 January 1944 when it crashed on take-off from Boscombe Down during an overload test, the aircraft breaking up after coming down in a field at Larkhill. *(Richard Riding)*

New Zealand pilots of 109 Squadron pictured in front of OBOE-equipped B.IX LR504 'HS-P' ('The Grim Reaper') at Little Staughton. OBOE was a precision blind-bombing system employing secondary radar principles. Devised by Alec Reeves of Standard Telephone & Cables Ltd in conjunction with Frank Jones of the TRE, OBOE consisted of two ground stations emitting pulses on a single carrier frequency but with different recurrence frequencies. One ground station was known as the tracking station while the other was referred to as the releasing station. The Mosquito would fly on a course of constant radius about the tracking station until it arrived over the target area. When the calculated point of bomb release had been reached the releasing station would send a signal to the aircraft automatically releasing the bombs. OBOE was initially pioneered on 109 Squadron's Mosquito B.IV Series iis, but the more powerful B.IX could fly faster and higher, increasing OBOE range as well as immunity from interception.

The tenth production B.IX, LR504 flew a total of 200 sorties, serving with both 109 and 105 Squadrons. It was delivered to 109 Squadron on 31 May 1943 and flew its first operation (target Krefeld) on 21 June 1943. After completing sixty sorties LR504 was assigned to 105 Squadron on 13 March 1944, receiving the unit codes 'GB-H'. The aircraft's 100th sortie was completed on 28 September 1944, by which time it sported a night under surface finish and 'needle'-blade propellers. LR504 returned to 109 Squadron in October 1944 but was damaged on 6 December after the undercarriage collapsed on return from an operation to Duisberg. The aircraft was repaired and had flown a further forty operations by VE Day, including four during 'Operation Manna'. At some point after August 1944 LR504's under surfaces were refinished in Medium Sea Grey and the 'needle'-blade propellers replaced by 'paddle'-blade units. Note LR504's extensive mission 'tally' together with the painted Perspex nose and bomb-aimer's glass panel. *(Bill Simpson, via Stuart Howe)*

LR495, the first Mosquito B.IX, is seen again, this time at Hatfield on 9 April 1943. Note the bomb mounted on the port wing's underwing hardpoint, the B.IX being the first Mosquito Bomber version to feature this facility. *(BAE SYSTEMS)*

Pilot Geoffrey Perks (right) and navigator Don Brown pose with a pristine 571 Squadron B.XVI at RAF Oakington in 1945. Judging by the absence of exhaust staining on the cowlings, coupled with the lack of a mission 'tally' on the nose, this Mosquito was probably a new delivery to the Squadron. 571 Squadron was formed at Downham Market on 7 April 1944 during the expansion of No 8 Group's Light Night Striking Force. Equipped with Mosquito B.XVIs, 571 flew its first operational sortie (target Osnabruck) on 12 April 1944.

The B.XVI was developed from the B.IX but differed from the earlier variant through provision of a pressurised cockpit, modified canopy and (aside from the first twelve production aircraft) bulged bomb bay doors. The latter feature, well illustrated in this picture, enabled the B.XVI to carry a 4,000lb 'Cookie' blast bomb. 571 Squadron dropped a large number of 'Cookies' on Berlin and also laid mines to disrupt the German waterways system. Note the curved demarcation line on the nose camouflage (a feature of some Hatfield-built Mosquito Bombers), together with the 'paddle'-blade propellers and 100-gallon drop tanks. After the war, Geoffrey Perks flew Mosquito B.35s as a Flight Commander with 14 Squadron in Germany. *(Geoffrey Perks)*

692 Squadron B.XVI MM141 'P3-H' lies inverted in a ditch after overshooting the runway at Warboys on the night of 30 September 1944. This Hatfield-built B.XVI was assigned to 109 Squadron on 15 June 1944 before passing to 692 Squadron on 5 July. At 1825hrs on 30 September 1944 MM141 took off for Hamburg at the start of its forty-second operational sortie. Returning to Warboys at 2028hrs, it overshot the runway into a nearby field where it struck a hedge and overturned. Both crew members survived but the aircraft was damaged beyond repair. Equipped with Mosquito B.IVs, 692 Squadron formed at Graveley on 1 January 1944. By July the Squadron was equipped exclusively with the Mosquito B.XVI and became an instrumental part of 8 Group's Light Night Striking Force. *(Stuart Howe collection)*

These two views of 98 Squadron B.XVI RV297 'VO-H' were
taken over Germany in 1946. Formerly equipped with
Mitchells, 98 Squadron received its first Mosquito B.XVIs in
September 1945 and moved from Melsbroek to Wahn (as
part of the BAFO) in March 1946. Hatfield-built in
December 1944, RV297 was initially delivered to 692
Squadron, but also saw service with 128 (as 'M5-F'), 139 and
571 Squadrons before allocation to 98 on 8 November 1945.
It remained on the Squadron's strength until November
1947, when B.35s began replacing the B.XVIs. On 26
November RV297 flew to 9 MU for storage, eventually being
sold as scrap to John Dale Ltd on 5 August 1948.
(Both Wally Froud, via Stuart Howe)

Airmen refuel an unidentified 98 Squadron B.XVI ('VO-A')
from a bowser at Melsbroek in 1946. Many of 98 Squadron's
B.XVIs were war veterans and soldiered on until replaced
by B.35s between 1947 and 1948. The B.XVI was classified
obsolete in April 1949. *(Wally Froud, via Stuart Howe)*

Early production B.35 TA638 photographed at Boscombe Down in May 1945. The B.35 represented the pinnacle of Mosquito Bomber development and first flew in March 1945. An updated version of the B.XVI, it was equipped with fuel-injected Merlin 113 and 114 series engines, but arrived too late for wartime operational service. B.35s were originally earmarked for Far East operations with 'Tiger Force' and many received modifications for this role including the installation of tropical filters in the lower cowling air intakes. Modification and preparation work delayed the B.35's introduction to RAF squadron service until 1947. Following trials work at the A&AEE at Boscombe Down, TA638 was converted to TT.35 status by Brooklands Aviation before being sold for scrap on 25 January 1957. The aircraft wears the standard Mosquito Day Bomber scheme of Ocean Grey and Dark Green camouflaged upper surfaces with Medium Sea Grey under surfaces. *(Richard Riding collection)*

These two shots show armourers loading a 4,000lb 'Cookie' into the bomb bay of a B.XVI. These are staged pictures taken at Hatfield in 1944, possibly during filming of the Cecil J. Gurney production *de Havilland Presents The Mosquito*. This B.XVI had just come off the Hatfield production line and is likely to be MM118. In the second picture, note the armourers manually winching the bomb into position using handles slotted through the port fuselage side panel. Two special winches were provided for this purpose, both permanently attached to the wing centre section. The winch handles engaged with a universal

coupling, the rear winch featuring an adjustable cable guide enabling the bomb to be offered up straight to the release gear. To prevent overloading of the winches and hoisting cables, a friction device was incorporated in both winch handles at their point of attachment to the winch shafts. Note the factory buildings to the right of the second picture, with a Fighter Mosquito parked outside. MM118 served with 571 and 692 Squadrons, eventually being lost on 17 September 1944 when it crashed near Graveley on return from a raid to Cologne. *(Both BAE SYSTEMS)*

MOSQUITO

The most efficient air weapon

A British achievement

DE HAVILLAND

(BAE SYSTEMS)

Round the clock: a B.XVI departs from RAF Wyton at the start of another sortie as USAAF B.17 'Flying Fortresses' pass by on return from a daylight raid. This Mosquito is likely to be an aircraft from the resident 128 Squadron. Note the 100-gallon drop tanks and the bulged bomb bay. Mosquito Bombers could fly to Berlin and back in 4 hours, as opposed to the same trip in a four-engined heavy bomber, which took almost twice that. Mosquitoes of 8 Group's Light Night Striking Force regularly flew to the German capital twice in one night. *(Howard Lees)*

A formation of 98 Squadron B.35s performs a low-level run and break over another B.35 at RAF Wahn in 1949. The leading aircraft is believed to have been flown by Flt Lt 'Jock' Cassels, with Ken Hirst and Flt Lt Roger Topp as numbers two and three. 98 and 14 Squadrons were the only Mosquito Bomber units stationed in Germany at the time and formed part of the British Air Forces of Occupation (BAFO). Note that the tailwheels have been locked permanently down, a peacetime practice adopted to minimise hydraulic problems. *(R. L. Topp)*

An unidentified 98 Squadron B.35 flown by Flt Lt Ken Hirst is photographed from another B.35 (flown by Flt Lt 'Jock' Cassels) during a cross-country flight from Wahn on 8 August 1949. 14 and 98 Squadrons took part in many of the postwar Fighter and Bomber Command air exercises over the UK, flying from and returning to their base in Germany. Sometimes the Mosquitoes flew at medium or high level in order to give the 'defending' fighters a chance of interception, but the Mosquito crews much preferred low-level 'attacks' on fighter airfields. *(Frank Joliffe, via Stuart Howe)*

B.35s of 98 Squadron take off from Celle in 1949. The leading aircraft is believed to be VP181, built by Airspeed at Christchurch in 1947. Following five months in storage at 15 MU, VP181 joined 98 Squadron at Wahn in May 1948 where it was coded 'VO-B'. 98 Squadron operated the aircraft until 28 February 1951, when it was flown to 38 MU Llandow for storage. In July 1953 it was delivered to Brooklands Aviation at Sywell, near Northampton, for conversion to TT.35 status, this work being completed by February 1954. VP181 spent the remainder of its life in storage with 38 MU and was sold as scrap to Lowton Metals on 16 April 1957. *(Geoffrey Perks)*

At RAF Wahn in 1949 is immaculate B.35 VP202 of 14 Squadron. Built at the Airspeed Christchurch factory in October 1947 (under Air Ministry Contract 3527), VP202 was retained at Christchurch for modifications before delivery to 15 MU at Wroughton on 30 April 1948 for storage. On 2 July 1948 VP202 was assigned to 14 Squadron at RAF Wahn in Germany, becoming the regular mount of Flt Lt Mike Levy, who recalls the aircraft as 'my pride and joy'. VP202 was written off by another 14 Squadron pilot on 29 April 1949 after undershooting Wahn during a practice single-engine landing (Mike Levy was on leave at the time).

The aircraft is finished silver overall and carries the 14 Squadron crest on both sides of the fin. The spinners are painted yellow as are the Squadron code letters, which are also outlined in black. The aerial under the rear fuselage is for the 'BABS' (Beam Approach Beacon System) navigation aid, while those on the wingtips are di-pole director and reflector aerials for the IFF AR 5610 installation. The latter incorporated a Type 3624 transmitter-receiver floor-mounted in the battery compartment forward of fuselage bulkhead four. *(Both Mike Levy)*

A primary role of the BAFO Mosquito B.35 Squadrons was low-level bombing, regular practice being carried out over the Fassberg and Nordhorn Ranges. Demonstration bombing was usually conducted in box formations of four aircraft, and this photograph (taken from the under-fuselage F.24 camera using an angled mirror) features four 98 Squadron B.35s releasing 500lb bombs over the Fassberg Range in 1948. The postwar Mosquito Bomber Squadrons maintained the aircraft's reputation for precision low-level strikes. *(Frank Jolliffe, via Stuart Howe)*

Up close and personal is 14 Squadron B.35 TJ141 'CX-Y', flown by Flt Lt Mike Levy with Navigator 2 Bert Fulker in the right-hand seat. This picture was taken by the under-fuselage camera (using an angled mirror to take rear-view oblique pictures) of B.35 TA695 'CX-W', flown by Fg Off Neville Cornwall (with Navigator 3 Saxby) on 9 September 1948. Both aircraft were on a local low-flying and formation exercise from their base at Wahn. The object protruding in the upper right-hand corner is the under-fuselage aerial for the 'BABS' (Beam Approach Beacon System) navigation aid. On 30 October 1948 Neville Cornwall (together with Mike Levy's regular navigator, Flt Lt Williams) were lost in TJ141 after an engine fire caused the aircraft to crash into the sea off Gozo during a flight from Malta to Wahn. Note the fairing for the fuel cooler radiator (visible beneath the starboard wing root) mounted on the rear section of the starboard fuselage underwing side panel. *(Mike Levy)*

139 Squadron B.35 RS699 'XD-J' on a 'Sunray' detachment to
Shallufa in November 1949. 'Sunrays' were long-range
overseas navigation flights designed to provide concentrated
training during the winter months when flying in UK skies
was spasmodic. The first B.35 produced by the Airspeed
Christchurch factory, RS699 was ready for collection on 28
February 1946. Following brief spells with 274 and 37 MUs, it
returned to Christchurch for modifications on 17 April 1947.
In January 1948 it was delivered to 231 OCU, serving with
this unit for just over a year before joining 139 Squadron at
Coningsby on 25 February 1949. As 'XD-J' RS699 remained
with 139 until 2 February 1951, when it flew into the ground
during a practice bombing run over the Wainfleet Ranges. 139
Squadron pilot Harold Stillwell recalls RS699 as 'a particularly
smooth specimen of the breed'. Note the 100-gallon drop
tanks and the 'Signal Red' spinners, the latter a feature of 139
Squadron's postwar Mosquitoes. Keen-eyed observers will
spot the Lincoln and Proctor in the background. During its
Shallufa detachments 139 Squadron also conducted low-level
shallow dive bombing practice flights. *(Harold Stillwell)*

The port engine of a 139 Squadron B.35 (probably VP179) is receiving attention at Shallufa in 1949. Note the coolant header tank mounted on the front top of the engine, and the intercooler radiator just forward of the fitter's right knee. Early production Mosquito B.35s were equipped with Merlin 113 and 114 engines, each producing 1,690hp at 13,000 feet with 18lb boost. The Merlin 114 was installed in the port side and drove a Marshall cabin supercharger to maintain 2lb per sq in cabin pressure differential. The Merlin 100 series engines were developed from the two-stage, two-speed supercharged Merlin 70 series (fitted to the Mosquito B.IX, PR.IX, B.XVI, PR.XVI and NF.30), but differed from the earlier versions through provision of an SU fuel-injection pump and improved blower. The first Mosquito version to be equipped with 100 series Merlins was the PR.32 (Merlin 113/114), which first saw operational service over Europe in December 1944. Merlin 113A and 114A engines were equipped with anti-surge supercharger diffusers and were fitted to the Mosquito PR.34A, B.35, TT.35, NF.36 and NF.38. The identity of this particular engine fitter is presently unknown. *(Harold Stillwell)*

The starboard engine and propeller of 139 Squadron B.35 VP179 undergo inspection at Shallufa during a 'Sunray' detachment in November 1949. Airspeed-built in 1947, VP179 served with 231 OCU before transfer to 139 Squadron at Coningsby, where it was allocated the unit codes 'XD-B'. It was written off on 17 October 1950 after crashing during a single-engine landing at Hemswell. *(Harold Stillwell)*

Here is B.35 RS699 'XD-J' again at Shallufa, this time ground-running its uncowled port engine. The Mosquito to RS699s right is VP179 'XD-B', and the picture was taken from beneath the Shallufa Station Flight Beaufighter TT.10 SR916. *(Harold Stillwell)*

B.35 TH984 'P' of 231 OCU photographed at RAF Coningsby in February 1949. Formed from a detachment of 16 OTU on 15 March 1947, 231 OCU's primary role was the training of Mosquito Bomber and Photographic Reconnaissance crews. Based at Coningsby and equipped with Mosquito B.XVIs and B.35s, 231 OCU disbanded on 4 December 1949 before re-forming two years later (at Bassingbourn) to train Canberra jet bomber crews.

Hatfield-built in 1945, TH984 was prepared for service at 218 MU Colerne before allocation to 142 Squadron in August 1945 (together with several other B.35s including TH976, TH979 and TA722). TH984 returned to 218 MU in September 1945, remaining there until 6 October 1948 when it was delivered to 231 OCU. It eventually passed to the Coningsby Station Flight and was destroyed in a night-flying accident on 20 December 1949 when it crashed south of Waddington. TH984 is finished in the standard day bomber camouflage scheme with the addition of a yellow training band on the rear fuselage. Note the two silver-finished B.35s to TH984's left. The objects in the foreground are parachutes. *(Geoffrey Perks)*

B.35s of 98 Squadron at RAF Celle shortly after the Berlin Airlift. Previously based at Wahn, the Squadron moved to Celle in September 1949. Note the PSP (Pierced Steel Planking) aerodrome surface.
(via Frank Jolliffe and Stuart Howe)

98 Squadron aircrews discuss the flight plan prior to taking off from RAF Wahn in 1949. Second from the left is navigator Pat Fell, with his Polish pilot, Joe Butryn, second from the right. The Mosquito behind them is one of 98 Squadron's B.35s, still resplendent in its factory-applied day bomber camouflage scheme (several of the Squadron's B.35s had been re-finished overall silver by this time). Note the groundcrew member locking the Dzus fasteners on the port engine lower cowling; these often proved awkward to engage, requiring a large screwdriver or 'Dzus Key' to lock them in position. The Mosquito in the background is probably an FB.VI from the resident 11 Squadron. *(via Frank Jolliffe and Stuart Howe)*

98 Squadron B.35 TJ133 'VO-A' airborne from RAF Celle. A subsidiary role of the BAFO Mosquito Bomber squadrons was the conduct of daily meteorological flights, as BAFO did not possess a dedicated meteorological unit. These were undertaken by a single aircraft at first light and noon each day, the duty being shared on alternate months between 14 and 98 Squadrons. The Mosquitoes were fitted with wet- and dry-bulb thermometers, readings being taken in straight and level flight at 500, 1,000 and 1,500 feet. The readings were then logged at every drop of 50 millibars until 300 millibars had been reached (approximately 30,000 feet). Additionally, visual observations were made regarding cloud levels, condensation trails and icing conditions, this information being passed to HQ BAFO for transmission to all meteorological stations.

TJ133 left the Hatfield factory in October 1945 for storage at 27 MU Shawbury. In January 1947 it was flown to Marshalls at Cambridge for modifications before returning to store in March 1948, this time at 19 MU. On 30 June 1949 the aircraft was assigned to the BAFO Reserve Aircraft Pool at Luneberg, being allocated to 98 Squadron at Celle on 13 October 1949. It served with 98 Squadron until March 1951 when it returned to 27 MU, eventually being sold as scrap on 26 November 1954. *(Patrick Fell, via Stuart Howe)*

14 Squadron aircrews photographed at the unit's Celle base in approximately 1950. The Mosquito B.35 behind them is possibly VP180 or VP189, the latter currently preserved at the Alberta Aviation Museum where it has been converted to represent a 418 Squadron RCAF FB.VI. Back row (left to right): Master Navigator G. Reed; Navigator F. Suskiewicz (Polish); Pilot 3 Ray Cocks; Flt Sgt Goodyear; Fg Off O. Bergh (South African); (unknown); Fg Off P. Taylor; (unknown); (unknown); Navigator 2 Merideth. Front row (left to right): Flt Lt Fry; Flt Lt Sargent; Commanding Officer Sqn Ldr Greenleaf (see page 102); Flt Lt G. D. Perks; Flt Lt M. Levy; Flt Lt Ramaof. *(Geoffrey Perks)*

September 1948 saw the first major United Kingdom air defence exercise since the Battle of Britain. Code-named 'Operation Dagger', participants included RAF Fighter, Bomber, Coastal, Training and Reserve Commands, together with the USAF, British Army Anti-Aircraft Command and the Royal Observer Corps. This is the scene at RAF Wahn on 5 September as 98 Squadron's B.35s prepare to take off for a simulated attack on RAF Horsham St Faith near Norwich. Both BAFO Mosquito Bomber Squadrons (14 and 98) took part in the exercise, the Mosquito in the foreground being flown by Flt Lt (later Air Cdre) Roger Topp, with Frank Jolliffe as navigator. The 'attack' was a great success, the Mosquitoes avoiding interception and arriving over Horsham St Faith to discover the resident 'defending' Meteor Squadrons still on the ground! The Mosquitoes dropped toilet rolls over the aerodrome, each inscribed with rude messages from the Wahn groundcrews to their opposite numbers at Horsham St Faith. Roger Topp later formed the 'Black Arrows' aerobatic team of 111 Squadron, leading the famous twenty-two-Hunter formation loop at the 1958 Farnborough Air Show. Note that Flt Lt Topp's Mosquito appears to have a replacement starboard elevator and features newly applied fabric on the starboard wingtip. *(Frank Jolliffe, via Stuart Howe)*

This striking view is from the cockpit of a 14 Squadron B.35 during a formation practice flight from West Malling in September 1950; the Squadron was rehearsing for the annual Battle of Britain flypast over London. Note the 100-gallon wing drop tanks and the bulged bomb bay doors, the latter a prominent feature of the B.XVI and B.35. *(Mike Levy)*

During a formation take-off from Celle on 28 September 1950, 14 Squadron B.35 TK617 flew into the slipstream of the lead aircraft shortly after lift-off, causing the port undercarriage assembly to hit the ground. The port undercarriage subsequently jammed and would neither lower nor fully retract. TK617, flown by Flt Lt Geoffrey Perks, remained airborne to burn off fuel before making a belly-landing back at Celle. During the landing both propellers were torn away, the port unit chopping off the aircraft's nose and narrowly missing Geoffrey Perks's legs! After TK617 came to rest Geoffrey leant forward to disengage the magneto switches, but all four had disappeared! Note that a single blade from the starboard propeller has chopped its way through the starboard radiator leading edge structure. The nose section has been destroyed and the undercarriage doors and lower cowlings crushed. The crew survived this incident but TK617 was written off. *(Both Geoffrey Perks)*

Taken around ten days before the previous picture, 14 Squadron B.35 TK617 'CX-D' seen from the navigator's seat of another B.35 during formation practice for the 1950 Battle of Britain flypast over London. The apparent distortion of the aircraft's forward fuselage and mainplane is due to the curvature of the photographic aircraft's cockpit canopy Perspex. TK617 was built at Hatfield in late 1945 and issued to 14 Squadron at Wahn in 1947. *(Mike Levy)*

TA695, a 14 Squadron B.35, probably at Sylt in April or May 1950. This Hatfield-built B.35 was despatched to 27 MU Shawbury for storage on 6 June 1945. In April 1947 it was delivered to Air Service Training at Hamble for modifications, which were completed by 12 February 1948 when it flew to 10 MU for further storage. In July 1948 the aircraft, still wearing its factory camouflage scheme, was assigned to 14 Squadron at RAF Wahn, receiving the unit codes 'CX-W'. TA695 was flown on several occasions by Flt Lt Mike Levy and in 1950 took part in the RAF Display at Farnborough (by which time it had been refinished in overall silver dope), continuing to serve with 14 Squadron until February 1951 when the unit re-equipped with Vampire FB.5s. TA695 went into store at 22 MU Silloth on 27 February 1951, remaining there until October 1953 when it was delivered to Brooklands Aviation at Sywell for conversion to TT.35 standard. It emerged as a TT.35 on 7 January 1954 before returning to store, this time with 38 MU Llandow. This aircraft saw no further service, being sold as scrap to Eyre & Company on 25 January 1957. *(Mike Levy)*

Navigator 1 Felix Suskiewicz (left) pictured with two unidentified 14 Squadron groundcrew at West Malling. The date is 8 July 1950 and 14 Squadron (together with 98) was about to depart for the second day of the RAF Display at Farnborough, where it conducted a re-enactment of the 1944 Amiens prison raid. The aircraft behind them is B.35 VR799, built by the Airspeed Christchurch factory in 1947 and serving with 14 Squadron and the Bassingbourn Station Flight before being sold as scrap on 29 November 1954. Note the Mosquito NF.36 parked in the distance to the left, probably an aircraft belonging to the resident 25 Squadron. *(Mike Levy)*

The 1950 RAF Display at Farnborough featured a spectacular re-enactment of 'Operation Jericho', the wartime precision raid on Amiens prison. Twelve Mosquito B.35s from 14 and 98 Squadrons bombed a mock-up of the prison located on the west side of Farnborough aerodrome. Live commentary on the 'attack' was broadcast by BBC correspondent John Ellison from 98 Squadron B.35 RS716 flown by Flt Lt Roger Topp, who kept his thumb firmly on the radio transmit button (located on the control column 'wheel') throughout the entire sequence, as John Ellison had no facility to transmit his broadcast commentary. Consequently Roger Topp was unable to receive messages from the formation leader and 'just followed the crowd of Mossies'. In this photograph Roger Topp (left) and John Ellison are seen at West Malling prior to taking off for Farnborough. RS716 served with 98 Squadron from April 1950 until February 1951 and bore the unit code letters 'VO-W'. Following conversion to TT.35 status, RS716 was assigned to 229 OCU before being sold as scrap to Lowton Metals on 30 August 1957. Note the peeling silver dope on the aircraft's nose. *(Roger Topp)*

The cockpit view of a B.XVI or B.35 at Hatfield in 1946 shows the hinged inner entry door with the ladder stowage compartment immediately ahead. The blind flying panel is located forward of the control column 'wheel' with the engine instrumentation in a bank on the left. The throttle and pitch control levers are mounted in a box on the left-hand side of the cockpit wall, with the TR 1143 (or 1430) radio controller directly beneath them. Selector levers for the bomb doors, undercarriage and flaps are located below the right-hand side of the blind flying panel, with the aileron trim wheel positioned slightly further down. On the right-hand cockpit wall are the fuel content gauges and radiator shutter controls. Note the DR Compass Repeater mounted centrally above the blind flying panel. *(BAE SYSTEMS)*

The shadow of 98 Squadron B.35 TJ133 ('VO-A') races low over Farnborough aerodrome during the Amiens prison raid re-enactment at the 1950 RAF Display. TJ133 was flown on this occasion by Sgt John Perry with Patrick Fell as navigator. This photograph was taken by TJ133's under-fuselage camera. *(Patrick Fell)*

TA654, a silver-doped B.35 of 98 Squadron, is seen after a landing accident at Celle on 18 September 1950. TA654 was built at Hatfield in April 1945, one of the second batch of B.35s. Delivered to 10 MU Hullavington on 27 April, the aircraft passed to 218 MU Colerne on 18 July. A week later it arrived at Marshalls of Cambridge for modifications and the installation of radio and navigation equipment. This work took five months to complete, following which TA654 entered storage at 22 MU Silloth. In October 1947 it returned to Marshalls for further modifications, remaining there until September 1948, when it entered another period of store, this time at 27 MU Shawbury. In April 1950 it was issued to the BAFO in Germany and assigned to 98

Squadron at Celle. It was damaged at West Malling on 30 April 1950, repairs being conducted on site before the Mosquito returned to Celle. Further damage occurred three months later, TA654 again being repaired on site. In August 1950 98 Squadron was detached on exercise to Malta, TA654 being flown by Sgt Bolton with Patrick Fell as navigator. During the outward trip TA654 suffered an engine failure over the Mediterranean, leading to a diversionary landing at Istres. After an engine change the aircraft flew home to Celle, but was written off after it crashed on landing. Note the missing starboard propeller, which was torn off during the crash impact. The crew survived. *(Patrick Fell)*

B.35s of 14 Squadron (seen from the cockpit of another B.35) take off from West Malling in 1950. Before take-off the pilot would taxi forward to straighten the tailwheel before slowly opening the throttles, any tendency to swing to port being checked by coarse use of rudder (combined with differential throttle movement) until effective rudder control had been gained. Once comfortably airborne the wheels were braked and the undercarriage raised. With flaps up or 15 degrees down, single-engine safety speed at full load and take-off power was 185 knots. This dropped to 175 knots at plus-12lb boost, it being recommended therefore that full take-off power only be used when necessary. After lift-off, rpm would be reduced to 2,850 as soon as possible, providing that boost did not exceed plus-12lb per sq in. Note that the familiar wartime camouflage scheme has now given way to an overall silver-doped finish. *(Mike Levy)*

This impressive line-up of twelve B.35s from 14 and 98 Squadrons was photographed at West Malling in July 1950. The Mosquitoes had flown in from RAF Celle in Germany to take part in the RAF Display at Farnborough.

Nearest the camera are 14 Squadron aircraft TH999 'CX-A', RS708 'CX-Z' and TA695 'CX-W'. Imagine the sound made by this little lot! *(Mike Levy)*

This line-up of 14 Squadron B.35s is probably at Sylt in 1950. Nearest the camera is RS704 'CX-B', which was ready for collection from the Airspeed Christchurch factory on 30 March 1946. Delivered to 38 MU Llandow for storage on 8 April, RS704 later underwent modifications at Martin Hearn before returning to store, this time at 22 MU Silloth. Issued to the BAFO Reserve Pool in December 1949, it was assigned to 14 Squadron at Celle in January 1950, serving until 2 February 1951 when it returned to 22 MU for extended storage. Brooklands Aviation at Sywell converted RS704 to TT.35 standard between October 1953 and January 1954, the aircraft spending the rest of its days in storage at 38 MU before being Struck Off Charge on 29 June 1956. This Mosquito was eventually sold as scrap to Eyre & Company Ltd on 1 January 1957. RS704 is finished silver overall with yellow spinners and black underwing serial numbers. The fuselage code letters are applied in yellow with black outlines and the aircraft sports 100-gallon underwing drop tanks. Note that the rear fuselage hatch is in the open position, providing access to equipment such as the aircraft's batteries, hydraulic services panel, oxygen cylinders and radio gear. *(Mike Levy)*

14 Squadron B.35 TH999 'CX-A' suffered a take-off accident at RAF Fassberg in February 1951; note the fuselage fracture just aft of bulkhead number four and the port engine nacelle's distorted rear section, bent vertical by the crash impact. TH999 was built at Hatfield in September 1945 as the last in a batch of twenty-four B.35s commencing with aircraft TH976. TH999 went to 27 MU at Shawbury for storage in September 1945, remaining there until December 1947, when it passed to Martin Hearn for modifications . This work was complete by 20 February 1948, TH999 being

delivered to 9 MU on 27 February for further storage. Just under a year later, on 25 February 1949, it arrived at No 1 Break Down Recovery & Salvage Depot (1 BRSD) and went from there to the Reserve Pool at Luneberg on 25 April 1949. TH999 was then issued to 14 Squadron, serving with the latter until 1 February 1951, when it swung on take-off at Fassberg, the undercarriage being raised to bring the aircraft to a halt. TH999 was Struck Off Charge the following day. *(Patrick Fell, via Stuart Howe)*

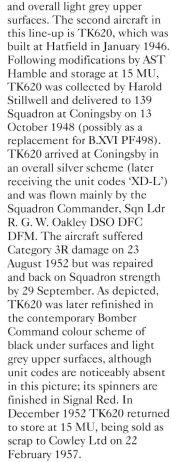

These 139 Squadron B.35s are probably at Hemswell in 1951. Note the postwar RAF Night-Bomber scheme of black under surfaces (extending to the top of the fuselage sides) and overall light grey upper surfaces. The second aircraft in this line-up is TK620, which was built at Hatfield in January 1946. Following modifications by AST Hamble and storage at 15 MU, TK620 was collected by Harold Stillwell and delivered to 139 Squadron at Coningsby on 13 October 1948 (possibly as a replacement for B.XVI PF498). TK620 arrived at Coningsby in an overall silver scheme (later receiving the unit codes 'XD-L') and was flown mainly by the Squadron Commander, Sqn Ldr R. G. W. Oakley DSO DFC DFM. The aircraft suffered Category 3R damage on 23 August 1952 but was repaired and back on Squadron strength by 29 September. As depicted, TK620 was later refinished in the contemporary Bomber Command colour scheme of black under surfaces and light grey upper surfaces, although unit codes are noticeably absent in this picture; its spinners are finished in Signal Red. In December 1952 TK620 returned to store at 15 MU, being sold as scrap to Cowley Ltd on 22 February 1957. *(Colin Armstrong via Stuart Howe)*

Flt Lt Mike Levy standing by the tail of 14 Squadron B.35 TJ143 at Wahn in 1948. Following an RAF Short University course at Southampton, Mike began flying training in 1945. Between 1948 and 1950 he flew Mosquito B.35s with 14 Squadron at Wahn, Celle and Fassberg before returning to the UK to become a Flying Instructor and Flight Commander on Meteors at Driffield. Following a spell as Flt Cdr Recruit Training at Bridgnorth, together with a Squadron Leader's posting at the Air Ministry, Mike returned to flying duties in 1958 with 213 Squadron at Bruggen. For the next two years he flew Canberra B(1)6s with 213 before joining the Atomic Operations staff at 2 ATAF, Rheindalen. Mike's final posting was to the Operational Requirements section of the Air Ministry, where he was responsible for the Martel and Nord AS.30 missiles as well as the SNEB 68mm rocket. Mike took voluntary early retirement from the RAF in 1968.

Hatfield-built in August 1945, TJ143 served only with 14 Squadron before being abandoned near Wahn following a cockpit fire on 2 April 1949. The 14 Squadron badge on the fin features a winged plate charged with a cross and surmounted by the head and shoulder pieces of a suit of armour. *(Mike Levy)*

98 Squadron B.35 TJ138 photographed at RAF Fassberg in 1951. The aircraft was built at Hatfield and delivered into storage at 27 MU in August 1945. Between February and May 1948 it was resident at RAF Martlesham Heath before returning to 27 MU. Assigned to 98 Squadron at Celle on 31 October 1950, TJ138 received the unit codes 'VO-L' (it is believed that it arrived on the Squadron in its original factory-applied camouflage scheme, this overall silver finish being applied at a later date). TJ138 served with 98 Squadron until 20 February 1951, when it returned to the UK for storage at 38 MU Llandow. Later converted to TT.35 status, the aircraft was delivered to No 5 Anti-CAACU at Llanbedr, being allocated the unit code letter 'Z'.

In January 1958 5 CAACU moved to Woodvale, TJ138 passing to the resident THUM (Temperature and Humidity) Flight, run by Short Brothers Ltd. To obtain meteorological information the THUM Flight made daily ascents to 30,000 feet and, in addition to TJ138, operated three Spitfire

PR.XIXs and another Mosquito TT.35, TA722. TJ138 made the last THUM Flight Mosquito sortie in April 1959 before returning to 27 MU Shawbury for disposal on 9 June 1959. A month later it became instructional airframe number 7607M for exhibition purposes, joining the Air Historical Branch Collection at Thorney Island. Displayed at Horse Guards Parade in 1960, TJ138 eventually found its way to RAF Colerne, where it was exhibited alongside other historic aircraft in the Station Museum. Over the next twenty-five years TJ138 was kept at Finningley, Swinderby and St Athan before moving to the RAF Museum at Hendon in February 1992. In May 2003 it was re-located to the new 'Milestones of Flight' exhibition gallery at Hendon where it now forms a most impressive spectacle. Note the rank pennant on the starboard side of the nose, indicating that TJ138 was the personal aircraft of the Squadron Commander. The spinners are finished in red, as are the code letters, which are outlined in black. *(Pat Fell, via Stuart Howe)*

Mosquito Fighters

The Mosquito was developed into arguably the most successful night-fighter of the Second World War. The initial Air Ministry Contract for fifty Mosquitoes comprised the prototype W4050 and forty-nine production bombers. However, this initial Contract was extensively modified to eventually include three Fighter Prototypes, twenty-two production Fighters and four production Trainers, the latter a dual-control version of the fighter design.

W4052 served as the Fighter Prototype, receiving the designation Mosquito F.II and making its maiden flight on 15 May 1941. The F.II was a day and night long-range fighter and intruder, the NF.II Night-Fighter version being equipped with Airborne Interception (AI) Mk IV or AI Mk V radar. F.IIs and NF.IIs were formidably armed with four .303in Browning machine-guns in the nose together with four 20mm cannon under the cockpit floor. 157 Squadron received the first NF.IIs to enter RAF service when W4087 and W4098 were delivered on 9 March 1942. The first NF.II operational sortie took place on 14 April 1942 when DD603 of 157 Squadron took off to intercept a German night raid on Norwich. F.II's conducted long-range ocean patrols and intruder missions, and NF.IIs were still flying operationally on Bomber Support duties in April 1944. F.IIs/NF.IIs were powered by Merlin 21, 22 or 23 engines, had a maximum speed of 370mph and a ceiling of 36,000 feet.

The next Mosquito Fighter development was the NF.XII, which employed AI Mk VIII radar in place of the nose machine-guns. This represented a great advance over AI Mk IV and V and was the first British-designed centimetric AI radar. The radar dish of AI Mk VIII rotated about its axis and gradually deflected sideways, tracing a 'spiral scan' in the sky up to approximately 45 degrees. Production NF.XIIs were all converted from F.IIs by Marshalls of Cambridge, the AI Mk VIII radar being housed in a distinctive 'thimble' nose radome. The NF.XII entered service with 85 Squadron in February 1943 and immediately enhanced the RAF's UK night defence capability. They were particularly effective against Luftwaffe 'hit and run' raiders operating over the South Coast and destroyed a large number of bomb-carrying Focke Wulf Fw190s. NF. XIIs also operated from Malta and remained in front-line service almost until the end of the war. The NF.XII had a climb rate of 3,000 feet per minute, a maximum speed of 370mph and a range of 1,750 miles.

The 'basic' strengthened wing of the FB.VI provided the basis for the next Night-Fighter variant, the NF.XIII. Equipped with AI Mk VIII radar in the 'thimble' or Universal 'bull-nose' radome, the NF.XIII exploited the FB.VI wing's facility for underwing drop tanks (increasing the range to 1,860 miles) or bombs, though the latter were rarely carried. An Me 410 became the NF.XIII's first victim, being destroyed by HK367 of 488 Squadron on 8 November 1943. Powered by 1,460hp Merlin 21s or 23s, the NF.XIII had a maximum speed of 370mph. Fifty were equipped with nitrous oxide injection, temporarily boosting their maximum speed by 47mph to enable the interception of fast Luftwaffe intruders.

In response to the threat posed by Luftwaffe high-altitude raiders, the Mosquito pressure cabin Bomber prototype, MP469, was hurriedly developed into a high-altitude fighter. Specially lightened, equipped with four .303in machine-guns and powered by Merlin 61s, MP469 had a wingspan of 59 feet and first flew on 14 September 1942, only a week after conversion work commenced. MP469 was soon reaching altitudes beyond its 43,000-foot design target and later attained 45,000 feet with the RAF High Altitude Flight. Concerns that the UK could be subject to high-altitude night bombing led to MP469 being fitted with AI Mk VIII radar in a nose 'thimble' radome, the four .303in machine-guns being repositioned to a ventral 'belly pack'. This led to the conversion of four B.IV airframes to the high-altitude fighter role under the designation Mosquito NF.XV. Similar to MP469, these aircraft featured a 62-foot wingspan and were powered by Merlin 70 series engines. NF.XVs entered service with the Fighter Interception Unit and 85 Squadron but never encountered any Luftwaffe aircraft.

Between June and September 1943 Marshalls of Cambridge converted more than ninety F.IIs to take the American SCR 720/729 or British AI Mk X radar in a Universal 'bull-nose' radome, producing the Mosquito NF.XVII. AI Mk X was a modified version of SCR 720 and radiated 0.75 microsecond pulses in the centimetric band at 9.1cm. The operator was provided with a two-tube display (as opposed to the single tube of AI Mk VIII); the left tube or 'C' scope displayed the target as a spot on an azimuth/elevation grid and the right or 'B' tube featured an azimuth calibration on the horizontal axis, while the vertical axis displayed the range of the target. SCR 720 proved superior to AI Mk VIII in dealing with 'Duppel', a German counter-measure to British radar (equivalent to the British 'Window'). HK285 of 25 Squadron became the first NF.XVII to destroy a German aircraft when it shot down a Ju 188 on 20 February 1944. NF.XVIIs also claimed several Heinkel He 111 bombers acting as V-1 rocket air-launch platforms.

The NF.XIX represented the ultimate in two-speed, single-stage supercharged Merlin Mosquito Night-Fighter development and was originally conceived as a long-range fighter for Coastal Command. Similar to the NF.XIII, the NF.XIX also featured the 'basic' wing of the FB.VI but differed principally from the NF.XIII through the installation of Merlin 25 engines of 1,635hp. The NF.XIX sported a Universal 'bull-nose' radome capable of accommodating either the American SCR 720/729 or British AI Mk VIII or Mk X radar. HK364 was the Prototype NF.XIX and more than 200 were built, many serving overseas with SEAC.

In April 1944 MM686, the first Mosquito NF.30, made its maiden flight. The NF.30 was basically an NF.XIX airframe fitted with two-speed, two-stage supercharged Merlin 70 series engines and equipped with AI Mk X radar. Initial deliveries were to 219 Squadron in June 1944, and the first NF.30 operational sortie resulted in the destruction of two German aircraft. Exhaust shroud problems restricted NF.30 operations until late 1944, following which this most potent aeroplane made its mark on the European war. NF.30s equipped with 'Monica' rearwards-facing radar flew on Bomber Support duties with 100 Group while others dropped napalm-filled drop tanks on German airfields. After the war they soldiered on with Auxiliary Air Force Squadrons, and several reconditioned examples were sold to the Belgian Air Force. The NF.30 had a still-air range of 1,180 miles at 30,000 feet and a maximum speed of 424mph.

The final Mosquito Night-Fighter to see RAF squadron service was the NF.36. Designed to bridge the gap between the NF.30 and the first generation of jet night-fighters, the NF.36 was powered by Merlin 113/114s and equipped with AI Mk X radar. MT466, a converted NF.30, was the Prototype and deliveries to the RAF began in May 1945. NF.36s equipped the postwar home defence night-fighter force as well as two Squadrons of the RAF Middle Eastern Air Force. The NF.36 had an all-up weight of 21,400lb and a maximum ceiling of 36,000 feet. NF.36s were replaced by Vampire and Meteor night-fighters during the early 1950s, the last example being retired in 1954.

The NF.38 was the final production Mosquito Night-Fighter variant and proved a great disappointment to the RAF. The Prototype (RL248) was converted from an NF.36 and featured the British-designed AI Mk IXb radar, the installation of which necessitated a lengthening and redesign of the forward fuselage. This shifted the centre of gravity too far aft, leading to unacceptable stability and handling characteristics. Additionally, the performance of AI Mk IXb proved inferior to AI Mk X and consequently no NF.38s entered RAF squadron service. In all, 101 production NF.38s were built, the final example, VX916, rolling out of the de Havilland Chester factory on 15 November 1950. Sixty NF.38s were sold to Yugoslavia and served in various roles until the early 1960s.

W4052 served as the Mosquito Fighter Prototype and, like W4050, was constructed in great secrecy at Salisbury Hall. To save valuable time dismantling and transporting W4052 to Hatfield, Geoffrey de Havilland Junior flew the aircraft from a field bordering Salisbury Hall on the evening of 15 May 1941. To make the maiden flight of an untested prototype from a non-aerodrome site was a brave decision but typical of Geoffrey's great confidence and ability. Accompanying Geoffrey was Salisbury Hall works foreman Fred Plumb, who had bet Geoffrey £1 that he would never

do it! W4052 took off at 1925hrs, the port wing dropping fairly steeply on lift-off, probably due to a strong gust as W4052 was taking off about 30 degrees out of wind. During the short 15-minute flight to Hatfield several points were noted, including the unsatisfactory nature of the throttle and propeller pitch controls and the existence of considerable play (both lateral and vertical) in the control column. The undercarriage warning lights were regarded as 'completely misleading', but, noted the 'Experimental Aircraft Pilot's Test Record': 'A commendable point on this machine (as opposed to the Reconnaissance version) is the fact that the crew have a clear view of the chassis, when lowered, through the side windows.' This picture was taken at Hatfield in September 1941 and clearly shows W4052's short-span (19ft 5½in) 'No 1' tailplane, the exhaust manifold cooling intakes and exit ducts on the engine side cowlings, and the nose-mounted 'arrowhead' transmitting aerial for the Airborne Interception (AI) Mk IV radar. W4052 is finished Night overall. *(BAE SYSTEMS)*

Taken at Salisbury Hall in 1941, this photograph depicts the Merlin 21 engine installation on one of the Mosquito Fighter Prototypes (believed to be W4052). Note the exhaust manifold ducting system with its exit pipe located in line with the engine's mid rear section. This exhaust arrangement was a characteristic of the initial prototypes together with all PR.1 and B.IV Series 1 Mosquitoes. Two-speed, single-stage supercharged Merlin Mosquito variants were fitted, with a number of engine-driven accessories including a Heywood air compressor (port engine only), propeller governors, vacuum pumps, Lockheed hydraulic pumps and electric generators (an 80-volt, 500-watt AC generator on the port engine and a 24-volt, 1,500-watt generator on the starboard). The engine cowlings featured cooling air ducts to the electric generator, air compressor, fuel pump, magnetos and exhaust manifolds. Pesco relief valves and oil drain traps were provided for the vacuum pumps on each engine. The drains from the Lockheed pump, engine vent, fuel pump and supercharger were channelled to the square-shaped tank visible under the rear lower section of the port engine bearer. *(BAE SYSTEMS)*

W4052 under construction in the Salisbury Hall hangar on 25 April 1941, three weeks prior to its maiden flight. The armament of four 20mm cannon and four .303 machine-guns has already been installed, but the canopy frame, nose cone and under-fuselage cannon fairing have yet to be fitted. Note the hinged single-piece access door for the nose machine-guns, this being replaced by two separate doors on later production aircraft. The circular panel directly under the nose provided access to the chamber for spent machine gun rounds and links. *(BAE SYSTEMS)*

The epitome of power and grace: W4052 roars low across Hatfield aerodrome on 5 September 1941. By this time three Mosquito Prototypes had taken to the air, W4050, W4051 and W4052. These were soon joined by a fourth when Bomber Prototype W4057 made its maiden flight three days later. Aerobatics were initially performed with W4052 on 11 June 1941 (during the course of its eleventh, twelfth and thirteenth test flights), Geoffrey de Havilland Junior subsequently reporting: 'The machine does all normal aerobatics such as loops, rolls in either direction, and rolls from the top of a loop with exceptional controllability and smoothness: there is adequate aileron control for performing really quick rolls from the top of a loop. With the elevator gearing at its present setting 4G turns may be done with relative ease.' The Mosquito's Chief Designer, R. E. Bishop, accompanied Geoffrey during the twelfth test flight. *(BAE SYSTEMS)*

This unusual aspect of W4052 (believed to have been taken at Boscombe Down in 1941) accentuates the streamlined form of the Mosquito design. Note the extended engine nacelles protruding aft of the wing trailing edge, W4052 being the first Mosquito constructed in 'long' nacelle form. Following W4052's first three test flights, Geoffrey de Havilland Junior commented on the effectiveness of the extended nacelles in relation to the tail buffeting encountered with W4050: 'The machine is beautifully smooth, no tail buffet of any description being apparent. There is a very slight mechanical vibration noticeable on the stick but this may be disregarded.' Following its initial twenty-five test flights (all in the hands of Geoffrey de Havilland Junior) W4052 was delivered to the A&AEE at Boscombe Down for acceptance trials on 23 June 1941. The object appearing to protrude from the rudder's upper leading edge is the opened access door to the nose machine-guns. A Bristol Beaufort and Curtiss Tomahawk are visible in the distance beneath W4052's port wing. *(Aeroplane)*

This shot of W4052 is believed to have been taken in late 1941 during acceptance trials at the A&AEE. W4052 had a long and varied career, being employed on many aspects of Mosquito design development including investigations into longitudinal stability (involving trials with three sizes of tailplane) as well as tests of exhaust stubs, flame-damping shrouds, long-range tanks, air brakes, braking propellers and experimental ailerons. On 3 April 1943 W4052 was allotted to the Fighter Interception Unit at Ford, but returned to de Havilland's a month later, where it continued its development work.. Note the absence of a longitudinal stiffening strake above the rear access hatch; from December 1942 this strake became a standard feature of production Mosquitoes and was added to reinforce the fuselage shell above the weak point of the hatch cut-out (existing aircraft also receiving this modification). The strake also helped to disperse water from the edges of the hatch cut-out, several early production aircraft suffering from severe water soakage in this area. W4052 is finished Night overall with the serial numbers applied in red. *(Aeroplane Monthly)*

W4053, the Turret Fighter Prototype, pictured at Hatfield in late 1941. W4053 was constructed at Salisbury Hall between May and September 1941, and equipped with a four-machine-gun Bristol turret located behind the cockpit. This was in accordance with Air Ministry instructions to complete two of the initial batch of fighters with gun turrets, the armament of the latter replacing the nose machine-guns. W4053 made its maiden flight (in the hands of Geoffrey de Havilland Junior) from Salisbury Hall on Sunday 14 September 1941, losing part of its turret on the way to Hatfield.

Ted Lovatt (the chargehand responsible for the installation of hydraulic and pneumatic systems in the Salisbury Hall-built prototypes) once flew in W4053 with Geoffrey de Havilland Junior while John de Havilland rode in the turret. Ted recalls: 'John went in the turret but we didn't have intercom so if we wanted to talk to John I had to turn round and try and make out what he was talking about. So off we went, got up to a reasonable speed, then John tried out the turret. All the way round the back of him everything worked beautifully, but when he tried to turn the turret forwards over the top of the cockpit – which was the rest position for the guns and, incidentally, the only position in which you could get in and out , the thing just stalled on him because of the force of the slipstream. We had two more flights like that, then it was banned – nobody was allowed to fly in it. On one occasion, as the machine was taxying out I saw a head pop up inside the turret. We managed to contact Geoffrey and stop it and it was a bloke trying to get a flight without anyone knowing he was there…'

W4053 flew to RAE Farnborough for trials work on 29 December 1941, following which it was concluded that the turret was unnecessary, largely due to the effectiveness of

the nose machine-guns. W4053's turret was subsequently removed and faired over, the aircraft later being fitted with dual controls to act as a prototype for the Mosquito T.3 (initially referred to as the 'F.II Dual Control'). W4053 was allocated to 151 Squadron for trials and pilot conversion, serving until 7 May 1942, when it passed to 264 Squadron. This Mosquito later entered service with 1655 MTU, where it remained until 25 November 1944 when it was damaged in a landing accident. Following repairs it went to 16 OTU and was destroyed during a single-engine landing at Barford St John on 1 July 1945, the crew being killed. *(BAE SYSTEMS)*

W4052 following a single-engine forced landing at Holwell Hyde (later known as Panshangar) aerodrome on 19 April 1942. The aircraft had recently been fitted with redesigned engine cowling side panels incorporating flame-damping exhaust shrouds. The Mosquito's original ducted exhaust system proved troublesome and was replaced by a 'saxophone' manifold with two 'fishtail' stubs exiting in line with the exhaust ports (as opposed to the original layout whereby the combined manifold exited from a faired duct on the side cowling's mid rear section). The new 'saxophone' manifolds were enclosed within flame-damping exhaust shrouds designed for night operations. Geoffrey de Havilland Junior was conducting a fuel consumption test flight to build up flying hours on the new cowling design when the port engine failed over Bedfordshire. While approaching Hatfield for a single-engine landing W4052 was hindered by a Proctor taking off from the aerodrome. With the undercarriage and flaps retracting very slowly, Geoffrey gingerly opened up the starboard engine and flew low over Welwyn Garden City before belly-landing at Holwell Hyde (which was also the home of No 1 EFTS). Apart from the starboard engine and both propellers, damage was confined to W4052's lower cowlings, engine nacelles and flaps. Following repairs the Mosquito was flown back to Hatfield on 5 May 1942. Note the 'Circle P' (for 'Prototype') marking on the port side of W4052's fuselage. *(Both BAE SYSTEMS)*

W4052 sports a bellows-type air brake mounted peripherally on the fuselage immediately aft of the inboard flaps. This air brake was developed by de Havilland's to provide an efficient means of decelerating Mosquito night-fighters while approaching enemy bombers from astern. A Youngman 'frill' brake had previously been tested on W4052, but the bellows design consisted of a series of rectangular plates hinged to open against the slipstream. Each plate was attached to its neighbours by a flexible material, the air brake taking the form of three arcs of a circle when the bellows were filled with air. The lower arc was of approximately 180 degrees with the remaining two arcs set at approximately 70 degrees each. The brake was operated by a venturi (visible beneath the fuselage) and butterfly valve, the latter controlled by the pilot via a Bowden cable. During normal flight the valve remained open, causing suction that kept the brake shut. With the valve closed the venturi acted as a pressure head and opened up the air brake against the slipstream (when flying at 250mph ASI the brake took about 3 seconds to fully open). With the throttles closed and no air brake, W4052 took 45 seconds to reduce speed from 250 to 150mph ASI. With the air brake deployed this time was reduced to 30 seconds. However, tests conducted at the A&AEE at Boscombe Down revealed that the brake caused severe buffeting and vibration, which, it was believed, would eventually lead to airframe structural failure. The A&AEE regarded the brake as unacceptable and 'the retarding effect not sufficiently adequate'. The first picture shows the normal position of the air brake with W4052 stationary (the lower arc would close in flight), while the second picture depicts the brake when fully open. *(Both de Havilland Aircraft Museum Trust collection)*

Four pictures of W4052 taken at Hatfield on 29 April 1943, during an early demonstration of the Mosquito to the Press. On this occasion W4052, in the hands of Geoffrey de Havilland Junior, gave a highly spirited display that included aerobatics and single-engine flying. Just over a week later, on Saturday 8 May 1943, Geoffrey displayed W4052 over Old Welwyn during a 'Wings for Victory' parade. During the display routine one of W4052's main undercarriage units dropped off its uplock (due to non-incorporation of a modification designed to eliminate this scenario) and was torn away in the slipstream, carrying the engine nacelle away with it. Geoffrey returned to Hatfield and made a very skilful landing on the remaining undercarriage unit, controlling W4052 down to a very low speed (and switching off the 'down side' engine) in order to minimise damage when the propeller and wingtip

contacted the ground. Shortly after W4052 landed, Experimental Flight Test Department Inspector Dick Whittingham recalls a van from Old Welwyn roaring across the aerodrome with the remains of W4052's undercarriage and nacelle in the back!

By this time W4052's original Night finish had given way to the standard Night-Fighter scheme of overall Medium Sea Grey with Dark Green camouflaged upper surfaces. Note the Perspex observation window on the crew entry door, a modification peculiar to W4052 and one applied in connection with trials work. B.IV Series ii DZ585 and early production FB.VI HJ768 are visible in the top left-hand corner of the first picture, while the cine film shot by the gentleman standing on the car in the fourth picture (page 131) now resides with the Imperial War Museum. *(Times/Topical Press/Times/BAE SYSTEMS)*

W4052 is seen at Hatfield on 2 June 1944 during filming of the Cecil Musk production *de Havilland Presents The Mosquito*. The aircraft was re-enacting the scene of its historic maiden flight, which originally took place from Salisbury Hall on 15 May 1941. Directly beneath the starboard propeller are Chief Test Pilot Geoffrey de Havilland Junior (left) and experimental shop foreman Fred Plumb (wearing a parachute), the actual crew on W4052's maiden flight. For filming purposes W4052 was repainted in a scheme approximating its original Night finish, having previously worn the standard Night-Fighter scheme of Medium Sea Grey and Dark Green camouflage. Experimental shop foreman Rex King (wearing his Home Guard uniform) is standing to the left of W4052's cockpit entrance ladder.

W4052 worked very hard during its career, often being used for demonstration purposes and carrying out more development test flying than W4050. It was eventually grounded (date unknown) after an RAF test pilot (attached to the Hatfield Experimental Flight Test Department)

reported that the port engine was 'nodding' in flight. Experimental Flight Test Department Inspector Dick Whittingham checked the engine bearers and their mounting points on the main spar, but could find nothing wrong. The RAF test pilot who originally reported the fault subsequently asked Dick to accompany him on a test flight in W4052. Once safely to height, the pilot began to fly W4052 in a 'porpoising' motion, moving the stick slowly forwards and backwards. Dick was then asked to check the attitude of the starboard engine, but noticed nothing amiss and all appeared normal. However, transferring his attentions to the port engine, Dick was alarmed to find that it was visibly moving up and down, a likely indication that the main spar structure (at the engine bearer mounting points) was breaking up. W4052 returned to Hatfield and never flew again, eventually being Struck Off Charge on 26 November 1946, although it was probably scrapped long before that date. *(BAE SYSTEMS)*

NF.II DD612 photographed on the Hatfield production line in early 1942. Note the coolant pipes running from the rear of the port engine bay to the top of the radiator matrix in the wing leading edge. The electro-pneumatic ram located through the rear section of the radiator structure inboard mounting rib is for actuation of the port radiator flap. Ammunition boxes and feed chutes for the four .303in Browning nose machine-guns are clearly visible, as is the 'arrowhead' transmitting aerial for the AI Mk IV radar. The inscription 'M/C 63' on the port engine's outboard inner exhaust shroud stands for 'Machine 63' and refers to DD612's Hatfield factory construction number '98063'.

DD612 made its maiden flight in the hands of de Havilland test pilot George Gibbins on 7 March 1942. A week later it was delivered to 30 MU, where it was prepared for active service and fitted with AI Mk IV radar before issue to 157 Squadron on 29 March. DD612 shot down a Dornier Do 217 on the night of 22 August 1942 and continued to serve with 157 Squadron until 15 April 1943, when it landed at Colerne with the tailwheel retracted. The subsequent damage was not repaired, DD612 being allocated instead to No 3 School of Technical Training as Instructional Airframe 3802M. DD612's airframe wears its factory-applied silver dope finish, but this would soon be covered by an overall Night scheme. *(Crown Copyright)*

NF.II DD621 never entered RAF service, crashing on take-off from Hatfield during its delivery flight to 32 MU on 29 March 1942; it was wrecked as it came down just outside the airfield perimeter. Note the 'balloon' tailwheel tyre (entangled in barbed-wire during the crash), and the fabric-covered elevators. DD621 is finished in Night Type 'S' and wears the Red, White, Blue and Yellow (1-3-5-7 proportioned) roundels on the fuselage sides, together with the correspondingly dimensioned Red, White and Blue fin flashes. These markings were considered too conspicuous for night operations (especially when coned in searchlights), so their yellow and white proportions were modified by reducing the roundel ring sizes and narrowing the white band of the fin flash. *(Both BAE SYSTEMS)*

This close-up shot shows an early production NF.II shortly after emerging from the Hatfield paint shop in early 1942. It is finished in the matt Special Night scheme, which was then standard for RAF night-bombers and fighters. There were concerns that the rough texture of this finish would incur a drag penalty on level speed performance, and this was confirmed by de Havilland's following two separate trials with NF.II W4082. The aircraft was initially tested in its Smooth Night undercoat finish and measured a maximum level speed of 378mph at 22,000 feet. Following the application of a top coat of Special Night, W4082 achieved only 352mph, a reduction of 26mph representing a total drag increase of 20 percent. A&AEE Boscombe Down repeated the test using NF.II W4076, recording maximum level speeds of 358mph and 366mph respectively. The A&AEE considered that 'the matt black ("Special Night") finish in our tests was thought by us to be slightly less rough and that the smooth black was slightly less smooth than during the de Havilland tests.' Improper application of the Special Night scheme was also considered to be a factor in performance loss. Consequently, the Special Night scheme was replaced with the less rough Night Type S or Smooth Night finish from March 1942 onwards. Note the 'arrowhead' transmitting aerial for the AI Mk IV radar and the four .303in Browning machine-guns mounted in the nose. The muzzles for the four 20mm cannon are just visible beneath the forward fuselage. Also worthy of note is the locking stay located inside the forward section of the port ventral bay door; these doors provided access to the 20mm cannons and could only be opened manually. *(BAE SYSTEMS)*

23 Squadron NF.II DD673 'YP-E' following an argument with a steam-roller at Manston during the early hours of 24 August 1942. The night before DD673 had set out to patrol Deelen airfield when the port engine failed close to the Dutch coast. During the subsequent single-engined landing at Manston the aircraft overshot the runway and collided with the steam-roller. Merlin 21-powered DD673 was built at Hatfield in June 1942 and delivered direct to 19 MU on 28 June. Allocated to 23 Squadron at Manston on 11 July 1942, it suffered this accident only six weeks later. Repairs were undertaken by Martin Hearn Ltd and took six months to complete, DD673 being ready for collection on 30 March 1943. Following storage at 27 MU it was delivered to 51 OTU on 17 May 1943, and from there went to 60 OTU, where it again suffered accident damage, this time on 6 June 1943. Following repairs at Hatfield it joined 141 Squadron on 24 March 1944 where it received the unit codes 'TW-T'.

DD673 conducted patrols over Paris during the early hours of D-Day and was written off following battle damage on 9 June 1944. Manston's inadequate night facilities for Mosquitoes landing on one engine were considered a secondary cause of the accident shown here. *(Crown Copyright)*

NF.II DD750 ready for a test flight from Hatfield in the late summer of 1942. This aircraft was delivered to 30 MU Sealand on 10 September 1942 for the installation of AI Mk IV radar. Following a month in storage at 27 MU it was allocated to 25 Squadron at Church Fenton on 22 October 1942. At 2046hrs on 22 March 1943 DD750 crashed at White Craig, Bilsdon (near Keighley), while returning from an operational patrol. It had been inadvertently positioned over high ground by the aerodrome controller and struck a hill while turning to land. *(BAE SYSTEMS)*

This second view of NF.II DD750 at Hatfield shows the factory buildings in the right background. Mosquito F.II/NF.IIs had a maximum speed of 370mph and were equipped with two-speed, single-stage supercharged Merlin 21, 22 or 23 engines of 1,460hp each. Several F.IIs were fitted with additional fuel tanks for long-range intruder operations while others were employed on ocean patrols in the Bay of Biscay. NF.IIs equipped with Serrate were the first Mosquitoes to serve with 100 (Bomber Support) Group, and in 1944 many were re-engined to improve their operational reliability. *(BAE SYSTEMS)*

F.II DZ238 'YP-H' of 23 Squadron photographed at Hatfield on 5 May 1943 shortly after returning from a tour of operational service in Malta. A Hatfield-built F.II, DZ238 was delivered to 27 MU in October 1942 before allocation to 23 Squadron on 9 December the same year. Following the installation of long-range tanks, DZ238 flew to Malta where 23 Squadron began intruder operations over North Africa, Sicily and Southern Italy from 28 December. On 5 May 1943, following 138 hours' flying time, DZ238 returned to Hatfield for a major inspection and overhaul, this work being completed by 22 May, when it was delivered to 30 MU. DZ238 spent the remainder of its life serving with 60 and 13 OTUs, being damaged on four occasions, the last occurring on 11 May 1945 (while on the strength of 13 OTU) when it flew into a hail storm near Melton Mowbray. Repairs were completed by 26 June, after which it returned to service before being Struck Off Charge on 12 November 1945. Note that it wears the Intruder scheme of Night under surfaces with Medium Sea Grey and Dark Green camouflaged upper surfaces. The Squadron code letters are applied in red. FB.VIs began to arrive at 23 Squadron from May 1943 and eventually completely replaced the F.IIs. The inscription on the nose reads 'Babs'. *(Both BAE SYSTEMS)*

These two pre-delivery shots of NF.II DD758 were taken at Hatfield in the summer of 1942. DD758 was delivered direct from Hatfield to 30 MU on 9 September 1942, where it was prepared for active service and fitted with AI Mk IV radar. In October 1942 the aircraft entered storage with 27 MU before allocation to 25 Squadron on 9 September 1943. Nine days later it was re-assigned to 141 Squadron at Wittering, this unit forming part of 100 (Bomber Support) Group, which controlled the operation of radio counter-measures against German night-fighters. 141 Squadron's Mosquito NF.IIs were equipped with extra fuel tanks and Serrate, a homing device designed to pick up German night-fighter radar transmissions, which could track the enemy aircraft from a distance of 100 miles but indicated only bearing, not range. Serrate would be used to detect the enemy fighters before (when range was sufficiently reduced) AI Mk IV took over for the final interception. A common set of Cathode Ray Tube displays was employed for both radars, a switch converting from one to the other.

DD758 served with 141 Squadron until 9 June 1944, when it was lost in a crash-landing at Ford while returning from a Serrate patrol. In poor weather conditions and with the port engine shut down, the pilot was forced to make a belly-landing but collided with two parked Spitfire IXs, all three aircraft being destroyed. At the time Ford aerodrome was packed to capacity with parked aircraft (including some within the perimeter track), leaving little room for manoeuvre. DD758 wears an overall Night Type S finish, although the aluminium under fairing between the rear fuselage and tailcone has yet to be painted. Note the AI Mk IV radar's nose-mounted 'arrowhead' transmitting aerial, and the azimuth and elevation aerials on the wings. *(Both BAE SYSTEMS)*

456 Squadron (RAAF) F.II DZ681 photographed at RAF Valley in 1943. Hatfield-built in January 1943, DZ681 was delivered to 19 MU on 13 January, where it was prepared for active service. On 1 February 1943 it was assigned to 456 Squadron at RAF Valley, where it received the unit codes 'RX-L'. On 15 January 1944 DZ681's pilot lost control of the aircraft following failure of the port engine's constant speed unit. The Mosquito was subsequently written off in the resulting crash Fairwood Common. 456 Squadron was formed at Valley on 30 June 1941, initially equipped with Defiants and Beaufighters. Mosquito F.IIs began to replace the Beaufighters in December 1942, the Squadron's first operational Mosquito sortie being flown on 22 January 1943. 456's F.IIs flew many 'Ranger' and intruder missions over occupied Europe, attacking airfields and destroying enemy railway communications. Note the 'needle'-blade propellers and shrouded exhausts, the latter very necessary for night operation. DZ681 is finished in the standard Night-Fighter scheme of overall Medium Sea Grey with Dark Green camouflaged upper surfaces.
(Bob Richardson, via David Vincent and Stuart Howe)

For a sense of SECURITY

Even when a crash landing is inevitable there is comfort in the knowledge that the strong ductile metal blades will cushion the impact and minimise the damage

DE HAVILLAND PROPELLERS

(BAE SYSTEMS)

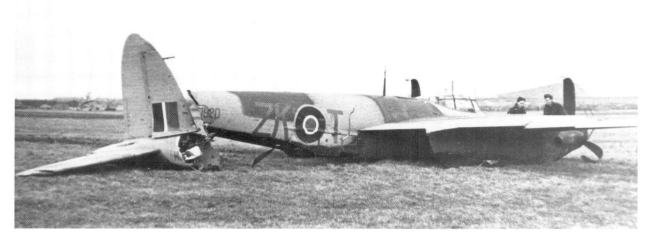

25 Squadron NF.II HJ920 'ZK-T' has force-landed at its Acklington base in January 1944. Built at Leavesden, Merlin 21-powered HJ920 was delivered to 30 MU on 25 October 1942, where it was prepared for service and fitted with AI Mk IV radar before allocation to 25 Squadron on 22 November. 25 Squadron was engaged on 'Ranger' and Intruder operations during 1943, and replaced its Mosquito NF.IIs with NF.XVIIs in late January 1944. HJ920 served with 25 Squadron until 20 January 1944, when hydraulic problems forced the pilot to make a belly-landing with the result depicted here. The damage was extensive enough for the aircraft to be written off and reduced to spares. HJ920 is finished in the Intruder scheme of Medium Sea Grey and Dark Green camouflaged upper surfaces with the under surfaces in Night. *(P. Small, via Stuart Howe)*

LAC John Claxton, a 141 Squadron armourer, is pictured with one of the unit's Mosquito NF.IIs at Wittering in 1943. Note the nose-mounted Type 19 'arrowhead' transmitting aerial for the AI Mk IV radar. It is believed that this particular aircraft was also equipped with Serrate. *(Don Aris, via Stuart Howe)*

With the starboard engine feathered, F.II DD664 makes a low fly-past over the 'Riverside Hatchery', possibly at Bankstown or Mascot in around December 1942. DD664 was shipped from the UK in September 1942 as a pattern aircraft for Australian Mosquito production. Note the RAAF Anson in the foreground. *(Sun)*

DD744, an F.II of 60 Squadron SAAF, flying from Castel Benito in February 1943. Constructed as a tropicalised F.II, DD744 left the Hatfield factory equipped with flame-damping exhaust shrouds and finished in an overall silver dope scheme. It was delivered to 27 MU on 3 September 1942 and to the Overseas Aircraft Preparation Unit three weeks later. Following a month at the Ferry Training Unit, DD744 returned to Hatfield in late November 1942 for modifications. This work probably included the fitting of tropical filters to the carburettor air intakes (note the 'chin' extensions on the lower cowlings) and the replacement of the flame-damping exhaust shrouds by individual exhaust stacks (six on the outboard side and five on the inboard) as seen here.

This second view of F.II DD664 is believed to have been taken shortly after its first flight in Australia. Hatfield-built in June 1942, DD664 was delivered to 30 MU on 16 June, where it was prepared for overseas shipment as a pattern aircraft for Australian Mosquito production. Following an equipment check at 27 MU, it arrived for packing at 47 MU during July, before shipment from Liverpool on 11 September. DD664 made its first flight from Bankstown on 17 December 1942 in the hands of de Havilland Australia test pilot Bruce Rose. Re-serialled A52-1001, it was subsequently fitted with Packard Merlin 31s (the intended powerplants for local Mosquito production), making its initial flight in this form on 23 March 1943. Delivered to Mascot for assessment, A52-1001 later served with 5 OTU at Williamtown before conversion to components in 1946. In this picture it still wears its original Night finish applied at the Hatfield factory. Note the RAAF national markings including the starboard underwing roundel. A Beaufighter and Wirraway are visible in the background. *(Sun)*

DD744 and DD743 were flown to the Middle East in January 1943 to assess the Mosquito airframe's resistance to desert climatic conditions. However, upon arrival at Kasfareet on 22 January both were diverted to 60 Squadron SAAF for reconnaissance duties. A single camera was installed in the forward fuselage of each aircraft before they were flown to 60 Squadron's Castel Benito base on 5 February 1943. DD744 flew 60 Squadron's first operational Mosquito sortie on 15 February and served with the Squadron until 17 August 1943, when the undercarriage collapsed following a take-off accident at Hal Far, Malta; it never flew again and was Struck Off Charge in November 1943. Note that the original silver dope finish has given way to a camouflage scheme, although the under surfaces may have remained partly silver. *(Stuart Howe collection)*

Extended carburettor air intakes became a feature of some production two-speed, single-stage supercharged Merlin Mosquitoes from 1943. These gave a pronounced 'chin' appearance to the lower engine cowlings and were designed to house air filters necessary for operations in tropical conditions. The filters could be switched in or out by the pilot and were controlled by an electro-pneumatic ram-operated scoop in the intake's forward section. The ram was connected to a lever on a shaft, the opposite end of which featured two sprockets (connected by a chain) attached to the intake shutter. Activated by a switch on the pilot's instrument panel, the scoop deflected air upwards through the cleaner elements before entering the right-angle bend to the carburettor. When the filters were not required, the scoop deflected air downwards, beneath the cleaner elements, before entering the carburettor. The installation was tested on NF.II W4096 (illustrated) and included trials to determine the effect on range of activating the filters in flight. These tests showed that filters decreased range by no more than 0.75 percent, a still-air range of 2,500 air miles being obtained (with the filters in or out) using medium supercharger gear at 20,000 feet (at an indicated airspeed of approximately 170mph). Two types of ice guard attachment were employed with tropical filters, the first flush-mounted on an extension of the air intake's lower lip (as shown here), the second being the more usual design located at four attachment points on the intake's upper and lower lips. Among the first Mosquitoes to be fitted with tropical filters were F.IIs DD743 and DD744, despatched to the Middle East in January 1943 (see the previous photograph). The tropical filter installation became a standard feature on later production FB.VIs, T.3s and TR.33s, the filters being by-passed for operations in non-tropical conditions. Several Canadian and Australian-produced Mosquitoes also received the tropical filter installation. *(via DHAMT Ltd)*

The port Merlin 23 of F.II DD723 fitted with an underslung radiator in place of the conventional leading-edge-mounted unit. DD723 was constructed at Hatfield in 1942 and delivered to 30 MU for the installation of AI Mk IV radar on 16 May. After a brief period with 27 MU it was allocated to 85 Squadron at Hunsdon on 6 September, suffering accident damage just over two months later. Following repairs, DD723 was assigned to Rolls Royce at Hucknall on 26 June 1943 for engine cooling trials work. The aircraft's radiators and oil coolers were substituted by wooden leading-edge structures and both engines placed in 'Consus'-type mountings. 'Marston' standard Lancaster-type underslung radiators and oil coolers were installed and trials conducted to assess engine cooling on the climb and in level flight. Radiator suitability requirements under tropical conditions on the climb were nearly met, the port radiator being 2 percent down while the starboard radiator was

recorded as 'unity'. Results were compared with a standard Merlin 23-powered FB.VI (LR352) and revealed that radiator suitability was slightly improved on the underslung radiator installation, but oil cooling was marginally worse.

DD723 later received further damage, being despatched to Marshalls at Cambridge for repairs on 11 December 1944. The aircraft never flew again and was re-categorised as a write-off on 21 April 1945. Note the electro-pneumatic ram (for actuation of the radiator flap) with its mechanical linkage positioned beneath the engine's rear section. The radiator flaps were controlled by a three-way switch (with 'Open', 'Automatic' and 'Closed' positions) and was thermostatically controlled in the automatic position. This photograph provides a good illustration of the exhaust inner shroud with the rear two exhaust ports served by a single combined stub.
(BAE SYSTEMS)

This close-up shot shows the 'thimble' nose radome on NF.XII HK117. The NF.XII was the first Mosquito Night-Fighter version to be equipped with centimetric AI radar, in this case the Mk VIII, which employed a dish-based scanning system in place of the AI Mk IV's static-aerial system. AI Mk IV operated on a 1.5-metre frequency, but it was soon realised that radar efficiency would be greatly improved by a practical microwave system operating in the 10-centimetre waveband. Such a system would provide a tighter beam, higher resolution and prove less susceptible to ground return signals. The invention of the Cavity Magnetron in February 1940 provided the necessary leap forward in microwave technology and led to the development of AI Mk VIII by the Telecommunications Research Establishment (TRE). AI Mk VIII's radar scanner dish was 28 inches in diameter and rotated at 200rpm, at the same time tilting up and down and from left to right, thus tracing a 'spiral' scan ahead of the aircraft at up to 45 degrees. A new type of indicator display was also developed for AI Mk VIII, providing the radar operator with all the information he required on one screen. F.II DD715 was the first Mosquito converted to carry AI Mk VIII, the new radar replacing the four .303in nose machine-guns and more than compensating for the loss in offensive fire power. Ninety-seven NF.XIIs were produced, all converted from new F.II airframes by Marshalls of Cambridge. Production of AI Mk VIII was undertaken by GEC and EKCO, the latter company producing around 5,000 sets during the war. *(Richard Riding collection)*

In this forward view of NF.XII HK117 taken in March 1943, note the shrouded exhausts and 'needle'-blade propellers. Originally built at Leavesden as an F.II, HK117 was delivered to Marshalls of Cambridge on 2 February 1943 for conversion to NF.XII status. This work included the installation of AI Mk VIII radar and was completed by 23 March, when HK117 was allocated to 10 MU. Following preparatory work at 218 MU, HK117 entered service with 29 Squadron at Bradwell Bay on 12 June 1943, but was damaged in a flying accident on 27 September, repairs being effected by Martin Hearn Ltd. HK117 was ready for collection nine months later and passed to 10 MU on 28 June 1944. In May 1945 it was damaged once more, rectification work being carried out by 71 MU before the aircraft found its way to 44 MU on 25 June 1945. HK117 was eventually Struck Off Charge and sold as scrap on 25 October 1946. The aircraft wears the standard Night-Fighter scheme of overall Medium Sea Grey with Dark Green camouflage upper surfaces. Note the 'balloon' tailwheel tyre, the Marstrand anti-shimmy type having yet to be introduced. The 'thimble' nose radome appears to be finished in black. *(Richard Riding collection)*

This shot of 256 Squadron NF.XII 'JT-R' (possibly HK131) is likely to have been taken during a flight from Malta in 1943. Note the 'thimble' nose radome for the AI Mk VIII radar, together with the shrouded exhausts. Formerly equipped with Beaufighters, 256 Squadron converted to Mosquito NF.XIIs at Ford in May 1943, beginning defensive patrols off the South Coast shortly afterwards. In July 1943 a detachment from 256 flew to Malta in support of the Sicilian invasion, the remainder of the Squadron arriving in October. During its stay in Malta 256 Squadron flew convoy patrols in addition to providing night defence for the beleaguered island. Leavesden-built HK131 was delivered to Marshalls of Cambridge on 6 March 1943 for the installation of AI Mk VIII radar. Allocated to 256 Squadron on 9 May 1943, HK131 flew to Malta the following July and served with 256 until March 1944 (eventually being Struck Off Charge on 30 August 1945). The small aerial mounted midway along the centre fuselage formed part of the IFF installation. NF.XIIIs began to replace 256 Squadron's NF.XIIs from November 1943. *(Ken Bernau, via Stuart Howe)*

Another 256 Squadron NF.XII (possibly HK136) photographed from a fellow 256 Squadron aircraft in around 1943. Production NF.XIIs were converted from Leavesden-built NF.IIs by Marshalls of Cambridge, the aircraft being delivered direct from the factory for fitment of their radar equipment. The NF.XII was powered by Merlin 21 or 23 engines of 1,460hp each, had a maximum speed of 370mph and a range of 1,705 miles. AI Mk VIII radar replaced the NF.II's nose machine-guns, but the four 20mm cannon were retained. HK136 joined 256 Squadron direct from 218 MU on 18 May 1943. Detached to Malta in August 1943, it continued to serve with 256 until delivered to 156 MU at Blida on 1 February 1944. HK136 later returned to 256 Squadron and was written off at Brindisi on 7 October 1944 after the undercarriage collapsed during a single-engine landing. HK136 was Struck Off Charge on 28 March 1945. *(Ken Bernau, via Stuart Howe)*

There can be no doubt that the Mosquito was a very beautiful aeroplane, its sleek form well illustrated here by NF.XIII HK428 'RO-K' of 29 Squadron. The NF.XIII was the first Mosquito Night-Fighter variant to feature the strengthened or 'basic' wing of the FB.VI, increasing the fuel load from 547 to 716 gallons. Equipped with Merlin 23 engines, Leavesden-built HK428 was delivered to 218 MU on 12 November 1943 before joining 29 Squadron at Ford on 28 January 1944. As 'RO-K', it served with 29 Squadron until suffering a landing accident at Hunsdon during a night-flying test on 22 October 1944. In poor visibility and with an overheating starboard engine and unserviceable flaps, HK428 overshot the Hunsdon runway and struck a hedge, the starboard undercarriage collapsing shortly afterwards. Following repairs at Hatfield, it was issued to the Central Gunnery School at Catfoss on 27 April 1945 before despatch to 10 MU for storage on 4 June 1945. HK428 was Struck Off Charge on 16 September 1946 and reduced to scrap. Note the 'thimble' nose radome and the chutes in the ventral bay doors for ejection of spent 20mm cannon shell cases and links. This photograph was taken on 1 March 1945. *(BAE SYSTEMS)*

264 Squadron NF.XIII HK480 'PS-P' is probably at Church Fenton in 1944. HK480 was delivered direct to 218 MU from the de Havilland Leavesden factory on 12 December 1943 and, after preparation for active service, was delivered to 264 Squadron at Church Fenton on the 30th. At the time 264 Squadron was engaged in bomber support operations over Europe, but switched back to home defence duties in early 1944. In May 1944 the Squadron moved to Hartford Bridge to take part in preparations for the Normandy invasion. At 2254hrs on the night of 5 June 1944 HK480 took off for a jamming patrol between St Martin and St Pierre, becoming the first 85 Group aircraft to fly over the Normandy beachhead. Crewed by Flt Lt J. D. Fox and Plt Off C. A. Pryor, it eventually went missing on the night of 24 June 1944 during another beachhead patrol. HK480 is finished in the standard Night-Fighter scheme of overall Medium Sea Grey with Dark Green camouflaged upper surfaces. The unit codes 'PS-P' are applied in red and the serial number in Night. *(James Earnshaw)*

The Mosquito was no exception to the application of nose art during the war, this 'sharkmouth'-adorned NF.XIII belonging to 604 Squadron. The identities of the majority of this group are unknown with the exception of navigator D. E. Wilson, who is believed to be second from the left. Note the 'eye' painted on the Universal 'bull-nose' radome. In common with most NF.XIIIs this aircraft is fitted with 'needle'-blade propellers. *(via David Oliver)*

264 Squadron NF.XIII HK470 'PS-D' is probably at Gilze Rijen in April 1945. Leavesden-built in November 1943, HK470 was delivered to 410 Squadron (RCAF) on 12 December 1943 and assigned the unit codes 'RA-X'. During service with 410 Squadron HK470 was damaged twice but shot down a Ju 88 on the night of 18 June 1944. On 21 September 1944 it was allocated to 604 Squadron before passing to 264 Squadron in April 1945. The aircraft was written off on 24 July 1945 after crashing into sand dunes while approaching to land at Knocke. Note the port engine's lower cowling lying on the grass between the wing and tailplane. The Typhoons in the background belong to 609 Squadron. *(James Earnshaw)*

This damage to the nose of an unidentified NF.XII or NF.XIII was probably caused by return fire from a German bomber or night-fighter. The large hole appears to have been recently covered by a temporary fabric patch, perhaps for a ferry flight to a repair MU. The Mosquito is finished in the standard Night-Fighter scheme of overall Medium Sea Grey with Dark Green camouflaged upper surfaces. Note the ice guard attached to the carburettor intake on the starboard lower cowling. *(Stuart Howe collection)*

A 604 Squadron crew (believed to be Fg Offs Ralph McIlvenny and Jack Haddon, but also reported as Fg Off W. Coates and Flt Lt P. Sandeman) pose for the camera at Colerne during the summer of 1944. At the time 604 Squadron was engaged in night defence patrols in support of the Allied invasion forces in Normandy. The Mosquito in the background is NF.XIII MM465 'NG-G', built at Leavesden in February 1944 and allocated to 604 Squadron on 1 March 1944, serving with that unit until 3 March 1945 when it passed to 264 Squadron, then based on the continent at Lille. MM465 was stored at 57 MU from 30 August 1945 and eventually sold as scrap to Lanzer & Company on 7 August 1947. Note the black and white bands (unofficially known as 'invasion stripes') on the fuselage and wings in accordance with SHAEF Operational Memorandum No 23; these were applied to all Allied aircraft taking part in 'Operation Overlord', the invasion of Normandy. MM465 sports a 'thimble' nose radome for its AI Mk VIII radar, later production NF.XIIIs being equipped with the Universal 'bull-nose' radome. *(Key)*

This 264 Squadron NF.XIII (possibly HK518) flew through the exploding debris of its victim, believed to be a Ju 88, in August 1944; note that the fabric covering on the fuselage and wing upper surfaces has been largely burned away, although the fuselage still bears traces of the 264 Squadron unit code letters 'PS'. The canopy glazing and 'bull-nose' radome are badly scorched, and the aircraft also lost its entire rudder fabric during this incident. This photograph was taken on an airfield in Normandy while 264 Squadron was operating in support of the invasion forces. HK518 survived the war to be Struck Off Charge on 1 January 1947. This picture was brought back from France by Mr Hugh Wootton on 1 September 1944. *(Crown Copyright)*

A 604 Squadron crew pose with their NF.XIII, possibly at Hurn in June 1944. Formerly equipped with Beaufighters, 604 Squadron converted to Mosquito NF.XIIIs at Church Fenton in April 1944 following transfer to 85 Group 2nd TAF. The Squadron moved to Hurn in May where it commenced operations in support of the Allied invasion forces in Normandy; it later re-equipped with Mosquito NF.30s and disbanded at Vandeville on 18 April 1945. Note the cover protecting the carburettor intake on the starboard lower cowling. *(Key)*

J. P. Smith of the Mosquito design team is seen at Hatfield on 16 September 1942 with the first high-altitude Fighter Mosquito, MP469. Originally built as the pressure cabin Bomber Prototype (and equipped with Merlin 61s), MP469 was converted into a high-altitude fighter in response to high-altitude bombing raids over the UK by Luftwaffe Junkers Ju 86Ps. Conversion work was completed within a week, the Hatfield design office and experimental shop staff working round the clock. MP469 was specially lightened for its new role and fitted with extended wingtips, increasing the overall wing span to 59 feet. One of the more unusual aspects of the conversion was the grafting of a four .303in machine-gun fighter nose on to MP469's bomber fuselage. This fighter nose originated from F.II DD715, which had been converted to carry AI Mk VIII centimetric radar as a Prototype for the NF.XII. Not until the postwar feature films would we see the bomber cockpit and fighter nose configuration, the latter albeit in mock-up form, represented again. *(BAE SYSTEMS)*

This second view of MP469 at Hatfield on 16 September 1942 clearly shows the extended 59-foot wingspan and the four-bladed propellers, which were originally tested on W4050 and had been fitted to MP469 on 13 September. For its high-altitude fighter role, MP469's fuselage and outer wing fuel tanks were removed, leaving only the inboard tanks with a total capacity of 287 gallons. A fighter-type control column replaced the bomber 'wheel' and a plywood panel was substituted for the pilot's back armour. Smaller-diameter main wheels were later fitted, but MP469 still retains the standard units in this picture.

In its new configuration MP469 first flew on 14 September 1942 and was soon reaching altitudes beyond its 43,000-foot design objective (it possessed a climb rate of 500 feet per minute). On 16 September the aircraft was delivered to the High Altitude Flight at Northolt in anticipation of further bombing raids by Luftwaffe Ju 86Ps, which, in the event, never materialised. In response to fears of high-altitude night raids on the UK, MP469 was later fitted with AI Mk VIII radar (in a 'thimble' nose radome), necessitating re-location of the nose machine-guns to an under-fuselage 'belly pack'. In this configuration MP469 was designated NF.XV and successful trials led to the production of four more, all converted from B.IV airframes and each equipped with Merlin 70 series engines and featuring a 62-foot wingspan. MP469 also served with the Fighter Interception Unit and 85 Squadron before ending its days at the School of Aeronautical Engineering, RAF Henlow, as Instructional Airframe 4882M. It has Dark Sea Grey and Dark Green camouflaged upper surfaces and PR Blue under surfaces. The spinners are likely to be finished in Dark Sea Grey. *(BAE SYSTEMS)*

F.II DZ659 was selected on the Hatfield production line as a trials installation aircraft for the American SCR 720 AI radar. SCR 720 was developed by the Massachusetts Institute of Technology and produced by the Western Electric Corporation and the Bell Telephone Laboratory. Operating in the 10-centimetre waveband, it had a range of approximately ten miles and was generally resilient to enemy jamming. The Telecommunications Research Establishment (TRE) at Defford delivered an SCR 720 set to Hatfield in January 1943 and a mock-up of the proposed installation in DZ659 was ready for inspection by 10 February. Installation work was overseen by Western Electric and completed by 23 March, DZ659 becoming, in effect, a prototype for the NF.XVII. This Mosquito also pioneered the Universal or 'bull-nose' radome capable of housing either SCR 720/729 or the British-produced AI Mk X radar.

DZ659 was flown to the Fighter Interception Unit (FIU) at Ford on 1 April 1943 for operational trials before flying back to Hatfield for special examination on 21 April. Returning to the FIU on 7 May 1943, the aircraft passed to the Signals Intelligence Unit at Defford on 18 May. By now sporting Night under surfaces, November 1943 saw it back at Ford, where it was used to test the installation of AI Mk X and SCR 729 radars. A take-off accident at Wittering on

10 June 1944 resulted in an undercarriage collapse, but DZ659 was repaired on site and serviceable again by 8 August. Further damage occurred on 27 November 1944, repairs not being completed until 10 February 1945. Allocated to 10 MU for storage in May 1945, DZ659 was eventually Struck Off Charge as obsolete on 28 February 1946. During its later service with the Fighter Interception Unit it wore the unit codes 'ZQ-H'. Production NF.XVIIs were all converted from Leavesden-built F.II airframes, their radar sets and 'bull-nose' radomes being installed by Marshalls of Cambridge. DZ659 is seen here at Hatfield on 31 March 1943 shortly before delivery to Ford.
(Both BAE SYSTEMS)

This picture was taken at Hatfield on 31 March 1943 and features the SCR 720 radar installation in DZ659. The large cylindrical unit on the fuselage bulkhead is the radar high frequency unit, the parabolic scanning dish (with its vertical dipole) being located forward within the plastic upper section of the nose radome. SCR 720 was developed by the Massachusetts Institute of Technology and built by the Western Electric Corporation and the Bell Telephone Laboratory. It was an improved version of the earlier SCR-520 and was also fitted to the Northrop P-61 Black Widow and the Grumman Tigercat. *(BAE SYSTEMS)*

255 Squadron NF.XIX TA408/G is pictured at Rosignano in March 1945. A Hatfield-built Mosquito, TA408 was delivered to 27 MU on 9 September 1944 before passing to 218 MU on 10 October . Five days later it arrived at No 2 Aircraft Preparation Unit in readiness for overseas service, and was later delivered to No 1 Ferry Unit and flown to the Mediterranean Theatre on 13 October, arriving at 144 MU the following day. TA408 was among the initial batch of Mosquito NF.XIXs allocated to 255 Squadron at Rosignano (its first, TA428, being delivered on 26 January 1945), where it received the unit codes 'YD-D'. 255 Squadron was engaged in intruder operations over the Balkans and began using Mosquito NF.XIXs in February 1945. On 22 April 1945 TA428 was written off in a take-off accident at Rosignano, eventually being Struck Off Charge on 6 September 1945. Note the 'G' suffix at the end of the serial number, indicating that TA408 required an armed guard due to the installation of secret equipment (possibly as this was one of the first NF.XIXs received by 255 Squadron). It wears the standard Night-Fighter scheme of overall Medium Sea Grey with Dark Green camouflaged upper surfaces and is equipped with 'paddle'-blade propellers. *(Philip Hyson, via Stuart Howe)*

157 Squadron NF.XIX TA446 'RS-Q' lies shattered at Shipdham following a belly-landing at 1400hrs on 17 January 1945. TA446 was returning to its Swannington base following failure of the port engine shortly after take-off. The propeller was feathered but the port undercarriage would not retract, the subsequent drag preventing TA446 from maintaining height. In the ensuing forced landing the aircraft was written off after the fuselage separated aft of number four bulkhead (the cause of the engine failure turned out to be inadvertent operation of the engine fire extinguisher). Hatfield-built in August 1944 and equipped with Merlin 25s, TA446 was delivered to 218 MU on 5 August 1944. On 12 September it was allocated to 85 Squadron at Swannington, but re-assigned to 157 Squadron (also at Swannington) on 21 October. On the night preceding the incident shown here, TA446 destroyed a Junkers Ju 188 while engaged on a bomber support operation. Nine days later, on 26 January 1945, it was officially Struck Off Charge. TA446 wears the standard Night-Fighter scheme of overall Medium Sea Grey with Dark Green camouflaged upper surfaces. The unit code letters are finished in red. *(Keith Goodchild)*

255 Squadron personnel photographed at Hal Far, Malta, in August 1945. Equipped with an assortment of Mosquito NF.XIXs and NF.30s, 255 Squadron moved to Malta from Rosignano in September 1945. In January 1946 the Squadron was posted to Gianaclis in Egypt, where it disbanded on 31 March 1946. The Mosquito in the background is Hatfield-built NF.XIX TA440 'YD-G'. *(Philip Hyson)*

157 Squadron burned this effigy of Hermann Goering during the VE Night celebrations at RAF Swannington. One of the Squadron's NF.30s is visible in the background. *(Stuart Howe collection)*

This is a postwar shot of NF.30 NT497, built at Leavesden in February 1945 and serving with both 219 and 23 Squadrons before being sold as scrap to F. W. Ward in November 1953. Note the flame-damping louvred exhaust shrouds, which were introduced on the NF.30 and became a standard feature of most Mosquito Night-Fighters equipped with two-speed, two-stage supercharged Merlin engines. Considerable problems were encountered with the NF.30's inner and outer exhaust shrouds following the type's introduction to squadron service in June 1944, and modifications were required to ensure efficient operation coupled with good flame-damping qualities. The louvred or 'slotted' shroud eventually cured the flame-damping problems, the new design being tested on 219 Squadron NF.30 MM690 during July 1944. These tests proved the louvred shroud to be 'very satisfactory for fighter use', although it remained visible at a considerably larger angle from astern than the shrouded double ejector 'saxophone' exhaust of the NF.II. Special anti-glow paint was applied to the exhausts of MM690 and MM688 to determine whether this could be used as an interim measure pending production of the louvred shroud; however, trials revealed that the exhausts still produced an excessive red glow that was considered unsafe for operational use against anything but flying bombs. *(Eddy Gosling)*

151 Squadron crew Abdul (on the left, his full name not known) and Jock Adamson are photographed with their NF.30 at Lubeck in 1946. 151 Squadron received its first NF.30s in October 1944, having previously been equipped with NF.XIIs and NF.XIIIs together with a small number of FB.VIs. In February 1945 the Squadron commenced low-level intruder flights over Germany, often attacking German night-fighters landing at their home airfields. The NF.30 was equipped with two-speed, two-stage supercharged Merlin 72s or 76s, had an operational ceiling of 35,000 feet and possessed a maximum speed of 424mph at 26,500 feet. Note the 'paddle'-blade propellers and louvred exhaust shrouds. This picture was taken by 151 Squadron navigator Fg Off Frank Baker. *(Simon Baker)*

151 Squadron NF.30 NT498 'DZ-E', possibly at Lubeck in 1946. NT498 was delivered from the Leavesden factory to 218 MU on 25 February 1945, and three weeks later was allocated to 406 Squadron (RCAF) and assigned the unit codes 'HU-P'. Damaged on 25 April 1945, repairs were carried out by a team from 71 MU and completed by 21 June. NT498 passed to 151 Squadron in July 1945, remaining with 151 until 24 October 1946, when it flew to 9 MU for storage. This NF.30 was sold as scrap to John Dale on 5 August 1948. *(Simon Baker)*

151 Squadron NF.30 NT564 'DZ-M' is seen from another NF.30 in 1946. This Leavesden-built Mosquito was the regular mount of navigator Frank Baker and joined 151 Squadron on 19 April 1945, serving with 151 until entering storage at 9 MU on 24 October 1946. Note the 'BABS' (Beam Approach Beacon System) aerial positioned beneath the rear fuselage at bulkhead number five. The A.1271 beam approach amplifier, used in conjunction with TR.1430 radio equipment, was mounted on the inner fuselage aft of bulkhead number four. NT564 was eventually sold as scrap to John Dale on 5 August 1948. *(Simon Baker)*

151 Squadron NF.30 NT547 'DZ-G' lies damaged following a landing accident at Weston Zoyland on the morning of 17 September 1946. Returning from a practice interception flight, NT547's starboard tyre burst, causing the aircraft to swing and leading to the collapse of the starboard undercarriage. NT547 was built at Leavesden in early 1945 and delivered to 218 MU for storage on 22 March. On 16 July it was delivered to 151 Squadron, with which it served until suffering the accident depicted here. The aircraft was subsequently written off, being Struck Off Charge on 2 November 1946. In the first view note the cockpit escape hatch lying on the starboard wing. The second, close-up, shot features the damage caused to NT547's starboard engine nacelle, outer undercarriage door and wing leading edge. Note the fire extinguisher located on the outboard side of the engine bulkhead (between the engine bearer mounting points), and the lack of louvred exhaust shrouds. *(Both Simon Baker)*

A new NF.36 takes off for a test flight from Leavesden. The final Mosquito Night-Fighter version to see RAF squadron service, the NF.36 was designed to bridge the gap between the Mosquito NF.30 and the RAF's first generation of jet fighters. Basically an updated version of the NF.30, it was equipped with fuel-injected Merlin 113/114 engines (in place of the NF.30's Merlin 70 series) together with a later version of AI Mk X radar. A converted NF.30 (MT466) served as a Prototype for the NF.36, and 256 production aircraft were ordered from the de Havilland Second Aircraft Group factory at Leavesden (under Air Ministry Contract 1576). With the cessation of hostilities in Europe this order was cut back to 163 aircraft, the final example (RL268) leaving the factory on 28 March 1947. The last NF.36s in RAF squadron service were retired in March 1954. *(Richard Riding collection)*

An unidentified NF.36 tucks in close to the camera aircraft during a training flight from West Malling in 1949. Note the SCR 729 aerial beneath the lower forward fuselage, and the inverted 'T'-shaped aerial beneath the starboard wing, the latter for the radio altimeter. This is likely to be a 25 Squadron aircraft with only the forward section of the spinners painted in 25's red markings. The nose radome's upper section has been left unpainted, a normal peacetime practice on RAF Mosquito Night-Fighters. *(John Gerrish)*

264 Squadron NF.36 RL134 'PS-G' lands at Acklington on 2 June 1950. At full load and with 18lb boost (flaps up or 15 degrees down), the NF.36's single-engine safety speed was 186 knots. If an engine failed on take-off, once the safety speed had been attained the NF.36 would climb at full load provided the propeller of the failed engine had been feathered and the flaps fully raised. Leavesden-built RL134 was delivered from the factory to 27 MU on 1 July 1945. On 13 October 1949 it was allocated to 264 Squadron at Coltishall, where it was assigned the unit codes 'PS-G'. In July 1950 Airwork at Gatwick modified RL134 in accordance with Special Technical Instruction (STI) 109b, following which it returned to 264 Squadron. This NF.36 continued to serve with 264 until 1 February 1952, by which time Meteor NF.11s had replaced the Mosquitoes and RL134 entered storage with 22 MU. The aircraft was ultimately sold as scrap to David Band on 22 April 1954. *(Mike Gray)*

23 Squadron NF.36 RL184 'YP-N' being refuelled by Willie Wardle and 'Doc' Turner (23 Squadron's Medical Officer) at Coltishall on 15 March 1951. Leavesden-built RL184 was delivered direct from the factory to 27 MU on 21 August 1945. On 6 November 1950 it was allocated to 264 Squadron at Church Fenton, but diverted to 23 Squadron at Coltishall five days later. In December 1950 it underwent modifications (in accordance with Special Technical Instruction 109b) with Scott Clann at Prestwick before returning to Coltishall in January 1951. Five months afterwards it passed to 228 OCU at Leeming (by which time it had acquired blue-painted spinners), where it served until the night of 14 November 1951 when it hit a tree within the Leeming circuit and crashed east of the aerodrome. Note the open ventral bay doors, which provided access to the four 20mm cannons. To open the doors, five securing hooks had to be unscrewed from the starboard side and the doors lowered by hand (port and starboard in sequence) before being secured by stays at their front and rear corners. The doors featured chutes in their forward sections for the ejection of spent cannon shell cases and links. RL184 is finished in the standard Night-Fighter scheme of overall Medium Sea Grey with Dark Green camouflage upper surfaces. The unit code letters are applied in red and the serial number in Night. *(Mike Gray)*

NF.36s of 23 Squadron lined up at Coltishall on 3 April 1951. 23 Squadron carried out a number of roles during this period including night-fighting, all-weather day operations, low-level intruding and radio countermeasures. For the latter several of the Squadron's NF.36s were equipped with 'Hookah', a device enabling them to home into radio and radar jamming transmissions from enemy aircraft. 'Hookah' was a development of Serrate but differed in the band of frequencies capable of being swept. 'Hookah Bat' detected radar frequencies and 'Hookah Mouse' detected VHF frequencies. The 'Hookah' Cathode Ray Tube was approximately 3 inches in diameter and was fixed into the visor of the AI Mk X radar display, the picture being viewed on a mirror placed between the B and C scopes of the display. Aerials for 'Hookah' were fixed outboard on the port and starboard wing leading edges and are clearly visible on the second NF.36 in this line-up, RL135. 23 Squadron regularly practiced with 'Hookah' against the Lincoln bombers of 100 Group.

RL135 was built at Leavesden in June 1945 and initially stored at 15 MU. On 10 October 1947 it was allocated to 23 Squadron at Coltishall where it received the unit codes 'YP-F'. In February 1950 all NF.36s were grounded following the discovery that propeller feathering was a possible cause of engine fires. Modifications were introduced (under Special Technical Instruction STI 109b) to prevent this, RL135 undergoing the necessary work at Leavesden in May 1950. RL135 was later re-coded 'YP-T' and continued to serve with 23 Squadron until 23 July 1952 when it entered storage at 38 MU. RL135 was eventually sold for scrap to David Band & Company on 3 January 1955. The red and blue insignia of 23 Squadron is represented on the spinners, which are finished in concentric rings of blue, red and blue. Beyond RL135 are RL183 'YP-E' and RK998 'YP-A'. *(Mike Gray)*

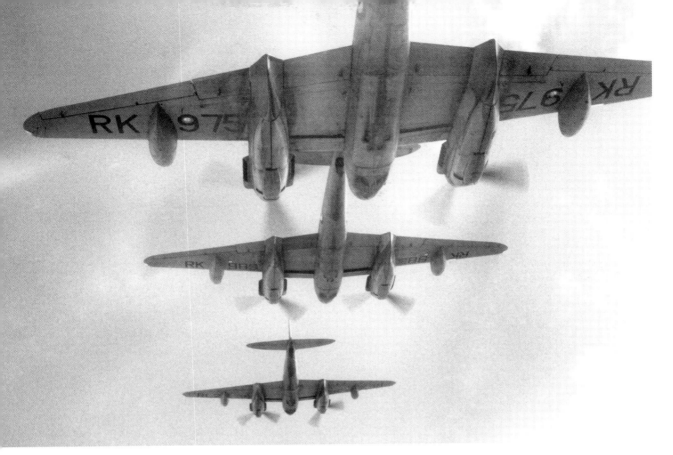

39 Squadron NF.36s in line-astern formation during a flight from Nicosia to Kabrit on 30 May 1952, returning from Nicosia's Armament Practice School, which provided annual concentrated gunnery training for 39 Squadron's pilots. This photograph was taken from NF.36 RL130 by 39 Squadron navigator Peter Verney. The leading aircraft is RL236, with RK983 and RK975 bringing up the rear. All three aircraft were built at the de Havilland Leavesden factory in 1945, RK975 serving with 219 and 39 Squadrons before being sold as scrap to International Alloys on 23 April 1954. RAF Middle Eastern Air Force (MEAF) NF.36s rarely flew without underwing drop tanks. *(Peter Verney)*

This photograph demonstrates very close formation of 39 Squadron NF.36s flying from Kabrit in 1952. In the Egyptian climate Mosquito cockpit temperatures could reach as high as 70°C, leading to very uncomfortable conditions for the crew. *(Peter Verney)*

A 39 Squadron NF.36 seen from the navigator's seat of another over the Nile Delta in 1952. Note the flame-damping exhaust shroud on the photographic aircraft's starboard inner engine. *(Peter Verney)*

An NF.36 of 39 Squadron photographed over Egypt's Little Bitter Lake in 1952. 39 Squadron reformed at Khartoum in March 1949 (with Tempest F.6s) before moving to Egypt later the same year as the RAF's only Middle East-based night-fighter squadron. Equipped with Mosquito NF.36s, the Squadron was initially based at Fayid in the Canal Zone under the command of Sqn Ldr R. D. Doleman DSO DFC. In 1951 the Squadron moved to Kabrit on the Great Bitter Lake where they were joined by 219 Squadron, which was also equipped with NF.36s. Most of 39 Squadron's flying took place over the Sinai Desert, where it conducted practice interceptions under GCI control. Aerial gunnery training took place on a range at Shallufa (often used for bombing practice by the UK-based B.35 Squadrons during 'Sunray' detachments) situated 15 miles from Kabrit. Note the 39 Squadron markings, which appeared on both sides of the fuselage and consisted of a black horizontal band with two yellow pyramids either side of the roundel. *(Peter Verney)*

This was the scene at 228 OCU Leeming following a night taxying accident between NF.36s RL267 (seen in the first photograph) and RL121 (in the second) on 10 December 1951. While taxying out for a training flight at 2135hrs, RL267 struck the stationary RL121, causing severe damage to both aircraft, which were subsequently written off. Note that the nose of RL267 has been completely destroyed together with the port outer wing and aileron of RL121. Both Mosquitoes were built at the de Havilland Leavesden factory and served with the Central Fighter Establishment (CFE) before allocation to 228 OCU. The gentleman leaning on RL267's starboard propeller is 'Doc' Crossley. A Miles Martinet is visible through the hangar doors on the right. *(Both Mike Gray)*

The remains of 39 Squadron NF.36 RL234 are seen behind the Technical Wing hangar at Kabrit in August 1952. RL234's condition was the result of a landing accident on the night of 12 August 1952 following a Practice Interception (PI) flight. Kabrit's main runway was then under repair so pilots were instructed to use the aerodrome's shorter 1,500-foot runway. RL234 overshot on landing, the pilot raising the undercarriage to avoid entering the Great Bitter Lake, which was situated fairly close to the runway. No blame was attached to the pilot as the margins of error allowed by the runway for night operations were too small. RL234 was built at Leavesden in October 1945 and placed in store before delivery to 39 Squadron at Kabrit on 9 December 1949. It served with 39 Squadron until 6 June 1952, when it suffered accident damage (which was repaired on site), the aircraft returning to operational status on 29 July. Following the damage illustrated here RL234 was Struck Off Charge on 31 August 1952. *(Peter Verney)*

Sqn Ldr John Cogill (left) and Sgt Peter Verney are pictured with NF.36 RL141 at Benson on 25 July 1953. By March 1953 Meteor NF.13s had replaced 39 and 219 Squadrons' Mosquito NF.36s for defence of the Canal Zone, and the remaining unserviceable NF.36s were repaired and gradually ferried back to the UK for disposal. The last NF.36 to leave was RL141, which was ferried home by 39 Squadron CO John Cogill accompanied by navigator Peter Verney. Departing Fayid at 0640hrs on 24 July 1953, they reached Luqa in 4hrs 35mins and, after refuelling, took off for Istres, arriving at 1700hrs GMT. The following morning RL141 left Istres at 0635hrs bound for Benson, where it landed at 0940hrs. Due to radio problems Peter Verney had to rely on dead reckoning and map-reading for much of this final leg, but arrived over the English coast at precisely the calculated position. An ex-219 Squadron aircraft, RL141 had previously served with 23 Squadron and was sold as scrap on 22 April 1954. *(Peter Verney)*

Following the accident that befell RL234 (upper picture), 39 Squadron's night-flying sorties temporarily ended at Fayid while runway repairs were completed at Kabrit. The aircrews would then be driven back to Kabrit before returning the following day to collect their aircraft. As a result, 39 Squadron aircrew log books featured several entries for 10-minute 'Fayid to Kabrit' ferry flights. Here we see three of the Squadron's NF.36s at Fayid in August 1952 ready for the short hop back to Kabrit. *(Peter Verney)*

An airman secures the nose access doors of an unidentified 25 Squadron NF.36 at West Malling. Note the parabolic scanning dish of the AI Mk X radar clearly visible beneath the transparent nose radome. Protruding from the centre of the dish is the vertical dipole used for both transmission and reception of radar signals. Located beneath the starboard nose access door is the camera gun housing. The spinners are finished in red. *(John Gerrish)*

United States Air Force night-fighter crew Captain 'Mac' Macbeth (pilot, left) and Major Jack Lawler (navigator) stand with 23 Squadron NF.36 RL184 at Coltishall on 3 May 1951. Both men were on an exchange posting with the RAF, their usual mount being the North American F-82 Twin Mustang. *(Mike Gray)*

Mosquito Night-Fighters are participating in the annual Battle of Britain flypast over London during September 1947. This three-'Vic' formation consists of NF.36s from the West Malling Wing, with 25 Squadron forming the first 'Vic', 29 Squadron the second and 85 Squadron the third. *(Philip Hyson)*

141 Squadron NF.36 RL188 'TW-B' ready for a sortie from Coltishall in September 1950. By now the Mosquito's days as a front-line night-fighter were numbered for it lacked the performance necessary to deal with the threat of Soviet high-altitude raiders. Nevertheless, the NF.36 fulfilled its design requirement of bridging the gap between the NF.30 and the RAF's first generation of jet fighters.

RL188 was ready for collection from the Leavesden factory on 11 August 1945, being delivered to 19 MU for storage five days later. On 2 February 1946 it was delivered to 85 Squadron, where it received the unit codes 'VY-M' before transfer to 141 Squadron at Coltishall (initially as 'TW-G' and later as 'TW-B') ten months later. In June 1950 it returned to Leavesden for modifications (in accordance with Special Technical Instruction STI 109b), which were complete by the 16th. A heavy landing in August 1950 caused Category 3 damage, which was repaired on site, RL188 returning to service on 28 September. In November 1950 the aircraft passed to 23 Squadron at Coltishall where it was re-coded 'YP-P', this being changed to 'YP-V' in 1951. 228 OCU received RL188 on 29 November 1951, retaining it until February 1952, when it entered storage at 22 MU. Declared Non-Effective Stock in April 1953, RL141 was sold as scrap to David Band & Company a year later. Note the 141 Squadron badge on the fin. *(Mike Gray)*

RK998 'YP-A', a 'Hookah'-equipped NF.36 of 23 Squadron, photographed from another NF.36 on 3 April 1951. The 'Hookah' aerials are clearly visible on the wing leading edge and bear some similarity to the aerials of the wartime German Lichtenstein radar. The 23 Squadron colours are represented on the spinners, which are finished in concentric rings of red, blue and red. Note the absence of a louvred exhaust shroud on the port engine outer side cowling, the exhaust stubs (a specialist 'multi-blister' flame-damping type developed for Mosquito Night-Fighters) exiting directly into the slipstream. RK998 was ready for collection from the Leavesden factory on 13 June 1945 and delivered into storage at 27 MU two days later. In May 1949 it was allocated to 23 Squadron at Coltishall and underwent modifications (in accordance with Special Technical Instruction 109b) at Leavesden a year later. During a flight to Hatfield on 20 December 1951 RK998 landed at Leavesden in error and was damaged in a ground loop after overshooting the runway. Repairs were carried out by de Havilland's, RK998 returning to 23 Squadron on 7 July 1952. Three weeks later it entered storage at 27 MU before being declared Non-Effective Stock in June 1953. RK998 was sold as scrap to Aluminium Refineries on 31 March 1955. *(Mike Gray)*

NF.36 RL183 'YP-E' of 23 Squadron undergoing a gun harmonisation check at Coltishall on 2 February 1951. Note that the aircraft has been jacked in the neutral incidence or 'rigging' position (measured using longitudinal level datum blocks positioned inside the rear fuselage aft of bulkhead four) with the tail trestled and secured at fuselage bulkhead six. Leavesden-built RL183 was ready for collection on 31 July 1945 and delivered to 27 MU for storage on 5 August. Allocated to 23 Squadron at Coltishall on 25 April 1949 (to replace RL249, which crashed shortly after take-off on 14 February 1949), RL183 was issued with the unit codes 'YP-E'. The aircraft returned to Leavesden on 13 June 1950 for modifications (in accordance with Special Technical Instruction 109b), which were completed by 3 July when the aircraft flew back to Coltishall. RL183 was later recoded 'YP-N' and eventually retired to 38 MU on 23 July 1952. On 3 January 1955 this NF.36 was sold as scrap to David Band & Company. *(via Mike Gray)*

25 Squadron aircrews pose for a group photo at West Malling in 1947. The Mosquito behind them is one of the Squadron's NF.36s, probably RL117 'ZK-B'. together with 29 and 85 Squadrons, 25 formed part of the West Malling Night-Fighter Wing and received its first NF.36s from 29 Squadron when the latter was reduced to peacetime strength in October 1946. Each West Malling Night-Fighter Wing squadron retained eight NF.36s, the individual squadrons distinguished by different coloured spinners and code letters: 25 Squadron boasted red spinners and codes, 29 Squadron yellow and 85 Squadron blue. Additionally, the Wing's squadrons were assigned separate batches of individual aircraft code letters, 25 Squadron using the letters A to H, 85 Squadron J to Q, and 29 Squadron S to Z. Note the two black bars flanking the individual aircraft letter 'B' on the nose radome, these markings being individual to 25 Squadron. RL117 was built at Leavesden in June 1945 and entered storage with 27 MU later the same month. Allocated to 29 Squadron on 20 September 1946, it passed to 25 Squadron three weeks later. On 13 September 1948 RL117 crashed near West Malling after colliding with 85 Squadron T.3 VT612. *(Philip Hyson)*

In a scene at Coltishall on 3 April 1951, engine fitters Briggs (left) and Cpl Les Farley (right) work on the port Merlin 114 of 23 Squadron NF.36 RL243 'YP-L'. The NF.36 equipped with fuel-injected Merlin 113/114s (of 1,690hp each) providing this version of the Mosquito with a maximum speed of 404mph. Note that the cowling side panel lacks the outer louvred flame-damping exhaust shroud normally associated with two-stage Merlin Mosquito Night-Fighters. RL243 previously served with the Central Fighter Establishment at West Raynham as 'ZE-C', 25 Squadron as 'ZK-G' and 264 Squadron as 'PS-C'. Two months after this photo was taken, RL243 was allocated to 228 OCU before passing to 48 MU on 10 March 1952. Declared Non-Effective Stock in June 1953, RL243 was sold as scrap on 15 October 1954. The spinners are finished in concentric rings of red, blue and red. (Mike Gray)

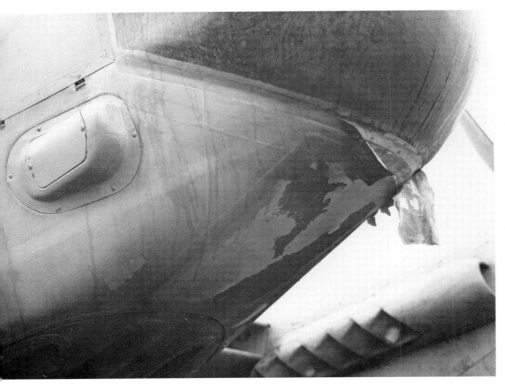

The effects of cannon blast on the lower section of an NF.38's nose radome can be seen here – note the loosened fabric strips between the radome and lower forward fuselage. Such damage was not uncommon with operational Mosquito Night-Fighter squadrons, one former navigator describing the experience of the four 20mm cannons being fired 'as though there was someone belting the floor beneath with a baulk of timber'. Note the camera gun housing beneath the starboard nose access door. (BAE SYSTEMS)

NF.36 RK993 'G' of 228 OCU pictured at its Leeming home base in late 1948. 228 OCU formed on 1 May 1947 through an amalgamation of Nos 13 and 54 OTUs. The unit's primary role was to provide instruction for night-fighter crews and, in addition to the Mosquito NF.36, it was also equipped with the Brigand T.4 and Wellington T.18. RK993 was built at Leavesden in 1945 and delivered direct from the factory to 15 MU on 11 June. On 29 September 1947 it was assigned to 228 OCU, serving until 15 June 1950 when it was damaged beyond repair in a take-off accident at Leeming. *(John Gerrish)*

A 39 Squadron NF.36 being re-armed at Kabrit in 1952. In common with all centimetric-radar-equipped Mosquito Night-Fighters, the NF.36 featured an armament of four 20mm Hispano cannons fitted with pneumatic firing units and Martin Baker spring-type blast tubes. The cannons were positioned in the underside of the fuselage, the outboard pair mounted approximately 14 inches further rearward than the inboard pair. The front cannon mountings were of the ball-and-socket type, while those for the rear worked on a 'swinging link' system, consisting

of an inverted U-shaped bracket pivoted at its apex. Two pairs of ammunition tanks, each tank holding 150 rounds, were mounted between the three cannon support frames, the forward pair feeding the inboard cannons and the rear pair the outboard cannons. Ammunition belts were laid in each tank with the open side of the link uppermost and the projectiles facing forward. Left-hand belts were used for the port tanks and right-hand belts for the starboard. The ammunition belt passed over rollers (fitted at the outboard side of each tank) at the point of entry to the fixed feed chute. During air-to-ground firing practice over the Shallufa range 39 Squadron crews regularly witnessed local women and children collecting spent 20mm shell cases as they fell from the aircraft. Note the armourer holding an ammunition drum (lower right). *(Peter Verney)*

219 Squadron NF.36 RK994 running up, possibly at Kabrit in 1951 or 1952. A Leavesden-built aircraft, RK994 was despatched to the MEAF in February 1951 and assigned to 219 Squadron at Kabrit on 13 April. On 24 October 1952 it passed to 39 Squadron before being retired to 19 MU in the UK during March 1953. The aircraft was sold as scrap to David Band & Company on 27 May 1954. *(Mrs Cunningham)*

NF.36 RL265 of 228 OCU following a single-engine belly-landing at Leeming on the afternoon of 21 January 1949. One of the last NF.36s produced, RL265 left the Leavesden factory on 13 September 1946 for storage at 19 MU. On 6 October 1947 it was delivered to 228 OCU at Leeming; it served there until 21 January 1949 when the starboard engine failed during an air test. Unable to feather the starboard propeller, the pilot commenced a landing descent from 4,000 feet as the aircraft would not maintain height. RL265 was written off in the subsequent forced landing, breaking its back and losing the port propeller; it was Struck Off Charge five days later. *(J. K. Rogers, via Stuart Howe)*

An NF.36 of 264 Squadron starts up in readiness for a sortie from Coltishall. 264 Squadron formed part of 12 Group's Eastern Sector and arrived at Coltishall in 1948, sharing the aerodrome with 23 and 141 Squadrons. 264 received its first Mosquito (NF.II W4086) in May 1942 and went on to complete nearly ten years of Mosquito operations before Meteor NF.11s replaced the NF.36s in late 1951. Note the ground crewman operating the Ki-gass priming pump in the port engine nacelle. The engines were started with the main fuel cocks set to 'OUTER TANKS'; it was recommended that the engines be started in a different order each time to check operation of the vacuum pumps. Once the engines were running satisfactorily the pilot would release the starter and booster coil push buttons and switch on the booster pumps, the latter remaining on at all times. This aircraft is likely to be RL252, which joined 264 Squadron in January 1949, serving until 28 August 1950, when it crashed on landing at Church Fenton. The spinners bear 264 Squadron's black and yellow concentric ring markings. (Bob Jacobs, via Mike Gray)

These three views show VT653, the third production NF.38, following roll-out from the Hatfield factory in January 1948. The final production Mosquito variant, the NF.38 was designed to accommodate the British-designed AI Mk IXb radar. Unlike the AI Mk X, this featured a stabilised search 'lock on' capability, but proved inferior in overall performance to both the Mk X and the earlier Mk VIII versions. Installation of AI Mk IXb in the Mosquito necessitated extensive modification and lengthening of the forward fuselage, increasing weight and shifting the centre of gravity aft. Enlarged elevator horn balances were fitted to improve handling, but trials at the Central Fighter Establishment, West Raynham, revealed the NF.38 unsuitable for RAF squadron service due to its inferior radar, poor performance and instability. Of the 101 NF.38s produced, sixty were sold to the Yugoslav Air Force and served in various roles until the early 1960s.

VT653 was ready for collection on 20 February 1948 and delivered for trials at the Central Fighter Establishment on 10 March. It passed to the Handling Squadron at Boscombe

Down in June 1948 before entering storage with 22 MU on 27 January 1949. In 1952 it was sold to the Yugoslav Air Force (receiving the Yugoslav Air Force serial '8028') and delivered to its new owners (via No 1 Overseas Ferry Unit Abingdon) by RAF ferry pilot Richard Livermore on 9 April 1952. Note the raised and extended cockpit canopy (which was 5 inches longer than previous Mosquito Fighter canopies and equipped with less framing), and the 'paddle'-blade propellers. VT653's fuselage, tailplane, elevators and top cowlings have still to be finished in Medium Sea Grey and Dark Green. *(All Richard Riding collection)*

The engines and propellers of NF.38 VX860 under inspection at 22 MU Silloth on 29 March 1951. Constructed at the de Havilland Chester factory, VX860 was delivered into storage at 22 MU on 25 February 1950. In 1951 it was sold to the Yugoslav Air Force as '8047' and flown to No 1 Overseas Ferry Unit Abingdon on 12 December in preparation for delivery. '8047' departed

Abingdon on 19 December 1951, arriving in Yugoslavia on 3 January 1952. Note the wingtip-mounted receiving aerials (Types 357A, 397 and 398 running inboard from the wingtip) for the ARI 5610 radio installation, the latter's transmitting aerial fitted on the underside of the rear fuselage aft of bulkhead number five. *(Mike Gray)*

These three views of NF.38 7142M (ex-VT697) of 1119 (Shrewsbury) Squadron ATC show it being dismantled by a team from 9 MU Cosford. Chester-built VT697 was delivered into storage at 27 MU on 14 December 1949. By this time the RAF had no use for the Mosquito NF.38 and VT697 remained in store for the next four and a half years, being declared Non-Effective Stock on 5 May 1953. On 20 May 1954 it was allocated to 1119 (Shrewsbury) Squadron

ATC as Instructional Airframe 7142M, where it stayed until moved by 9 MU (in 1956 or 1957), being eventually scrapped. The first picture shows to advantage the raised and lengthened cockpit canopy of the NF.38 with its modified Direct Vision sliding windows. Note the whip aerial for the ARI 5083/ARI 5782 radio installation extending rearwards from the cockpit, the aerial and loading unit being mounted direct to the canopy roof.

VX916 photographed at Chester in November 1950 prior to its maiden flight. Standing in front of the aircraft are (left to right) flight shed Superintendent Mr Andrews, test pilot Pat Fillingham, and Factory Manager Mr S. G. Statham. *(Fotocraft)*

Pat Fillingham takes the final production Mosquito, NF.38 VX916, aloft from Chester on the occasion of its maiden flight. Constructed under Air Ministry Contract 2468, VX916 was ready for collection on 22 December 1950 and passed to 48 MU the same day. Sold to the Yugoslav Air Force as '8027', VX916 left the UK on 6 December 1951. It still has to undergo final finishing as evident from the unpainted lower forward fuselage, flaps, elevators and port engine outer side cowling. Note the enlarged elevator horn balances. *(Fotocraft)*

Sgt Jeff Hewes is at the controls of 264 Squadron NF.36 'PS-F' at Coltishall. This aircraft is probably RL209, a former 141 Squadron aircraft that joined 264 Squadron on 30 October 1951 before passing to 228 OCU just over a month later. Following storage at 38 MU, RL209 was sold as scrap to R. J. Coley on 19 January 1954. Note the 264 Squadron yellow and black concentric ring markings on the spinners. *(Bob Jacobs, via Mike Gray)*

'Tea up!' There's a queue for the NAAFI wagon at RAF Coltishall on 18 January 1951. Note the 264 Squadron NF.36 on the far right. *(Mike Gray)*

23 Squadron groundcrew personnel – left to right, Williams, Bloxham, Clements and Fox – are pictured with NF.36 RL183 'YP-E' at Coltishall on 6 October 1951. RL183 was built at Leavesden in July 1945 and entered storage with 27 MU on 5 August. In April 1949 it was assigned to 23 Squadron (as a replacement aircraft for RL249) and received the unit code letters 'YP-E'. Modifications (in accordance with Special Technical Instruction 109b) were carried out at Leavesden in June 1950, RL183 returning to 23 Squadron on 3 July. This aircraft was later recoded 'YP-N' before retirement to 38 MU in July 1952. Declared Non-Effective Stock on 16 June 1953, RL183 was sold as scrap to David Band and Company on 3 January 1955. *(Mike Gray)*

The drone of eight Merlins can be heard over Church Fenton as four 141 Squadron NF.36s carry out a practice flypast during Battle of Britain Day 1950. *(Mike Gray)*

'Hookah'-equipped NF.36 RL201 'YP-C' is seen at Coltishall on 30 October 1951. RL201 left the Leavesden factory for storage at 19 MU on 27 August 1945, then on 27 February 1946 it was allocated to 85 Squadron, receiving the unit code letters 'VY-P'. Eight months later the aircraft passed to 141 Squadron (as 'TW-D'), but suffered accident damage during early September 1948. Following repairs, RL201 was assigned to 23 Squadron in March 1949, initially receiving the unit codes 'YP-C', later changed to 'YP-O'. Modifications (in accordance with Special Technical Instruction 109b) were carried out by Airwork at Gatwick in July 1950, RL201 returning to 23 Squadron on 15 July. This NF.36 later passed to the RIDS at West Raynham before retirement to 22 MU on 8 October 1952; it was eventually sold as scrap on 22 April 1954. *(Mike Gray)*

Mosquito Trainers

The Mosquito Trainer version was developed to convert pilots from other twin-engine aircraft types to the Mosquito. Initially produced to train pilots for Mosquito Night-Fighter squadrons, examples of the Trainer variant served with the majority of RAF Mosquito squadrons, as well as several specialist training and second-line units. Based upon the F.II airframe, the British Trainer version received the designation T.3 and more than 350 were built before production ceased in 1948. Turret fighters W4053 and W4073 were converted into T.3 Prototypes by removing all armament (including the turrets) and equipping the cockpits with dual controls. Leavesden-built W4075, W4077, W4079 and W4081 were the first production T.3s, these aircraft originally being designated 'F.II Dual Control'. Wartime T.3s were manufactured by the de Havilland Second Aircraft Group shadow factory at Leavesden, which specialised in Mosquito Fighter and Trainer variants. Early examples were powered by Merlin 21 or 23 engines, but later aircraft received the more powerful Merlin 25s, together with the 'basic' strengthened wing of the FB.VI. Pending delivery of locally produced Mosquito trainers, T.3s were shipped to Canada and Australia, while others were loaned to BOAC in the UK.

After the war smaller batches were produced at Leavesden and Hatfield, the final aircraft (VT631) leaving the Hatfield factory in October 1948. T.3s were operated by the air forces of several foreign countries, including Norway, Israel, Yugoslavia, New Zealand, Turkey and Belgium (some Belgian T.3s later being converted into target tugs). Due to their high power and low weight, T.3s were light on the controls and generally regarded as a pleasure to fly.

The T.3 had a loaded weight of 20,319lb and a climb rate of 2,500 feet per minute; its range was 1,560 miles and maximum speed around 384mph. A number of foreign air force FB.VIs were also converted into dual-control trainers.

Trainer versions of the Mosquito were also manufactured in Canada and Australia, all based on locally produced Fighter-Bomber airframes. The first of three Canadian Trainer variants, the T.22, was developed from the FB.21 and received power in the form of Packard Merlin 31s or 33s. Six T.22s were constructed, all incorporating dual-control conversion parts shipped from Hatfield. The FB.21 was superseded by the FB.26 and led to the next Canadian Trainer Mosquito, the T.27. Powered by Packard Merlin 225s, T.27 production amounted to forty-nine aircraft, many serving with 313 Ferry Training Unit at North Bay, Ontario. Due to a shortage of cannon armament and radio equipment, more than thirty FB.26 airframes were completed as dual-control trainers and re-designated T.29. The T.29 was the final production Canadian Trainer variant and, like the T.27, was powered by Packard Merlin 225s. In addition to the RCAF, T.29s served with the Nationalist Chinese Air Force as well as several UK-based Mosquito Night-Fighter squadrons.

The sole Australian-built Mosquito Trainer variant was the T.43. Twenty-two were produced (serialled A52-1051 to A52-1071) by converting existing FB.40 airframes. Powered by Packard Merlin 33s, the T.43 retained the FB.40's bomb bay but featured a re-designed cockpit instrumentation layout. Some T.43s were armed with nose machine-guns.

The cockpit of an early T.3 clearly shows the instructor's control column on the right-hand side. The columns were coupled by a torque tube for elevator control and by a chain and tie rods for aileron control. To ease exit in an emergency, the instructor's control column could be uncoupled from the elevator control (by removing a pin on the connecting torque tube), enabling it to be pushed fully forward. Note the standard RAF blind flying panel situated forward of the left-hand column, with the engine instrumentation in a bank on the left. The magneto switches are located in the top right-hand corner, with the engine starter and booster coil push buttons slightly above and to their left. The throttle and pitch control levers are mounted in a quadrant attached to the left-hand side of the cockpit wall. The instructor was also provided with throttle controls, which can be seen directly to the left of the right-hand control column, immediately below the fuel contents gauges. The lever at the bottom centre provided height adjustment for the instructor's seat. Note the gunsight mountings at the top of the instrument panel. T.3s had provision for four .303in machine-guns, but these were rarely fitted to RAF aircraft although several foreign air force machines were so equipped. T.3s were generally regarded as a pleasure to fly, due principally to their high power and low weight. *(BAE SYSTEMS)*

This picture of the final assembly of one of the first Leavesden-built Mosquitoes. was taken on 15 October 1941 and probably features T.3 W4075 (originally designated as an 'F.II Dual Control'). de Havilland's began construction of the Leavesden factory in 1940 under the Second Aircraft Group shadow organisation. Large orders for Mosquito Fighters were anticipated, assisting sub-contracting plans and the dispersal of Hatfield factory production to lower the bombing risk. The Leavesden factory specialised in the manufacture of Mosquito Night-Fighter and Trainer variants and included dispersal sites at the Alliance factory on Western Avenue (Acton) and the Aldenham bus depot. W4075 served with 105 Squadron and 1655 MTU, eventually being written off in a flying accident on 17 February 1944. This aircraft has still to receive a finishing coat of silver dope over its red-doped wings and fuselage. Note the underwing fuel tank panel propped up on the floor behind the starboard wing. The Leavesden factory was still undergoing completion at this time. *(BAE SYSTEMS)*

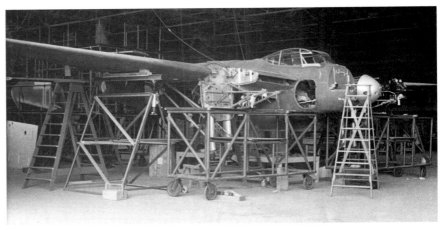

This production line shot taken in 1942 shows the cockpit entrance hatchway of another early T.3. Note the instructor's hinged bucket seat visible immediately inside the hatchway, and the second control column's torque tube linkage running along the cockpit floor. On all other versions of the Mosquito the navigator's position was set slightly aft and to the right of the pilot in order to provide greater space for both crew members, but on Mosquito Trainer versions the instructor occupied the right-hand crew position, a bucket seat being installed to bring him side-by-side with the pupil pilot. During acceptance trials of the second T.3 Prototype (W4073) at A&AEE Boscombe Down, the seating was reported as 'very cramped and for two large pilots would be almost impracticable'. *(BAE SYSTEMS)*

In this close-up shot of a T.3 following roll-out from the de Havilland Leavesden factory in 1942, note the 'needle'-blade propeller and the uncowled starboard Merlin 21 with its 'saxophone' exhaust manifold's two 'fishtail' stubs. The exhaust manifold was enclosed within a flame-damping shroud attached to the engine cowling side panel, the shroud featuring ducts in its lower section to provide cooling air for the 'fishtails'. Mosquito engine bearer frames were of tubular steel construction bolted to both the front spar and the fixed section of the undercarriage mounting structure (they were interchangeable between port and starboard engines). A lack of shell case ejection chutes in the ventral bay doors denotes that this is a Trainer version of the Mosquito, further confirmed by the instructor's bucket seat just visible inside the crew entrance hatchway. This T.3 (possibly HJ866) has yet to have its crew entrance door fitted and will soon receive a coat of camouflage over its silver-doped finish. The cylindrical object attached to the outside edge of the engine firewall is the Graviner fire extinguisher. Hanging beneath the starboard wing is the access panel for number three fuel tank's contents gauge transmitter unit. *(Crown Copyright)*

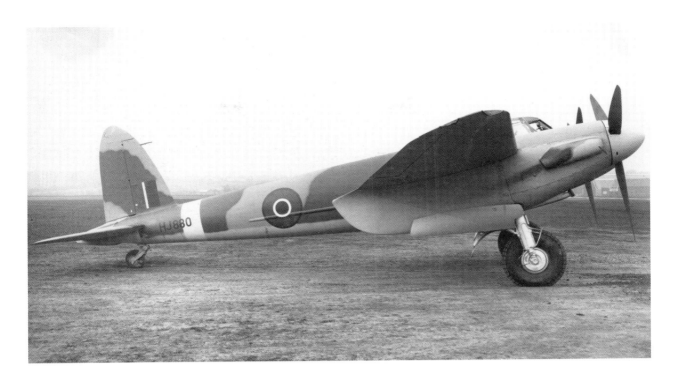

These two views show Merlin 21-powered T.3 HJ880 at the de Havilland Second Aircraft Group (SAG) Leavesden factory in March 1943. Delivered to 19 MU on 24 March 1943, this T.3 passed to 47 MU three weeks later, where it was prepared for overseas shipment to Canada. HJ880 arrived in Halifax aboard the SS *Curacoa* on 15 May 1943 before issue to the RCAF at Amerhurst on 27 May. In July 1943 it was assigned to 36 OTU at Greenwood (receiving the unit code '9') before transfer to 7 OTU at Debert some time after June 1944. As 'S 13' HJ880 served with 7 OTU until it was destroyed in a flying accident at Debert on 23 November 1944. While in Canada HJ880's shrouded exhaust system was replaced by individual exhaust stubs. Note the Sky-painted rear fuselage band and spinners. This picture was taken on orthochromatic film, hence the black appearance of the yellow striped wing leading edges and the fuselage roundel's yellow outer ring. *(Both Crown Copyright)*

Brand new T.3 LR585 photographed by Eddie Riding at the de Havilland Leavesden factory in October 1944. This was the last aircraft in a batch of fifty-nine Leavesden-built T.3s delivered between December 1943 and October 1944. Note the 'paddle'-blade propellers and the 50-gallon underwing drop tanks. LR585 is finished in the standard Mosquito Trainer scheme of Ocean Grey and Dark Green camouflaged upper surfaces, Medium Sea Grey under surfaces, Sky rear fuselage band and spinners, with yellow striped wing leading edges. LR585 was delivered to 10 MU on 9 October 1944 and to No 1 Ferry Unit on 14 November. Following work at No 1 Overseas Aircraft Preparation Unit (OAPU), it was delivered to the Mediterranean Theatre, arriving in Italy on 29 November 1944, where it was assigned to 255 Squadron at Rosignano (255 was a Night-Fighter Squadron equipped with Mosquito NF.XIXs and NF.30s). On 2 February 1945 LR585 was written off after ground looping on take-off from Rosignano, eventually being Struck Off Charge on 19 July 1945. *(Richard Riding collection)*

(BAE SYSTEMS)

A very early T.3, probably W4077, is seen at Lasham during the summer of 1944. The second production T.3 (originally designated 'F.II Dual Control'), Leavesden-built W4077 made its maiden flight in the hands of de Havilland test pilot George Gibbins on 10 March 1942. Geoffrey de Havilland Junior cleared W4077 as ready for acceptance on 13 March, the aircraft entering service with 151 Squadron just over a month later. W4077 underwent damage repairs between 15 November 1942 and 2 February 1943, only to be damaged once more, this time at Wittering on 6 March 1943, after a tyre burst on landing led to collapse of the undercarriage. Serviceable again by 21 April, W4077 passed to 10 MU on 2 September before spending another three months under repair, this time at Hatfield between November 1943 and January 1944. This T.3 was assigned to 4 Squadron in March 1944 before allocation to 613 Squadron at Lasham on 8 June, remaining with 613 until delivery to No 2 GSU in November. 54 OTU was the final recipient of W4077, the veteran Mosquito arriving at this unit on 1 February 1945. W4077 was Struck Off Charge on 12 March 1945 but is recorded as due for repairs at Marshalls of Cambridge in August 1945, presumably being scrapped not long afterwards. Note the stub exhausts and the Night-Fighter scheme of overall Medium Sea Grey with Dark Green camouflaged upper surfaces. *(Key)*

Brand new T.3 TV960 pictured with flight shed personnel at the de Havilland Leavesden factory during the summer of 1945. Second from the right is production foreman H. G. Harris, with Aeronautical Inspection Directorate (AID) Chief Inspector Eddie Riding to his left (sitting on the tailplane). Eddie Riding worked at Leavesden between June 1944 and February 1946, signing out new NF.XIIIs, NF.XIXs, NF.30s, NF.36s, T.3s and TR.33s. He regularly accompanied the factory test pilots on delivery or test flights, enjoying some spectacular trips in the process! While at Leavesden Eddie flew in well over seventy different Mosquitoes, including the first pre-production TR.33, TS444. TV960 was delivered to 13 OTU on 30 August 1945, serving with this unit until the night of 5 February 1946 when the undercarriage collapsed while taxying at Croft. The aircraft was placed in storage with 38 MU on 20 May 1946 and Struck Off Charge twenty-two days later. The aircraft immediately preceding TV960 on the Leavesden production line, TV959, is currently owned by the Washington-based Flying Heritage Collection and stored in the UK pending restoration. *(Richard Riding collection)*

With the main wheel chocks in position, Eddie Riding raises TV960's tail during a power check at Leavesden. Although a spectacular sight, this practice was naturally frowned upon! *(Richard Riding collection)*

These examples of artwork adorn the crew entrance and nose door of unidentified T.3 'Snogger the One'. In the smaller picture note the Type 90 aerial protruding through the underside of the fuselage immediately forward of the ventral bay doors; this formed part of the ARI 5025 radio equipment installation, the aerial being connected to a type R.3090 receiver mounted inside the fuselage aft of bulkhead number three. The control unit for ARI 5025 was positioned forward of fuselage bulkhead number two on the starboard side. For ease of stowage, the crew entry ladder was telescopic and featured two lugs on its upper section designed to engage with locating holes on the cockpit floor (when not in use the ladder was retained on clips inside the entrance door). A first aid kit was located in a box aft of the pilot's seats (as outlined on the stencilling beneath the hatchway). Also noteworthy are the faired-over cannon ports. *(Both Stuart Howe collection)*

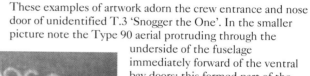

This unidentified T.3 is probably at a Maintenance Unit in the Mediterranean Theatre towards the end of the war. Note the standard Mosquito Trainer colour scheme of Ocean Grey and Dark Green camouflaged upper surfaces, Medium Sea Grey under surfaces, Sky rear fuselage band and spinners, and yellow striped wing leading edges. *(Stuart Howe collection)*

T.3 LR527 'DF-S' is pictured while on the strength of the Central Bomber Establishment at Marham. Originally equipped with Merlin 21s, this Leavesden-built Mosquito was delivered to 1655 MTU on 27 April 1944, remaining with the latter when it was redesignated 16 OTU on 1 January 1945. During its first two years of service LR527 was damaged on at least three occasions before allocation to the Central Bomber Establishment in June 1946. The CBE was formed at Marham on 25 September 1945, engaged principally on experimental work with Lancasters and Lincolns. In addition to T.3 LR527, the CBE also operated Mosquito B.XVIs PF498 and PF556, and later formed the nucleus of the Bomber Command Bombing School.

LR527 later passed to 228 OCU in March 1950 and to 1689 FPTF in February 1952. Six months later it was assigned to the Ferry Training Unit at Benson, remaining there until 20 April 1953 when it crashed during asymmetric landing practice. While on final approach and crossing the Benson aerodrome boundary, power was increased on the live (starboard) engine, and LR527 subsequently climbed steeply to port before crashing. The primary cause of the accident was loss of control, probably due to the increased output on the live engine while the aircraft was below the critical single-engine safety speed. LR527 sports grey upper surfaces and Night under surfaces, with white code letters and serial numbers. The Anson C.12 NL231 'XE-D' (to the right of LR527) acted as a Central Bomber Establishment communications aircraft, while the B.XVI in the background is probably PF556. *(Jim D. Oughton)*

204 AFS T.3 TV967 'FMO-A' is seen at Turnhouse in late 1948. Note the drop tank release gear fairing beneath the port wing, and the silver-doped fabric sealing strips at the joint between the tailplane and rear fuselage/tailcone. A Leavesden-built T.3, TV967 entered storage with 19 MU on 8 November 1945. On 17 May 1946 it was delivered to 54 OTU but suffered accident damage three weeks later. Following repairs by Martin Hearn Ltd it was assigned to the Central Flying School at Little Rissington, remaining there until transfer to 204 AFS in October 1948. TV967 underwent major servicing at Brooklands Aviation between October and November 1949 before rejoining 204 AFS on 7 December. It was written off by a pupil pilot practising single-engine landings at Swinderby on 26 April 1951 (the aircraft swung on touch-down, causing the undercarriage to collapse). TV967 sports white code letters and a yellow training band on the rear fuselage. *(R. Hepburn, via Francois Prins)*

23 Squadron T.3 TV970 suffered a mid-air collision with 74 Squadron Meteor F.4 VT133 on 21 April 1949. Both aircraft survived the incident, the Meteor pilot being blamed for failing to keep a good look out. TV970, in the hands of Flt Lt C. Hughes, flew for 15 minutes in this condition before making a perfect landing at its Coltishall base. Note the missing starboard tailplane tip and elevator outer section, which were torn away by the collision impact.

A Leavesden-built T.3, TV970 was delivered from the factory to 19 MU on 8 November 1945. In February 1946 it was allocated to 64 Squadron, but passed to 219 Squadron five months later, where it received the unit codes 'FK-V'.

By 26 September 1946 TV970 was on the strength of the Station Flight at Wittering, remaining there until April the following year when it joined the Station Flight at Coltishall. 23 Squadron (also at Coltishall) was next to receive TV970, the Mosquito being transferred in July 1948; it served with 23 as a continuation trainer for the Squadron's NF.36s. TV970 spent the remainder of its working life with 23 Squadron, eventually being written off in a take-off accident at Coltishall on 31 May 1951. Note that TV970 still bears the 219 Squadron code letters 'FK' (applied in red) despite having been on 23 Squadron's strength for almost a year. *(Both BAE SYSTEMS)*

Another view of 23 Squadron T.3 TV970 at Coltishall, by now wearing 23's 'YP' unit code letters. *(Mike Gray)*

T.3 TW105 is being towed out from the Leavesden factory in February 1946, probably for initial engine runs. Transferred to the Royal Navy and stored at Culham, this T.3 was delivered to 762 Squadron (Fleet Air Arm) at Ford on 21 March 1946. During the course of its two and a half years of service with 762 Squadron, TW105 wore the unit codes (in successive order) 'FD6C', '452/FD' and '452/CW'. On 27 November 1948 it returned to de Havilland's at Leavesden before entering long-term storage with the Aircraft Holding Unit at Stretton on 25 May 1949. TW105 returned to Culham in February 1950, where it remained until flown to the Aircraft Holding Unit at Lossiemouth on 8 January 1953. TW105 was eventually sold as scrap to R. A. Short on 11 August 1955. *(Richard Riding collection)*

T.3s and FB.VIs lined up at No 1 Ferry Unit Pershore in 1947. No 1 FU formed at Pershore on 16 March 1944 through an amalgamation of No 301 Ferry Training Unit and No 1 Ferry Crew Pool. The Unit processed large numbers of Mosquitoes and Beaufighters and was eventually retitled the 'Overseas Ferry Unit' when it transferred to Manston on 17 May 1948. The T.3s (both finished in Trainer Yellow) are second and third from the left in this line-up. *(Richard Livermore)*

609 Squadron (Royal Auxiliary Air Force) T.3 VA883 photographed at Yeadon in April 1947. During the course of its career this 1946 Leavesden-built T.3 served with 609 Squadron, the Celle Station Flight, 231 OCU, the Home Command Examining Unit and the Ferry Training Unit. Equipped with Mosquito NF.30s, 609 Squadron re-formed at Yeadon in May 1946, VA883 being attached to the Squadron for dual assessment and continuation training. Note the 609 Squadron badge on the forward fuselage, featuring a rose in front of two hunting horns with the motto 'Tally Ho'. The

vertical rectangular 'slots' on the engine cowling side panels (immediately forward of the leading exhaust stub) are manifold cooling ducts, which formed part of the inner exhaust shrouds. VA883 was ultimately sold as scrap on 14 July 1959. The identity of the airman in the foreground is presently unknown. *(Alan G. Harwin)*

In addition to VA883, 609 Squadron also operated T.3 VA926, seen here at Yeadon in 1947. VA926 was completed at Leavesden in December 1946 and delivered to 609 Squadron (Royal Auxiliary Air Force) on 16 December for continuation and dual assessment training. On 26 October 1947 it swung on landing at Linton-on-Ouse, the resultant damage being repaired by 11 August 1948. Five days later

VA926 flew to 22 MU but was damaged once more, repairs being conducted on site. Between December 1949 and April 1952 the aircraft served with 204 AFS, but, following a period in storage, was allocated to the Home Command Examining Unit on 24 September 1953. This T.3 was Struck Off Charge and sold as scrap on 23 February 1955. VA926 is finished Trainer Yellow overall. *(Alan G. Harwin)*

204 AFS T.3 VA927 'FMO-B' ready for a sortie from Driffield on 24 April 1949. Note the trolley accumulator parked beneath the trailing edge of the port wing; this would be connected to the external current supply plug (located on the port side of the fuselage above the inboard port flap) to provide electrical power for engine starting. VA927 was constructed at Hatfield in December 1946, immediately entering storage (initially with 37 MU then 9 MU) before allocation to 204 AFS on 10 February 1949. Seven months later it suffered a flying accident and, after repair, passed to 41 Squadron (then equipped with the de Havilland Hornet) on 2 June 1950. 58 Squadron at Benson received VA927 in July 1951, operating the aircraft until 10 February 1953 when it flew into rising ground near Ewelme, Oxfordshire, during a GCA calibration flight. VA927 is finished silver overall with a yellow training band around the rear fuselage. 204 AFS student pilot Mike Gray made his first Mosquito solo in VA927 on 14 March 1949 *(Both Mike Gray)*

189

Canadian-produced Mosquito Trainer variants were based on the FB.21 and FB.26 airframes (Canadian equivalents of the British FB.VI). Utilising dual-control conversion components shipped from Hatfield, the initial Canadian Trainer version was powered by Packard Merlin 31s or 33s and designated T.22. The T.27 succeeded the T.22, but differed from the latter through the installation of Packard Merlin 225s. KA888 depicted here was the twelfth aircraft from a total production run of forty-nine T.27s. Due to a shortage of cannon armament and radio equipment, many FB.26s were completed on the assembly line as trainers, receiving the designation T.29. In common with the majority of Canadian-built Trainers, KA888 remained in Canada. *(Public Archives of Canada)*

This Canadian-built Trainer Mosquito (possibly a T.27) was photographed by Geoffrey Perks at No 313 Ferry Training Unit, North Bay, Ontario, in September 1945. Formed as No 313 Ferry Training & Conversion Unit on 1 March 1944, its role was to train ferry crews for the overseas delivery of aircraft produced in Canada and America. Types instructed on included the Lancaster B.X, Hudson VI, Mitchell II, and Mosquito B.XX and T.27. On 5 July 1944 the unit was retitled No 313 Ferry Training Unit before disbanding on 18 October 1945. Geoffrey Perks served with 313 and flew several Mosquito T.27s including KA892, KA893 and KA890. Note the 100-gallon underwing drop tanks and the Hamilton Standard-built 'paddle'-blade propellers. *(Geoffrey Perks)*

de Havilland Hatfield test pilot Pat Fillingham demonstrates RAAF T.3 A52-1005 (ex-HJ960) to the Australian press at Bankstown. Pat Fillingham arrived at Bankstown (direct from the de Havilland Canada Downsview plant) on 19 October 1943 to advise the Australians on Mosquito flight-test methods. The cameraman on the car is likely to be Eric Bierre of Movietone News. *(BAE SYSTEMS)*

Former RAAF T.3 A52-1006 at Whenuapai on 8 November 1946 following delivery to the RNZAF. Constructed at Leavesden as HJ968 in August 1943, this aircraft became one of fourteen T.3s allocated to the RAAF pending delivery of locally produced Mosquito T.43s. HJ968 was shipped to Australia aboard the SS *Orari* on 11 October 1943, arriving in Sydney six weeks later. As A52-1006, HJ968 served with the RAAF at 5 OTU Williamtown before sale to the RNZAF in 1946. After the war the RNZAF ordered surplus FB.VIs from Britain and desperately required Mosquito Trainers to convert pilots assigned to ferrying these FB.VIs back to New Zealand. A52-1006 was one of four former RAAF T.3s sold to the RNZAF in September 1946, being delivered to Ohakea via Amberley, Norfolk Island and Whenuapai by Sqn Ldr R. M. McKay and Flt Lt G. S. Martin. A52-1006 was re-serialled NZ2302 in RNZAF service and placed in storage during July 1947. After being declared surplus, NZ2302 was sold as scrap under Government tender on 20 April 1953. *(J. B. Coll, via Stuart Howe)*

In the larger of these two shots of T.3 A52-1003, the aircraft is landing while serving with the RAAF at Williamtown in Australia. The second photograph (taken at Norfolk Island on 7 November 1946) depicts the same aircraft during its delivery flight to the RNZAF. Originally constructed at Leavesden as HJ893, this T.3 was delivered direct from the factory to 27 MU on 30 May 1943. Allotted to the RAAF, HJ893 was prepared by 47 MU before despatch to Australia aboard the SS *Northumbria* on 30 June 1943. Arriving in Australia two months later, HJ893 received the RAAF serial number A52-1003. Following re-assembly and the installation of Packard Merlin 31s (all RAAF T.3s were shipped from the UK minus engines), A52-1003 entered service with 5 OTU RAAF at Williamtown. Due to a shortage of armed Mosquitoes, in 1944 some RAAF T.3s were fitted with four .303in machine-guns, A52-1003 being one of them. It was later sold to the RNZAF (as one of the latter's initial batch of four T.3s), arriving at Ohakea on 8 November 1946, where it received the RNZAF serial NZ2304. In the second picture, note A52-1003's nose machine-guns and the replacement of the wartime camouflage scheme by an overall silver-doped finish. NZ2304 was sold as scrap by Government tender in May 1953. *(Hawker de Havilland/J. B. Coll, via Stuart Howe)*

Silver-doped T.43 A52-1056 of 87 (PR) Squadron RAAF takes off from Fairbairn in 1952. This aircraft was originally laid down as FB.40 A52-8, but was completed as a T.43 and re-serialled A52-1056. Powered by Packard Merlin 33s, the T.43 was a Trainer version of the FB.40, retaining the latter's bomb bay but featuring dual elevator trim tab controls, a redesigned cockpit instrument layout and, on some examples, nose machine-guns. Strictly speaking, the T.43 was not an Australian version of the British T.3, being more akin to a production Trainer version of the FB.VI, had such an aircraft existed. The T.43's nearest overseas production equivalent was the Canadian T.29. A52-1056 remained in Australia throughout its career, serving with the CFS, the ARDU and 87 (PR) Squadron. From September 1952 it went into storage, latterly with 1 AD at East Sale Victoria before sale to R. H. Grant & Company on 28 April 1958. Note the six exhaust stubs on the engine outboard side, a feature common to all Australian-produced two-speed, single-stage supercharged Merlin Mosquitoes. *(Noel Sparrow)*

An unidentified Canadian-built Mosquito seen at RCAF Edmonton in the late 1940s. Judging by the faired-over cannon ports and the presence of a Sky rear fuselage band and yellow wing leading edges, this aircraft appears to be a T.27 or a T.29. Unusually, however, it is equipped with four .303in machine-guns, a non-standard fitment on Mosquito Trainers built in Britain and Canada. *(W. Cottrell, Alberta Aviation Museum Collection)*

Dated 22 October 1947, these photographs depict T.27 KA890, the first Canadian Mosquito prepared for export to the Nationalist Chinese Air Force. One of more than 200 Canadian-built Mosquitoes (mainly FB.26s) sold to Nationalist China, KA890 formerly served with No 313 Ferry Training Unit at North Bay, Ontario. For their journey overseas, the Chinese Mosquitoes were transported (from Downsview) by rail to Canadian east coast ports, from where they were shipped to Shanghai. In readiness for its forthcoming trip, KA890's airframe has

been thoroughly sealed before receiving an external coat of preservative. In the second photograph KA890's engines are visible on the rail transport trailer's front and rear sections (immediately beneath the port and starboard wing leading edges). The location is believed to be Downsview. *(Both de Havilland Canada)*

58 Squadron T.3 VT589 'OT-Z' was ready for collection from the de Havilland Hatfield factory on 22 August 1947 and was delivered to 19 MU three weeks later. Assigned to 58 Squadron at Benson on 3 November 1947, it passed to 540 Squadron (also at Benson) on 3 December the same year, and received the unit codes 'DH-Z'. VT589 remained with 540 Squadron until 24 May 1951 when it swung on landing at Benson and the starboard undercarriage collapsed. The aircraft was scheduled for repair but was written off shortly afterwards, being Struck Off Charge on 27 June 1951. It was equipped with Merlin 25s and 'paddle'-blade propellers. In this pleasing view the T.3 is finished in Trainer Yellow overall with Night underwing/fuselage serial numbers. T.3s were fully aerobatic, 220-270 knots being recommended for rolls, 350 knots for loops and 350 knots-plus for climbing rolls. *(Stuart Howe collection)*

T.3 RR313 'ZQ-W' is pictured while on the strength of the twin-engined flight of the Bomber Command Instructors School. RR313 was built at Leavesden during the summer of 1945 and delivered to the School at Finningley on 22 June. Two years later it passed to the Coningsby Station Flight before allocation to 109 Squadron in September 1948 and 231 OCU in January 1949. Delivered to the Reserve Pool at Luneberg in January 1950, RR313 moved to RAF Celle in February 1950 and suffered an accident the following September. Repairs were conducted by Brooklands Aviation before RR313 passed to 228 OCU at Leeming. This much-travelled T.3 was eventually written off while serving with the Far East Training Squadron at Seletar on 29 March 1954, the undercarriage collapsing after the aircraft swung on landing. *(via J. D. Oughton)*

Leavesden-built T.3 TV983 was stored at 27 MU from 1 February 1946 before allocation to 500 Squadron ten months later. In November 1948 it was damaged in a flying accident, repairs being carried out by Brooklands Aviation and completed by 7 July 1949. In March 1950 it was allocated to the Central Flying School before returning to 27 MU in February 1951. 13 Squadron at Fayid received the aircraft in December 1951, but after only three months it passed to 39 Squadron at Kabrit. Returning to the UK in October 1952, TV983 entered service with the Ferry Training Unit at Benson on 31 May 1953. Its last posting was to the Armament Practice Station at RAF Sylt, where it arrived in June 1956. Declared Non-Effective Stock on 31 May 1958, TV983 was later sold as scrap to R. J. Coley. These pictures are likely to have been taken at Sylt in 1957. TV983 is finished silver overall with yellow training bands on the wings and rear fuselage. *(Both Gus Weedon)*

Memorable Mosquito: this is T.3 RR299, the aeroplane that inspired a whole new generation of Mosquito admirers (the author included) and thrilled crowds at UK air displays for more than thirty years until its tragic loss on 21 July 1996. When on the strength of 204 AFS it is seen flying from the unit's Brize Norton base in October 1949, finished silver overall with yellow training bands on the wings and rear fuselage. The 204 AFS code letters 'FMO-(bar)B' are applied in black, as is the serial number on the rear fuselage. RR299's service with 204 AFS ended at 1212hrs on 19 December 1949 when it swung on landing at Brize Norton in the hands of a Burmese Air Force student pilot (the Burmese had been considering the purchase of surplus RAF Mosquitoes, but this never materialised). RR299 suffered extensively in this incident, the port undercarriage assembly being torn away and the fuselage and port wing receiving major damage; repairs were carried out by Brooklands Aviation and took eight months to complete. 204 AFS student Roy Quantick made his first Mosquito night solo in RR299 and later went on to fly PR.34s with 81 Squadron. Note that RR299's tailwheel has not retracted and remains in the locked-down position. This picture was taken from a 204 AFS T.3 or FB.VI. *(Roy Quantick)*

A line-up of 204 AFS FB.VIs and T.3s photographed at Driffield on 9 March 1949. Nearest the camera is FB.VI HR252 'FMO-X' with T.3s RR297 'FMO-D' and VT590 next in line (the identity of the FB.VI next to VT590 is unknown). Standard Motors-built HR252 served with 1692 Flt, 169 Squadron, 16 OTU and 204 AFS before conversion as Instructional Airframe 6654M on 26 April 1949. Leavesden-produced RR297 was allocated to 16 OTU, 204 AFS, No 1 Overseas Ferry Unit, 231 OCU and the Ferry Training Unit at Benson before transfer to the FEAF in December 1954. RR297 was Struck Off Charge on 1 September 1955. VT590 was built at Hatfield and assigned to the Central Flying School, 204 AFS and 33 and 45 Squadrons before being Struck Off Charge on 22 January 1954. The two FB.VIs are distinguishable from the T.3s by their colour scheme of overall Medium Sea Grey with Dark Green camouflaged upper surfaces. Note that RR297's starboard engine is fitted with three of the combined exhaust stubs normally fitted to the rear two cylinders (engine outboard and inboard sides) of single-stage Merlin Mosquitoes made in Britain and Canada, a feature of many postwar RAF Mosquito T.3s and FB.VIs. *(Mike Gray)*

Pupil pilot Jason Spokes taxying 204 AFS T.3 RR308 'FMO-(bar)A' at the start of a dual training sortie from Driffield on 28 April 1949. A Leavesden-built T.3, RR308 was delivered to 489 Squadron on 11 June 1945 before passing to 132 OTU two months later. In June 1946 it entered service with 60 OTU and underwent repairs at Hatfield between June 1947 and February 1948. Following storage at 19 MU it was issued to the Central Flying School in August 1948 and to 204 AFS at Driffield three months later. After three years' service with 204 AFS (during the course of which it was damaged twice) RR308 was issued to the FEAF on 14 February 1952, passing to 45 Squadron where it received the unit codes 'OB-Z'. In November 1952 it was allocated to 33 Squadron before being declared surplus on 20 January 1955 and Struck Off Charge the following day. The bar above the 'A' signified that RR308 was the second of two serving 204 AFS Mosquitoes to carry this individual unit code letter. *(Mike Gray)*

FB.VIs and T.3s of 204 AFS seen through the office window of Flt Lt P. H. Cleaver (204 AFS 'B' Flight Commander) at Driffield on 13 March 1949. The T.3s were used for dual instruction, the FB.VIs being employed for solo flights as well as training sorties by pupil pilots with their newly crewed navigators. Nearest the camera is FB.VI RF890 'FMO-T'. *(Mike Gray)*

Immaculate silver-doped T.3 RR307 'Y' of 141 Squadron is seen at Church Fenton on 15 September 1950. Over the course of its ten-year life, this 1945 Leavesden-built T.3 served with 489 Squadron (RNZAF), 8 OTU, 58 Squadron, 141 Squadron and 226 OCU. Allocated to the FEAF in October 1954, RR307 was Struck Off Charge eleven months later. The spinners feature 141 Squadron's black and white concentric ring markings, and the squadron badge is carried on the fin. The badge represented 141's night-fighter role and featured a leopard's face with the motto 'Caedimus Nocta' ('We slay by night'). T.3s were retained on operational Mosquito squadrons for the purpose of conducting instrument ratings and continuation training. Note the 141 Squadron NF.36 parked beyond RR307. *(Mike Gray)*

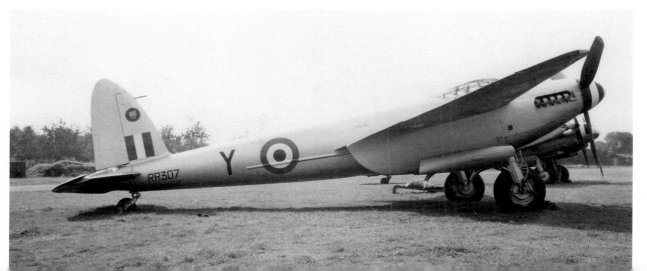

231 OCU T.3 RR305 'Y' was photographed from the starboard wing of a B.XVI at Coningsby in 1948. Throughout its career this Leavesden-built Mosquito served with 231 OCU, eventually being written off in a landing accident at Hemswell on 31 May 1951. Note RR305's silver-doped finish and the fabric repairs to the fin leading edge. This picture was taken by Stuart Redfern who for many years was an Inspector on BAe's T.3 RR299/G-ASKH at Hawarden. A 109 Squadron Mosquito B.XVI is visible in the distance to the left of the hangar. *(Stewart Redfern)*

Mosquito fuselages on the scrap dump at 49 MU Colerne in July 1953. On the right is Leavesden-built T.3 HJ898, which entered service with 8 OTU on 6 July 1943. Following repairs at Marshall's it was loaned to BOAC, but swung on landing, leading to the collapse of the undercarriage, during an acceptance test flight at Leuchars on 23 April 1945. HJ898 returned to RAF charge three weeks later and repairs were completed by Martin Hearn in January 1946. In September 1946 it was issued to 16 OTU, remaining with the latter unit when it was retitled 204 AFS in 1947. The Empire Test Pilot's School took charge of HJ898 in April 1949 (where it received the fuselage code '23' seen here), but by June 1952 it had been transferred to RAE Farnborough. HJ898 was Struck Off Charge on 31 March 1953. *(Mike Gray)*

762 Squadron (Fleet Air Arm) T.3 VT607 lands at Culdrose in 1949. Final approach for landing would commence at 125 knots, this speed being reduced to no less than 105 knots over the start of the runway. In order to maintain rudder effectiveness upon touch-down, tail-down 'wheeler' landings were recommended, although three-point landings (in the hands of a competent pilot) were possible. Constructed at Hatfield among the last batch of T.3's, VT607 was allotted to the Royal Navy and flown to the Receipt & Despatch Unit at Culham on 3 February 1948. Seven months later it was delivered to 762 Squadron (Fleet Air Arm) at Culdrose before passing to Airwork at Brawdy in January 1950. Brooklands Aviation at Sywell overhauled VT607 during July 1950, after which the aircraft was based at Yeovilton between January and July 1951. Later stored at Culham and Abbotsinch, VT607 was Struck Off Charge on 11 August 1955 and condemned to the Abbotsinch fire dump. VT607 is finished in Trainer Yellow overall with Night underwing serial numbers. 762 Squadron (Fleet Air Arm) was a Heavy Twin Conversion Unit specialising in the training of Fleet Air Arm Mosquito pilots. In addition to T.3s, 762 Squadron was also equipped with Mosquito FB.VIs. *(Ken Lambert, via Stuart Howe)*

T.3 VT619 '464 CW' of 762 Squadron (Fleet Air Arm) is seen at Culdrose in 1949. One of the final production T.3s, VT619 was ready for collection from the Hatfield factory on 11 June 1948, being delivered to the Receipt & Despatch Unit at Culham twelve days later. VT619 served with 762 Squadron (Fleet Air Arm) at Culdrose between January and September 1949 before passing to Airwork at Brawdy in January 1950. In July 1951 Brooklands Aviation at Sywell began a major overhaul, the aircraft returning to Culham in January 1952, where it remained for a year. VT619 reached the Aircraft Holding Unit at Abbotsinch in July 1953, where it was Struck Off Charge on 11 August 1955. In 1957 this Mosquito ended its days on the Abbotsinch fire dump. In common with the remainder of the final T.3 production batch, VT619 is in overall Trainer Yellow. *(Ken Lambert)*

A sad end to a fine aeroplane: 762 Squadron (Fleet Air Arm) T.3 VT630 lies shattered in a field a mile south of Culdrose on 19 October 1949. With the port engine feathered, VT630 had been on final approach to land at Culdrose when the starboard engine failed at 800 feet. During the resultant crash-landing VT630 was written off, being Struck Off Charge the following day. A late production T.3, VT630 was built at Hatfield but had a relatively short life. Assigned to the Royal Navy, it was delivered to the Receipt & Despatch Unit at Culham on 14 October 1948 before allocation to 762 Squadron (Fleet Air Arm) at Culdrose in September 1949. As '452/CW' it served with 762 Squadron for only a few weeks before suffering the damage shown here. VT630 is finished in Trainer Yellow overall. *(Ken Lambert, via Stuart Howe)*

VA880, a rather forlorn T.3 of 762 Squadron (Fleet Air Arm), suffered a landing accident at Culdrose on 31 October 1949. VA880 was built at Leavesden in the summer of 1946 and assigned to the Royal Navy. On 2 August it entered storage at the Receipt & Despatch Unit at Culham before joining 762 Squadron at Ford in January 1948. Assigned the 762 Squadron codes '458/CW', VA880 was damaged in a belly-landing on 20 March 1948 after the port engine cut during an overshoot. The aircraft later moved with 762 Squadron to Culdrose, repairs following the incident shown here being completed by January 1951. The Aircraft Holding Unit at Abbotsinch received VA880 in July 1953, the aircraft eventually being Struck Off Charge on 11 August 1955 and ending its days on the station fire dump. *(Both Ken Lambert, via Stuart Howe)*

T.3 VP343 pictured during a delivery flight from the UK to Seletar on 19 October 1954. A postwar Mosquito, VP343 was built at Hatfield in January 1947 and allocated to 36 Squadron four months later. Entering storage with 19 MU on 16 January 1948, VP343 was issued to 228 OCU at Leeming on 1 June the same year. While serving with 228 OCU, VP343 was damaged three times, the last incident occurring on 22 December 1950 when it swung on take-off from Leeming. After repairs it returned to service in February 1951 before entering store at 15 MU a year later. VP343 passed to 231 OCU on 9 July 1952 before allocation to the FEAF in September 1954. Ferry pilot Richard Livermore and navigator Sgt Bradley carried out the delivery flight, Sgt Price replacing Sgt Bradley at Calcutta. This picture was taken from Hornet PX342 (flown by F. S. Lanowski) during the final leg between Calcutta and Seletar. VP343 is finished silver overall with yellow training bands on the wings and rear fuselage; the fuselage and underwing serial numbers are applied in Night. Note the 100-gallon underwing drop tanks, which, when full, increased a T.3's fully loaded weight from 19,554lb to 20,319lb. VP343 was Struck Off Charge at Seletar on 9 September 1955. *(Richard Livermore)*

Here is another shot of T.3 VP343 during the course of its delivery to Seletar, taken at Bahrain on 9 October 1954 and featuring navigator Sgt Bradley (left) and ferry pilot Richard Livermore. Flying Mosquitoes on long delivery flights could be very arduous, the high noise factor, caused by the close proximity of the exhaust stubs to the cockpit, proving very fatiguing. *(Richard Livermore)*

This postwar shot features the foam-covered wreck of T.3
TW110 at Tengah. Leavesden-built in April 1946, TW110
was delivered direct from the factory to 27 MU on 4 April
1946. Allocated to ACSEA, it arrived at 390 MU on 25 July
1946 and was placed in storage until issued to 81 Squadron
on 13 January 1948. TW110 later served with 45 Squadron
and was written off in this take-off accident at Tengah on
24 June 1948. *(Stuart Howe collection)*

Ferry Training Unit T.3 VP347 is seen at RAF Benson in
1954. Constructed at the de Havilland Hatfield factory,
VP347 was ready for collection on 11 April 1947. During its
career the aircraft served with the Manston Station Flight,
540 Squadron at Benson, as well as the Ferry Training Unit.
VP347 suffered several accidents, the last occurring on 26
October 1954 when it was written off in a forced landing at
Benson following engine failure (it was declared scrap on 1
December 1954). VP347 is finished silver overall and
features yellow training bands on the wings and rear
fuselage. *(Richard Livermore)*

In 1953 this unidentified T.3 swung on landing at Seletar, leading to the collapse of its undercarriage. The whole incident was witnessed by 390 MU Aircraft Painter and Finisher Brian Rose, who was repainting a Valetta outside a hangar. After landing on its belly the Mosquito slid towards Brian's Valetta, coming to a halt just 25 yards away! This aircraft is likely to be TW113 of the Far East Training Squadron, which suffered a landing accident at Seletar on 4 July 1953. *(Brian Rose)*

T.3 VP354 has passed through a rainstorm during a ferry flight to Seletar in October 1951. The first picture was taken at Habbaniya on 6 October and the second one at Bangkok four days later. Note that the rain has worn away VP354's silver finish to reveal the original Trainer Yellow colour scheme. A postwar T.3, VP354 was ready for collection from the de Havilland Hatfield factory on 30 May 1947. Delivered to 616 Squadron at Finningley on 17 June, it remained with 616 until 9 June 1949, when it suffered a Category B flying accident. Following repairs by Brooklands Aviation, VP354 entered storage with 15 MU in March 1950 before passing to 27 MU just over a year later. In September 1951 it was

allocated to the FEAF at Seletar, departing via Abingdon on 3 October crewed by RAF ferry pilot Richard Livermore and navigator Flt Sgt Pender. On arrival at Seletar VP354 was allocated to 81 Squadron, serving until 11 January 1954, when it was written off in a landing accident. *(Both Richard Livermore)*

This shot of T.3 TV959 dates from the late 1950s during its service with the Home Command Examining Unit at White Waltham. Constructed at Leavesden in the summer of 1945, TV959 entered service with 13 OTU on 29 August before allocation to 266 Squadron just over a year later. Following service with 54 OTU and 228 OCU it was delivered to 204 AFS in July 1951. TV959's stay with 204 AFS was brief, for it was damaged in a flying accident on 11 September 1951, repairs being carried out by Brooklands Aviation and completed by 4 February 1952. Following storage at 27 MU, TV959 was assigned to the Home Command Examining Unit at White Waltham in May 1952 before suffering further damage in August 1953, repairs once again being effected by Brooklands Aviation. Returning to White Waltham in December 1955, TV959 remained on the Home Command Examining Unit strength until transfer to the Headquarters Fighter Command Communications Squadron at Bovingdon on 17 February 1959. The aircraft's final posting was to N. 3 CAACU at Exeter, where it arrived in April 1959, receiving the unit code letter 'Y' and serving alongside T.3s RR299 and TW117. TV959's role at 3 CAACU was to renew instrument ratings and to conduct

annual standardisation checks for the unit's TT.35 pilots.

The aircraft was Struck Off Charge on 31 May 1963 and is believed to have been transported to Bovingdon for ground use in the Mirisch Films production *633 Squadron*. On completion of filming, TV959 was transferred to the Imperial War Museum and displayed at Lambeth (minus its starboard outer wing, which was sawn off due to space restrictions) for many years until traded to 'The Fighter Collection' at Duxford. TV959 is currently owned by the Washington-based Flying Heritage Collection and stored in the UK awaiting restoration. *(Stuart Howe collection)*

Stripped-down T.3 VA875 out to grass at White Waltham in 1958. This Mosquito was ready for collection from the de Havilland Leavesden factory on 26 June 1946, and over the next eleven years it served with 54 OTU, the Linton-on-Ouse Station Flight, 64 Squadron, 204 AFS, the Home Command Examining Unit and the Home Command Communications Squadron. VA875 was Struck Off Charge as surplus but recoverable for spares breakdown on 10 April 1957. *(Peter Arnold)*

T.3 LR539 in the process of being stripped for spares at 27 MU Shawbury in July 1956. LR539 was built at Leavesden in April 1944, serving with 54 OTU, 51 OTU, 13 OTU, the Central Flying School and 228 OCU during its twelve-year career. Declared Non-Effective Stock on 29 May 1956, LR539

was sold as scrap to Henry Bath & Son four months later. In addition to the propellers and engine nacelles, note that the cockpit canopy structure has been removed leaving only the windscreen in situ. Parked beyond LR539 is T.3 LR554, which was also being stripped of useful parts. *(Philip Birtles)*

Home Command Examining Unit T.3 TV959 is undergoing inspection and servicing at White Waltham. This aircraft served with the Unit from May 1952 until February 1959, when it was assigned to the Headquarters Fighter Command Communication Squadron at Bovingdon. It is one of only two surviving T.3s in the world. *(Bob Tatum collection)*

T.3 RR299 photographed outside the flight test hangar at the de Havilland Hatfield aerodrome in 1957. RR299 was then on the strength of the Home Command Examining Unit at White Waltham, where it served alongside fellow Leavesden-built T.3 TV959. In 1963 RR299 was purchased by Hawker Siddeley Aviation for use a display aircraft, becoming a regular sight at Hatfield from 1965 onwards. Although Hatfield aerodrome no longer exists, today the flight test hangar is used as a gymnasium. Note the de Havilland Canada Beaver visible beneath RR299's starboard wing. *(BAE SYSTEMS)*

RR299, in the hands of Pat Fillingham, flies over a sea of clouds during a photographic sortie from Hatfield in 1969. RR299 had recently taken part in the Oakmont Productions film *Mosquito Squadron*, for which it gained this camouflage scheme together with the fictitious (for a Mosquito squadron) unit code letters 'HT-E'. *(Philip Birtles)*

Mosquito Fighter-Bombers

Perhaps more than any other version of the Mosquito, the Fighter-Bomber epitomised the design's tremendous versatility and undertook some of the most audacious precision raids of the Second World War. Night and day, Fighter-Bomber Mosquitoes flew deep into enemy territory, attacking aerodromes, communications systems and industrial objectives, and annihilating specialist targets with lethal accuracy. They roamed the Bay of Biscay and the coast of Norway sinking German U-boats and shipping targets, while BOAC examples raced between Scotland and Sweden carrying important mail, freight and occasionally passengers. Engaged on bomber support duties in the night skies over Germany, the Fighter-Bombers played a principal role in electronic countermeasures warfare and assisted in the destruction of Luftwaffe night-fighters. Fighter-Bombers shot down more than 600 V-1 flying bombs and conducted an intensive campaign to destroy their launch sites in Northern France. They attacked the Japanese in India, Burma and New Guinea, and stood by to intercept Japanese fire balloons launched against Canada's west coast. After the war, Fighter-Bombers patrolled the skies over Indonesia and French Indo-China and formed an integral part of several foreign and Commonwealth air forces. Israeli examples operated almost with impunity during the Sinai campaign and several Yugoslavian aircraft were still flying into the 1960s. Fighter-Bomber versions accounted for the majority of Mosquito production and represented nearly a third of total output.

Plans for a Mosquito Fighter-Bomber were considered long before the first F.IIs entered RAF service. The projected new variant became the Mark VI and was originally planned in two versions: the Mk VIA Night-Fighter and the Mk VIB Fighter-Bomber, intruder and long-range fighter. Mosquito Night-Fighter development negated the need for a Mk VIA, but the Mk VIB formed the basis of the FB.VI, and the first Prototype, HJ662/G, made its maiden flight on 1 June 1942. F.IIs had enjoyed considerable success in the intruder role but lacked any bomb-carrying capability. The FB.VI addressed this deficiency, combining the formidably armed Mosquito Fighter with a proportion of its Bomber counterpart's offensive load. This was achieved through marrying the 'basic' strengthened wing (originally tested on Bomber Prototype W4057) to the Fighter airframe, enabling the carriage of two bombs on underwing hardpoints together with two more in the rear of the ventral bay (behind the cannons). Series 1 FB.VIs carried four 250lb bombs, this load being increased to four 500lb bombs on Series 2 aircraft. Power came in the form of either Merlin 21s, 22s or 23s, with the higher-rated 25s installed for increased performance at low level. For extra range, a 63-gallon fuel tank could be installed in place of the fuselage bomb load. Like the F.II, the FB.VI was highly manoeuvrable but lacked the former's rate of climb due to increased weight.

Demand for other Mosquito variants slowed the introduction of FB.VIs on to the assembly lines until early 1943, 418 Squadron (RCAF) becoming the first unit to be equipped with the new version in May the same year. 605 and 23 Squadrons followed, the latter flying its first FB.VIs on intruder flights from Malta. The range and bomb load of the FB.VI made it an extremely potent weapon, which was exploited to good effect on Ranger and Intruder missions. However, it was daylight precision strikes on specialist objectives that arguably became the hallmark of the FB.VI and greatly enhanced the Mosquito's reputation in the public eye. FB.VIs of 2 Group, 2nd Tactical Air Force, specialised in such work, 464 Squadron (RAAF) and 487 Squadron (RNZAF) carrying out the Group's first operation (against power stations in Northern France) on 2 October 1943. Techniques were honed over the following months, 2 Group FB.VIs carrying out the famous raids on Amiens prison, the Shellhaus building in Copenhagen and the Gestapo Headquarters at Aarhus University. After D-Day FB.VIs provided close tactical support to the Allied armies advancing into Germany, several squadrons remaining with the British Air Forces of Occupation (BAFO) following the Nazi surrender. The long range and great striking power of the FB.VI made it ideal for Coastal Command anti-shipping operations and led to its only production development, the FB.XVIII. Equipped with a 57mm six-pounder gun, the FB.XVIII's primary role was to destroy German U-boats and shipping targets. Coastal Command FB.VIs could also be equipped with underwing-mounted rocket projectiles, employed with great success by the Banff Strike Wing Squadrons during anti-shipping operations off the Norwegian coast.

Following the rectification of structural problems, Mosquito Fighter-Bombers operated very successfully against the Japanese in the Far East, while RAAF aircraft operated from Borneo during the war's closing stages.

Mosquito Fighter-Bombers were also produced in Canada and Australia. The initial Canadian version was based on the FB.VI and designated Mosquito

FB.21. Two pre-production FB.21s were constructed (KA100 and KA101), both powered by Packard Merlin 33s, a third aircraft (KA102) receiving two-speed, two-stage supercharged Packard Merlins in connection with development of the proposed (Packard Merlin 301-powered) FB.24 high-altitude Fighter-Bomber. Production of the FB.24 did not proceed, the FB.21 being superseded by the Packard Merlin 225-powered FB.26. Output was small in comparison to the FB.VI, but more than seventy FB.26s were delivered to the RAF, some serving with 249 Squadron in Kenya, others with 55 Squadron in Greece. The majority of FB.26s were retained in Canada, nearly 200 later being sold to the Nationalist Chinese Air Force.

Australian Mosquito production concentrated entirely on the Fighter-Bomber airframe, which received the local designation FB.40. Also based on the FB.VI, the FB.40 was powered by Packard Merlin 31s or 33s, the first example, A52-1, making its maiden flight on 23 July 1943. The RAAF received its first FB.40s during the first half of 1944, wing manufacturing problems then delaying deliveries until August the same year. More than 200 FB.40 airframes were produced, six being converted into PR.40s, twenty-two into T.43 trainers and twenty-eight into PR.41s, the latter equipped with two-speed, two-stage supercharged Packard Merlin 69 engines. The projected Merlin 69-powered FB.42 (as with the Canadian FB.24) did not enter production.

FB.VIs were manufactured at the de Havilland Hatfield factory, Standard Motors at Coventry and Airspeed at Portsmouth, the latter constructing the final example (VL732) in July 1946. In addition to those squadrons based in Germany, FB.VIs served the postwar RAF in various training and second-line units including 204 AFS, 228 OCU and the Central Gunnery School.

The FB.VI first Prototype, HJ662/G, in the Hatfield Erecting Shop during early 1942. The most prolific and versatile mark of Mosquito, the FB.VI was originally planned in two versions, the Mk VIA Night-Fighter and the Mk VIB Fighter-Bomber, intruder and long-range fighter. Mosquito Night-Fighter development negated the need for a Mk VIA but the Mk VIB provided a basis for what eventually became the FB.VI. Retaining the armament of the F.II, the FB.VI introduced the strengthened or 'basic' wing (initially tested on Bomber Prototype W4057) to the Fighter airframe. The FB.VI differed principally from the F.II through its ability to accommodate both an internal and external bomb load, which, on the intruder version, consisted of two bombs in the fuselage ventral bay (aft of the cannon) and two more on streamlined underwing hardpoints (mounted outboard at wing rib number eight). Series 1 FB.VIs carried four 250lb bombs, this load being increased to four 500lb bombs on Series 2 machines. To increase range, the fuselage bomb load could be replaced by a 63-gallon fuel tank, which occupied the space behind the cannons. The ventral bay doors were split into four separate panels, the forward pair providing access to the cannon armament, the rear pair acting as bomb doors to the fuselage bomb bay/fuel tank compartment; in this photograph HJ662/G appears to be fitted with the full-span doors of the F.II. The raised inspection panel on the starboard wing top surface covered the aileron centre hinge and differential control. *(BAE SYSTEMS)*

This second view of HJ662/G in the Hatfield Erecting Shop is a close-up shot of the tail assembly. HJ662's airframe was originally intended for completion as a B.IV Series ii bearing the serial number 'DZ434', but that number was subsequently allocated to another B.IV, which served with 109 Squadron until written off on 23 October 1943. Note the 'balloon' tailwheel tyre (a contrast to the double-ridged Marstrand anti-shimmy unit that became a standard feature of later production aircraft) and the tailcone with its twin navigation/formation tail lamps. The curved panel at the bottom of the picture is the aluminium under fairing between the rear fuselage and tailcone; the strip in the lower rudder fabric provides access to the rudder trim tab linkage. The chalk inscription on the rudder's upper section reads 'FOR INTRUDER'. *(BAE SYSTEMS)*

This close-up shot shows HJ662/G's starboard underwing bomb carrier enclosed within its streamlined fairing. Located at wing rib number eight, the FB.VI's underwing hardpoints were capable of accommodating a variety of different loads including bombs, rockets, depth charges and fuel tanks. The key to this capability was the strengthened or 'basic' wing, which greatly increased the Mosquito's offensive versatility, making the FB.VI much in demand by RAF Commands both at home and abroad. *(BAE SYSTEMS)*

A 250lb bomb is mounted on HJ662/G's port underwing bomb carrier. This aircraft represented the intruder version of the FB.VI with provision for two 250lb bombs in the fuselage and two more on the wings. The first production FB.VIs (Series 1 aircraft) carried the same bomb load as HJ662/G, but later (Series 2) machines could accommodate four 500lb bombs. This photograph was taken during HJ662/G's brief handling and diving trials at the A&AEE at Boscombe Down in June/July 1942. During the course of these tests the underwing bombs were replaced by two 315lb Smoke Curtain Installation (SCI) containers. Trials with underwing bombs were made at an all-up weight of 20,835lb, this rising to 20,950lb with the SCI containers. The A&AEE regarded HJ662/G's manoeuvrability as 'particularly good' and the controls well harmonised. Stability was also praised, but the 'increase in weight above the Fighter type has noticeably reduced the rate of climb, but not to a serious degree'. HJ662/G is finished in Medium Sea Grey and appears to have suffered a serious oil leak from the port engine. The dark appearance of the yellow 'Circle P' (for 'Prototype') marking on the fuselage side indicates that this photograph was shot on orthochromatic film. *(via DHAMT Ltd)*

HJ662/G is seen at A&AEE Boscombe Down in the summer of 1942. Equipped with Merlin 21s, the aircraft made its maiden flight from Hatfield on 1 June, and was delivered to Boscombe Down on the 13th for 'Brief handling and diving trials of Intruder version'. Trials commenced on 17 June and covered handling and diving characteristics while fitted with 250lb bombs or 315lb SCI containers beneath the wings. These tests consisted of general handling, an assessment of longitudinal stability, and dives with the bomb doors open and closed. The A&AEE concluded that 'the aeroplane is very pleasant to fly, the controls being sufficiently light and well harmonised to indicate that, apart from strength considerations, full aerobatics would be practicable … the fitting of two SCI containers under the wings does not adversely affect the handling characteristics.' HJ662/G's 'brief' handling trials were indeed brief, for the aircraft crashed at Boscombe Down on 10 July after the port engine failed to give full power on take-off. The pilot attempted to lift HJ662/G over two parked Beaufighters but struck both aircraft, severely damaging Mk II R2311 with the Mosquito's undercarriage and tail unit. The pilot survived but HJ662/G was declared a write-off and Struck Off Charge on 6 August. Subsequent inspection of the port engine revealed no defect, the cause of failure being described as 'obscure'. FB.VI handling trials were resumed at Boscombe Down with HJ663 in April 1943. Note the Wellington in the distance beneath HJ662/G's starboard wing, and the tail of a Beaufort visible on the right. *(via DHAMT Ltd)*

The FB.21 was the initial Canadian-built Fighter-Bomber version (based on the British FB.VI), and two pre-production aircraft (KA100 and KA101) equipped with Packard Merlin 33s were constructed at Downsview. The FB.21 design was later revised, emerging as the Packard Merlin 225-powered FB.26. This photograph depicts KA100. *(BAE SYSTEMS)*

This rare shot of Canadian-built Fighter-Bomber KA102 is believed to portray the FB.24 development aircraft, equipped with two-speed, two-stage supercharged Packard Merlin engines. Projected as a Packard Merlin 301-powered high-altitude fighter-bomber, work on the FB.24 did not progress beyond KA102. This aircraft is unarmed and the spinners appear to be finished in Sky. Two-speed, two-stage supercharged Merlin Mosquito variants never entered Canadian production. *(de Havilland Canada)*

FB.40 A52-1, the first Australian-built Mosquito, poses at the de Havilland Bankstown aerodrome in around mid-1943. The FB.40 was the Australian equivalent of the British FB.VI and formed the basis of all Australian-produced Mosquito variants. The Australian de Havilland Company had considered Mosquito manufacture as early as November 1941, despatching its supplies director and a senior engineer (John Byrne and John Mills respectively) to de Havilland Canada and the USA to investigate project feasibility and the supply of Packard-built Merlin engines. In March 1942, following approval by the Australian War Cabinet, de Havilland Australia was instructed to proceed with the manufacture of Mosquito Fighter-Bombers for the RAAF. Delays in the receipt of drawings, jigs and components from Hatfield, coupled with a lack of local engineering resources, set back production schedules, but the first Australian aircraft was ready for testing by July 1943. Note that A52-1 is finished in silver overall with the exception of the fin and rudder, which are finished in the RAAF 'Mosquito Attack' scheme of Foliage Green and Earth Brown. It is likely that A52-1 was not fully camouflaged at this stage due to the urgency of the flight test programme. *(BAE SYSTEMS)*

A52-1 runs up its Packard Merlin 31s, probably during a press demonstration at Bankstown in 1943. The aircraft made its maiden flight on 23 July 1943 in the hands of de Havilland Australia test pilot Wing Cdr Gibson Lee. A52-1 was not the first Mosquito to grace Australian skies, as Bruce Rose had flown F.II DD664 (the pattern aircraft shipped from Hatfield) from Bankstown on 17 December the previous year. DD664's initial Australian flights were made with its original Merlin 22 engines, but these were soon replaced by American-built Packard Merlin 31s, the intended power units for locally produced Mosquito FB.40s. DD664's first flight with Merlin 31s took place on 23 March 1943 and, although a challenging exercise, this engine installation proved a success. Both Merlin 31s were later removed from DD664 and fitted to A52-1, powering the latter on its maiden flight. Note the six exhaust stubs on the engine outboard side, a contrast to the five stubs normally fitted to the FB.40's British contemporary, the FB.VI. *(BAE SYSTEMS)*

An extremely purposeful-looking aeroplane: this fine shot of A52-1 banking away from the camera aircraft was taken during a filming and photo session from Bankstown in 1943. Note that large sections of the mainplane and flap under surfaces have still to be finished in silver dope. A52-1 wears the RAAF national markings of blue and white roundels and fin flashes. *(Sun)*

213

A52-1 starts its engines in preparation for another sortie, probably from Bankstown. By this time the aircraft's original silver finish had given way to the RAAF's first 'Mosquito Attack' colour scheme of Earth Brown and Foliage Green upper surfaces and Sky Blue under surfaces. Although A52-1 first flew in July 1943 it was not delivered to the RAAF until 4 March 1944. This delay was due to the usual problems associated with introducing a brand new type into production, and included modifications to the aileron controls, engine cowlings, instrument panel and oil pipelines. A52-1's RAAF service was very short, for it was written off at Laverton after an air bottle exploded on 24 June 1944. Note the high position of the camouflage demarcation line on the rear fuselage.
(Photographer unknown, via BAE SYSTEMS)

FB.40 A52-3, the third Australian-built Mosquito, photographed at No 1 Aircraft Performance Unit, Laverton (Victoria), in around May 1944. November 1944 saw A52-3 return to the de Havilland Bankstown factory, where it was converted to T.43 standards and re-serialled A52-1050. In September 1946 the aircraft entered storage at 3 AD Amberley, remaining there until transferred to Archerfield in July 1953. This Mosquito was eventually sold in February 1954 and dismantled four months later. A52-3's upper surfaces are finished in Foliage Green and Earth Brown with the under surfaces in Sky Blue. *(Both RAAF, via Frank Smith)*

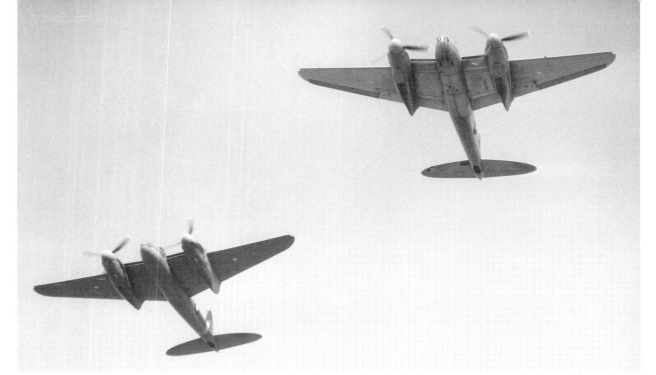

FB.40 A52-1 (right) in formation with British-built T.3 A52-1005. This picture may have been taken during filming of the 'Movietone News' production 'Latest Mosquito planes now made in Australia', which was shot by Eric Bierre. A52-1005 was constructed at Leavesden as HJ960 in June 1943; travelling via 10 and 47 MUs, it was shipped to Australia on 30 July 1943, arriving in Sydney two months later. Following re-assembly and the installation of Packard Merlin 31s, A52-1005 entered service with 5 OTU RAAF before being sold to the RNZAF as NZ2303 in 1946. NZ2303 was allocated to 75 Squadron at Ohakea before entering storage at Woodbourne in December 1949. The aircraft was eventually sold as scrap in around November 1952. *(Sun)*

Within the confines of a sandbagged anti-shrapnel bay (possibly at Hunsdon), armourers Col Davies and 'Smithy' Smith prepare a 140 Wing FB.VI in readiness for another sortie. 'Smithy' is checking the four 20mm cannon while Col Davies steadies a 500lb bomb that is being winched into the bomb bay. As a permanent part of the fuselage structure, a bomb loading winch was mounted on the floor of the rear compartment forward of bulkhead number four. The winch hoisting cable, with its ball end attachment, wound on to a deeply grooved pulley driven from the winch shaft by a sliding plate and pegs. To hoist the bombs, the cable was threaded over separate pulleys on each bomb crate, but when not in use was wound on the pulley with its ball end stowed in a clip beneath the rear floor. Series 1 FB.VIs carried two 250lb GP or SAP bombs in the bomb bay and two more on underwing bomb racks. On Series 2 aircraft this load was increased to two 500lb GP or MC bombs (with short tails and tail fuse only) in the bomb bay and two on the underwing bomb racks. The 'U'-shaped fittings at the forward end of the gun bay are the front ammunition chutes for the 20mm cannon (note the gun heating tubes running adjacent to the chutes). This photograph captures the essence of the FB.VI, a Fighter Mosquito combining a proportion of the Bomber's offensive load. *(John Stride collection)*

This striking view features the nose of a new FB.VI at the Hatfield factory in 1943. In common with the Mosquito F.II/NF.II, the FB.VI was equipped with four 20mm cannon beneath the cockpit floor (note the cannon ports exiting through the aluminium under fairing) as well as four .303in Browning machine-guns in the nose. The circular panel immediately behind the nose cone provided access to a chamber for spent .303in ammunition rounds and links; spent cannon shell cases were ejected through chutes in the ventral gun bay doors. The spent .303in ammunition cases had to be contained in order to prevent the slipstream from directing them into the cannon ports. Worthy of comment is the 'W/T' stencil forward of the crew entrance door; 'W/T' stood for 'Wired Throughout' and signified that the airframe had been bonded (the electrical connecting of two or more conducting objects not otherwise connected) to eliminate the build-up of static charge. The 'DTD S3A' stencil beneath it indicated the Air Ministry 'Directorate of Technical Development' paint/dope specification applied to the aircraft. Note the protective coverings on the barrels of the machine-guns and cannons. *(BAE SYSTEMS)*

HJ732/G, the Prototype FB.XVIII 'Tsetse' Mosquito, pictured at Hatfield on 11 August 1943. Developed for Coastal Command anti-submarine operations, the FB.XVIII was a modified FB.VI adapted to carry a 57mm six-pounder gun in place of the four 20mm cannon. The gun's feed mechanism was designed and built by the Molins Company of Peterborough, which was more normally associated with the production of cigarette manufacturing machines. An extremely accurate weapon, the 57mm gun was used to good effect by FB.XVIIIs operated by 248 and 254 Squadrons against U-boats and shipping targets. HJ732/G became the development prototype, making its maiden flight on 8 June 1943. Seventeen production aircraft followed, the first two being used for acceptance trials at the A&AEE at Boscombe Down. Note the gun muzzle protruding from the lower nose section, and the external armour plating beneath the nose machine-guns. Some production FB.XVIIIs were adapted to carry only two nose machine-guns (fed from enlarged ammunition tanks), these being employed for sighting purposes in addition to defence.

Although not featured on HJ732/G, production FB.XVIIIs were fitted with external armour plating around both sides of the nose. The under surfaces of HJ732/G's inboard flaps were severely damaged by gun blast during air and ground firing trials of the 57 mm gun. Damage to the starboard flap was more severe due to the gun's installation 4 inches to starboard of the centre-line. To counter this problem, the inboard flaps of production FB.XVIIIs incorporated external strengthening ribs on their lower surfaces. FB.XVIIIs were nicknamed 'Tsetses' Mosquitoes after the deadly African tsetse fly. *(BAE SYSTEMS)*

Inside the gun bay of an FB.XVIII (looking forward) we can see the rear of the 57mm cannon (top left). Note the modifications to the starboard gun bay door, its forward section featuring a blister fairing for the cannon installation. On production FB.XVIIIs, 3/8-inch armour plate was fitted externally to both gun bay doors along approximately three-quarters of their length. The large duct located inside the rear of the starboard door is the shell case ejection chute. The first three FB.XVIIIs (HJ732/G, HX902/G and HX903/G) were despatched to A&AEE Boscombe Down for proofing trials prior to service use. The A&AEE reported that the shell case ejection chute 'is considered to be adequate' but 'under continued ejection, denting of the deflector plate still occurs, and the sides continue to be lightly struck by the gun at its limit of recoil. Further alteration to overcome these two minor faults is not necessary.' This photograph was taken in 1943 and illustrates the FB.XVIII development Prototype, HJ732/G. *(BAE SYSTEMS)*

MOSQUITO
(Rolls-Royce Merlin engines)

The flying field gun

DE HAVILLAND *In the attack today — on the trade routes of the future*

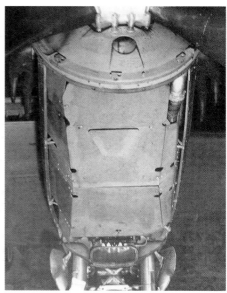

These two photographs taken at Hatfield on 8 February 1944 show armour plating fitted beneath the port engine of a production FB.XVIII. The FB.XVIII's primary role was the destruction of surfaced German U-boats operating from Biscay ports. This dangerous work demanded maximum protection for the attacking Mosquito and, in addition to the engines, 3/8-inch armour plate was added to the cockpit floor, ventral gun bay doors, radiator housings, radiator flaps and nose. This vital necessity imposed an additional weight penalty of some 900lb. Note the shallower depth of the port gun bay door in relation to the starboard unit, necessary due to the 57mm cannon installation. The de Havilland Company 'Mosquito News' report for May/July 1944 included the following: 'Mk XVIII aircraft, mounting 6 pounder guns, are attached to No 248 Squadron at Portreath, and apart from certain trouble due to gun blast, have been operating successfully. Sholto Douglas, Commander-in-Chief, Coastal Command, thinks highly of it and applied in April for an immediate establishment of 6, increasing to a full squadron, but the request was turned down by the Air Staff; at present there are two with the squadron, and we are building two more.' *(Both BAE SYSTEMS)*

A 500lb bomb is loaded beneath the starboard wing of a 140 Wing FB.VI at Hunsdon, being hoisted into position using Type A 'Hockey Stick' hand winches. Mk III Universal Carriers were used on all FB.VI wing bomb installations, but separate underwing fairings were required for 250lb and 500lb loads. *(John Stride collection)*

The .303in Browning machine-guns of 613 Squadron FB.VI LR275 are reloaded at Lasham. Merlin 23-powered LR275 was built at Hatfield in November 1943 under Air Ministry Contract 555. After preparation at 10 MU it was issued to 305 Squadron on 25 November 1943, but passed to 613 Squadron the following day. On 9 December LR275 collided with FB.VI HX980 in a taxying accident at Lasham, repairs and modifications delaying its return to 613 Squadron until 4 February 1944. The next day it was damaged once more, repairs being completed by 2 March before the aircraft transferred to 305 Squadron two weeks later. LR275 eventually went missing during a night intruder sortie over Normandy on 8 June 1944. Note that the machine-gun ammunition boxes are marked with the aircraft's serial digits.
(613 (City of Manchester) Squadron Association)

Constructed at Hatfield in December 1943, Merlin 25-powered FB.VI LR356 was assigned to 21 Squadron on 1 February 1944, receiving the unit codes 'YH-C'. Two weeks later, during a ferry flight in poor weather conditions, it was damaged in a landing accident at Hatfield. Following repairs, LR356 was retained by de Havilland's for tests with 500lb underwing bombs before returning to 21 Squadron (via 417 ARF) in late April 1944. Recoded 'YH-Y', LR356 flew twenty-two operational sorties with 21 Squadron but received damage on 5 July 1944, repairs taking three weeks to complete. 613 Squadron took delivery of LR356 on Christmas Eve 1944 and by 29 January 1945 had flown eleven sorties with the aircraft. On 2 February 1945, crewed by Flt Lt D. A. Sheppard and Flg Off A. G. Martin, LR356 failed to return from a night intruder operation to Hanover and Elze. This picture was taken by a de Havilland photographer at Hatfield during the underwing bomb tests previously referred to. Note the lower section of the unit code letter 'C', visible immediately forward of the fuselage roundel. *(BAE SYSTEMS)*

MOSQUITO

Latest and fastest
night interceptor

DE HAVILLAND

In the attack today
On the trade routes of the future

(BAE SYSTEMS)

FB.VI PZ202 fitted with the two-tier rocket rail arrangement designed to enable rocket-armed Mosquitoes to carry drop tanks. Rocket projectiles were a reasonably cheap and accurate weapon and proved extremely effective during Coastal Command anti-shipping operations. Rockets were produced in two forms, the 25lb solid armour-piercing type and the 60lb semi-armour-piercing with a high-explosive warhead. de Havilland's adapted the FB.VI to carry eight 60lb rockets (on four rails per wing located between ribs seven and eleven) during the autumn of 1943, but this installation, which later became standard, precluded the fitting of underwing drop tanks.

In October 1943 HJ719 became the first FB.VI to fly with rocket rails, subsequent trials with HX918 at Boscombe Down establishing an optimum dive angle for firing of 20 degrees. During operations the rockets could be fired in pairs, but were normally released in one salvo, harmonised to strike the superstructure, waterline and engine room of enemy shipping targets. Extremely destructive and with no recoil, the salvo from eight 60lb rockets was comparable to the broadside from a six-inch-gun cruiser. The two-tier arrangement shown on PZ202 permitted the rocket's striking power to be combined with the extra range afforded

by drop tanks. A guard frame was later fitted between the rocket rails and drop tank (also tested on PZ202) to stop the latter from fouling the rails when jettisoned.

A Hatfield-built FB.VI, PZ202 was retained by de Havilland's for trials work until allocated to the A&AEE in February 1945. It was later sold to Turkey and, following overhaul by Fairey Aviation, became '6679' with 3 Aaly/4 BI of the Turkish Air Force in 1947. The drop tank illustrated is of the 100-gallon type, and the photograph was taken at Hatfield on 6 January 1945. *(BAE SYSTEMS)*

Armourers clean and re-load the .303in Browning nose machine-guns of a 140 Wing FB.VI. Each of the four ammunition boxes could accommodate up to 750 rounds of mixed ammunition types. When the boxes were removed for refilling, the inboard pair were refitted first to enable the inboard guns to be cocked. Viewed from the nose looking rearwards, the guns were numbered (left to right) '4 3 2 1' respectively, their individual numbers painted on the armour-plated bulkhead immediately aft of the ammunition boxes. *(John Stride collection)*

This close-up shot was taken at Hatfield in August 1944 and shows the Serrate installation in a 100 Group FB.VI. A homing device, Serrate indicated bearings on transmissions from German night-fighter radar equipment, principally the FuG 202/212 and 220 sets. 100 Group Mosquito NF.IIs and FB.VIs were normally fitted with both AI Mk IV radar and Serrate, the latter sharing the radar's transmitting aerial and Cathode Ray Tube display. These aircraft were equipped with Serrate Mk II (devised to locate FuG 202/212 radar transmissions), but it would appear that some 100 Group FB.VIs received the later Serrate Mk IV. Serrate indicated an enemy aircraft's range but not its bearing, so AI Mk IV radar was employed for the final interception. Serrate-equipped Mosquito NF.IIs and FB.VIs were flown by 141, 169 and 239 Squadrons. In this photo note how the Serrate equipment has replaced the nose machine-guns. The black box on the right-hand face of the armour-plated bulkhead is the windscreen wiper motor. The hinged section on the bulkhead's left side provided access to the rear of the instrument panel. This FB.VI is equipped with 'saxophone' exhaust manifolds. *(BAE SYSTEMS)*

HJ716 featured among the initial batch of FB.VI Series 1s built at Hatfield in 1943. These were equipped with either 1,460hp Merlin 23s or the more powerful 1,635hp Merlin 25s, the latter necessary for increased performance during low-level operations. Delivered to 27 MU on 22 April 1943, HJ716 passed to No 1 Overseas Aircraft Preparation Unit on 27 May. Flown to Malta on 20 June 1943, HJ716 arrived on the beleaguered island the following day and was assigned to 23 Squadron at Luqa (then equipped with Mosquito F.IIs). Initially equipped with F.IIs, 23 Squadron welcomed the range and bomb-carrying capabilities of the FB.VI and soon began intruder operations over Sicily and Southern Italy. HJ716 flew 23 Squadron's first FB.VI intruder sortie on 17 July when Fg Off Menks attacked airfields near Rome. HJ716 was eventually lost in a landing

accident (following engine failure) at Gerbini on 5 September 1943. This picture was taken during a test flight from Hatfield on 21 April and shows to advantage the Medium Sea Grey and Dark Green camouflage finish. During service in Malta HJ716 sported the Intruder scheme with its under surfaces refinished in Night. Note the underwing bomb carriers. *(BAE SYSTEMS)*

With bomb doors open, an FB.VI of 140 Wing carries out low-level attack practice shortly after the Wing replaced its Venturas with Mosquitoes in the summer of 1943. 140 Wing's Senior Admin Officer, Sqn Ldr Chas Wood, reported at the time: 'We are equipped with Mark VI Mosquito aircraft with Merlin 21s and 25s, we are promised all 25s and everyone will be pleased when this comes about. Our operatoinal role is Low Level daylight and mostly on constructional works on the French coast, the much talked of gun emplacements. The boys are all very happy on the job, all working well together and are dead keen on the aircraft.' *(John Stride collection)*

Factory-fresh FB.VI LR248 photographed at Hatfield in October 1943. Worthy of comment are the extended carburettor air intakes (housing tropical filters) and the 50-gallon underwing drop tanks. The first FB.VI in the 'LR' series production batch, LR248 is finished in the standard Mosquito Night-Fighter scheme (applied to the majority of production FB.VIs) of Medium Sea Grey overall with Dark Green camouflaged upper surfaces. The aerial-shaped object beneath the nose (right of the cockpit entrance ladder) is the tube for the trailing aerial. Note the Mosquito NF.II in the distance beneath LR248's starboard wing. *(Aeroplane Monthly)*

618 Squadron FB.VI HR619 'E 1' is seen shortly after re-assembly at Mascot in July 1945. this Merlin 25-powered aircraft was constructed by Standard Motors in November 1944 and delivered to 47 MU early the following month. Prepared for shipment to 618 Squadron in Australia, it left Liverpool on 16 December 1944, arriving in Sydney on 28 February 1945. HR619 made its first air test from Mascot in the hands of 618 Squadron pilot Flt Lt Foss, the second flight being carried out by Flt Lt Clutterbuck (with Roley Manning as observer on both occasions). This FB.VI is finished in the Night-Fighter scheme of Medium Sea Grey overall with Dark Green camouflaged upper surfaces, the Dark Green extending to the fin and rudder (a deviation from this scheme's standard application). The fuselage roundels and fin flashes are applied in white and blue (in accordance with RAAF national insignia), while the squadron code letters are believed to be in red. *(Both Roley Manning)*

These two further shots of HR619 date from 1947. Following 618 Squadron's disbandment at Narromine in July 1945 (see Mosquito Bombers), its aircraft were sold off at public auction. Farmer Roland Shepherd purchased HR619 (minus engines) for $30, towing the aircraft to his property 25 miles from Narromine. The first picture was taken during transit, while the second one depicts HR619 at its final resting place on Roland's 'Kokoda' farm. The wings were pruned to enable passage over railway level crossings!
(Mary Shepherd, via Ross Shepherd)

This photograph was taken at Mascot in July 1945 and shows 618 Squadron airframe fitter LAC Roley Manning with his wife-to-be. The Mosquito behind them is FB.VI HR580 'T I', which had recently been assembled and was awaiting delivery to Narromine. After the war Roley Manning settled in Australia, where he still lives today. HR580 was sold by public auction at Narromine in 1947. *(Roley Manning)*

One for the modellers: this close-up shot shows the 82 Squadron unit code letters on FB.VI HR558 'UX-G'. HR558 was built by Standard Motors in November 1944, serving with 82 Squadron in the Far East before being Struck Off Charge on 11 July 1946. It is finished overall in glossy aluminium dope with fuselage roundels in dark blue and SEAC white. The Squadron code letters are approximately 27 inches high and applied in Night. This photograph was taken at Joari, Cox's Bazar. *(Vic Hewes)*

This pleasing shot portrays an unidentified 82 Squadron FB.VI (possibly RF665 'UX-C') – note the colourful artwork on the crew entrance door, which incorporates the inscription 'Charlie'. Previously equipped with Vultee Vengeance dive-bombers, 82 Squadron began conversion to Mosquito FB.VIs at Kolar in July 1944. The Squadron's brief was to destroy Japanese lines of communication in

Burma (whether road, rail or river-based). Following a move to Ranchi, the Squadron commenced Mosquito operations in October 1944, but was grounded on 20 October after HP919 crashed due to structural failure. This led to an inspection of all Mosquitoes based in the Far East for three months or more (together with those that had spent up to four weeks in the Middle East), revealing that airframe structural integrity had been impaired by heat and humidity, mainplane glue joints being particularly badly effected. This problem was especially apparent on aircraft constructed with organic-based casein glue, those manufactured using formaldehyde resin passing inspection. All Mosquitoes manufactured using casein (including newly completed airframe components) were subsequently scrapped. This FB.VI is finished in glossy aluminium dope (to reflect heat from the airframe) and is equipped with exhaust shrouds, the latter for night intruder operations. *(George Mahony, via Howard Sandall)*

Taken at 18,000 feet over the Chin Hills, this picture portrays FB.VIs of 82 Squadron returning from a strike on Japanese locomotives at Myindaik. Following the structural failure that occurred to an 82 Squadron aircraft on 20 October 1944, Far East Mosquito operations resumed (with aircraft that had passed inspection) in November 1944, 82 Squadron commencing day and night intruder operations from 19 December. Targets included Japanese aerodromes as well as rail, road and river communications around Meiktila and Rangoon, 269 sorties being flown during March 1945 alone. *(Vic Hewes)*

204 AFS FB.VI RF936 'FMO-V' photographed at Driffield by student pilot John Gerrish during the summer of 1948. This Mosquito was built by Standard Motors in April 1945, serving with the Central Gunnery School and 204 AFS before being Struck Off Charge on 23 December 1948. John Gerrish flew RF938 three times during his 204 AFS course, carrying out low flying, navigation and night flying training sorties. RF938 wears the Night-Fighter scheme of overall Medium Sea Grey with Dark Green camouflaged upper surfaces. It is believed that several 204 AFS FB.VIs featured red spinners, RF938 appearing to be one of these. *(John Gerrish)*

FB.VIs RF856 (left) and TE869 are at No 1 Ferry Unit, RAF Pershore, awaiting delivery to the RNZAF in August 1947. Both constructed by Standard Motors, RF856 previously served with 404 Squadron (RCAF) and 132 OTU before departing for New Zealand, where it became NZ2366. Following a period in store, TE869 was delivered to the Far East in April 1946 before returning to the UK six months later. Departing the UK on 15 August 1947, TE869 became NZ2361 in RNZAF service. *(Richard Livermore)*

FB.VIs of 107 Squadron are seen at their RAF Wahn base in 1948. A wartime 2 Group unit, 107 Squadron moved from Melsbroek to Gutersloh in November 1945 as part of the British Air Force of Occupation (BAFO). Two years later 107 relocated to Wahn and was renumbered as 11 Squadron on 4 October 1948. 11 Squadron initially retained 107's 'OM' unit code letters, but these were later changed to 'EX'. Second from the right is TA581 'OM-O', a Hatfield-built FB.VI that was written off in a take-off accident on 26 May 1949. The aircraft in the immediate foreground is probably TA120 and carries the 107 Squadron badge on its fin. The badge portrays a double-headed eagle, gorged with a collar of fleur-de-lys, and bears the motto 'Nous y serons' ('We shall be there'). A former 464 Squadron (RAAF) machine, TA120 was damaged beyond repair while being towed at Wahn on 5 May 1949. *(Mike Levy)*

FB.VIs of 36 Squadron form up over Portsmouth in preparation for the 1947 Battle of Britain flypast over London. 248 Squadron (the famous wartime coastal strike unit) was renumbered 36 Squadron in October 1946, retaining 248's original 'DM' unit code letters. The aircraft in the foreground is Hatfield-built RS622 'DM-M', which was delivered to 248 Squadron in February 1945 before entering storage at 15 MU in November 1947. Transferred to Non-Effective Stock three years later, RS622 was sold as scrap to David Band & Company on 10 November 1954. Beyond RS622 is RF932, a Standard Motors-built FB.VI that was delivered to 36 Squadron in July 1947. Following 36 Squadron's disbandment in October 1947, RF932 entered storage at 15 MU before being sold as scrap to International Alloys on 17 January 1951. Note the silver finish on both aircraft, and the underwing rocket rails. *(via Bill Binnie, Stuart Howe collection)*

Following a minor inspection, this unidentified FB.VI is about to undergo an air test from RAF Heliopolis in around 1946. With the starboard engine already running, the member of the groundcrew on the right is operating the Ki-gass priming pump (accessible through a hinged panel on the forward inboard side of the engine nacelle) in readiness for starting the port engine. Note the fabric repairs beneath the forward section of the nose. The trailing aerial tube (located on the starboard underside of the nose) is particularly evident in this shot. *(Ken Allen)*

Colour Section

Watched by an armourer (left), a 139 Squadron pilot signs the Form 700 prior to boarding a B.35 at Hemswell. This aircraft has recently been armed, probably in readiness for a bombing exercise over the Wash. The light grey upper surface and Night under surface finish was applied to 139 Squadron's aircraft following their move from Coningsby to Hemswell in March 1950 (the paint job on this particular B.35 appears to be fairly recent). Yellow stencilling on the nose outlines stowage positions (within the fuselage) for the crash axe and fire extinguisher, while the sign in the armourer's hand reads 'BOMBED UP – LIVE BOMBS'. Judging by the rank pennant on the nose, this aircraft was assigned to the Squadron Commander. Note the Signal Red spinners. *(Aeroplane Monthly)*

A 'Vic' formation of three 139 Squadron B.35s viewed from the nose of another B.35 during the early 1950s. The aircraft in the centre (probably VP194) wears the postwar Bomber Command scheme of light grey upper surfaces and Night under surfaces, the aircraft to its right (TK620 'XD-L') featuring the earlier all-silver finish. 139 Squadron relinquished its Mosquito B.35s for Canberra B.2s in November 1953. *(Aeroplane Monthly)*

No 3 CAACU TT.35 RS712 '50' is seen during the early 1960s – note the target drogue stowed externally on the aft ventral bay/fuselage under fairing. RS712 was equipped with an ML Type G (Mark 2) wind-driven winch, its rear section just visible beneath the port outer undercarriage door. Mounted on the tailplane tip is the support structure for the control surfaces cable guard frame, the latter designed to prevent winch drogue cables from fouling the elevator and rudder. Despite this safety feature, incidents did occur including one alarming situation in the mid-1950s involving a No 3 CAACU TT.35. On this occasion the pilot carried out a steep turn while towing a drogue target over northern Somerset. Shortly afterwards the control column was forced forward, causing the Mosquito to enter a 'bunt' (an outside loop) manoeuvre. Assuming that the drogue cable had wrapped round one of the elevators, the pilot applied further forward pressure on the control column, which had the effect of releasing the cable and freeing the elevators. On return to Exeter the aircraft was thoroughly examined, and slight scrape marks were discovered on the port elevator top surface. This obviously indicated that the drogue cable had travelled across the tailplane, but no fault could be traced to explain why. RS712 was declared Non-Effective Stock in May 1963.
(Chris Buck, Stuart Howe collection)

RG302 photographed at Seletar in the mid-1950s. Constructed at Hatfield as a PR.34, RG302 was delivered direct from the factory to 44 MU on 22 October 1945. Three years later it passed to 22 MU Silloth, remaining there until 30 December 1949 when it was transferred to Leuchars. Allocated to 540 Squadron at Benson in March 1950, RG302 received the unit code letters 'DH-B' and served until 17 May 1951, when it flew to Marshalls for PR.34A conversion. Emerging as a PR.34A in November 1951, RG302 was assigned to the Central Signals Establishment (CSE) on 10 December, and to 192 Squadron the same day. 38 MU

Llandow stored RG302 from 7 November 1952, the aircraft later being issued to the Far East Air Force for delivery to the Maintenance Base Far East (MBFE) at Seletar. Issued to 81 Squadron at Seletar on 4 May 1954, RG302 was Struck Off Charge in October 1955 and later scrapped. Note the single-piece Perspex nose and the aft positioning of the starboard fuselage roundel. The small window immediately forward of the roundel is for the DR Master Compass Unit, a feature of RG302's PR.34A conversion, which was suspended from a bracket attached to the roof of the rear fuselage. *(SAC E. Wilkins, 81 (PR) Squadron, Seletar)*

This unusual aspect shows TT.35s of the Towed Target Flight, RAF Schleswigland, undergoing maintenance. The photograph was taken by New Zealander Dave Cooke, who served as a Target Towing Operator (TTO) at Schleswigland between November 1954 and August 1956. During this period he flew in more than ten TT.35s, including RS715, TJ113, TJ127, TJ136, TK599, TA634, TA609 and TA699. As a part of its maintenance schedule, the Mosquito in the far corner has been jacked up using two 10-ton hydraulic bipod jacks positioned on the outboard side of each engine. The jack adapters engaged with jacking pins screwed into the picketing eye socket on the outboard side of each nacelle. In order to prevent the aircraft from tipping forward, a weighted strop has been placed over the rear fuselage. Note the engine cowling panels neatly stacked on a mobile trestle forward of the nose. The aircraft in the foreground appears to have a well-weathered port spinner and is equipped with an ML Type G (Mark 2) wind-driven winch. *(Dave Cooke)*

LAC Ian Donaldson marshals in 81 Squadron PR.34A PF656 at Seletar on completion of another photographic sortie over the Malayan jungle. As a PR.34, this Percival-built Mosquito emerged from the Luton factory on 16 February 1946, entering storage with 274 MU just under a month later. Transferred to 51 MU the following November, PF656 relocated to 27 MU in February 1950 before delivery to Marshalls for PR.34A conversion in April. Conversion work took just under a year to complete, PF656 going on to serve with 540 and 81 Squadrons before being Struck Off Charge on 22 October 1955. Note the Harvard and Meteors in the background to the right. *(SAC E. Wilkins, 81 (PR) Squadron, Seletar)*

This unidentified Norwegian FB.VI is possibly at Kjevik. Note the Norwegian flag colours on the spinners, originating from the war years when Norwegian Mosquitoes otherwise carried standard RAF markings. Like many Norwegian FB.VIs, the nose machine-guns have been removed from this aircraft. *(via Bjorn Olsen)*

Colour photos of Norwegian Mosquitoes are rare. Standard Motors-built FB.VI RF764 'F-AB' joined 'B' Flight of 333 Squadron on 10 April 1945, receiving the unit code letters 'KK-E'. Later recoded 'F-AB', RF764 became 'RI-D' in 1951 and was eventually Struck Off Charge on 12 January 1952. However, unlike other remaining Norwegian Mosquitoes, RF764 was granted a new lease of life as an instructional airframe at Kjevik (Kristiansand) Air Base. It made the last flight by a Norwegian Mosquito when it was delivered from Sola to Kjevik on 21 April 1952. During its career this FB.VI logged 433hrs 55mins flying time. (via Bjorn Olsen)

Freshly painted TT.35s lined up at Bovingdon in 1963 for the filming of *633 Squadron*. The aircraft in the foreground is the Skyfame Museum's TA719/G-ASKA, marked up as 'HJ898 HT-G'. Four TT.35s were employed for the aerial sequences in the film, namely RS709, RS712, TA639 and TA719. These were supplemented by T.3 TW117, the latter wearing the film markings 'HR155 HT-M'. The two aircraft next to TA719 have yet to receive nose 'machine-guns'. *(Bob Tatum collection)*

Mexican-registered Mark 35 XB-TOX of the Fotogramex SA de CV Company is seen in the late 1950s or early 1960s. Originally constructed at Hatfield as B.35 TA717, this Mosquito was delivered direct from the factory to 44 MU on 6 July 1945. Passing to Martin Hearn on 4 February 1948, TA717 underwent modifications before transfer to 15 MU Wroughton in late April. For the next eight years it remained in storage at Wroughton and was declared Non-Effective Stock on 10 January 1955.

In May 1956 TA717 was sold to the Aviation Export Company of California and placed on the US civil register as N9911F. The aircraft had been purchased on behalf of the American McIntyre & Quiros (M&Q) surveying company, which, in collaboration with the Mexican company Fotogramex SA de CV), required it for aerial survey work in Mexico. After overhaul and repainting, N9911F was ferried to California where it was re-registered N6867C in June 1956. Shortly afterwards it flew to Mexico in preparation for a photographic survey of the country's central region, this work being supervised by Ing Miguel Perez Elias, manager of Fotogramex. Receiving the Mexican civil registration XB-TOX, the Mosquito is believed to have been flown until the early 1960s, and passed to Aero Services SA when Fotogramex went bankrupt. Stored outside (in a enclosed area) at Mexico City Airport for more than thirteen years, XB-TOX eventually succumbed to the Mexican climate and fell derelict. In 1979 its remains were acquired by Mike Meeker of British Columbia for use in the restoration of former Spartan Air Services Mark 35 VR796/CF-HML, but have since been dispersed. Note the light blue and orange paint scheme, the latter colour extending to the propeller blades. XB-TOX is remembered with great affection by Miguel and Charbel Perez Caram, the children of Fotogramex manager Miguel Perez Elias. 'Fotogramex' is emblazoned on the side of XB-TOX's nose. *(Miguel and Charbel Perez Caram)*

T.3 TV983 (left) and TT.35 TK608 are believed to have been photographed at the Armament Practice Station, Sylt, during the late 1950s. TV983 (see Chapter 5) had a long career serving both at home and abroad before being declared Non-Effective Stock in May 1958. Originally constructed as a B.35 at Hatfield, TK608 served with 236 OCU and the Armament Practice Station at Sylt, eventually being sold as scrap on 9 June 1959. *(Stuart Howe collection, via Jan Olaf)*

One of the TT.35s used in the filming of *Mosquito Squadron* is seen at Bovingdon in 1968. This aircraft is probably RS712/G-ASKB, which (among others) wore the markings 'RF580 HT-F' during the production. The unidentified gentleman posing by the cockpit entrance is believed to be a member of the aerodrome firecrew. Currently owned by American collector Kermit Weeks, RS712 is presently on display in the Air Venture Museum of the Experimental Aircraft Association (EAA) at Oshkosh, Wisconsin. Note the flag for the port undercarriage lock hanging beneath the wheel well. The grey under surface film paint has been removed from the Perspex nose glass section. *(Bob Tatum collection)*

Four Mosquitoes in close formation is a sight that will probably never be seen or heard again. Taken in July 1968 during the filming of *Mosquito Squadron*, this photograph depicts TT.35s RS709 (bottom), RS712 and TA634, together with T.3 RR299 (third aircraft down) making a low flypast over Bovingdon aerodrome. Nearly twenty years later RR299 and RS712 would briefly fly formation (prior to the latter's departure for its new home in the USA), but the making of *Mosquito Squadron* marked the last occasion when four Mosquitoes were seen in the air together. *(Bob Tatum collection)*

PR.41 VH-WAD pictured at Guildford Airport, Perth, on 29 April 1965. A detailed history of this particular Mosquito has been recounted many times before, but it is worth noting that it was originally laid down as FB.40 A52-210 but completed to PR.41 standard and re-serialled A52-319. Delivered to the RAAF in February 1948, A52-319 spent its entire RAAF career in storage and was declared surplus in March 1953. Captain James Woods then purchased the aircraft with the intention of entering it in the 1953 London to New Zealand Air Race, the aircraft being allocated the Australian civil registration VH-WAD. Sponsorship for Captain Woods's participation in the race did not materialise, VH-WAD subsequently falling into dereliction at Perth Airport. Later sold to a US owner but not delivered, the Mosquito became the subject of a legal wrangle but was eventually acquired by the Australian War Memorial in January 1979. By this time its condition was extremely poor, so it was transported back to Bankstown for a thorough and detailed restoration by Hawker de Havilland apprentices. This task took some seventeen years to complete, the aircraft eventually being rolled out at Bankstown (once again marked as A52-319) in 1996.

Today A52-319 is on display at the Australian War Memorial building in Canberra, resplendent in its original silver dope scheme but featuring tri-colour marked spinners (red, white and blue) as worn on several 87 (PR) Squadron RAAF PR.41s during the early 1950s. Note the port for the oblique camera installation positioned on the lower fuselage directly beneath the longitudinal stiffening strake. In this shot the Mosquito is finished in silver overall with the spinners in red (the nose cone was also finished in red); the civil registration 'VH-WAD' is still clearly visible on the fin. Lancaster VII NX622 of The Air Force Association (Western Australia) is parked next to VH-WAD. *(R. Hourigan)*

An unidentified TT.35 'beats up' the Bovingdon control tower during the filming of *Mosquito Squadron* in July 1968. *(Bob Tatum collection)*

TT.35 TA669 of the RAF Schleswigland Towed Target Flight was photographed from TT.35 TK609 during the mid-1950s. Hatfield-built as a B.35 in May 1945, TA669 entered storage with 44 MU on 24 May before passing to 19 MU on 16 March 1948. Delivered to Brooklands Aviation at Sywell in September 1953, TA669 was converted to TT.35 standard, this work being complete by April 1954, when it passed to 38 MU. Issued to the Armament Practice Station at Sylt on 20 May 1955, TA669 later served with the Towed Target Flight at Schleswigland, where it was written off in an emergency landing following problems with the port engine on 20 November 1956. Note the target drogues stowed externally on the starboard ventral bay door and on both sides of the aft ventral bay/fuselage under fairing. The blades of the ML Type G (Mark 2) winch 'windmill' appear to be set in the feathered position. *(Dave Cooke)*

139 Squadron pilot Harold Stillwell took this colour shot of Mosquitoes at Coningsby in October 1948. Nearest the camera is B.XVI PF498 'XD-D', believed to be the last B.XVI to serve with 139 Squadron and the only Mosquito in the Coningsby Wing (at that time) to be finished in Night-Bomber camouflage. Beyond PF498 are three of 139 Squadron's B.35s, the variant with which the Squadron had just begun to re-equip. Bomber Command's postwar Mosquito strength consisted of just two Squadrons, 139 and 109, acting in the target-marker role for the Lancaster and Lincoln force. The RAF's remaining B.35 Squadrons were based in Germany with the British Air Force of Occupation. 139 Squadron was the second (and longest-serving) RAF Mosquito Bomber Squadron, flying its first sortie on 25 June 1942 using aircraft borrowed from 105 Squadron. 139 eventually replaced its Mosquitoes with Canberra B.2s in November 1953.

PF498 (occasionally referred to in 139 Squadron as 'the black dog') featured in Volume 1 of *de Havilland Mosquito – An Illustrated History* (page 36) and sections of its wing are incorporated in Tony Agar's composite Mosquito restoration at the Yorkshire Air Museum. This print was made from a 'Dufaycolor' (additive system) transparency. In the late 1940s colour film was not readily available to amateur photographers and few possessed 35mm cameras able to take Kodachrome. Most of the available second-hand 'Leica' and 'Contax' cameras had been 'liberated' from Germany. *(Harold Stillwell)*

TT.35 TA634 (G-AWJV) taxies at Bovingdon during the filming of *Mosquito Squadron* in July 1968. TA634 wears the code letters 'HT-C', but also sported 'HT-G' and 'HT-L' at various points in the production. The cable guard frame forward of the tailwheel (a legacy of the Mosquito TT.35 conversion) had been removed from the other airworthy TT.35s (RS709 and RS712) employed for the film, making TA634 readily identifiable in certain scenes. Neil Williams piloted TA634 throughout the filming, having conducted his first Mosquito solo flight on this particular aircraft. Following TA634's acquisition by the Mosquito Museum in 1970, Neil Williams regularly visited to sit in the cockpit of 'his' Mosquito. Note the dummy machine-guns on the nose Perspex. TA634's original Perspex nose (complete with its 'machine-gun' attachment holes) is today installed on the Imperial War Museum's TT.35 TA719 at Duxford. *(Bob Tatum collection)*

FB.VI N9909F (ex-PZ474) at Whitman Air Park, San Fernando, California, during the late 1950s. Photographed while under the ownership of California Air Charter, the aircraft languished outside at Whitman Air Park until 1970, by which time it had fallen into a state of extreme dereliction. N9909F's remains were subsequently acquired by Jim Merizan, who intended to restore the aircraft to an airworthy condition. Although much work was undertaken to achieve this goal, PZ474 has yet to be completed and its wing is currently in outside storage at Chino Airport. Note the open ventral bay doors and the oil-streaked engine lower cowlings. *(Bernard B. Deatrick, via Stuart Howe collection)*

This picture was taken by 8 Group (Pathfinder Force) Photographic Officer Howard Lees during a Russian Air Force visit to RAF Wyton in 1945. The Mosquito under scrutiny is a Percival-built B.XVI, possibly from 128 Squadron, which was based at Wyton between September 1944 and June 1945. An 8 Group (Pathfinder Force) Squadron, 128 operated a mix of Mosquito B.XXs, B.XXVs and B.XVIs with the Light Night Striking Force, flying a total of 1,416 sorties until May 1945. Note the yellow spinners, a feature of 128 Squadron's Mosquitoes that continued postwar when the unit was re-numbered 14 Squadron. *(Howard Lees)*

T.3 RR299 photographed in around 1966 during the early days of its career as a display aircraft. Allocated the civil registration G-ASKH in 1965, RR299 was initially demonstrated in this overall silver dope scheme, the spinners later being re-painted yellow. The inscription on the nose reads 'DE HAVILLAND MOSQUITO – TWO ROLLS ROYCE MERLIN 25 ENGINES'. *(John Stride collection)*

The old and the new: T.3 RR299 photographed with a 23 Squadron Tornado F.3 on 11 May 1991. Flown by Tony Craig (then Chief Test Pilot at British Aerospace Chester), RR299 was on its way to display at 23 Squadron's Leeming base. The Mosquito and Tornado were briefed to rendezvous over the bay by Lancaster University, the Tornado then escorting RR299 into Leeming as the cameras made the most of this rare photo-opportunity. This trip marked Tony Craig's last display in RR299, which he had been demonstrating (with great panache) for British Aerospace since early 1984. The outing was especially fitting for Tony as during his RAF career he had previously served with 23 Squadron, the great wartime exponents of the Mosquito, which operated the type until May 1952. *(23 Squadron, via Tony Craig)*

FB.40 A52-110 of 94 (Attack) Squadron RAAF photographed at Castlereagh, NSW, in August 1945. The final RAAF Mosquito Squadron formed during the Second World War, 94 came into being at Castlereagh on 30 May 1945 but disbanded only four months later. During the V-P celebrations on 16 August 1945, three 94 Squadron FB.40s flew under Sydney Harbour Bridge in close formation! A52-110 joined 94 Squadron on 2 August 1945 but entered storage in 1946 and was Struck Off Charge in July 1949. Note the tail of FB.VI A52-537 (ex-HR577) to A52-110's left.
(Frank Smith, via Stuart Howe)

This newly completed FB.40 has been rolled out from the Australian de Havilland factory at Bankstown. Note the underwing bomb carriers and 'needle'-blade propellers, the latter a feature of the first 100 (Packard Merlin 31-powered) Australian-built Mosquitoes. Subsequent FB.40s were equipped with Packard Merlin 33s and 'paddle'-blade propellers. This FB.40 is finished in Foliage Green overall.
(Milton Kent, Hawker de Havilland)

94 Squadron RAAF FB.40 A52-92 was photographed probably at Castlereagh in August 1945. A52-92 was built at Bankstown in May 1945 and delivered to 94 Squadron on 17 August. Following 94 Squadron's disbandment the aircraft entered storage with 2 AD in September 1945, being disposed of four years later. A52-92 is finished in silver overall with black spinners. The RAAF national markings are applied in white and blue with the fuselage serial number in Night.
(Frank Smith, via Stuart Howe)

FB.40 A52-62 at the de Havilland Bankstown factory in 1945. A52-62 was later converted into a PR.41 and re-serialled A52-324. Following a period in storage, it was sold to Sqn Ldr A. J. R. 'Titus' Oates in November 1952 for entry in the 1953 England to New Zealand International Air Race. As 'VH-KLG' ('KLG' in recognition of KLG Spark Plugs, one of the aircraft's sponsors), A52-324 underwent modifications at Bankstown including the installation of additional fuel tanks in the ventral bay (enclosed within a 'bulged' fairing protruding beneath the lower line of the fuselage). Sadly, navigational problems forced VH-KLG to ditch off Mergui during the flight to England on 3 October 1953, thus ending the career of a very potent racing aeroplane. In this photograph A52-62 is finished in Foliage Green. *(Milton Kent, Hawker de Havilland)*

Taken at the Bankstown factory in November 1946, this picture shows de Havilland staff with one of the 212 Mosquito airframes produced in Australia. From left to right, the people depicted in this photograph are Fred Glenloud, Bill Hawkins, Harry Broe, Bill Haase, Ron Lambert, Fred Lowe, Harry Regan, Dick Aldred and Charlie Luxmore. Australian Mosquito variants were all based on the FB.40 airframe, six being converted into PR.40s, twenty-two into T.43s and twenty-eight into PR.41s. Judging by the nose machine-guns and faired-over cannon ports, this particular machine may be a T.43 (although it lacks the 'paddle'-blade propellers normally associated with the Australian Trainer version). Note the incomplete lower engine cowlings and the unpainted cockpit entrance and machine-gun access doors. *(Hawker de Havilland)*

FB.40 A52-50 served with 5 OTU at Williamtown NSW before disposal in 1949. By the time of the Japanese surrender in August 1945, 108 FB.40s had been produced by the de Havilland Australia Bankstown factory. *(Milton Kent, Hawker de Havilland)*

No 1 Squadron (RAAF) Mosquito FB.VI A52-526 'NA-E' is undergoing major servicing at Kingaroy, Queensland, in 1945. Note that the ventral gun bay doors are in the open position, allowing access to the four 20mm cannon. Standard Motors-built as HR506, A52-526 served with No 1 Squadron throughout its operational career and was eventually scrapped in 1950. A52-505 'NA-Q' (ex-HR366) can be seen to the left of the picture. *(Frank Smith/R. A. Little, via Stuart Howe)*

FB.VIs A52-515 'NA-V' (ex-HR408) and A52-508 'NA-L' (ex-HR307) of 1 Squadron (RAAF) are pictured at Labaun Island, Borneo, in 1945. The first 1 Squadron FB.VI to operate from Labuan was A52-521 (ex-HR488) in July 1945, the remainder of the unit's aircraft arriving the following month. On 8 August 1945 seven of the Squadron's FB.VIs raided Kuching, losing one of their number (A52-510, ex-HR412) in the process. With the Japanese surrender imminent, 1 Squadron spent the remainder of the war flying seaward reconnaissance patrols before operations ceased on 15 August. Standard Motors-built A52-515 served only with 1 Squadron and was sent to the DAP for disposal in 1949. A52-508 (another Standard Motors-produced aircraft) was converted to components in 1946. Note that A52-515 is fitted with exhaust shrouds while the aircraft on the far right features open stubs. All three Mosquitoes are equipped with 100-gallon underwing drop tanks, and A52-515 carries the inscription 'Mid-Night' on the crew entrance door. *(Frank Smith, via Stuart Howe)*

This spectacular shot depicts FB.VIs of 1 Squadron RAAF in July 1945. The aircraft nearest the camera is Standard Motors-built A52-500 (ex-HR302), which was lost after it crashed during take-off from Labuan on 11 August 1945. *(RAAF, via BAe Systems)*

This 'Vic' formation of 1 Squadron (RAAF) FB.VIs comprises (left to right) A52-526 'NA-E' (ex-HR506), A52-500 'NA-A' (ex-HR302) and A52-505 'NA-J' (ex-HR336). Following the Japanese surrender, 1 Squadron remained on Labuan Island flying tactical reconnaissance flights until the end of August 1945. In October the Squadron was ordered to shepherd aircraft of the RAAF's 81 Wing to Japan as they were required for occupation duties. However, the Labaun wet season severely affected the adhesion of the Mosquitoes' mainplane fabric and 1 Squadron's aircraft were ordered back to Australia before the situation worsened. By the close of November 1945 the Squadron's aircraft had been despatched to No 2 AD at Richmond. A52-526 was scrapped after being sold in 1950, A52-500 crashed taking off from Labaun on 11 August 1945, and A52-505 was converted to components in 1946. 1 Squadron officially disbanded at Narromine on 7 August 1946. Originally delivered in the factory camouflage scheme, 1 Squadron's FB.VIs were later refinished in silver overall in order to reflect heat from their airframes. *(RAAF, via BAe Systems)*

FB.VI TA373 photographed during its delivery flight to the RNZAF in 1947. A Hatfield-built Mosquito, TA373 was delivered direct from the factory to 27 MU on 18 March 1945. Allocated to 305 Squadron, it received battle damage on 12 April, repairs being undertaken by Martin Hearn and taking six months to complete. On 10 November 1947, following two years in storage, TA373 was flown from 27 MU to No 1 Overseas Ferry Unit at Pershore by ferry pilot Richard Livermore. Here it was prepared for delivery to New Zealand, Richard carrying out an air test and 3-hour cross-country flight in order to evaluate the aircraft's cruising performance and fuel consumption. Fitted with 100-gallon underwing drop tanks, TA373 left Pershore on 14 November 1947 on the first stage of its flight to New Zealand. Flown by Richard and navigated by New Zealander Flt Sgt Bob Greig,

TA373 escorted two Spitfire IXs to Egypt for the first leg of the trip before proceeding solo to New Zealand, which was reached on 18 December after 55hrs 45mins flying time.

Assigned the RNZAF serial number NZ2373, TA373 was ferried to Woodbourne shortly after delivery, where it remained in storage until declared surplus under RNZAF Surplus Return 4106. In April 1953 the aircraft was sold by GSB tender 4980 and later scrapped. The first picture was taken at Malta on 17 November, while the second one features TA373 at Darwin on 3 December. Note that the spinners are almost completely devoid of their black paint, which was stripped off by rain during the delivery flight. Although a late production FB.VI with Merlin 25s, TA373 is equipped with 'needle'-blade propellers.
(Both Richard Livermore)

An unidentified FB.26 retracts its undercarriage shortly
after take-off from RCAF Edmonton in the late 1940s.
(Bill Cottrell, Alberta Aviation Museum Collection)

FB.26 KA133 'A' pictured at RCAF Edmonton during 'Air
Force Day' on 11 June 1949. At that time KA133 is believed
to have been on the charge of the Winter Experimental
Establishment and still wears the distinctive nose marking
applied during its former service with 133 Squadron
(RCAF). During the Second World War 133 Squadron was
the only home-based RCAF unit to fly Mosquitoes
operationally. Stationed at Patricia Bay, British Columbia,
133 stood by to intercept long-range fire balloons released
from Japan. Note the identification letter 'A' beneath the
forward section of the nose (applied to the spent .303in
ammunition chamber access panel), and the protective
covering on the machine-guns. KA133 is equipped with
Hamilton Standard-built 'paddle'-blade propellers. The
nose marking is believed to have been applied in red.
(W. Cottrell, Alberta Aviation Museum Collection)

FB.26 KA143 at RCAF Edmonton in the late 1940s. The FB.21 was intended as the initial Canadian Fighter-Bomber version, and two pre-production aircraft were constructed in late 1943. Serialled KA100 and KA101, they were powered by Packard Merlin 33s and were equivalent to the British-built FB.VI Series 1. Canadian production then focused on Mosquito Bomber versions, latterly the B.XXV with Packard Merlin 225 engines. The first 'true' production Canadian Fighter-Bombers appeared in October 1944 and were also powered by Merlin 225s, receiving the designation Mosquito FB.26. The majority of FB.26s were retained in Canada by the RCAF (many later being sold to Nationalist China), but more than seventy were delivered to the RAF, some serving with 249 Squadron in Kenya, others with 55 Squadron at Hassani in Greece. KA143 remained in Canada, its armament removed by the time of this picture. Note the Canadian practice of extending the Dark Green camouflage up the fin and rudder of Mosquito Fighter-Bomber versions. *(Bill Cotterell, Alberta Aviation Museum Collection)*

This postwar shot depicts FB.26 KA539 bogged down at RCAF Edmonton; it appears to have suffered a take-off, landing or taxying accident, but damage seems confined to the tailwheel and rear fuselage. Note the lack of exhaust stubs on the starboard engine outboard side. KA539 was sold to China on 5 April 1948 and assigned the Chinese Air Force serial number '126'. Both of KA539's propellers are in the feathered position. *(Bill Cottrell, Alberta Aviation Museum Collection)*

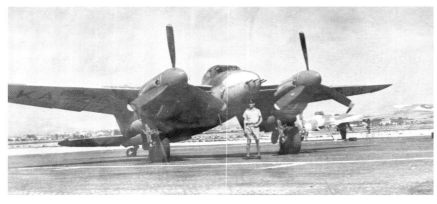

55 Squadron FB.26 KA263 photographed at Hassani in Greece during 1946. KA263 was built by de Havilland Canada and flown to the UK during July 1945. Delivered to 10 MU on 19 July, the aircraft went to 13 MU on 6 November. In February 1946 KA263 passed to No 1 Ferry Unit before despatch to the Mediterranean Theatre on 23 March. Two days later it arrived at Hassani, where it entered service with 55 Squadron. Later stored, KA263 was eventually Struck Off Charge on 31 December 1946. This Mosquito was one of the relatively few FB.26s to enter RAF squadron service. *(Stuart Howe collection)*

Lt Cdr S. M. P. Walsh DSO DSC & Bar, the Commanding Officer of 811 Squadron Fleet Air Arm, is pictured with one of the Squadron's FB.VIs at Ford. A former wartime Wildcat Squadron, 811 re-formed at Ford in September 1945. Initially equipped with FB.VIs, the Squadron received twelve Sea Mosquito TR.33s in April 1946, half of them being withdrawn on the unit's move to Brawdy later the same year. 811 Squadron disbanded on July 1947, re-forming with Sea Furies at Arbroath six years later. *(Bill Holdridge, via Stuart Howe collection)*

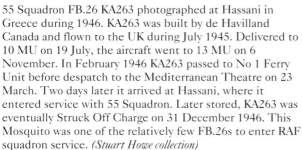

FB.VI TE710 'FD-4K' of 811 Squadron (Fleet Air Arm) takes off from Ford in 1946. Standard Motors-built TE710 was assigned to the Royal Navy on 24 August 1945, passing to 811 Squadron at Ford in January 1946. It later served with 790 Squadron at Dale and Culdrose, suffering a landing accident on 10 January 1948 that caused the port undercarriage to collapse. Embalmed at Stretton in July 1950, TE710 was eventually sold as scrap to R. A. Short on 18 November 1953. *(Bill Holdridge, via Stuart Howe)*

FB.VI TE708 of 762 Squadron (Fleet Air Arm) is at the Royal Navy shore base HMS *Seahawk* (Culdrose) in 1949. This Standard Motors-built FB.VI was assigned to the Fleet Air Arm on 24 August 1945, passing to 811 Squadron at Ford (as 'FD4G') in 1946. TE708 also served with 787 Squadron at West Raynham before transfer to 762 Squadron at Culdrose on 19 October 1948. Following storage at Culham and Lossiemouth, this FB.VI was sold to R. A. Short on 28 November 1953. Note that the aircraft's nose machine-guns have been removed. *(R. Neep, via Ken Lambert and Stuart Howe)*

FB.VIs of 811 Squadron (Fleet Air Arm) are lined up at their Ford base in 1946. Nearest the camera is TE701 'FD4A', which was assigned to the Royal Navy on 24 August 1945, passing to 811 Squadron by January 1946. This FB.VI was transferred to 780 Squadron at Peplow on 9 September 1946 before delivery to the Aircraft Holding Unit at Stretton two

weeks later. Following overhaul at the de Havilland Leavesden factory, TE701 flew to the Receipt & Despatch Unit at Culham in November 1950, later passing to the Aircraft Holding Unit at Stretton, where it was sold as scrap to R. A. Short in November 1953. *(Bill Holdridge)*

762 Squadron (Fleet Air Arm) FB.VI TE829 '465 CW', seen at Culdrose in 1948, was a Standard Motors-built aircraft assigned to the Royal Navy on 9 October 1945, and passing to 762 Squadron at Ford in February 1946. TE829 moved with 762 Squadron to Culdrose before entering storage at Stretton, where it remained until July 1950. Following a spell at Yeovilton, it was stored at Culham and Lossiemouth before sale as scrap in November 1953 to R. A. Short, who sold it on to the Israeli Air Force. TE829 is finished in silver overall with yellow training bands on the wings and rear fuselage. Note the trolley accumulator parked next to the port side of the fuselage. *(R. Neep, via Ken Lambert)*

Mosquitoes of 762 Squadron (Fleet Air Arm) are pictured at Culdrose in 1948. Formed at Yeovilton on 23 March 1942, 762 Squadron was an Advanced Flying Training School Squadron initially equipped with Fairey Fulmars. The Squadron later moved to St Merryn, receiving Grumman Martlets and Miles Masters before returning to Yeovilton in September 1942. Re-equipped with Sea Hurricanes, 762 disbanded into 761 Squadron in June 1943. Nine months later 762 Squadron re-formed as the 'Twin Engine Conversion Unit' (formerly part

of 798 Squadron) flying Beauforts and Oxfords at Yeovilton before moving to Halesworth on 3 December 1945. Here it was enlarged to include a Mosquito conversion section, the Squadron being retitled the 'Heavy Twin Conversion Unit' when it moved to Ford in January 1946. 762 finally moved to Culdrose in May 1948, where it was disbanded in December the following year. The Mosquito second from the right is FB.VI TE829 '465 CW'. Note the Airspeed Oxford on the right. *(R. Neep, via Ken Lambert)*

Photo Reconnaissance Mosquitoes

The Mosquito opened and closed its front-line RAF operational career as a Photographic Reconnaissance aircraft. This role is fundamental to the Mosquito story, for despite being designed as an unarmed bomber the type was initially accepted by the Air Ministry as a high-speed reconnaissance aircraft. The first batch of fifty Mosquitoes included one Prototype (W4051) and nine production reconnaissance aircraft designated Mosquito PR.1. Broadly similar to W4050 (the original Mosquito Prototype), PR.1s featured short engine nacelles and were powered by Merlin 21s. On 17 September 1941 PR.1 W4055 of No 1 PRU carried out the first operational sortie by a Mosquito.

Several F.IIs were adapted to carry cameras, including W4089, DD615, DD620 and DD744, but their range was restricted, so the B.IV provided the basis for the next batch of Photographic Reconnaissance Mosquitoes, the PR.IVs. B.IV Series 1 W4067 had previously been adapted for photographic reconnaissance duties, but more than thirty B.IV Series iis were converted into PR.IVs, the first operational flight being undertaken by DK284 in April 1942. PR.IVs served well, but their performance capabilities were limited by their single-stage engines. Several had long lives, including DZ383, which began its career with 540 Squadron before transferring to the RAF Film Production Unit for the remainder of the war.

The demand for increased altitude and speed performance led to the PR.VIII, a converted B.IV equipped with two-speed, two-stage supercharged Merlin 61 engines. Five PR.VIII conversions were built before the introduction of the PR.IX, a refined production version of the PR.VIII fitted with Merlin 70 series engines. The PR.XVI was developed from the PR.IX, but featured a pressurised cockpit enabling aircraft to operate at increased altitudes, thereby decreasing the chances of interception.

One of the most capable Photographic Reconnaissance Mosquito versions was the PR.32, of which four were built. Based on the PR.XVI but substantially lightened and fitted with extended wingtips, PR.32s were powered by Merlin 113/114 engines and operated at altitudes of more than 40,000 feet, with a top speed of more than 425mph.

The ultimate Photographic Reconnaissance Mosquito was the PR.34, an ultra-long-range version that could be described as a flying fuel tank. The PR.34 featured enlarged ventral bay doors to accommodate two long-range fuel tanks, which, coupled with the aircraft's ability to carry 200-gallon drop tanks, provided the PR.34 with a maximum fuel load of 1,267 gallons and a range of 3,340 miles. PR.34s arrived just in time to take part in the war, operating long-range flights with 684 Squadron from the Cocos Islands. PR.34s served with the postwar RAF in the UK and the Middle and Far East. On 15 December 1955 81 Squadron PR.34A RG314 made the last front-line operational sortie by an RAF Mosquito.

A small number of B.35s were converted into PR.35s for night photographic reconnaissance and photographic training. Several of these served with 58 Squadron at Benson. PR.35 conversions included TA650, TJ124, TK632 and VR805.

A small number of Canadian-built B.VII and B.XX Mosquitoes were converted into Photographic Reconnaissance aircraft for the USAAF and received the designation F-8-DH. A failure in their intended role, several later served as bombers with the RAF.

Two Photographic Reconnaissance versions of the Mosquito were produced in Australia, the PR.40 and the PR.41. The PR.40 was an adaptation of the FB.40 airframe, the first example (A52-2) being the second Mosquito constructed in Australia. The first PR.40 operational flight took place in June 1944 and a total of six aircraft were built. The PR.41 was a conversion of the FB.40 but powered by two-speed, two-stage supercharged Packard Merlin 69 engines. Twenty-eight were manufactured, the last example being delivered to the RAAF in July 1948. PR.41s were used extensively on postwar aerial survey work over Western Australia.

With Geoffrey de Havilland Junior at the controls, PR.1 Prototype W4051 climbs away from Hatfield on the occasion of its maiden flight. A Salisbury Hall-built prototype, W4051's original fuselage was diverted to W4050 after the latter was damaged during A&AEE trials on 24 February 1941. W4051 was subsequently fitted with a production PR.1 fuselage and on 10 June 1941 became the third Mosquito to fly. Note the full 54ft 2in wingspan (as opposed to W4050's 52 feet) and the short-span (19ft 5½in) 'No 1' tailplane. Also apparent are the single-piece trailing edge flaps associated with the short nacelle configuration. *(BAE SYSTEMS)*

W4051 illustrates the PR.1's sleek form during a flight from Boscombe Down in the summer of 1941. The first Mosquito version to enter RAF service, the PR.1 was powered by Merlin 21s and initially equipped with three vertical cameras (two positioned at the forward end of the ventral compartment and one in the aft lower section of the rear fuselage), this later being increased to four, including an obliquely mounted unit on the fuselage port side. Ten PR.1s were built, four of them (W4060, W4061, W4062 and W4063) as long-range aircraft with an overload 151-gallon fuel tank (the PR.1's normal fuel load was 536 gallons) installed in the fuselage. The contents of this tank were supplied to the main system by an electrically driven immersed fuel pump. W4062 and W4063 were tropicalised and featured altered radiator flap settings in comparison to earlier production aircraft.

Although a Prototype aircraft, W4051 (together with W4054 and W4060) was employed on PR.1 acceptance trials at the A&AEE, Boscombe Down, being used for radio tests as well as an evaluation of camera and cabin temperatures. W4051 later flew operationally with No 1 PRU (as 'LY-U') from Benson and Leuchars, and in September 1942 was fitted with a long-range fuel tank. This aircraft was later allocated to 521 (Meteorological) and 540 Squadrons before transfer to 8 OTU in August 1943. Damaged on 19 April 1944, it was due for repair but was re-categorised as a write-off on 17 May 1945. In addition to being the prototype PR.1, W4051 was also the first Mosquito delivered to the RAF. Note the rear fuselage camera port and the short engine nacelles. At the time of this picture W4051's upper surfaces are believed to have been finished in Medium Sea Grey and Olive Green with the under surfaces in Sky Blue. During service with No 1 PRU W4051's under surfaces were refinished in PRU Blue. *(Aeroplane Monthly)*

On 13 September 1941 the Secretary of State for Air, Sir Archibald Sinclair, made an official visit to No 1 PRU at RAF Benson. While he was there he received a 15-minute flight in a Mosquito PR.1 flown by Sqn Ldr Rupert Clerke. Here Sir Archibald is about to board the aircraft, which was probably W4056. *(Wg Cdr J. H. Weaver, RAF Museum)*

Sqn Ldr Rupert Clerke of No 1 PRU is pictured with PR.1 W4056 at Benson. On 17 September 1941 Sqn Ldr Clerke (with navigator Sgt Sowerbutts) carried out the first Mosquito operational flight when he flew W4055 on a reconnaissance sortie to Brest and the Spanish-French frontier. W4055 performed well, but the mission was unsuccessful due to electrical problems that prevented the cameras from working. In addition to flying the first Mosquito operational sortie, Rupert Clerke later carried out the first Mosquito day combat (flying 157 Squadron F.II DD607) when he shot down a Ju88 off the Dutch coast on 30 September 1942.

W4056 was delivered from Hatfield to No 1 PRU on 27 August 1941 and was shot down over Stavanger during a reconnaissance flight on 3 April 1942. Its lower surfaces are likely to have been finished in PRU Blue with the upper surfaces in Medium Sea Grey and Olive Grey. Note the 42-inch '1-3-5-7'-proportioned red, white, blue and yellow fuselage roundel. No 1 PRU informally christened its PR.1s after varieties of liqueur, including 'Curacoa' and 'Benedictine', the latter applied to W4055. *(Wg Cdr J. H. Weaver, RAF Museum)*

PR.IV DZ383 pictured while on the strength of 540 Squadron at Benson in May 1943. Converted from a B.IV Series ii on the Hatfield production line, DZ383 was delivered to 540 Squadron on 30 November 1942, and served with it until damaged in a flying accident on 29 July 1943. Following repairs by Martin Hearn, DZ383 entered storage at 27 MU before allocation to the RAF Film Production Unit for use within 138 Wing, 2nd Tactical Air Force. It often accompanied 138 Wing's FB.VIs during their low-level precision operations, filming and photographing attacks such as the raid on Egletons School by 613 Squadron on 18 August 1944. In order to take part in these operations, DZ383's PR Blue paint scheme gave way to the standard Mosquito Day Bomber finish (complete with '?' marking on the fuselage sides forward of the roundel). Additionally, extra nose glazing was installed to facilitate a wider field of view for the cameraman. This much-travelled aircraft was eventually retired to 44 MU on 5 July 1945 and Struck Off Charge thirteen months later. *(Alan Brackley collection)*

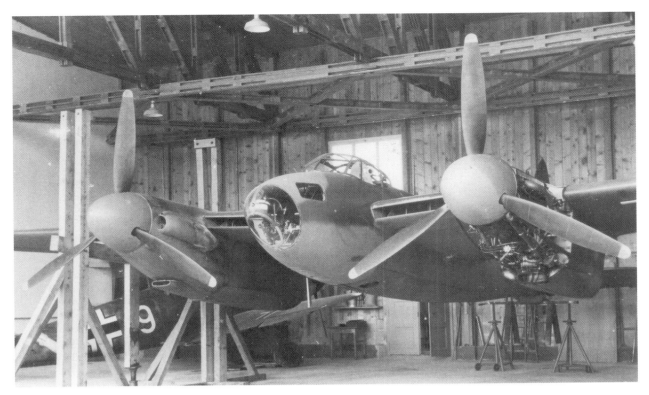

PR.IV DK310 of No 1 PRU took off from Benson on 24 August 1942 to photograph Italian cruisers under construction in the Adriatic ports of Venice, Trieste, Pola and Fiume. Crewed by Canadian pilot Flt Lt Gerald Wooll and navigator Sgt John Fielden, DK310 left Benson at 0925hrs and headed for Ford aerodrome, where DK310's fuel tanks were topped up before departing for Venice. During the outward flight, south-westerly winds blew DK310 slightly off course, causing it to infringe the Swiss border north of Baden. Around this time the port engine temperature began to increase and, despite corrective measures, glycol fumes began to emit from the overflow vent. Flt Lt Wooll shut down the engine and feathered the propeller, continuing on at reduced speed to a point where the Swiss, Italian and German borders merged. The crew were not particularly concerned at the prospect of a single-engine flight over the target area, but knew that they would be in trouble on the return trip, especially if the Germans realised that they were over Italian naval yards (not to mention the difficulty of crossing the Alps).

However, approximately 2 hours after take-off the crew were alarmed to see paint peeling off the starboard engine cowlings, and initially thought that the engine was on fire. The situation was obviously now drastic, and DK310 was committed to a forced landing. Descending through broken cloud at 10,000 feet, Flt Lt Wooll spotted 'a nice green

field straight ahead, within gliding distance' where he landed 2hrs 15mins after leaving Ford. DK310 had arrived at Belpmoos aerodrome, five miles from Berne. The crew were interned and DK310 locked up in a hangar with two Luftwaffe Messerschmitt Bf109Fs that had inadvertently landed at Belpmoos a month before.

DK310 was meticulously examined by the Swiss, revealing that the port radiator shutter had jammed in the closed position, leading to coolant loss and engine overheating. The starboard engine problems were caused by an oil leak. Following a year of negotiations DK310 passed to the Swiss Army as 'E-42' before transfer (as HB-IMO) to Swissair; the aircraft's ultimate fate is detailed in the Civil Mosquitoes chapter. Flt Lt Wooll and Sgt Fielden were later repatriated to the UK in exchange for the two German pilots whose Messerschmitts shared the same hangar as DK310! Flt Lt Wooll returned to Canada as a test pilot on Canadian-built Mosquitoes at Downsview. He and Sgt Fielden had previously flown DK310 on a 4hrs 50mins flight from Gibraltar photographing landing spots for 'Operation Torch'.

Here we see DK310 at Belpmoos undergoing examination by the Swiss during the summer of 1942. Note one of the interned Messerschmitts parked beyond it.
(Archiv Flieger Flab Museum, Dubendorf)

Geoffrey de Havilland Junior brings PR.IX MM230 close to the camera aircraft during a test flight from Hatfield on 7 October 1943. A refined version of the PR.VIII, the PR.IX was the first two-speed, two-stage supercharged Merlin Mosquito variant to enter quantity production, the initial example (LR405) making its maiden flight in April 1943. PR.IXs were powered by Merlin 70 series engines (72/73 or 76/77) and ninety were built before being superseded by the pressure-cabin-equipped PR.XVI on the Hatfield production lines. MM230 was retained for trials work at Hatfield and Ford, which included testing of the exhaust shrouds developed for the Mosquito NF.30. In January 1946 MM230 entered storage at 44 MU before being Struck Off Charge ten months later. It is finished in PRU Blue and carries 50-gallon underwing drop tanks. Although not featured on this aircraft, many PR.IXs were equipped with an observation blister on the canopy roof escape hatch. Note that the canopy starboard direct vision quarter window is in the open position. *(BAE SYSTEMS)*

The first Mosquito PR.VIII, DK324, made its maiden flight from Hatfield on 20 October 1942. A conversion of the B.IV Series ii airframe, the PR.VIII was the first operational Mosquito version to be powered by two-speed, two-stage supercharged engines, in this case 1,565hp Merlin 61s; these were necessary to increase speed and altitude performance during long-range flights over Europe. Four additional B.IV Series iis were converted to PR.VIII standard (DZ342, DZ364, DZ404 and DZ424), these acting as a stop-gap pending arrival of the first production two-stage Merlin variant, the PR.IX. On 28 November 1942 DK324 was delivered to the A&AEE at Boscombe Down for acceptance trials and drop tank tests, these being followed by an evaluation of climb performance during January 1943. In April 1943, after further trials at Boscombe Down, DK324 was transferred to RAF Benson before issue to 540 Squadron the following month.

DK324 flew operationally until damaged in a take-off accident at Leuchars on 2 September 1943, repairs (which probably included conversion to B.IX standard) not being completed until February 1944. Transferred to 1409 Flight on 2 March, DK324 passed to 139 Squadron two weeks later, where it was allocated the unit code letters 'XD-R'. Operating to Cologne on 21 March, DK324 had completed a total of fifty-eight operations by 7 August and was transferred to 109 Squadron shortly afterwards. It flew nine sorties with 109 Squadron, the last on 15 September 1944, after which it underwent repairs between October 1944 and March 1945. 44 MU took delivery of DK324 on 2 April 1945, the aircraft remaining in storage until Struck Off Charge on 1 November 1946. *(Imperial War Museum)*

Bomber and Photo Reconnaissance Mosquitoes undergoing modifications at Marshalls Flying School, Cambridge, in around early 1944. On the right is a B.IV Series ii aircraft modified to carry the 4,000lb bomb (note the enlarged elevator horn balances). Marshalls Flying School is an integral part of the Mosquito story and made a huge contribution to the aircraft's success both during and after the war. Marshalls overhauled, modified and repaired Mosquitoes and was responsible for the NF.XII and NF.XVII conversion programmes (from F.IIs) in addition to modifying several 'Highball' and 4,000lb bomb-carrying B.IV Series iis (many of the 'Highball' machines being test-flown by Marshalls' test pilot Leslie Scratchland). The Mosquito has another very significant link with Marshalls Flying School in the form of Norman de Bruyne, who in 1929 became one of the Flying School's first three pupil pilots and later invented the synthetic glues used in Mosquito construction. *(The Marshall Group of Companies)*

In this rare formation shot of three PR.IXs, nearest the camera is LR432 'L1' of 544 Squadron, built at Hatfield and equipped with Merlin 72/73 engines. LR432 entered RAF service with 540 Squadron in September 1943 before passing to 544 Squadron a month later. Flown on several occasions by the celebrated Photographic Reconnaissance pilot John Merifield, LR432 completed a total of forty-three operations before passing to 8 OTU on 22 January 1945. Delivered to 71 MU on 31 August 1945, LR432 was Struck Off Charge twelve days later. *(Photographer unknown)*

Beautiful spy: PR.XVI NS705 is seen during a test flight from Hatfield in 1944. The PR.XVI was developed from the PR.IX, but featured a Westland Valve 2.5lb per sq in cabin pressurisation system (based upon that fitted to Mk XV MP469) enabling operations up to 36,000 feet. DZ540, a converted B.IV Series ii, acted as the Prototype PR.XVI and first flew in July 1943. During acceptance trials at the A&AEE, DZ540 was flown at the maximum permissible weight of 22,340lb with the centre of gravity 16.1 inches aft of datum. This corresponded to the photographic reconnaissance loading with 760-gallon overload tanks in the ventral bay as well as 50-gallon drop tanks. Some of the tests were made with bombs in place of the overload tanks to enable jettison (to lighten the aircraft) in the event of an emergency landing. DZ540's performance measurements were generally similar to B.IX LR495, making allowances for differences in weight and external equipment.

During tests of DZ540's cabin pressurisation system no internal misting was encountered, but above 23,000 feet some frosting occurred on the single-thickness portions of the canopy Perspex. The double-layer bulged side windows and upper front panel remained clear at all times. Noise from the cabin supercharger and piping 'generally was not considered excessive but the whine was scarcely audible if the fixed air supply opening was covered with the hand'. Despite successful trials with DZ540, the initial PR.XVIs to enter squadron service were not popular with crews due to canopy internal misting and icing problems, together with the lack of bulged side windows and cockpit roof observation blisters. The icing and misting difficulties were cured following trials with MM352, after which PR.XVIs really came into their own.

Delivered to Benson on 30 September 1944, Hatfield-built NS705 was despatched to the MAAF, where it was issued to 680 Squadron in December 1944. On 20 January 1945, crewed by Fg Offs Christiensson and Wheeler, it took off on a reconnaissance flight to Blechammer and Odertal but suffered engine problems twenty miles from the target and landed at Novi Sad near Belgrade. Following repairs NS705 returned to 680 Squadron, but suffered a landing accident at San Severo on 20 May 1945. The resulting damage was not repaired, NS705 being Struck Off Charge on 30 August 1945. Note the 100-gallon drop tanks. (Charles E. Brown, RAF Museum)

140 Squadron PR.XVI NS580 'Z' pictured at Melsbroek in early 1945. 140 Squadron received its first Mosquito PR.IXs in November 1943 and began photographic reconnaissance operations over Western Europe in preparation for the Allied invasion. On 4 February 1944 140 Squadron conducted the first operation by a Mosquito PR.XVI when MM279 flew to the Cabourg-St Aubin region. Bad weather and night photography were also undertaken by 140, its crews undergoing Gee and Rebecca-H training in early 1944. During July and August 1944 140 Squadron monitored enemy troop concentrations (and communications systems) by both day and night, the latter sorties being carried out using photoflash equipment. Moving from Northolt to Normandy (Balleroy) in September 1944, 140 arrived at Melsbroek on 26 September, where it remained until relocating to Eindhoven in February 1945. Hatfield-built NS580 was delivered to Benson on 24 July 1944 before passing to 218 MU on 27 November. Allocated to 140 Squadron on 4 January 1945, NS580 was retired to 9 MU eight months later and sold as scrap to Lanzers on 6 August 1947. Note the photo-electric cells and the TR 1143 beam approach aerial beneath the rear fuselage. NS580 was equipped with Rebecca-H. *(M. R. S. Cunningham MBE)*

Higher, farther and faster than ever, the Mosquito brings all Europe under the eyes of the Royal Air Force

DE HAVILLAND

In the attack today, on the trade routes of the future

(BAE SYSTEMS)

Typical of the work conducted by Photographic Reconnaissance Mosquitoes is this shot featuring the Baltic coast port of Gdynia. *(Stuart Howe collection)*

Pilots and navigators of 1409 Flight pictured at RAF Wyton on 19 April 1945. During the war Photo Reconnaissance Mosquito variants were operated on meteorological duties by both the RAF and the USAAF. Long-range meteorological flights over enemy territory were vital in order to provide detailed forecasts prior to Bomber Command and USAAF raids. This information would lower loss rates and reduce the level of abandoned sorties linked to poor weather conditions. Meteorological operations received the code name 'PAMPA', and 1401 Flight (attached to Coastal Command) was formed in August 1941 to undertake this specialist work. Initially equipped with Spitfires, 1401 received a converted Mosquito B.IV Series ii (DK285) in April 1942 and flew its first Mosquito 'PAMPA' sortie the following July. A month later 1401 Flight became 521 Squadron, and continued to operate Mosquito IVs until 31 March 1943, when they were allocated to the newly formed 1409 Flight at RAF Oakington. 1409 Flight came under the control of Bomber Command and continued the Mosquito 'PAMPA' operations flown by 521 Squadron. Mosquito crews received specialist meteorological training, enabling them to record and report comprehensive information that was often relayed home prior to landing. 1409 Flight later received Mosquito PR.IXs and PR.XVIs, and operated the celebrated PR.IX ML897 'D for Dorothy'.

The personnel featured in this group are (back row, left to right) Fg Off Jones, Harry Gilmour, Eric Adams, Wrey, Flt Lt Birchmore, John Kennedy and Fg Off Clive Bancroft; (front row, left to right) Fg Off Ted Royall, Bennet, Flt Lt Ricky Elias, CO Sqn Ldr Johnny Johnson, Lowther, Hughes and Fg Off George Dunn. Seated on the ground immediately in front is Fg Off Con Saunders holding George, the CO's pet dachshund. The Mosquito in the background is likely to be PR.XVI NS736, which was allocated to 1409 Flight on 29 October 1944 and received the code letter 'B' in January 1945. NS736 was written off in a landing accident at Lyneham on 14 March 1946. *(George Dunn)*

Aluminium-doped PR.XVI NS787 starts its engines in readiness for another sortie, probably from Alipore in early 1945. A tropicalised PR.XVI, NS787 was delivered from Hatfield to Benson on 23 November 1944 before despatch to No 1 OAPU three weeks later. Allocated to ACSEA, NS787 served with 684 Squadron and received the unit code letter 'M'. 684 Squadron flew deep-penetration reconnaissance flights over Burma and Siam and later sent a detachment of PR.34s to the Cocos Islands. NS787 survived the war to be Struck Off Charge on 26 September 1946. LAC R. S. Jones is operating the Ki-gass priming pump (located on the engine/undercarriage mounting structure aft of the fireproof bulkhead) through the access door on the starboard engine nacelle. *(Photographer unknown)*

684 Squadron PR.XVI NS645 receiving attention to its starboard propeller on the Cocos Islands in 1945. From June 1945 684 Squadron maintained a detachment (from Alipore) on the Cocos Islands for very-long-range reconnaissance flights over Malaya and Java. Equipped with PR.34s and long-range PR.XVIs, the first operation took place on 13 July when PR.34 RG185 'Z' (seen on the right behind NS645) flew to Point Pinto via Morib. 684 Squadron's PR.34s made some of the longest reconnaissance flights of the war, including a 2,600-mile (9hrs 5mins duration) sortie from the Cocos to Penang Island. Built at Hatfield and equipped with Merlin 72/73s, NS645 was delivered to Benson on 13 August 1944 before proceeding to 10 ADU on 8 September. Allocated to ACSEA and assigned to 684 Squadron, NS645 was eventually Struck Off Charge on 14 February 1946. It features aluminium-doped upper surfaces and PRU Blue under surfaces with National Markings applied in blue and SEAC white. Note the drop tank (from a Hawker Hurricane) fitted beneath NS645's forward fuselage; several 684 Squadron PR.XVIs carried these tanks, which were normally jettisoned after use but occasionally carried a forward facing F-24 camera. *(Francois Prins)*

PR.XVI A52-616 of the Survey Squadron RAAF undergoes a starboard engine inspection at Clonawry in June 1947. Originally constructed at Hatfield as RF975, this PR.XVI was transferred to the RAAF in 1945 and re-serialled A52-616. After the war the RAAF used its remaining wartime PR.XVIs for survey flights over Western Australia until they were replaced by PR.41s in 1947. Following its withdrawal from active service, A52-616 entered storage before being sold as surplus in 1954. Its airframe is finished in aluminium dope with the spinners and nose anti-glare panel in black. *(J. Jordan, via Stuart Howe)*

The PR.32 was developed to operate above 40,000 feet and provided a useful platform for eluding German jet and rocket interceptors. Based upon the PR.XVI airframe, the PR.32 was fitted with extended wingtips and specially lightened to increase altitude and speed performance. Development work on the aircraft's design was carried out using PR.XVI MM328, and a total of four production aircraft (NS586 to NS589) were constructed at Hatfield in late 1944. PR.32s were the first Mosquitoes powered by the new fuel-injected Merlin 100 series engines (Merlin 113/114) and possessed a service ceiling of 43,000 feet.

The final production PR.32, NS589 is fitted with 'paddle'-blade propellers and 100-gallon drop tanks. PR.IXs were the first Photographic Reconnaissance Mosquitoes to be fitted with 'paddle'-blade propellers, the installation affording a distinct improvement in speed and high-altitude capability. NS589 was allocated to 540 Squadron and carried out the first PR.32 operational sortie when it flew to Darmstadt and Mannheim on 5 December 1944. 544 Squadron received NS587, which attained an altitude of 42,500 feet during a sortie to Lake Constance on 9 April 1945. NS586, the first PR.32, was employed for trials of de Havilland four-blade hydromatic propellers incorporating double-acting governors, and in this configuration NS586 was tested at the A&AEE at Boscombe Down in March and April 1945. Three flights had been made by 8 April (only one of which was successful) before NS586 suffered structural failure and crashed four days later. PR.32s had an all-up weight of 22,122lb (with 100-gallon drop tanks) and were some 30mph faster than the standard PR.XVI. *(Stuart Howe collection)*

RG176, the first production PR.34, shows off the type's enlarged ventral bay doors, similar to those featured on the B.XVI. Developed from the PR.XVI, the PR.34 was designed for ultra-long-range reconnaissance, and featured increased internal fuel tankage and provision for the carriage of 200-gallon underwing drop tanks. The enlarged ventral bay doors enclosed two long-range fuel tanks mounted in tandem beneath the centre section tanks. The front tank was a short type (100 gallons capacity) enabling cameras to be fitted in the bay's forward section, while the rear tank held 152 gallons. Some PR.34s were equipped with 176-gallon forward tanks. but these could be changed for the 100-gallon type if cameras were installed. This extra tankage (coupled with the 200-gallon drop tanks) brought the PR.34s total fuel capacity to 1,267 gallons, providing a range of 3,340 miles. To lighten the aircraft and increase ceiling, all armour plating and fuel tank bullet-proofing was removed.

The third production PR.34 (RG178) was employed on handling trials at A&AEE Boscombe Down during March 1945. Underwing drop tanks were not carried on this aircraft, which weighed in at 22,510lb with the centre of gravity 17.2 inches aft of datum. In this condition RG178 was reported as 'very pleasant to fly and is considered acceptable for Service use. The ailerons are its most pleasant feature, and though the aircraft is difficult to trim accurately at high altitude, once trimmed it will hold a constant airspeed, even in disturbed air.' These comments were not generally borne out in squadron service, the PR.34 being markedly heavier and considered less tractable than earlier Mosquito versions.

RG176 served on trials work at Boscombe Down before conversion to PR.34A standard in 1950. Later allocated to 540 Squadron at Benson, RG176 was written off after the undercarriage collapsed during a single-engine landing on 6 June 1952. Note the enlarged elevator horn balances, necessary to improve stability and handling as the PR.34 operated at substantially higher weights than the PR.XVI. Early PR.34s featured the standard Bomber/Photo Reconnaissance Perspex nose with glass centre panel, this being replaced by a one-piece Perspex unit on later production aircraft. The bulge above the starboard ventral bay door is the housing for the fuel cooler radiator, which was mounted on the rear section of the starboard fuselage under wing side panel. *(BAE SYSTEMS)*

A pair of 81 Squadron PR.34s fly low over Victoria, Labaun, during the King's Birthday flypast on 7 June 1951. Roy Quantick is leading in RG299 (left) with PF668 on his port side. This rare sight only usually occurred when two aircraft returned from survey flights concurrently, thus indulging in a bit of formation practice! *(Roy Quantick)*

Mosquito PR.34A RG236 photographed at Hatfield on 19 November 1949. The PR.34 and PR.34A were identical structurally, but the latter variant incorporated additional equipment. This included an ARI 5083 Gee receiver positioned on the wing deck (the indicator being installed behind the pilot's seat) and a DR Compass suspended from a bracket attached to the roof of the rear fuselage. Rebecca Mk 4 (TR 3624) navigation equipment was mounted in the rear fuselage (with its indicator unit located on the instrument panel at the navigator's position), together with an Air Mileage Unit fitted to the rear fuselage port side. Two HX2 generators were installed (one on each engine) with AC supply obtained from a rotary converter mounted in the dinghy bay. The PR.34A was powered by two Merlin 114As, had a total fuel capacity of 1,267 gallons and possessed a maximum all-up weight (including two 100-gallon drop tanks) of 22,190lb. Note the Gee whip aerial extending from the rear of the cockpit canopy and the TR 1430 aerial positioned on top of the fuselage (forward of the roundel). The small circular window in the rear fuselage (immediately aft of the roundel) is for the DR Master Compass Unit, and the wingtip aerials are connected to the Rebecca navigation equipment. PR.34A conversions were undertaken by Marshalls at Cambridge. *(BAE SYSTEMS)*

This cockpit view of PR.34A RG236 shows the DR Compass Repeater Unit and Heading Indicator on the centre of the cockpit coaming, with the pilot's blind flying panel directly beneath it. The internal access door is hinged upwards and clearly shows the drift sight mounted within its aft section (the sight was protected by a cover when not in use). The throttle quadrant is mounted on the left-hand cockpit wall with the compass and engine instrumentation directly ahead of it. Visible forward of the pilot's seat are the rudder pedals and control column, with the brake lever located above the column's right-hand yoke. For leg reach, the rudder pedals were adjustable, fore-and-aft, by lifting them against the tension of the springs from one ratchet plate slot to another. The drop tank jettison switch is on the top far left of the cockpit immediately below the port direct vision quarter window. *(BAE SYSTEMS)*

With its starboard radiator removed and the propeller feathered, Overseas Ferry Unit PR.34 RG190 sits forlornly at Mauripur in January 1951. RG190 had been engaged on a 'Big Brother' escort flight, shepherding Vampires from Fayid to Singapore during the active period of the SW monsoon. Flown by Flt Sgt Richard Livermore and navigated by Flt Sgt Cliff Pemberton, RG190 left Fayid on 30 December 1950 with a Vampire convoy (together with a single Spitfire PR.XIX) bound for Mauripur as their first stop. Having successfully reached Mauripur the convoy took off on 2 January 1951 with Palam as its next destination. After around 50 minutes' flying time RG190's starboard engine temperature began to rise, so the propeller was feathered and the convoy returned to Mauripur. Inspection revealed that the starboard radiator had burst, so a signal was sent for a replacement unit. Mosquito PR.34 PF630 subsequently took over the convoy ferry to Singapore, RG190 returning to Fayid on 9 January following repairs.

Hatfield-built RG190 previously served with 544 Squadron, the Photographic Reconnaissance Development Unit and 540 Squadron, ultimately being sold as scrap to David Band on 27 May 1954. Note the single-piece Perspex nose, which was a distinctive feature of later production PR.34s. The vertical lines on the nose were applied as an aid to calculate drift during photographic runs.
(Richard Livermore)

In the ventral bay of PR.35 TK615 are three light series carriers for the aircraft's load of twelve 4.5-inch photo-flashes. A conversion of the B.35, the PR.35 was designed for night photographic reconnaissance and photographic training together with a secondary role of day photography. The twelve photo-flashes were employed for medium-level night photography, low-level night photography being undertaken using twelve 1.5-inch photo-flash cartridges in two multi-flash dischargers (the dischargers were mounted in the rear section of each engine nacelle with their flare chutes projecting downwards). Two cameras were located in the rear fuselage between bulkheads four and five, each camera mounted in a wooden crate bolted to ferrules in the inner fuselage skin. Four alternative split camera pairs could be installed, the various types consisting of K.19Bs with photo-electric cells; F.61s with speeded-up gear boxes; 20-inch-lens F.52s; or 36-inch-lens F.52s. Camera crates were not interchangeable and were clearly labelled with the aircraft's serial number, the type of camera carried and its position within the aircraft. The ventral bay photo-flashes were released via a switch marked 'FLASH JETTISON' located below the DR Compass Repeater on the cockpit coaming. Neither bombs nor long-range tanks were fitted to the PR.35.

PR.35s served with B Flight of 58 Squadron, including the first PR.35 conversion, RS700. Constructed at Hatfield, TK615 entered storage with 274 MU in December 1945, passing to 38 MU in June 1947. Converted to PR.35 standard by Marshalls in 1950, TK615 was allocated to the A&AEE at Boscombe Down in March 1951, where it was written off in a landing accident two years later. A total of fifteen B.35s were converted to PR.35 standard. This photograph was taken on 6 April 1951. *(BAE SYSTEMS)*

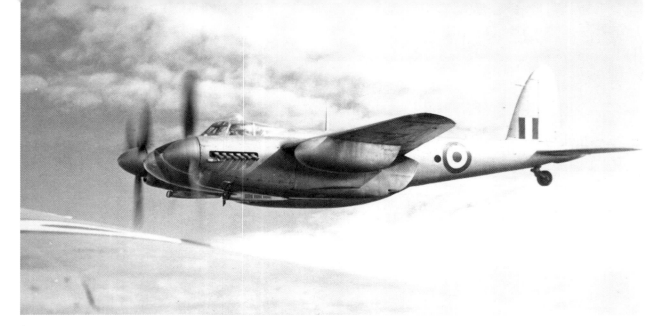

81 Squadron PR.34 PF677 en route from Labuan Island to Singapore on 30 September 1950. Note the camera port just forward of the fuselage roundel, and the 100-gallon underwing drop tanks. The deep belly profile of the PR.34 (well illustrated here) cut the aircraft's maximum speed by some 6mph. This picture was taken from 81 Squadron PR.34 PF668 flown by Roy Quantick. *(Roy Quantick)*

81 Squadron PR.34 PF677 undergoes inspection at Seletar in 1950. Built by Percival's Luton factory in May 1946, PF677 was delivered to 38 MU before allocation to the FEAF on 30 June 1950. Assigned to 81 Squadron on 13 September 1950, it was damaged in a take-off accident on 7 August 1951. During the course of this incident the aircraft swung to port, the swing being corrected to starboard in order to avoid a Dakota, before the Mosquito came to rest with a severely strained undercarriage and damaged tailplane. Following repairs it returned to 81 Squadron on 5 September 1951 before passing to 390 MU on 1 November 1952. PF677 ended its days as Instructional Airframe 7147M with the RAF Malaya Training School, being Struck Off Charge on 28 September 1954. PF677 wears an aluminium-doped finish (severely weathered on the spinners and fin leading edge) with serial numbers applied in Night. Note the camera port in the starboard ventral door's forward section, and the single-piece Perspex nose. *(Ken Dunbar)*

Roy Quantick and navigator Pop Reilly beat up the Labuan coral strip runway (originally constructed by the Japanese) in 81 Squadron PR.34 PF677. The date is 12 June 1951 and Roy has just returned from a 5hrs 35mins survey flight to Sarawak and Towns. On return from a sortie, 81 Squadron's Mosquitoes often carried out a low flypast if they had a full magazine of pictures. Note the locked-down tailwheel. *(Roy Quantick)*

81 Squadron groundcrew personnel SAC Ted Wilkins (right) and Cpl Turner take a break from servicing instruction at Seletar in around 1954. The Mosquito behind them is PR 34A RG205, which was built at Hatfield as a PR.34 in April 1945, serving with 544, 540 and 58 Squadrons before conversion to PR.34A standards between August 1951 and March 1952. Following a year in storage, RG205 was allocated to the FEAF and delivered to 81 Squadron at Seletar in February 1953. It was written off at Butterworth on 28 February 1955 after an undershoot on landing led to the collapse of the undercarriage. RG205's upper surfaces are finished in light grey with the lower surfaces and fin in PR blue. Note the thin black demarcation line between the fuselage colours. *(SAC E. Wilkins, 81 (PR) Squadron, Seletar)*

A picture you can hear! An unidentified 81 Squadron PR.34 (probably RG299), flown by Sgt Paddy Hood, beats up Labuan Island airstrip during a survey detachment from Seletar in 1951. 81 Squadron's primary task at Labuan was map-making photography utilising cameras with a slightly larger field of view than those normally carried in the aircraft. Existing maps of British North Borneo and Sarawak were inaccurate, so 81 Squadron flew numerous survey flights to record known and uncharted areas. The pictures were processed by No 2 Air Survey Liaison Unit of the British Army, which was permanently attached to 81 Squadron. The sighting and aligning of the survey run was controlled from the nose of the aircraft by the navigator. *(Roy Quantick)*

Taken at the end of its operational career, this picture
depicts PR.40 A52-2 'Old Faithful', the second Australian-
built Mosquito. A conversion of the FB.40 airframe, six
PR.40s were constructed in response to initial RAAF
requirements for a Photo Reconnaissance version of locally
produced Mosquitoes. In a remarkably short time A52-2
was equipped with two split F-24 8-inch cameras in the
nose, and one F-52 20-inch camera in the rear fuselage.
Delivered to No 1 PRU RAAF, A52-2 became the first
Australian-built Mosquito to operate against the Japanese
when it flew a reconnaissance mission from Coomalie
Creek to Ambon on 1 June 1944. It went on to complete a
total of thirty-eight operational sorties before conversion to
components following a mainplane inspection on 12 June
1945. Note the camera fairings beneath the nose, and the
lack of undercarriage doors on the starboard nacelle. A52-2
is finished in PRU blue. *(Milton Kent)*

This fine postwar shot is of PR.40 A52-6, the longest-serving example of this particular Mosquito variant. Six PR.40s were constructed (A52-2, A52-4, A52-6, A52-7, A52-9 and A52-26), the last five with provision for one vertical camera in the nose as well as two mounted obliquely in the aft fuselage. During the war A52-6 served operationally with 87 (PR) Squadron and later passed to the Survey Flight RAAF. However, the latter chose not to operate A52-

6 and standardised on the PR.XVI pending arrival of PR.41s. On 10 May 1949 this aircraft was allocated to No 3 AD Amberley for storage. Note the longitudinal stiffening strake on the fuselage and the oblique camera installation beneath the lower section of the fuselage roundel. A52-6 is finished in aluminium dope with the spinners in black. *(Photographer unknown)*

An unidentified PR.41 of 87 (Survey) Squadron RAAF photographed at Fairbairn by Noel Sparrow in 1952. The PR.41 was the only production two-speed, two-stage supercharged Merlin Mosquito variant to feature the original Fighter nose shape, albeit modified for the Photographic Reconnaissance role. A very handsome aeroplane, the PR.41's lines were pleasing in comparison to the British-built two-stage Merlin Mosquito Night-Fighters

with their 'bull-nose' radomes. This aircraft may be A52-302, which was originally laid down as FB.40 A52-193 but was later converted to PR.41 standard and re-serialled A52-302. Following service with 87 (Survey) Squadron, A52-302 was sold to R. H. Grant Trading Company in 1958 and later scrapped. It is finished in silver overall with black spinners and a black anti-glare panel immediately forward of the windscreen. *(Noel Sparrow)*

PR.41s of 87 (Survey) Squadron RAAF are being overhauled by the Service Department of the Australian de Havilland Company. PR.41s were employed extensively on aerial survey work over Australia, detachments often operating from unsealed strips and under adverse conditions of heat and dust. These aircraft replaced the RAAF Survey Squadron's PR.XVIs in 1947 (the unit being retitled No 87 (Survey) Squadron in March 1948), mapping large areas of north-west Australia with occasional detachments abroad, including Fiji and New Guinea. This work ceased in August 1953 when PR.41 A52-308 flew a survey run over Noonkanbah in Western Australia, and by the close of the year 87 (Survey) Squadron had been disbanded. The propellers on the Mosquito in the foreground appear to have been paint-stripped for inspection, this aircraft also displaying its port Merlin 69's intercooler radiator. Note the engine coolant header tanks visible on the right-hand aircraft. *(Visatone)*

81 Squadron aircrews are pictured with one of the unit's PR.34s at Seletar. The gentleman are (left to right) Flt Lt Fish, Flt Sgt 'Chas' Kirkham, Fg Off A. J. 'Collie' Knox, Fg Off Peter Cross, Sgt John Fordham and Flt Lt 'Tommy' Thompson. 81 Squadron's part in the history of the Mosquito should not be underestimated, but is often overlooked. The leading Photographic Reconnaissance Squadron in the FEAF, 81 Squadron saw the Mosquito through its final years of front-line RAF service and maintained an excellent serviceability rate. This is especially significant as the Squadron was operating in a climate that proved problematic during initial deployment of the type.

Between 1941 and 1946 81 Squadron served in the fighter role before re-forming at Seletar in September 1946 as the renumbered 684 Squadron. Equipped with Mosquito PR.34s and Spitfire PR.XIXs, the Squadron's initial postwar task was aerial survey work over Malaya, Thailand, Java, Hong Kong, Burma and Borneo. From June 1948 it was heavily involved in Operation 'Firedog', flying photographic reconnaissance missions over the Malayan jungle to locate Communist terrorist hideouts. In December 1955 an 81 Squadron Mosquito PR.34 (RG314) carried out the RAF's final front-line Mosquito operation, bringing the total number of 81 Squadron 'Firedog' sorties to 6,619. Former 81 Squadron personnel justly retain a tremendous pride for their Squadron and its achievements.
(Former SAC 'Wilbur' Wright, ex-81 PR Squadron)

LAC 'Red' Skelton supervises the refuelling of an 81 Squadron PR.34 that has just returned from an operational sortie. Over mainland Malaya large high-topped thunder clouds built up in the afternoon as the hot sun dispersed morning ground mists. Such conditions obviously negated photography, so 81 Squadron's Mosquitoes took off just after dawn (around 0630hrs) and returned at midday. The camera magazines were immediately removed and the pictures developed while groundcrews inspected and refuelled the aircraft in readiness for another early start the next day.

Note the camera port forward of the fuselage roundel. PR.34s featured mountings for the installation of cameras in six positions according to operational requirements. The installation arrangements were as follows. 1: Two F.52 cameras (working as a pair) with either 36-, 20- or 14-inch lenses mounted vertically (or obliquely) for split photography, at the rear of bulkhead four. Alternatively, the rear two mountings could accommodate a 12-inch-lens K.17 camera for vertical photography. 2: One K.17 camera (with 6-inch cone) mounted vertically forward of bulkhead five. 3: One F.24 camera, mounted for oblique photography, exposing through the window in the port side of the fuselage at 15 degrees depression angle. 4: Two F.52 cameras with 14-inch lenses mounted for split photography at the forward end of the ventral compartment. The camera control panel was situated in the nose aft of the Mark IX bombsight.
(SAC E. Wilkins, 81 (PR) Squadron, Seletar)

A second FB.VI was 'semi-navalised' as a back-up trials aircraft to LR359. This was LR387, seen here at Hatfield in later form as the Prototype Sea Mosquito TR.33. LR387 was flown to Farnborough on 1 March 1944, proceeding to RNAS Arbroath on 18 March for arrestor gear proofing trials. The following month it was based at Crail (with the Fleet Air Arm Service Trials Unit) and conducted deck landings aboard HMS *Indefatigable* during May 1944. To be more representative of the Sea Mosquito design, LR387 returned to Hatfield for extensive 'navalisation' modifications, emerging as the Prototype TR.33 in May 1945. This work included a major redesign of the wing structure (overseen by de Havilland designer W. A.

Tamblin) to facilitate folding of the outer wing panels, installation of American AN/APS-4 ASH radar (in a thimble-shaped nose radome), and provision for the carriage of a single 2,000lb 18-inch Mk XV or XVII torpedo. LR387 was employed on arrestor wire tests with the RAE before allocation to 778 Squadron (Fleet Air Arm) for deck landing trials aboard HMS *Illustrious*.

In the first picture note the torpedo beneath LR387 and the longitudinal stiffening strake mounted externally on the fuselage. The second shot shows to advantage the fold joint fairings on the wing upper surfaces. LR387 is thought to have ended its useful life as an instructional airframe at Yeovilton. *(BAe Systems/Richard Riding collection)*

This close-up shot shows the torpedo mounting points beneath TR.33 Prototype LR387. TR.33s carried a 2,000lb Mk XV or XVII torpedo released via a push button (which also operated the torpedo camera) on top of the control column. The torpedo was supported by a tube mounted on the lower boom of the forward main spar. An alternative under-fuselage load was a single sea mine or a 2,000lb bomb. Like the FB.VI, two 500lb bombs could be accommodated within the fuselage bomb bay, together with two more under the wings. Eight rocket projectiles (four per wing) could also be carried, this number being reduced to four when 50- or 100-gallon drop tanks were installed. *(BAE SYSTEMS)*

The port wing of TR.33 Prototype LR387 being folded at Hatfield on 12 June 1945. Had Sea Mosquito squadrons ever operated from aircraft carriers, this manual operation would have been performed by deck handling parties. Power folding was not introduced as this would require a complete redesign of the aircraft's hydraulic system, and its absence also saved weight. Four hinge castings were fitted on each side of the wing between the centre section and outer wing panels, bolted to spruce blocks incorporated within the wing structure between the spars. In the extended position the wings were locked by two pins engaging lugs on the outer wings at the front and rear spars. In the folded position the outer wings rested on two damper jury struts (the port one is just visible in this picture) inserted through holes running from the undercarriage bays through to the wing upper surface. Two tethering eyes at the wingtips and one each side of the cockpit canopy were used in conjunction with special reinforced bungee cable to secure the wings. To save disconnecting the aileron cables when folding the wings, doors were provided in the wing upper surface to allow the cables to fold without fouling the structure. To ensure the wings were locked in the spread position before take-off, the pilot would check that the indicator flag in the region of the rear spar (as viewed from the cockpit) was out of sight. The wings were not folded when 100-gallon drop tanks were fitted and filled. *(BAE SYSTEMS)*

For TR.33 handling trials, two fixed-wing pre-production aircraft were constructed at Leavesden. AID Chief Inspector Eddie Riding photographed the first of these, TS444, shortly after roll-out from the factory. During 1946 TS444 was employed on armament and handling trials at Boscombe Down and Farnborough before allocation to the Royal Naval Aircraft Repair Yard at Fleetlands. The latter move was rescinded, however, and TS444 flew to Hatfield for modifications in preparation for further trials work. During mid-1947 it conducted tests at Defford (in connection with propeller controlling characteristics) before returning to Hatfield on 17 July for major repairs. 790 Squadron (Fleet Air Arm) at Culdrose was next to receive TS444, the aircraft arriving in October 1948 before moving to Brawdy for Fleet Requirements duties (with Airwork) during May 1950. Following overhaul by Brooklands Aviation, TS444 entered storage at Culham, later moving to Stretton, where it was sold as scrap to R. A. Short in November 1953. Note the arrestor hook, four-bladed propellers, underwing rocket rails and the 'Circle P' (for 'Prototype') marking on the rear fuselage. TS444 appears to be finished in Slate Grey and Ocean Grey camouflaged upper surfaces with yellow under surfaces. Although not equipped with folding wings, TS444 carries fold joint fairings on the wing upper surfaces. *(Richard Riding collection)*

TS449, the second pre-production TR.33, photographed at Hatfield on 16 April 1946 following the installation of RATOG (Rocket Assisted Take-Off Gear) on the rear fuselage. Note the Lockheed oleo-pneumatic AIR 35792 undercarriage legs and the small-diameter main wheels. The Mosquito's aerofoil section (Piercy Section RAF 34 with modified camber) provided a low maximum lift coefficient resulting in a flat landing approach.

During deck landing trials the high power needed to maintain speed at safe limits led to a critical engine cut height with the conventional rubber-in-compression undercarriage legs. This became apparent during trials with LR359 as the undercarriage gave an excessive rebound ratio if the aircraft contacted the deck in anything but a three-point landing. To overcome this

problem, Lockheed long-stroke oleo-pneumatic undercarriage units were fitted to dampen the 'bounce' effect (being tested on TR.33 Prototype LR387).

TS449 carried out RATOG trials with the RAE and aboard HMS *Illustrious* during 1946 before allocation to 'C' Squadron of the A&AEE in November 1947. TS449 later served with 790 Squadron (Fleet Air Arm), at Culdrose (as '406'), and with Airwork at Brawdy before entering storage at Lossiemouth in July 1952. Sold as scrap to R. A. Short in August 1953, TS449 later entered service with the Israeli Air Force. Parts of the aircraft exist to this day and are being incorporated into the restoration of FB.VI TA122 at the de Havilland Heritage Centre, Salisbury Hall. TS449's upper surfaces appear to be finished in Ocean Grey with the under surfaces in Sky. *(BAE SYSTEMS)*

This close-up shot shows the RATOG (Rocket Assisted Take-Off Gear) installation on the fuselage of pre-production TR.33 TS449. For carrier take-offs in overloaded condition, RATOG would have been very necessary for Sea Mosquito operations. Lt Cdr Eric Brown flew TS449 on RATOG tests at Farnborough during May and June 1946 before the aircraft went on to conduct

further RATOG trials aboard HMS *Illustrious* the following August. For the Farnborough tests, TS449 was loaded to a weight of 22,560lb, which included a 2,000lb torpedo and two 250lb bombs. Four RATOG rockets were employed to simulate short carrier take-offs, the rockets being jettisoned shortly after the aircraft became airborne. *(BAE SYSTEMS)*

TS449 photographed with flight shed personnel at the de Havilland Leavesden factory in early 1946. Standing in front of the aircraft are (left to right) production foreman H. G. Harris, test pilot S. F. Offord and flight shed superintendent J. H. Simpson. TS449 is equipped with de Havilland four-bladed propellers (Type D/14/445/2) of 12ft 6in diameter, which provided a thrust improvement of between 5 and 10 percent over the more conventional three-bladed units. Four-bladed propellers were vital for the Sea Mosquito's shipboard role where maximum revs and thrust were required from the onset of the limited take-off run. Note the small-diameter main wheels and the Lockheed long-stroke oleo-pneumatic undercarriage legs. In contrast to the earlier photograph of W4096 (see page 141) this provides a good illustration of the second type of ice guard fixing on Mosquitoes equipped with tropical air intakes, the guard frame fixed at four points on the intake's upper and lower lips. Neither TS444 nor TS449 were equipped with folding wings. *(Richard Riding collection)*

During the war shortages of AI Mk X radar led to the installation of American AN/APS-4 radar in several 100 Group (RAF) FB.VIs. AN/APS-4 was originally designed as an 'X Band' ASV radar, but could be used for Airborne Interception work and possessed a range of approximately 3¾ miles. In RAF and Royal Navy service AN/APS-4 received the designation AI Mk XV, but was more commonly known as ASH (Air-to-Surface Home). Sea Mosquito TR.33s were equipped with ASH and this photograph is believed to depict the installation in either TS449 or an early production

TR.33. The nose radome (referred to as the ASH 'bomb') housed the ASH transmitter/receiver, the indicator control unit and amplifier being installed in the cockpit (in this photograph the ASH 'bomb' is hinged downwards in the servicing position). Note the radar junction box mounted centrally on the nose armour plate with the windscreen wiper motor to its right. The panel hanging beneath the nose provided access to the camera gun. In order to provide cooling air for the radar equipment, TR.33s incorporated suction louvres on their nose access doors. *(BAE SYSTEMS)*

This view through the cockpit entrance hatchway of an early TR.33 shows the navigator's chart board case (secured by bungee chord) with the Aldis signalling lamp coiled on top of it (the lamp lead was plugged into a socket located in the cockpit roof adjacent to the floodlight). The ASH indicator control unit is in the stowed position (on a hinged mounting) at the top of the cockpit, with the bomb door, undercarriage and flap selector levers to its left. The panel positioned lower right of the selector levers housed the switching arrangements for the fuselage bombs, mines and torpedo, as well as the wing bombs and drop tanks. This panel's top section also featured a master switch with three positions: 'GUN CAMERA-RP; TORPEDO-BOMBS; MINES-TORPEDO CAMERA'. This permitted the master firing switch on the control column to be used for the release of the torpedo, bombs, rocket projectiles or mines or for the independent operation of the gun camera or torpedo camera (when fitted). The TR.33 had provision for two F.52 cameras in the rear fuselage, both installed forward of bulkhead number five. *(BAE SYSTEMS)*

The cockpit of a TR.33 contained the ASH radar indicator control unit (Type 97) on the right-hand side. A Mk VI drift recorder could be mounted in the cockpit floor with its sighting head positioned between the navigator's knees (the sighting head was stowed on the starboard side of the cockpit when not in use). Note the GM2L reflector gun-sight on the cockpit coaming above the pilot's blind flying panel. The gun-sight's 'ON-OFF' switch is located on the starboard switch panel with its dimmer control positioned under the coaming. The throttle and pitch control levers are mounted in a quadrant on the left-hand side of the cockpit wall (the pitch control levers are visible over the top of the pilot's seat), with the compass and engine instruments directly ahead. The arrestor hook was released by means of a lever positioned just forward of the throttle quadrant, but could not be reset to the 'up' position from the cockpit. A Type G torpedo director (located immediately in front of the navigator), together with a computer in the nose, controlled the torpedo gyro-angling unit installed on the port bomb door. The TR.33's FB.VI ancestry is particularly evident in this shot. *(BAE SYSTEMS)*

299

The Sea Mosquito TR.37 Prototype, TW240, displays its elongated nose radome. Derived from the TR.33, the TR.37 was specifically developed to carry two 1,000lb 'Uncle Tom' rocket projectiles beneath the wings. 'Uncle Tom' required a specialist ASV Mk XIII radar installation, which was housed within the large radome. Alternative armaments were a single 18-inch Mk XVII torpedo beneath the fuselage or four rocket projectiles under each wing (or two rockets per wing when drop tanks were fitted). Additionally, in place of the 'Uncle Tom' rockets two 500lb Mk 8 sea mines could be carried. In contrast to the TR.33, TR.37s were armed with only two 20mm cannons, the centre gun louvres being faired over. The fourteenth production TR.33, TW240 was delivered from Leavesden to Hatfield in January 1946 for conversion to the TR.37 Prototype. Sea Mosquito fuselage modifications necessitated relocation of the rear access hatch (on the starboard side) to beneath the fuselage, the hatch illustrated in the open position in this picture. *(BAE SYSTEMS)*

This is a close-up shot of the ASV Mk XIII radar installation in TR.37 Prototype TW240. Transversely mounted forward of the armoured bulkhead is the Type 196/WW radar modulator unit; the Type 80A radar scanning unit was enclosed within the nose radome's front section (the TR.37 featured the longest nose radome of any radar-equipped Mosquito version). The transmitter-receiver (Type TR 3523A) is fitted in the port side of the nose with the amplifier directly behind it. The radar's power unit was positioned on fuselage bulkhead four with the strobe unit located on the rear face of bulkhead three. Note the bullet deflector plate on top of the forward fuselage. *(BAE SYSTEMS)*

The cockpit interior of TR.37 Prototype TW240 shows the ASV Mk XIII radar indicator unit (in the stowed position within a pivoting crate) on the right-hand side. Above the indicator unit are the propeller feathering buttons, which also incorporate warning lights for low engine oil pressure and coolant. Jettison switches for the underwing drop tanks and RATOG rockets are positioned top left above the engine instrumentation. The reflector gun-sight is located on the cockpit coaming, with the rudder trim control to the right. To assist with sighting of the 'Uncle Tom' rockets, a Type S wind computer was mounted on the canopy structure with a UT computer aft of the pilot's seat. The gun-sight incorporated a red warning light (visible at the top rear centre), a cancelling switch being fitted next to the throttle box with an 'ATTACK' switch installed on junction box B (the latter visible on the starboard cockpit wall next to the navigator). To record instrument readings, two bantam cameras were fitted in the cockpit canopy structure, their power drawn from the torpedo camera circuit; the left-hand camera centred on the ATM compass indicator, the right-hand one on the torpedo director control. Unlike the TR.33 and FB.VI, the TR.37's engine starter and booster coil push buttons were installed on junction box B (the NF.30, 36 and 38 being similarly equipped). *(BAE SYSTEMS)*

TR.37 Prototype TW240 is seen at Hatfield in August 1947 with a Hornet and two Vampires awaiting delivery in the background. TW240 passed to the A&AEE at Boscombe Down in December 1946 for handling trials with 'Uncle Tom' rockets before passing to the TFU at Defford for radar tests. June 1947 saw TW240 back at Hatfield for installation of an experimental static vent before proceeding to Boscombe Down for handling, position error and deck landing trials. 771 Squadron (Fleet Air Arm) operated TW240 from August 1949 before the aircraft entered storage at Stretton in January 1950, eventually being sold as scrap to R. A. Short on 18 November 1953. Mounting points for the 'Uncle Tom' rockets are just visible beneath TW240's wings. The TR.37 incorporated an additional pitot head located on the outboard leading edge of the starboard wing. In connection with development work on the Comet airliner, the Horsa glider on the right was fitted with a mock-up of the airliner's proposed nose design. *(Richard Riding collection)*

Twenty-six TR.37s were ordered for the Fleet Air Arm, but only six were constructed (at a cost of £13,832 each), the remaining twenty being cancelled. This photograph depicts the first production aircraft, VT724, shortly after roll-out from the de Havilland Chester factory in 1948. Between August and December of that year VT724 conducted trials work on the 'Uncle Tom' rocket installation before passing to the Receipt & Despatch Unit at Culham. Later entering storage at Stretton, VT724 was sold as scrap to R. A. Short on 23 July 1953. Note the RATOG attachment points on the lower fuselage, and the radio altimeter aerial beneath the starboard wing. Sea Mosquitoes were equipped with enlarged elevator horn balances, the starboard one just discernible in this picture. VT724 is not equipped with an arrestor hook. *(BAE SYSTEMS)*

This frontal shot of VT724 shows the four-bladed propellers and the ASV Mk XIII radar installation's nose radome. The TR.37 carried a single G.45B cine-camera in the port wing (visible immediately right of the port engine's outboard exhaust stubs), which operated automatically when the guns were fired. Additionally, an F.46 torpedo camera could be mounted under the starboard wing in place of a drop tank.

Aerobatics in the TR.37 were only performed when sufficient fuel, oil and ammunition had been expended (and all external stores jettisoned) to reduce the weight to 19,100lb. TR.37s had a maximum speed of 383mph at 20,000 feet and a still-air range of 1,100 miles. Note the newly completed Mosquito NF.38 in the background beyond VT724's starboard wing. *(BAE SYSTEMS)*

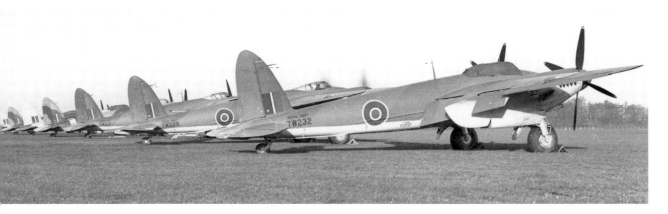

These brand new TR.33s, T.3s and NF.36s were photographed at Leavesden by Eddie Riding in late 1945. The initial four aircraft in this line-up are, from right to left, TR.33s TW232, TW229 and TW231, and T.3 TV973. TW232 served with 703, 771 and 790 Squadrons (Fleet Air Arm) before being sold as scrap to R. A. Short in July 1953. TW229 carried out radio trials work with the A&AEE and RAE before passing to 790 Squadron (Fleet Air Arm) at RNAS Dale. TW229 crashed after the port engine caught fire during an air test on 16 December 1946. TW231 served with the RN Air Section at RAF Defford until written off in a ground collision with a taxying Lancaster on 29 May 1947.

On 26 November 1945 Eddie Riding flew in TW231 during a test flight from Leavesden. The pilot on this occasion was S. F. Offord, who dived TW231 from 6,000 feet before low-flying between Watford and Dunstable. The final part of the test flight included a 'beat-up' of Eaton Bray with one propeller feathered! Note that the TR.33s sport Ocean Grey and Slate Grey camouflaged upper surfaces with their lower surfaces finished in Sky. The NF.36s are distinguishable by their Medium Sea Grey fins and rudders. An early production TR.33, TW232 features fixed wings and the conventional rubber-in-compression undercarriage legs. *(Richard Riding collection)*

This rare shot of TW227, the first production TR.33, was taken at Leavesden on 12 November 1945. Four days later TW227 was delivered to A&AEE Boscombe Down for general handling trials before passing to the ATDU at Gosport in July 1946. TW227 later served with Airwork from Brawdy, St David's and Hurn before entering storage at Lossiemouth in April 1953. The initial thirteen production TR.33s featured fixed wings and rubber-in-compression undercarriage legs. TW227 was Struck Off Charge in August 1953 and later scrapped. The Mosquito parked next to it is NF.36 RL245, which went on to serve with 68 and 85 Squadrons before being sold as scrap in March 1955. Note that TW227 is equipped with a nose radome fairing. *(Richard Riding collection)*

TR.33 TW279 '413 CW' of 790 Squadron (Fleet Air Arm) is taxying at Culdrose in 1948. Like all production TR.33s, TW279 was constructed at Leavesden, this particular aircraft being delivered into storage at the Receipt & Despatch Unit Culham on 31 July 1946. Allocated to 703 Squadron (Fleet Air Arm) in 1948, TW279 passed to 790 Squadron at Culdrose during August the same year, serving with 790 until July 1949. Between January and April 1950 it flew with Airwork at Brawdy before overhaul by Brooklands Aviation at Sywell. Following a spell at Yeovilton, this TR.33 returned to store at Culham before being sold as scrap to R. A. Short on 23 July 1953. The following year TW279 passed to the Israeli Air Force. Note the code letters for Culdrose ('CW') on the fin. *(Ken Lambert, via Stuart Howe)*

TR.33 TW247 '412 CW' of 790 Squadron (Fleet Air Arm) is seen at Culdrose. This aircraft was ready for collection from the Leavesden factory on 16 March 1946 and was delivered to the Receipt & Despatch Unit at Culham a month later. From October 1946 it served as 'FD4L' with 811 Squadron at Ford before entering storage at Stretton. 790 Squadron at Culdrose received TW247 in February 1948, retaining the aircraft until January 1950, when it was flown to Leavesden for overhaul. This Sea Mosquito spent the remainder of its active life with Airwork on FRU duties. The aircraft was later despatched to the Aircraft Holding Unit at Lossiemouth, where it was sold as scrap to R. A. Short on 25 November 1953. Note the nose radome fairing. *(Ken Lambert, via Stuart Howe)*

An unidentified 790 Squadron (Fleet Air Arm) TR.33 has suffered an undercarriage collapse or belly-landing at Culdrose in 1948. The circumstances surrounding this incident are presently unknown, but the aircraft may well be TW246, which was damaged on 23 October 1948 after the pilot accidentally retracted the undercarriage (instead of raising the flaps) after landing. Curiously, the propeller tips are bent forward, indicating that the aircraft was perhaps travelling sideways when the propellers made contact with the runway. Protruding from the cockpit canopy top section is the aerial rod for the ARI 5307 radio installation, the receiver (Type R.1585) being mounted on the forward starboard side of the ventral compartment. Following repairs TW246 went on to serve with Airwork at Brawdy and Hurn before being sold as scrap to R. A. Short in November 1953. *(Ken Lambert, via Stuart Howe)*

This line-up of 771 Squadron (Fleet Air Arm) TR.33s is possibly at Ford in 1948. 771 Squadron was originally allocated Mosquitoes while based at Gosport, but these were detached to Ford as Gosport was unsuitable for Mosquito operations. Second from the left is TW292 '595', which served with 771 Squadron between June 1947 and January 1950, later passing to Airwork at Hurn before sale as scrap to R. A. Short in August 1953. TW283 '591' is third from the left; this aircraft served with 771 Squadron between February 1947 and May 1948 before transfer to 762 Squadron at Culdrose as '466 CW'. Following storage at Culham and Stretton, TW283 was sold as scrap to R. A. Short in November 1953. Note that all four aircraft have their rear fuselage access hatches in the open position. *(Aeroplane Monthly)*

In this second view of 771 Squadron (Fleet Air Arm) TR.33 TW292 '595 LP', note the four-bladed propellers, small-diameter main wheels and Lockheed long-stroke oleo-pneumatic undercarriage legs. TR.33s were powered by Merlin 25 engines and had a maximum speed of around 376mph. Range was 1,265 miles and all-up weight 23,850lb. The code letters 'LP' on the fin stood for Lee-on-Solent. *(Bill Holdridge, via Stuart Howe)*

Here is a fine study of 771 Squadron (Fleet Air Arm) TR.33 TW286 '598 LP', which was delivered from the Leavesden factory to the Receipt & Despatch Unit at Culham on 21 October 1946. Eight months later it was allocated to 771 Squadron at Ford, where it became '598 FD', this changing to '598 LP' when 771 Squadron relocated to Lee-on-Solent. Between January and July 1949 TW286 received attention at the de Havilland Leavesden factory before entering storage at Stretton and later Culham. This TR.33 was eventually sold as scrap to R. A. Short on 23 July 1953. TW286 wears an overall silver dope finish with black spinners. In the hands of an experienced pilot aerobatics were permitted in the TR.33 (providing that the torpedo, bomb load, underwing stores and drop tanks had been jettisoned), but were not recommended due to the risk of causing damage to the radar equipment. Intentional spinning was prohibited. *(Bill Holdridge, via Stuart Howe)*

Senior Pilot David Parker photographed with 790 Squadron (Fleet Air Arm) TR.33 TW282 in 1949. TW282 was built at Leavesden in August 1946 and delivered to the Receipt & Despatch Unit at Culham early the following month. During its Fleet Air Arm career it served with 762 Squadron at Ford (as '471 FD'), 771 Squadron (also at Ford) and 790 Squadron at both Dale and Culdrose. TW282 later passed to Airwork at Brawdy before entering storage at Culham and later Lossiemouth, where it was sold as scrap to R. A. Short on 31 August 1953. Note the Culdrose code letters ('CW') above the fin flash. TW282 was purchased by the Israeli Air Force in 1954. *(Basil Nash, via Stuart Howe)*

Air mechanics Bob Rowling (left) and Ken Lambert sit atop 790 Squadron (Fleet Air Arm) TR.33 TW279 at Culdrose in 1948. The arrestor hook (with its pivot joint) is clearly visible beneath the rear fuselage. The Sea Mosquito fuselage was heavily modified to withstand carrier deck operations and featured an additional bulkhead (5A) for mounting the arrestor hook. The arrestor hook retaining catch and snap gear were fitted to the lower section of bulkhead six. For strengthening purposes two special longerons ran along the lower fuselage between bulkheads four and 5A. The arrestor hook was released by a cable control, the release lever positioned in the cockpit just forward of the throttle box. A microswitch on the left-hand arrestor arm illuminated a warning light in the cockpit when the hook was down between an angle of 47 and 70 degrees (ie fully extended). A damper strut was connected to the starboard arrestor arm immediately forward of the pivot joint. *(Ken Lambert, via Stuart Howe)*

TR.33 TW257 '590 LP' of 771 Squadron (Fleet Air Arm) is seen possibly at Ford in 1948. TW257 was delivered direct from Leavesden to the Receipt & Despatch Unit at Culham on 16 April 1946 before joining 739 Squadron (also at Culham) in May 1947. A month later it was transferred to 771 Squadron and detached to Ford, remaining with 771 until June 1948. 790 Squadron at Culdrose operated TW257 (as '405 CW') between July and October 1949 before the aircraft entered storage at Culham in July 1950. It was ultimately sold as scrap to R. A. Short in September 1953. TW257's upper surfaces are camouflaged in Slate Grey and Ocean Grey with the under surfaces in Sky. Note the longitudinal stiffening strake on the port side of the fuselage, and the serial number on the port wing under surface. The arrestor hook is just visible forward of the tailwheel. *(Aeroplane Monthly)*

This unidentified silver-doped TR.33 was photographed at Culdrose in 1948. It is believed to be TW248, which served with both 811 and 790 Squadrons (Fleet Air Arm) before passing to Airwork at Brawdy. Delivered to the Receipt & Despatch Unit at Culham in February 1952, TW248 was sold as scrap to R. A. Short on 25 November 1953. Note the hand-pump oil bowser next to the port main wheel. *(Ken Lambert, via Stuart Howe)*

771 Squadron (Fleet Air Arm) TR.33 TW256 '593 LP' is the subject of this photograph by Charles E. Brown. This aircraft was delivered from the Leavesden factory to the Receipt & Despatch Unit at Culham on 22 May 1946. The following month it passed to 703 Squadron at Thorney Island before transfer to 771 Squadron at Ford during May 1947. As '593 LP' TW256 remained on 771 Squadron

strength until flown to Leavesden for overhaul in January 1949. From January 1950 it was operated by Airwork and served on FRU duties until an engine fire on take-off from Hurn led to the collapse of the undercarriage. Following transport to Lossiemouth TW256 was Struck Off Charge on 15 June 1953. *(Charles E. Brown, RAF Museum)*

703 Squadron (Fleet Air Arm) TR.33 TW241 photographed at Coltishall during Exercise 'Emperor' in September 1950. TW241 had a long and varied career that began in April 1946 when it was delivered to RNAS Ford. TW241 was employed on deck landing trials by 778 Squadron (Fleet Air Arm) aboard HMS *Illustrious* during October and November 1946, during the course of which (on 6 November) it failed to engage an arrestor wire and was forced to take off again, the arrestor hook catching on the deck lift well before the aircraft left the ship (the original film of this incident is held by the RAF Museum Film Archive). In July 1947

TW241 passed to the Telecommunications Flying Unit at Defford for radar trials before allocation to the RAE (for air-to-air homing trials) in April 1949. 703 Squadron at Ford received TW241 in April 1950, the aircraft receiving the unit codes '043 FD' as seen here. This TR.33 later served with 771 Squadron (Fleet Air Arm) before entering storage at Lossiemouth in July 1953. The following month TW241 was purchased as scrap by R. A. Short and sold on to the Israeli Air Force. Note the 'Hookah' aerials on the leading edge of the port wing. An NF.36 is being refuelled to the right of TW241. *(Jack Cook, via Mike Gray)*

Unidentified crews of 790 Squadron (Fleet Air Arm) pictured with TR.33 TW239 '411' at RNAS Dale in 1948. 790 Squadron originally formed as a Target Towing unit in June 1941, but disbanded three months later when it became part of 772 Squadron. In July 1942 the Squadron re-formed with Fulmars and Oxfords and began training Fighter Direction Officers as part of the Fighter Direction School. 790 Squadron received its first Mosquito FB.VIs at Dale in July 1946, TR.33s arriving the following December (the Squadron also operated B.XXVs). 790 Squadron moved to Culdrose in December 1947, disbanding there just under two years later.

TW239 was delivered to the Empire Central Flying School on 15 January 1946, passing to 811 Squadron (Fleet Air Arm) at Ford a month later (where it became 'FD4R') before allocation to 790 Squadron at Dale in April 1947. Assigned to Airwork for FRU duties from Brawdy (as '416/BQ') and St David's, this TR.33 entered storage at Lossiemouth in February 1953. Bought as scrap by R. A. Short on 31 August 1953, TW239 was later sold to the Israeli Air Force. *(Basil Nash, via Stuart Howe)*

TR.33 TW286 is seen at Ford in 1947 with a camouflaged fixed-wing TR.33 behind. TW286 was then on the strength of 771 Squadron (Fleet Air Arm) and wore the unit codes '598 FD'. TW286 served with 771 Squadron between June 1947 and April 1948 before overhaul by de Havilland's at Leavesden in 1949. Following storage at Stretton and Culham, this TR.33 was sold as scrap to R. A. Short in August 1953. Note the enlarged elevator horn balances, necessary to improve handling due to the extra weight of the radar, naval equipment and wing folding gear. Enlarged elevator horn balances were also a feature of the TR.37, NF.38, PR.34, 4,000lb-bomb B.IV Series ii conversions, and several B.XXVs. A Supermarine Sea Otter amphibian is visible in the distance to the right. *(Bill Holdridge, via Stuart Howe)*

These 811 Squadron (Fleet Air Arm) TR.33s are at HMS *Peregrine* (RNAS Ford). The only front-line Sea Mosquito Squadron, 811 initially flew FB.VIs and received its first TR.33s in April 1946 at Ford. In December 1946 the Squadron moved to Brawdy before disbanding on 1 July 1947. Nearest the camera is TW245, which went on to serve with 790 Squadron at Dale and Culdrose before allocation to Airwork at Brawdy. Purchased as scrap by R. A. Short in August 1953, TW245 later entered service with the Israeli Air Force. The spinners appear to be finished in black with a white concentric ring on their forward sections. *(David Hughes, via Stuart Howe)*

Mosquito Target Tugs

Despite the success of W4050's initial flight trials, some Air Ministry critics believed that the Mosquito's only real application was as a high-speed target tug. This view was further reinforced by Admiralty requirements for a fast target tug aircraft, it eventually being agreed that 150 Mosquitoes be ordered for this purpose (divided between the RAF and the Fleet Air Arm). However, W4050's performance soon impressed the Air Staff, who quickly realised the design's great potential, especially as an offensive Fighter and Night-Fighter. Although a target-towing adaptation was studied, it was considered rather complex as well as a waste of precious Merlin XX engines. By mid-1941 official plans for a Mosquito Target Tug had been shelved, leaving the Fleet Air Arm to operate Target Tug conversions of existing types.

With the end of the Second World War the Admiralty again pressed for a target-towing Mosquito. This would be a conversion of existing aircraft (surplus examples then being readily available) and resulted in the first Mosquito Target Tug variant, the TT.39. Design and conversion work was undertaken by General Aircraft at Feltham (and later Lasham), which based the TT.39 on the B.XVI airframe. In addition to target-towing, the TT.39 was devised for photographic registering of towed-target firing together with radar calibration duties. To operate the target-towing equipment and photograph drogues hauled by other aircraft, the target operator occupied a compartment in the rear fuselage covered by a transparent cupola. The TT.39's most striking feature was an extended nose section featuring optically flat glass panels for photography. The hydraulically operated target-towing winch was housed in the ventral bay and powered by a retractable 'windmill'.

More than thirty TT.39 conversions were produced, many serving on fleet requirements duties from Malta and the UK. The least aesthetically pleasing Mosquito, this intricate machine had been withdrawn from use by 1954. During the early 1950s large numbers of surplus Mosquito B.35s remained in storage with RAF Maintenance Units, and between 1951 and 1954 more than 140 were converted into Target Tugs by Brooklands Aviation at Sywell. These aircraft were designated TT.35, the first conversion being carried out on B.35 RS719. Production conversions were equipped with either an ML Type G (Mark 2) wind-driven winch beneath the ventral bay doors or a target pack container mounted in the roof of the ventral bay. TT.35s served with the 2nd Tactical Air Force in Germany, and Civilian Anti-Aircraft Co-operation Units (CAACU), Operational Conversion Units and Station Flights in the UK. They provided target-towing services for air-to-air and ground-to-air gunnery practice and acted in support of all military training areas where air support and co-operation were fundamental in training military personnel. The last operational TT.35s served with No 3 CAACU at Exeter, which retired its final examples in May 1963. Most of these 'starred' in the 1963 feature film *633 Squadron* and account for the majority of surviving Mk 35 Mosquitoes in the world today.

Several Mosquito T.3s and FB.VIs were operated as Target Tugs by foreign air forces, including Belgium and Yugoslavia. The Belgian examples were converted by Fairey Aviation at Ringway, the Yugoslav aircraft being locally adapted.

It is significant that even in the secondary roles of target-towing and radar calibration, the Mosquito's high performance ensured its operation well into the jet age.

Between 1951 and 1954 146 surplus B.35s were converted into target-towing aircraft, receiving the designation TT.35. This photograph was taken in May 1951 and depicts the first TT.35 conversion, RS719. TT.35s were produced in two versions, the first equipped with an ML Type G (Mark 2) wind-driven winch capable of streaming drogue targets on a 6,000-foot cable, the second fitted with towing gear within the ventral bay. The former variant incorporated four 'sleeve' drogue targets (two per side, all secured by rubber bungees) stowed externally within underside recesses on the ventral bay doors and the aft ventral bay/fuselage under fairing. On the latter version three 'banner'-type drogue targets were streamed from a target pack container mounted in the roof of the ventral bay. RS719 was the Prototype ML Type G (Mark 2) winch-equipped TT.35, VR793 pioneering the ventral bay target pack container installation.

TT.35s were originally intended to operate at 25,000 feet, but trials with RS719 resulted in high engine temperatures caused by the drag of the external winch and the 'sleeve' targets. To overcome these problems, Marshalls carried out development trials of the ventral bay target pack using VR793, drag being further reduced by substituting 'sleeve' targets for the 'banner' type. TT.35s equipped with the external winch continued to operate but largely at altitudes below 25,000 feet.

As a B.35, Airspeed-built RS719 served with the Empire Test Pilots School and the Telecommunications Research Establishment before conversion as the Prototype TT.35. Following trials at A&AEE Boscombe Down, RS719 went on to serve with No 3 CAACU, the Meteorological Flight at RAF Woodvale, and No 5 CAACU. Damaged in an accident on 23 May 1958, RS719 was Struck Off Charge a week later. In this shot the ML Type G (Mark 2) winch is clearly visible beneath the forward section of the aircraft's ventral bay doors. RS719's upper surfaces are finished in silver dope, the under surfaces sporting black and yellow diagonal stripes. The blades of the winch 'windmill' were set vertical before opening the crew entrance door in order to avoid damage to the latter. Production TT.35 conversions were undertaken by Brooklands Aviation at Sywell. *(Richard Riding collection)*

This close-up shot of a TT.35's ML Type G (Mark 2) wind-driven winch is probably the prototype installation on RS719. The Type G winch was designed and manufactured by ML Aviation at White Waltham, where this photo is likely to have been taken. The winch was secured to a tubular steel mounting frame bolted to the wing centre rib together with a forward attachment bracket located on fuselage bulkhead two. The mounting frame incorporated a jettison mechanism with four sockets housing conical plugs. Each socket contained a pin, the centre portion of which was cut away to form a half-round section. With the jettison control lever in the locked position, the socket pins engaged with a semi-circular groove in the winch plug and provided a positive lock. In an emergency the pilot could jettison the winch by using a handle to the right of his centre instrument panel, (which was turned to the right then pulled back, thus cutting the cable and jettisoning the winch).

Aside from the Type G winch, target-towing equipment for this version of the TT.35 included a spring buffer unit, an exchange release unit, a cable cutter and four drogue targets. Operation of the winch was controlled by the Target Towing Operator (TTO) via electrical switches contained in a panel on the starboard cockpit wall. In addition to the electrical controls for winch operation, a mechanical linkage was provided between the buffer unit on the launching equipment and the holding brake on the winch. Winch fairings were mated to individual aircraft (to allow for variation in ventral bay door contour) and were not interchangeable. The ML Type G (Mark 3) winch was fitted to the Firefly TT.5, and the Type G (Mark 4) to the Meteor TT.20. The blades of the winch 'windmill' were fully feathering.
(ML Aviation, via F. R. Gordon, Berkshire Aviation Museum)

This nice air-to-air shot of Gibraltar Towed Target Flight TT.35 TJ114 'X' features 'the Rock' as a backdrop. Delivered direct from the Hatfield factory to 27 MU on 1 September 1945, TJ114 remained in store until 13 December 1951, when it flew to Brooklands Aviation for TT.35 conversion. Assigned to the Gibraltar Towed Target Flight in May 1953, TJ114 served until 6 February 1956, when it was declared scrap and Struck Off Charge. Note that the aircraft is equipped with target-towing gear within the ventral bay and does not feature the ML Type G (Mark 2) wind-driven winch. TJ114 is finished in silver dope overall with black and yellow diagonal stripes on the under surfaces. Yellow bands are carried on the rear fuselage and the outboard top surface of the wings. *(Steve Bond)*

TT.35 TJ154 of the Armament Practice Station at RAF Sylt is flanked by Vampire T.11 WZ502 and an unidentified Meteor T.7 (believed to be WL430). Originally constructed as a B.35 at Hatfield, TJ154 was delivered direct from the factory to 22 MU on 23 October 1945. Here it remained until 30 March 1951, when it passed to Marshalls for two months of modification/refurbishing work. Following storage with 15 MU, TJ154 flew to Brooklands Aviation at Sywell on 15 July 1952 for conversion to TT.35 standard. Between October 1953 and September 1955 it served with the Armament Practice Station at RAF Sylt and was later coded 'C' (this letter being applied to the rear fuselage immediately aft of the roundel). TJ154 flew back to the UK on 15 September 1955, entering storage with 22 MU where it was declared Non-Effective Stock two weeks later. This TT.35 was eventually sold as scrap to Eyre Smelting Company on 15 February 1957. TJ154's lines compare well with those of its formation partners. *(Betty Aherne, via Stuart Howe)*

TT.35 TK607 'W' is running up (probably at RAF Sylt) prior to another target-towing sortie. An ML Type G (Mark 2) winch-equipped TT.35, note the target drogue stowed externally on the aft ventral bay/fuselage under fairing. Four control handles or 'toggles', affixed to a bracket suspended from the canopy roof above the port wing decking, were activated by the Target Towing Operator (TTO) to stream the drogues. Mounted above each target stowage was a release bar featuring two spigots at either end. The spigots engaged with retaining bungees and were painted to correspond with coloured sleeves attached to the bungees. To ensure that the bungees engaged with the spigots in the correct sequence, each spigot was lettered (the letters being stencilled on the fuselage side adjacent to the spigots). The bungees engaged with the appropriate coloured spigots in alphabetical order, thereby ensuring that they did not become entangled and permitting the drogues to deploy cleanly.

A Hatfield-built Mosquito, TK607 left the factory as a B.35 in January 1946 and immediately entered storage with 22 MU. Converted to TT.35 standard by Brooklands Aviation between October 1951 and May 1952, TK607 passed to 38 MU before allocation to No 2 CAACU on 31 May 1953. No 5 CAACU received the aircraft in May 1955, operating it until the following September, when it was delivered to the Armament Practice Station at Sylt. TK607 later served with the Station Flight at RAF Schleswigland before returning to the UK in April 1958 for storage at 10 MU. Declared Non-Effective Stock on 31 October 1958, TK607 was sold as scrap to H. H. Bushell on 9 June 1959. A Meteor night-fighter is parked beyond TK607. *(Charlie Risborough, via DHAMT Ltd)*

TT.35s TA634 (leading) and TK607 are airborne from the Armament Practice Station at RAF Sylt in 1956. The APS provided target-towing services for air-to-air and ground-to-air gunnery practice (the latter comprising light and heavy ack-ack) and later moved to Schleswigland. Both aircraft feature ML Type G (Mark 2) winches and are equipped with target drogues under the ventral bay doors and the aft ventral bay/fuselage under fairing. TT.35s handled normally with 2- or 4-foot drogue targets in tow, the maximum towing speed for 2-foot targets being 280 knots, this reducing to 240 knots with 4-foot targets. With a target on short tow it was recommended that the aircraft never exceed 2.5g and 170 knots. Note that TK607's tailwheel has not retracted. This picture was taken from another TT.35. *(Charlie Risborough, via DHAMT Ltd)*

This rare photograph shows the ML Type G winch installation on an unidentified T.3. Note the towing cable buffer unit mounted beneath the fuselage immediately aft of the ventral bay doors. A target drogue is stowed on the under fuselage (directly forward of the rear access hatch) and a cable guard frame is fitted to the rear fuselage ahead of the tailwheel assembly. Worthy of comment is the lack of fairings surrounding the winch mounting structure. Six Belgian Air Force T.3s and three FB.VIs were converted to Target Tugs by Fairey Aviation at Ringway. *(ML Aviation, via F. R. Gordon, Berkshire Aviation Museum)*

Taken at Feltham on 23 May 1947, this photograph illustrates the extended nose compartment of TT.39 Prototype ML995. A conversion of the B.XVI, the TT.39 was developed and produced by General Aircraft Ltd (later Blackburn & General) in response to Royal Navy requirements for a Target Tug version of the Mosquito. The Royal Navy had long desired a Mosquito Target Tug, but only after the war did sufficient aircraft become available for conversion. A relatively complex aeroplane, the TT.39's principal roles were target towing for ground-to-air and air-to-air gunnery practice, photographic registering of towed-target firing, throw-off target and marking, and radar calibration. The observer normally sat next to the pilot, but in addition to acting as observer he also undertook the duties of photographer and target operator.

The target operator's position and camera equipment were located in the rear fuselage (beneath a transparent cupola), entry being gained through an access door beneath the fuselage. The extended nose compartment was used for photography only and featured a Vinten K-type camera (on a balanced swivel mounting) shooting through optically flat glass sections, the latter shown here in mock-up form. A knee pad and body rest were provided for the camera operator, the body rest also serving as a film storage compartment.

Note the retractable 'windmill' extending from the forward section of the ventral bay; this provided power for the TT.39's Miles Type H (Mark 1) target-towing winch, which was capable of deploying 6,000 feet of towing cable. Drogue targets of 2 or 4 feet were deployed in addition to a 16-foot winged target, the latter towed off (and landed on) a runway behind 200 feet of cable (32-foot winged targets could also be towed by the TT.39).

Constructed at Hatfield as B.XVI in May 1944, ML995 served with 105 Squadron during the war before transfer to General Aircraft at Feltham on 9 May 1946. Converted as a TT.39 Prototype, ML995 transferred to Royal Navy charge in August 1947 before undergoing handling trials at the A&AEE in July 1948. Later brought up to full TT.39 standard, ML995 was eventually scrapped at Lossiemouth in April 1953. The Mosquito in the background is either awaiting TT.39 conversion or spares breakdown. *(BAE SYSTEMS)*

The TT.39's less than pleasing lines led to this amusing contemporary caricature (by Chris Wren) appearing in *The Aeroplane*. *(Aeroplane Monthly)*

NAVAL AND NASAL

"Please, Sir Geoffrey, they can't do this to me!"

This view inside TT.39 Prototype ML995's ventral bay (looking forward) shows the retractable 'windmill' for the Miles Type H (Mark 1) target-towing winch. The 'windmill', which was operated by the main hydraulic system, drove a separate hydraulic system supplying power to three VSG pumps that in turn drove the winch.

The 'windmill' arm rpm indicator was located within the target operator's position in the rear fuselage (on the port side beneath the cupola). In this shot the three VSG pumps are clearly visible in the top left-hand corner of the ventral bay. The winch 'windmill' was constructed from laminated wood. *(BAE SYSTEMS)*

This close-up shot (looking rearward) shows the Miles Type H (Mark 1) target-towing winch mounted in the ventral bay of TT.39 Prototype ML995. Hydraulically operated, the winch derived its power from three VSG pumps driven by the retractable 'windmill'. A control valve mounted near to (and operated by) the selector control regulated the flow of fluid to the winch motor. From the control valve the pipe lines to the winch hydraulic motor (which served as supply and return lines depending on the direction selected) passed through a two-way pressurisation valve; this relief valve was provided to protect the winch motor if load on the winch exceeded the motor's power output during target-towing operations. In such an eventuality, the overloaded supply line would open the relief valve, thus permitting fluid to bypass into the return line (to the reservoir) via the control valve. The selector unit for operation of the control valve was mounted on the starboard side of the target compartment aft of the hydraulic-pneumatic panel. *(BAE SYSTEMS)*

728 Squadron (Fleet Air Arm) TT.39 RV295 '511' is airborne from Hal Far, Malta, and clearly visible on the rear fuselage is the target operator's compartment with its transparent plastic cupola. The target operator was responsible for operation of the winch control gear, the changing and release of the drogue targets, and photography of the sleeve targets towed by other aircraft (the latter task being undertaken used a modified K-type Vinten camera mounted integrally with the cupola). The cupola afforded a clear view aft and horizontally (30 degrees up on beam and 15 degrees down) and featured two optically flat glass windows. Manually rotated via a winding mechanism, it was possible to jettison the cupola in an emergency.

The target operator was provided with a crash seat (mounted on the control cable guard on the compartment's port side) for use during take-off and landing or when called to crash stations. A webbing strap-type seat (slung between the cupola attachment points) was utilised during operation of the Vinten camera. Most of the operator's target-towing equipment was fitted to the starboard side of the compartment, and included the winch controls and instruments together with the cable cutter handle. The drogue target chute was located in the centre of the

compartment immediately aft of fuselage bulkhead four, and the drogue target stowages were longitudinally positioned in the space between bulkheads three and four.

Originally constructed as a B.XVI at Hatfield, RV295 served with 571 and 109 Squadrons before transfer to General Aircraft at Feltham in November 1946. Following conversion to TT.39 standard, RV295 served with 728 Squadron (Fleet Air Arm) on fleet requirements duties between May 1949 and September 1950, eventually being Struck Off Charge on 21 March 1951. Note the cable guard surrounding the tailplane and fin; this ran from the fin leading edge to a guard tube on the port tip of the tailplane, continuing on to a similar tube on the starboard tip before returning to the fin (thus making a complete circuit). The guard was designed to prevent damage to the control surfaces in the event of drogue cable whip. The letters 'HF' on the fin signify that RV295 is based at Hal Far. It is finished in silver dope overall with black and yellow diagonal stripes on the under surfaces. Yellow bands have been applied to the rear fuselage and the inboard top surface of the wings. Aerobatics in the TT.39 were (understandably!) prohibited. *(DHAMT Ltd)*

This unidentified 728 Squadron (Fleet Air Arm) TT.39 is likely to be PF482, which made a wheels-up landing near Castel Benito in May 1951. Note that the rear fuselage cupola has been jettisoned, enabling the target operator to leave the aircraft. The Mosquito B.XVI fuselage was subject to extensive structural modifications during conversion to TT.39 standard. Aside from the extended nose compartment, modifications included cutting away the rear dorsal section to accept the cupola seating, deletion of the rear access door from the lower starboard side (together with the longitudinal stiffening strake directly above it), and the addition of an entrance door beneath the rear fuselage. Located immediately behind bulkhead five, this door provided access to the target operator's compartment and could be jettisoned in an emergency. The extended nose was detachable and was constructed of laminated wooden frames and stringers covered with plywood. Production TT.39 conversions were equipped with four-bladed propellers, specially cropped to clear the nose

extension. Thirty-one TT.39s are believed to have been produced, thirteen of them serving on fleet requirements duties with 728 Squadron (Fleet Air Arm) in Malta and six with 771 Squadron (Fleet Air Arm) at Ford. TT.39s had been withdrawn from use by 1954.

As a B.XVI, Percival-built PF482 served with 692, 571 and 163 Squadrons as well as 16 OTU before transfer to the Admiralty in 1947. Converted to TT.39 standard by General Aircraft at Feltham, PF482 joined 728 Squadron (Fleet Air Arm) at Hal Far in December 1950. On 24 May 1951 it made a belly-landing at Castel Benito following loss of directional control below 160 knots. Damage was so extensive that the aircraft was written off. Prior to a crash-landing in the TT.39, both underwing drop tanks (if fitted) would be jettisoned, together with the canopy roof escape hatch. It was recommended that an approach speed of 140 knots be maintained (with the undercarriage and flaps up) before lowering the flaps as required and carrying out a wheels-up landing. *(Peter Cook, via Stuart Howe)*

ML Type G (Mark 2) winch-equipped TT.35 TK609 is seen at RAF Sylt in 1957. Originally constructed as a B.35 at Hatfield, TK609 was delivered to 22 MU on 6 December 1945, where it began a six-year period in storage. Between 1 November 1951 and 8 April 1952 TK609 was converted to TT.35 standard by Brooklands Aviation before passing to 15 MU for further storage. 4 CAACU at Llandow received the aircraft in October 1953, operating it until 8 March 1954, when it swung on take-off and the undercarriage collapsed.

Following repairs by Brooklands Aviation, TK609 was assigned to 22 MU on 3 May 1955 before issue to the RAF Schleswigland Station Flight seven months later. It returned to the UK in April 1958 for storage with 10 MU where it was Struck Off Charge on 31 October 1958. TK609's ultimate fate was to be sold as scrap to H. H. Bushell on 9 June 1959. Note the tool box and servicing steps by the port main wheel. The spinners are finished in red. *(A. Pluck, via Stuart Howe)*

TT.35 TJ118 '53' of No 3 CAACU photographed at Exeter by Keith Saunders. One of No 3 CAACU's first TT.35s, TJ118 was constructed as a B.35 at Hatfield in September 1945. It spent the first seven years of its life in storage with 27 MU before passing to Brooklands Aviation at Sywell on 3 April 1952. Here it was converted into a TT.35 before delivery to No 3 CAACU at Exeter on 2 September 1952. TJ118 served there until 24 May 1957 when it re-entered storage with 27 MU. However, just under two an a half years later it returned to Exeter, resuming service with No 3 CAACU until 18 September 1961, when it was Struck Off Charge.

TJ118 remained at Exeter, eventually being acquired by Mirisch Productions for use in *633 Squadron*. Its dismantled remains were transported to Bovingdon, the wing (still in its target tug colour scheme) actually

appearing in one of the film's ground scenes. The fuselage was later moved to the MGM film studios at Borehamwood where the nose was cut off to film cockpit interior shots. The latter role was repeated during the making of *Mosquito Squadron* in 1968, the cockpit and dismembered fuselage (together with the fuselage minus cockpit of RS715) languishing at Borehamwood until recovered in 1973. TJ118's nose and fuselage are currently in storage with the de Havilland Aircraft Museum Trust (formerly the Mosquito Aircraft Museum) at Salisbury Hall, London Colney; interestingly enough, the Trust's TT.35 TA634 also wore the code '53' during service with No 3 CAACU. The Mosquito parked beyond TJ118 is TT.35 TA642 '48', destined to meet its end during the filming of *633 Squadron*. *(Keith Saunders)*

No 3 CAACU TT.35 TA634 '53' provides a demonstration of target-towing during an air display at Exeter in the early 1960s. Target-towing operations by No 3 CAACU were carried out at either low or high level; low-level operations (for small-calibre gunnery practice) took place at an altitude of 1,500 feet and employed 3,000 feet of towing cable, while high-level operations (for large-calibre gunnery practice) involved towing the maximum 6,000 feet of cable at heights of between 4,000 and 6,000 feet. During 180-degree turns to make the next run in for the guns, it was

not unusual (on high-level operations) to look out of the cockpit and see the target drogue travelling in the opposite direction! Consequently, it was very important to extend the runs before turning to re-approach the gun lines.

An exchange unit was attached to the end of the towing cable, enabling the Target Towing Operator (TTO) to exchange a damaged drogue or re-stream a new one. If a drogue was shot away it was necessary to ensure that the exchange unit was still attached, otherwise the next drogue launched would fly off the end of the cable. The procedure adopted was to wind in the cable until a length of about 1,000 feet was left trailing, while carrying out a gentle turn as the TTO endeavoured to spot the exchange unit. If it could not be sighted the crew assumed that they were trailing a cable and this had to be disposed off before landing. The cable could be wound in to an extent, but, without the weight of the exchange unit, it tended to jam the winch cylinder, leading to many hours of work for the ground staff. As all firing ranges were on the coast it was easy to drop the unwanted cable in the sea using a cutter installed in the aircraft. Like the TT.39, the TT.35 was equipped with a guard between the tailplane and fin to prevent winch cables from fouling the control surfaces. *(DHAMT Ltd)*

Believed to have been taken on 22 June 1963, this photograph shows former No 3 CAACU TT.35 RS718 at Exeter. The aircraft had been Struck Off Charge the year before, but remained at Exeter before transport to Bovingdon where it was destroyed during the making of *633 Squadron*.

Formed at Exeter Airport in April 1951, No 3 CAACU was one of five such civilian-run units operating under contract to the Air Ministry. By 1959 it had taken over the duties of the other four units and operated over the whole of the UK, including the Shetlands and Outer Hebrides. The unit's role was to provide services to all military training areas (both Army and Navy) where air support and co-operation were fundamental in training military personnel. No 3 CAACU took part in tactical exercises of all types including gun-tracking and live firing, the detection of camouflage units, searchlight training, and exercises for the benefit of RAF Fighter Controllers. During its twenty-year life span, No 3 CAACU

flew sixteen different aircraft types including the Beaufighter TT.10, Spitfire XVI, Mosquito T.3 and TT.35, Balliol T.2 and Meteor T.7. Mosquito TT.35s began to arrive in late 1952 and commenced target-towing duties in January 1953.

On occasions Mosquitoes were flown on non-target-towing missions including what became known as 'Mass Raids', during which a Mosquito would lead a formation of six or seven Spitfires for a high-level mock 'attack' on Manorbier camp in South Wales. Having 'attacked' from one direction, the formation flew off and re-formed to make a second 'attack' (from another direction) an hour later. The Mosquito would remain airborne between the 'attacks', the Spitfires returning to Exeter to refuel before re-joining the Mosquito. No 3 CAACU disbanded in December 1971, having flown a total of 75,386 hours, its duties being taken over by the re-formed 7 Squadron. Note that the cable guard has already been removed from RS718's tailplane and fin. *(via Jim Oughton)*

No 3 CAACU TT.35 TA639 '55' photographed at Exeter, with RS712 '50' behind. An early production B.35, TA639 left the Hatfield factory on 16 April 1945 for storage with 27 MU. It remained in store until May 1952, when it was delivered to Brooklands Aviation at Sywell for conversion into a TT.35. This work was complete by 30 September, TA639 being allocated to the Station Flight at Ballykelly on 17 October. Nearly two months later the aircraft transferred to the Aldergrove Station Flight, where it served until passing to 38 MU in December 1954. In January 1957 27 MU received TA639 once more, storing it until September 1959, when it was assigned to No 3 CAACU at Exeter. During its time with that unit it received the code '55', and on 9 May 1963 took part in the official flypast marking the Mosquito's retirement from service.

Struck Off Charge on 31 May 1963, TA639 went to the Central Flying School at Little Rissington, where it was prepared for a new career as a display aircraft. However, in July 1963 it was diverted to Bovingdon where it took part (as 'HT-B' 'HJ682') in the filming of *633 Squadron*. After the filming TA639 returned to Little Rissington and remained airworthy for a short while, eventually being transferred to the RAF Museum collection and stored at Henlow. This TT.35 was equipped with an ML Type G (Mark 2) wind-driven winch during service with No 3 CAACU (removed in this photograph but with its mounting points visible beneath the ventral bay doors). Note the black anti-glare panel on the nose forward of the cockpit. TA639 is today on show at the RAF Museum at Cosford. *(Martin Nesbit, via Harry Ellis and Stuart Howe)*

Unidentified TT.35 fuselages await their fate in a Midlands scrapyard during the 1950s. The wings have been sawn off close inboard revealing the spar boom laminations in the remaining stub centre sections. The port ventral bay door of the nearest fuselage still wears the black and yellow diagonal stripes applied to all TT.35s. Aside from the engines, radiators, undercarriage and control surfaces, the Mosquito's wooden airframe offered little of value to the scrap man. Note the Type 312 transmitting aerial (for the Type 3624 transmitter-receiver) mounted beneath the nose of the fuselage in the foreground. *(John Stride collection)*

324

Foreign Air Force Mosquitoes

During the Second World War Mosquitoes served with several foreign squadrons (including Polish and Norwegian) within the RAF, while the Americans operated PRXVIs and NF.30s independently within the USAAF. After the war, the plentiful supply of Mosquitoes in storage permitted a large export sales drive as foreign countries rebuilt their armed services. Surplus RAF Mosquitoes offered a relatively cheap means for overseas air forces to obtain significant numbers of a multi-role combat aircraft type. Fighter-Bomber variants naturally formed the majority of Mosquito exports, but Night-Fighters were also in demand, as were smaller numbers of Photographic Reconnaissance aircraft.

The Norwegian 333 Squadron returned home with its wartime FB.VIs, later supplementing these with ex-RAF examples. Sweden purchased sixty wartime NF.XIXs from RAF stocks, these forming the nucleus of that country's night air defence system. Under terms of the Western Defence Pact, Belgium received twenty-six NF.30s and a smaller number of FB.VIs and T.3s. The French Air Force became a major operator of Mosquitoes, the Armée de l'Air receiving more than 100 examples consisting largely of FB.VIs but also including T.3s, PR.XVIs and NF.30s. Large numbers of former French aircraft later formed the backbone of Israel's Mosquito force, these eventually being joined by ex-RAF FB.VIs and PR.XVIs together with thirteen former Royal Navy TR.33s. During the Sinai Campaign in 1956, Israeli Mosquito Fighter-Bombers inflicted significant damage on Egyptian ground forces without the loss of a single aircraft (no mean feat for an aircraft that was already more than ten years out of date).

Turkey received 135 ex-RAF FB.VIs and ten new-build T.3s, these aircraft serving until 1954 when they were replaced by American F-84 Thunderjets. The re-formed Czechoslovak Air Force equipped two of its Regiments with ex-RAF FB.VIs, but these were withdrawn shortly after the Communist take-over. The Dominican Military Aviation Corps purchased six FB.VIs from the UK in 1948, several being used to quell rebel landings on Dominica during 1949. The Dominican FB.VIs were later augmented by three ex-RCAF Trainer Mosquitoes in 1952. The Yugoslav Air Force (Jugoslovenska Ratno Vazduhoplovstyo – JRV) was a significant user of Mosquitoes, obtaining from the UK seventy-seven FB.VIs, sixty NF.38s and six T.3s. The JRV was the only air force to operate NF.38s, its quota including VX916, the very last Mosquito produced.

One of the most fascinating Mosquito exports concerns aircraft supplied to the Nationalist Chinese Air Force in 1947/48. Around 200 ex-RCAF Mosquitoes were sold to Nationalist China by the Canadian Government and shipped to Shanghai. This consignment largely featured FB.26s but also included T.27s and T.29s. Around sixty were destroyed in training accidents, but a small number flew operationally against the Communist forces before the latter over-ran the country in 1949.

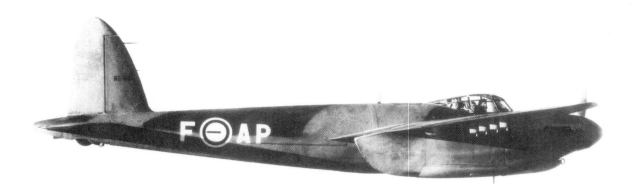

FB.VI RS610 'F-AP' belongs to No 334 Squadron Royal Norwegian Air Force. During the war No 333 Squadron was the only Norwegian unit to operate the Mosquito. Formed from No 1477 (Norwegian) Flight on 10 May 1943, the Squadron's 'A' Flight was equipped with Catalinas and based at Woodhaven, while 'B' Flight received Mosquito FB.VIs at Leuchars. 'B' Flight's Mosquitoes initially flew anti-shipping reconnaissance sorties off Norway, and in September 1944 moved from Leuchars to Banff. From there 'B' Flight flew as 'outriders' leading the Strike Wings from Banff and Dallachy on anti-shipping operations along the Norwegian coastline (in addition to its reconnaissance duties). On 26 May 1945 'B' Flight was re-designated 334 Squadron and returned home to Norway the following month, where it was based at

Gardermoen. From 21 November 1945 No 334 and all other Norwegian squadrons were transferred from RAF control to the Royal Norwegian Air Force ('Luftforsvaret' in Norwegian), and 334 Squadron became '334 skvadron'.

A latecomer to Norwegian service, Hatfield-built FB.VI RS610 was delivered to Norway by ferry pilot Richard Livermore on 18 August 1947. Following storage at Gardermoen RS610 was taken on charge by 334 Squadron in September 1949. A former 248 Squadron (RAF) aircraft, RS610 was eventually Struck Off Charge on 12 January 1952, having accumulated a total flying time of 524hrs 5mins. Note the underwing rocket rails and the application of the aircraft's serial number on the fin. *(Bjorn Olsen, via Sverre Thuve)*

This early postwar shot shows Norwegian FB.VIs in a hangar at Gardermoen. They retain their wartime Norwegian flag markings on the spinners, but Norwegian fuselage roundels have replaced the British ones. The aircraft on the right is Standard Motors-built RF831 'KK-G', which served with 333 Squadron 'B' Flight from 28 March 1945. During the course of its career RF831 was re-coded 'F-AD' (and later 'RI-D') before being Struck Off Charge on 12 January 1952 with a total flying time of 355hrs 25mins. *(via Bjorn Olsen)*

334 Squadron FB.VIs RF725 'KK-F' and RF831 'KK-G' overfly Stavanger harbour during the return flight home from Banff to Norway on 8 June 1945. Standard Motors-built RF725 was returned to the RAF following an accident at Kastrup (Copenhagen) on 26 October 1945. This photograph was taken by navigator Haakon Mathisen. *(Haakon Mathisen, via Bjorn Olsen)*

This photograph of Norwegian FB.VI's at Gardermoen was taken in around 1947/48. From August 1946 the Royal Norwegian Air Force abandoned the British system of squadron code letters, introducing a different system whereby a single-letter classified the aircraft type ('F' in the case of the Mosquito) with a further two letters identifying the individual aircraft. From January 1951 squadron codes were re-introduced, units that had previously served with the RAF reverting to their original wartime code letters. However, 334 Squadron was assigned the code letters 'RI' after the initials of its commanding officer, Major Reidar Isaksen. The aircraft on the left is RF831 'F-AD', with RF

874 'F-AF' on the right. Originally allocated to 404 Squadron (RCAF) at Banff, RF874 was transferred to 'B' Flight of 333 Squadron on 10 May 1945, receiving the unit code letters 'KK-K'. It was recoded 'RI-F' in 1951 but Struck Off Charge (together with the majority of the remaining Norwegian Mosquitoes) on 12 January 1952 with a total flying time of 282hrs 45mins. RF874 was subsequently scrapped at Sola. *(via Sverre Thuve/Bjorn Olsen)*

A ground crewman prepares a Norwegian FB.VI at Gardermoen, probably in 1949 before 334 Squadron's move to Sola on 4 October of that year. Visible in the background are a Vampire III, two newly delivered Vampire FB.52s, a Fairchild Cornell trainer/communications aircraft and a line-up of Spitfire IXs. All Norwegian Mosquitoes were grounded on 21 February 1951 following a fatal accident six days earlier when TE908 shed its port wing pulling out of a dive. The cause of the accident was structural failure, Norwegian Mosquitoes subsequently being maintained for emergency use only (it should not be forgotten that this was during the period of the Cold War in Europe and the war in Korea). From 12 January 1952 all Norwegian Mosquitoes were formally Struck Off Charge with the majority being scrapped at Sola. Note that the second aircraft in this line-up features unshrouded 'saxophone' exhausts on the outboard side of its port engine. *(via Sverre Thure/Bjorn Olsen)*

Turkish officials are pictured in the UK (probably at Ringway) with a newly refurbished FB.VI destined for their country's air force. Turkey originally ordered 108 FB.VIs and ten T.3s, but later added an additional twenty-four FB.VIs to equip two more squadrons. A total of 135 FB.VIs were eventually received by the Turks, this figure including three attrition replacements. The Turkish FB.VIs were reconditioned by Fairey Aviation at Ringway and allocated the delivery numbers 401 to 532 (serving aircraft were assigned Turkish Air Force serial numbers in the range 6650 to 6679).

The aircraft depicted here is Standard Motors-built HR184, which was delivered from the factory to 10 MU on 6 May 1944. Four months later it passed to 417 ARF before allocation to 418 Squadron (RCAF) on 4 January 1945,

receiving the unit code letters 'TH-Z'. During a formation flight on 22 February 1945 HR184 collided with RS613 after the latter pulled up to avoid drop tanks jettisoned by another Mosquito. The subsequent damage to HR184 had been repaired by 7 April, the aircraft eventually making its way to 27 MU in March 1946. Three months later it was sold to de Havilland's for resale to the Turkish Air Force, and flew to Ringway for refurbishing on 16 August 1947. Delivered to Turkey on 27 September 1947, HR184 became 6737 with the Turkish Air Force and served with 3 Alay (Bomber Regiment). The aircraft is finished in aluminium dope and wears its RAF serial number (in small letters) on the rear fuselage immediately forward of the tailplane. Note the four-bladed propellers. *(BAE SYSTEMS)*

Pat Fillingham positions Turkish Air Force T.3 '542' close to the camera during a pre-delivery test flight from Hatfield on 17 June 1947. Turkey purchased a total of ten Mosquito T.3s, all new-build aircraft as opposed to refurbished ex-RAF machines. These were serialled 6601 to 6610 in Turkish Air Force service ('542' becoming '6610') and bore delivery numbers in the range 533 to 542. The Turks also purchased £47,711 worth of Mosquito spares from de

Havilland's in February 1952, but the aircraft were replaced by American F-84 Thunderjets (supplied under the Marshall Aid Plan) in 1954. In accordance with the final batch of RAF T.3s, '542' was finished in Trainer Yellow overall. Note the Turkish national flag marking on the fin. It is believed that a small number of Turkish Mosquitoes were later employed on aerial survey work. *(BAE SYSTEMS)*

A refurbished FB.VI for the Dominican Military Aviation Corps is seen at Ringway in 1948. The Air Arm of the Dominican National Army was created in 1932 by the country's President, General Rafael Trujillo Molina. In 1947 a group of exiled Dominicans living in Cuba threatened to invade their home country and overthrow the president. The group formed their own air force, the Fuerza Aerea del Ejertico de la Revolucion Americana (FAERA), which operated largely from Havana and included PBY-5A Catalinas, B-25 Mitchells and P.38 Lightnings. Dominica possessed no suitable aircraft to oppose this threat and attempted to obtain bombers from both the USA and Canada. However, the USA refused to supply combat aircraft, knowing full well that a Dominican attack on the FAERA would provoke war with Cuba. President Trujillo's agents managed to obtain aircraft from elsewhere, including six Mosquito FB.VIs from the UK. All were refurbished by

Fairey Aviation and (like the Turkish examples) equipped with four-bladed propellers.

This FB.VI was formerly TE612 and became FAD '301' in Dominican Military Aviation Corps service. Constructed by Standard Motors, TE612 went direct from the factory to 10 MU on 17 July 1945. In October 1945 it passed to No 1 FU before despatch to Aden, where it arrived on 6 January 1946 for 114 Squadron. Returning to the UK in October 1946, it was stored at 9 MU until sold to de Havilland's in May 1948 for resale to Dominica. Delivered in July 1948, '301' was later re-serialled '2101'. Dominican Mosquitoes are believed to have initially seen action on 14 June 1949 when two aircraft (together with a Beaufighter) opened fire on a FAERA Catalina and two landing-craft at Luperon Bay. The FB.VIs were supplemented by three ex-RCAF T.29s (KA172, KA206 and KA243) in February 1952. All Dominican Mosquitoes are believed to have been withdrawn in 1954. *(Westland)*

During a visit to St Athan in 1951 (to collect a Brigand), No 1 Overseas Ferry Unit pilot Richard Livermore spotted this unidentified FB.VI destined for Yugoslavia. Seventy-seven FB.VIs were supplied to the Yugoslav Air Force under the Mutual Defence Aid Programme, the first examples arriving

during late 1951. In common with several other FB.VIs delivered to Yugoslavia (including TA484 '8117'), this aircraft's upper surfaces appear to be finished in Medium Sea Grey with the lower surfaces and spinners in a darker shade of grey. *(Richard Livermore)*

Jugoslav Air Force (JRV) NF.38 8030, probably from the 103rd Reconnaissance Regiment, makes its final approach for landing. Yugoslavia received a total of sixty NF.38s (serialled 8001 to 8060), the only country to make first-line use of this final production version of the Mosquito. The aircraft served with the 103rd Reconnaissance Regiment at Pancevo (close to Belgrade) and the 97th and 184th Aviation Regiments. Yugoslav NF.38s were withdrawn in 1960 when the 184th Reconnaissance Regiment retired its examples. At maximum landing weight, the NF.38's recommended final approach speed with flaps down was 110 knots, this being safely reduced by 5 knots at light loads. 8030 wears the standard RAF Night-Fighter scheme of Medium Sea Grey overall with Dark Green camouflaged upper surfaces. The Yugoslav national flag (red, white and blue with a red star centrally placed on the white section) is carried on the centre of the rudder, with Yugoslav roundels on the fuselage and the upper and lower mainplane surfaces. Note the enlarged elevator horn balances. *(Milan Micevski, via Stuart Howe)*

Yugoslav Air Force (JRV) FB.VI 8074 receives attention to its port engine. This aircraft was formerly TA586, a Hatfield-built FB.VI, which entered storage with 51 MU on 19 September 1945. In May 1950 it passed to 9 MU before allocation to 27 MU in January 1951. Following sale to the JRV it was delivered to No 1 Overseas Ferry Unit on 13 December 1951 and despatched to Yugoslavia six days later. From 1952, JRV FB.VIs served with the 32nd Bomber Division at Zagreb until the latter began re-equipment with other aircraft types in 1956. The 32nd's FB.VIs then passed to the 184th Reconnaissance Regiment, which operated this version of the Mosquito until 1960. FB.VIs also served with the 97th Aviation Regiment, at least four being converted to carry TR-45/A torpedoes. Yugoslav FB.VIs also served with a sea reconnaissance squadron, largely in the target-towing role for the Zadar anti-aircraft school, and were retired in 1963; these were the world's last operational examples of the FB.VI. Note the Yugoslav red star superimposed over the RAF roundel on the fuselage. The JRV serial number is carried on the fin, with the last two digits repeated on the rear fuselage. The port engine cowling panels are lying on the ground beneath the port wing. *(Milan Micevski, via Stuart Howe)*

This second photograph of Yugoslav Air Force (JRV) NF.38 8030 was probably taken at Pancevo. 8030 was built at Chester (under Air Ministry Contract 783) as VT696 in December 1949 and delivered direct from the factory to 22 MU for storage. Following sale to Yugoslavia, VT696 was delivered to No 1 Overseas Ferry Unit at Abingdon before despatch to Yugoslavia, where it arrived on 28 November 1951. *(Milan Micevski, via Stuart Howe)*

B.IV Series ii DK296 suffered a landing accident at the Soviet Scientific Research Institute of the Air Force (based at Sverdlosk in the Urals) on 15 May 1944. The only Mosquito received by the Soviet Air Force, DK296 was supplied to the Russians following a request to the British Government (in late 1942) for a single example of the design. DK296 was a particularly renowned Mosquito and made its maiden flight (in the hands of Geoffrey de Havilland Junior) from Hatfield on 12 June 1942. Cleared for service use the following day, DK296 was delivered to 105 Squadron on 21 June where it received the unit code letters 'GB-G'. This aircraft's first operational sortie took place on 25 June 1942 when 139 Squadron crew Sqn Ldr J. E. Houlston and Sqn Ldr Armitage flew a bombing mission to Stade. During the Flensburg raid of 11 July 1942, DK296 (on its third operation) was flown by Flt Lt Peter Rowland and navigated by Sgt Mike Carreck. On the way to the target their aircraft struck the roof of a house and returned to Horsham St Faith with a section of chimney pot embedded in the starboard side of the nose! After repair, DK296 operated to Osnabruck on 9 September 1942, but suffered flak damage during its nineteenth sortie (to the Stork works at Hengelo) on 20 January 1943, which resulted in a single-engine crash-landing at Marham. Repairs were not completed until 29 July 1943, the aircraft passing to 10 MU a month later.

Allocated to Russia, DK296 flew to 20 APU on 7 September 1943 to be prepared for its delivery flight to Vnukovo aerodrome in Moscow. Following protracted delays it left 305 FTU at Errol on 19 April 1944 flown by Soviet pilot Senior Lieutenant N. I. Polosukhin and navigated by Lieutenant Kekishev. Following its safe arrival in Moscow, DK296 flew to the Soviet Flight Research Institute at Kratovo for performance evaluation and an assessment of the type's potential for Soviet license production. The Mosquito was regarded favourably by the Russians, but its performance was considered no improvement over the Pe-2 or Tu-2, but then DK296 was a rather elderly B.IV Series ii. License production of the Mosquito was discounted in view of the difficulty of obtaining Merlin engines. On 15 May 1944 DK296 was flown to the Scientific Research Institute of the Air Force at Sverdlosk but swung on landing, leading to the collapse of its undercarriage. DK296 was not repaired, the aircraft being broken up and its various parts dispatched to aviation institutes and design bureaux. Note the Soviet Red Star markings on the fin and rudder. *(RAF Museum)*

A batch of NF.XIXs, newly refurbished for Sweden, pictured at Hatfield with Swedish Air Force (Flygvapnet) delivery crews on 25 February 1949. Sixty NF.XIXs were ordered by the Swedish Government as a relatively cheap way of acquiring a radar-equipped night-fighter force for Swedish air defence. The sixty aircraft were allocated Flygvapnet serial numbers in the range 30001 to 30060 and delivered between July 1948 and November 1949. As with so many other export Mosquitoes, these were all ex-RAF machines refurbished by Fairey Aviation at Ringway. After overhaul the Mosquitoes were flown from Ringway to Hatfield for collection by Flygvapnet crews, this particular consignment consisting of six aircraft. *(BAE SYSTEMS)*

The first NF.XIX for the Flygvapnet, TA286, pictured at Ringway following overhaul by Fairey Aviation. This Hatfield-built NF.XIX was bought by de Havilland in February 1948 for resale to Sweden. Serialled 30001 in Flygvapnet service, TA286 arrived at Vasteras on 16 July 1948 and entered service with No 1 Squadron of F1 Wing as 'Red A'. Note that the aircraft is finished in aluminium dope overall with the spinners in black. The majority of Flygvapnet Mosquitoes were delivered in their RAF Night-Fighter camouflage, but both 30001 and 30002 (ex-TA275) arrived in this silver scheme. 30001 remained in Flygvapnet service until August 1952. *(Westland)*

An unidentified Flygvapnet NF.XIX takes off from Hatfield on the first stage of its delivery flight to Sweden. Designated J.30 (J standing for 'Jakt', the Swedish for 'fighter') in Flygvapnet service, NF.XIXs equipped Nos 1, 2 and 3 Squadrons of F1 Wing at Vasteras. The three Squadrons were distinguished from each other by a separate uniform colour applied to their aircraft's spinners and code letters. No 1 Squadron's aircraft initially featured white spinners and code letters (although these were later changed to red), No 2's aircraft featured blue spinners and code letters, and No 3's sported yellow spinners and code letters. The letters were applied across the fin and rudder and featured white outlines (with the exception of No 1 Squadron's aircraft, which applied black outlines to the white letters, this later being altered to white with red letters). J.30s served the Swedes well, but several aircraft suffered structural failure attributable to fracture of the elevator static balance weight. In 1954 the J.30s were replaced in front-line Flygvapnet service by the de Havilland Venom. *(BAE SYSTEMS)*

The tailplane of Swedish Air Force J.30 30054 (probably 'Yellow D' of No 3 Squadron) forms a suitable conversation location for (left to right) Birger Lindberg of No 1 Squadron, a de Havilland representative (believed to be a Mr Carter), and Gunnar Lindahl of No 2 Squadron. Note the tailplane inboard incidence stencilling running longitudinally to the tailplane trailing edge. The stencilling was applied in 7-inch-high letters (outboard and inboard) on both the top and bottom surfaces of the tailplane. Like the majority of J.30s, this aircraft retains its RAF Night-Fighter scheme of overall Medium Sea Grey with Dark Green camouflaged upper surfaces. The dinghy box is lying on the port wing upper surface. This picture was taken in December 1951. *(Peter Kempe, via Stuart Howe)*

This rare shot depicts Belgian Air Force TT.3 MA-2 'B2-B'; constructed at Hatfield as VR335, it was delivered to 19 MU in May 1947 before sale to the Belgian Air Force the following July. Later converted to Target Tug configuration by Fairey Aviation at Ringway, MA-2 was one of six T.3s and three FB.VIs operated by the Target Towing Flight at Koksijde. MA-2's upper surfaces are finished in aluminium dope with the under surfaces in diagonal stripes of black and yellow. MA-2 was Struck Off Charge with the Belgian Air Force on 5 November 1954. Note the target drogue buffer unit beneath the fuselage. *(MAP)*

334

MB17, a newly refurbished NF.30 for the Belgian Air Force, is seen at Ringway in 1948. The total number of NF.30s supplied to Belgium (under the terms of the 'Western Defence Pact') amounted to twenty-six, two of which (NT450 and NT563) were employed as instructional airframes in the Technical Training School at Tongres. The remaining twenty-four received the Belgian Air Force serials MB1 to MB24, serving with Nos 10 and 11 Squadrons of the 1st Wing. MB17 was constructed at Leavesden as NT501 in February 1945. Delivered to 218 MU on 28 February, it was issued to 219

Squadron on 24 March and assigned the unit codes 'FK-D'. After the war NT501 was stored first at 51 MU, then 27 MU, before sale to the Belgian Air Force. Following overhaul by Fairey Aviation the aircraft was dispatched to Belgium on 21 December 1948. MB17 retains the standard RAF Night-Fighter scheme of Medium Sea Grey overall with Dark Green camouflaged upper surfaces, but does not appear to be fitted with a radar scanning dish. Note the Belgian Air Force roundel on the fuselage and the hastily applied fin flash, the latter markedly taller than its RAF equivalent. *(Westland)*

The port undercarriage of Belgian Air Force NF.30 MB19 'ND-A' of No 10 Squadron has collapse, probably during a take-off accident, at Beauvechain on 5 December 1952. Built at Leavesden as NT275, this aircraft was delivered to 27 MU on 2 December 1944 before passing to 218 MU early the following month. Allocated to 410 Squadron (RCAF) on 9 February 1945, NT275 remained with 410 until December 1945, when it entered storage with 51 MU.

Assigned to 27 MU in June 1948, NT275 returned to 51 MU three months later when it was sold to the Belgian Air Force. Following overhaul by Fairey Aviation at Ringway the aircraft was despatched to Belgium (as MB19) in December 1948. MB19 served with No 10 Squadron at Beauvechain and was Struck Off Charge on 17 October 1956. Note the damaged port propeller and the crushed aft lower section of the port engine nacelle. *(R. Binnemans, via Stuart Howe)*

Belgian Air Force NF.30 MB11 'KT-O' of No 11 Squadron photographed at Beauvechain in 1951. This NF.30 was built at Leavesden as NT377 and delivered to 218 MU in early January 1945. Allocated to 410 Squadron (RCAF) on 9 February 1945, it served with 410 until 16 June 1945 when it entered storage with 10 MU. Over the next three years NT377 passed between 27 and 51 MUs until sold to the Belgian Air Force in 1948. Following overhaul by Fairey Aviation, NT377 (as MB11) was flown to Belgium on 29 June 1948, where it entered service with No 11 Squadron at Beauvechain. Note the painted band on the aft section of MB11's spinners; this was applied in yellow and adorned the spinners of all No 11 Squadron Mosquitoes (aircraft from No 10 Squadron featuring the band in red). With the exception of MB24 (RK952), Belgian Air Force NF.30s were withdrawn from service in 1953 due to wear on their engine mountings and undercarriages. As illustrated on MB11, Belgian NF.30s later had the paint removed from the forward upper section of their nose radomes. *(R. Binnemans, via Stuart Howe)*

French Air Force (Armée de l'Air) FB.VI TE697 was constructed by Standard Motors in July 1945 and sold to the French in May 1946. The Armée de l'Air flew examples of the Mosquito T.3, FB.VI, NF.30 and PR.XVI, many of these later being sold to Israel. FB.VIs were operated against the Viet-Minh in Indo-China by 10/Groupe de Chasse 1/3 'Corse', which carried out its first sortie in January 1947. By May 1947 Groupe de Chasse 1/3 had flown more than 340 sorties (dropping more than 169,000lb of bombs) and redeployed to Rabat in Morocco the same month. At Rabat the unit was renamed Groupe de Chasse 1/6 'Corse' and continued operating FB.VIs until July 1949. In common with all Armée de l'Air FB.VIs, TE697 retains its RAF camouflage scheme and serial number. *(J. M. Petit, via Stuart Howe)*

Taken at Hatfield on 3 December 1945, this photograph illustrates the first entry of Free French Air Force personnel to attend the Mosquito Instructional School airframe course. The Mosquito behind them is an FB.VI equipped with 'needle'-blade propellers. *(BAE SYSTEMS)*

Aircrews of Groupe de Chasse 1/20 'Lorraine' (Armée de l'Air) pictured with one of the unit's PR.XVIs in North Africa. This unit formed at Dijon in 1945 and served in North Africa (at Agadir and Rabat) before moving to Tours in April 1952. French PR.XVIs were withdrawn from front-line service in 1953. Note the T.3 on the left. *(J. M. Petit, via Stuart Howe)*

Silver-doped FB.VI TE603 'KP-1' was acquired by the Czechoslovak Air Force (Ceskoslovenske Letectvo). Following the end of the Second World War, a new Czechoslovak Air Force was created using aircraft and personnel from Britain, Russia and Germany, together with the former Slovak Air Force. FB.VIs were supplied from the UK and served with No 24 Bomber Regiment and the 47th Air Regiment. The aircraft received the designation B-36 in Ceskoslovenske Letectvo service, or LB-36 when fitted with German cannon armament. Merlin 25-powered TE603 was constructed by Standard Motors in June 1945 and delivered to RAE Farnborough the following month. In August 1945 it was dispatched to the Middle East for 'special trials', returning (via Cairo and El Adem) to Farnborough on 2 October of the same year. TE603 joined the Northolt Station Flight in January 1946 but suffered accident damage a month later (repairs being carried out by de Havilland's). Following storage at 19 MU, TE603 was purchased by Czechoslovakia and departed the UK on 19 December 1946. As the Communists established power in 1948, all pro-Western and ex-RAF personnel were removed from the armed services and replaced by Russian advisers. Note the RAF roundel showing through on the port wing upper surface. Czech Mosquitoes were withdrawn from use in around 1950. *(Milan Janac, via Stuart Howe)*

G-AIRU/NS812) were bought in England and clandestinely ferried to Israel, although only G-AIRT reached its destination, G-AIRU crashing en route. In February 1951 Israel signed a contract with Société Nationale de Constructions (SNCAN) and Hispano for the refurbishment of sixty-three former Armée de l'Air Mosquitoes at a total cost of $387,300. This represented a relatively low-cost way of acquiring large numbers of a multi-role combat aircraft type for the Israeli Defence Force/Air Force. The aircraft comprised thirty-nine FB.VIs, twenty NF.30s and four PR.XVIs, refurbishment being carried out at Chateaudun and Rennes. These aircraft were later supplemented by two ex-Armée de l'Air T.3s, with at least four of the original FB.VIs being converted to dual-control standard. The first Israeli FB.VI unit was 109 Squadron of 4 Wing, which began operating Mosquitoes from Hatzor in early 1952. 109 was joined by the newly formed 110 Squadron in August 1953, the latter operating in a training capacity in addition to preparing for the night-fighter role. (Stuart Howe collection)

A formation of Israel Defence Force/Air Force FB.VIs is probably over Hatzor in 1954. Israel operated a total of eighty-seven Mosquitoes between 1948 and 1959 and became great exponents of the type. Following the Israeli War of Independence two PR.XVIs (G-AIRT/NS811 and

A TR.33 for the Israeli Defence Force/Air Force runs up at Blackbushe following refurbishment by Eagle Aviation. This was one of thirteen TR.33s and seven FB.VIs purchased by Israel from British scrap dealer R. A. Short in 1954. Several of the TR.33s had extremely low flying hours and were virtually new (a marked comparison to many of the Israeli FB.VIs previously acquired from the French), making a welcome addition to the Israeli Air Force inventory. During overhaul by Eagle Aviation the TR.33s had their arrestor hooks and radar equipment removed, but retained the four-bladed propellers. The refurbished Mosquitoes were allocated fictitious ferry markings in the range '4x3171' to '4x3190' and flown to Israel between November 1954 and August 1955.

This aircraft wears the ferry markings '4x3186' and was originally built at Leavesden as TW238 in December 1945. It served with 811 Squadron at Ford (as 'FD4Q') from April 1946, before entering storage at Stretton two months later. 790 Squadron at Culdrose took delivery of TW238 in August 1948, retaining the aircraft until January 1950. Following storage at Culham, it was sold as scrap to R. A. Short on 23 July 1953. TW238 was test-flown from Blackbushe by Israeli MoD chief test pilot Hugo Marom and delivered to Israel by Peter Nock. Note that TW238 retains its arrestor hook mounting points beneath the rear fuselage. (APN)

With its undercarriage retracting, an unidentified Israeli Defence Force/Air Force FB.VI climbs away after take-off. Several of the Israeli FB.VIs acquired from France were in quite poor condition, a fact that detracted from their flying qualities, particularly single-engine climb performance. This led to the type gaining a bad reputation, exacerbated by rumours of airframe woodworm and the fact that they were essentially 'third-hand' machines. On reflection this reputation was unfair as the aircraft had been properly maintained by the French and were being operated to their performance limits by the Israelis. Two aircraft were lost through structural failure but this was probably due to poor discipline on the part of the pilots. In 1956 the Israeli Mosquito Fighter-Bomber force began to be withdrawn, several aircraft being scrapped with the remainder entering storage. However, a mixed force of FB.VIs and TR.33s was re-activated and flown by 110 Squadron during the Sinai Campaign of October/November 1956. The Mosquitoes operated almost with impunity, attacking Egyptian vehicle convoys with bombs and rockets together with cannon and machine-gun fire. Throughout the Sinai Campaign not a single Mosquito was lost to enemy action. *(Stuart Howe collection)*

The remains of an Israeli Defence Force/Air Force TR.33 arrive at Kibbutz Beit Alfa in Northern Israel during the summer of 1960. Following their withdrawal from active use, several Israeli Mosquitoes were donated to Kibbutzes where they served as an amusement source for local children. To facilitate transport to Beit Alfa, this aircraft's fuselage was severed behind the wing, the rear section being propped up on a metal stand once the aircraft was in position at the Kibbutz. During the 1970s Rob Lamplough discovered the TR.33s remains at Beit Alfa and informed Stuart Howe of the Mosquito Aircraft Museum, Salisbury Hall. By now the fuselage had rotted away, leaving a fairly intact wing complete with engine nacelles, control surfaces and cowlings. Stuart travelled to Israel and negotiated donation of the aircraft's remains to the Mosquito Aircraft Museum, where (thanks to the generosity of El Al and several other companies) they arrived in July 1980. The wing has undergone a protracted and detailed restoration since 1985 and will one day be mated to the fuselage of Mosquito FB.VI TA122 at Salisbury Hall. The wing originates from one of two fixed-wing TR.33s, either pre-production aircraft TS449 or the seventh production machine, TW233. Note the Israeli national marking on the fuselage (in line with the break) and the forward section of the fuselage longitudinal stiffening strake *(Hillel Neuman, via Stuart Howe)*

Six B.VIIs and thirty-four B.XXs were supplied to the USAAF for photographic reconnaissance duties (being allocated serial numbers in the range 43-34924 to 43-34963). Designated F-8-DH, these aircraft were converted to Photographic Reconnaissance configuration by the Bell Niagara Modification Centre at Buffalo, New York. The majority of F-8-DHs remained in the USA, but nineteen were delivered to the European Theatre (this figure should have been twenty but KB326/43-34929 crashed en route). With its two-speed, single-stage supercharged Merlins, the F-8-DH lacked the altitude performance required for USAAF operations, American use of the Mosquito instead centring on the far superior PR.XVI. Three F-8-DHs are recorded as having been flown to North Africa, but eventually sixteen of the original nineteen aircraft delivered to Europe were transferred to the RAF (several going on to serve successfully as bombers). Early production F-8-DHs were equipped with a single vertical camera mounted in the forward section of the ventral bay, this installation

being changed to split vertical cameras on later aircraft.

This photograph of an F-8-DH was taken at Toronto and depicts 43-34943. Built by de Havilland Canada as KB149, it was transferred to the USAAF and flown to the Bell Niagara Modification Centre on 2 March 1944. Following conversion to F-8-DH standard, 43-34943 was delivered to Hunter Field on 2 May 1944 for the 3rd AAF. Eleven days later it flew to Romulus, but on 15 May 2/Lt H. Peattie ground-looped on take-off from Romulus after the starboard brake failed. Repairs were complete by 11 June but the following month 1/Lt F. Schrom had to make an emergency landing on the Willow Run-Detroit Expressway following engine problems. F-8-DHs were not popular with the USAAF, all remaining examples in the USA eventually being returned to the Canadian Government. An RAF crew ferried 43-34943, which had arrived in Canada by 1 January 1945 and was Struck Off Charge on 30 November. Note the USAAF 'star and bar' marking on the fuselage and the fabric repair to the port wing tip. *(BAE SYSTEMS)*

A USAAF Mosquito crew walk away from a fairly pristine PR.XVI. The Eighth Air Force operated two squadrons of PR.XVIs within the 25th Bombardment Group (Reconnaissance), formerly designated the 802nd Reconnaissance Group. Based at Watton, the Mosquito units were the 653rd Light Weather Squadron and the 654th Special Squadron. The spinners on 653rd Squadron Mosquitoes were finished in dark blue, 654th Squadron aircraft retaining their factory-finished PR blue spinners (changed to red following the end of the war); judging by its darker-coloured spinners this aircraft probably belongs to the 653rd. Note the mission tally symbols on the nose, consisting of a cloud with a bomb through the centre. The object forward and beneath the canopy direct vision quarter window is the intake for the cabin cold air louvre. *(Photographer unknown, via Stuart Howe collection)*

An unidentified PR.XVI of the 654th BS/25th BG peels
away from the camera aircraft. The 654th carried out day
and night photographic reconnaissance missions as well as
radar mapping sorties, the latter using modified PR.XVIs
equipped with American H2X radar. Night photography
flights were code-named 'Joker' and employed M-46 photo-
flashes (of 700 million candlepower) to illuminate the
target. Note the black and white 'invasion stripes' beneath
the fuselage and mainplane.

Major Hereward de Havilland (brother of Sir Geoffrey)
supervised the activities of de Havilland Company technical
representatives attached to Mosquito Squadrons and units.
Major de Havilland compiled a confidential quarterly report

(for 'in-house' distribution only) entitled 'Mosquito News'.
The May/July 1944 edition of this publication incorporated
the following paragraph regarding USAAF PR.XVIs stationed
at Watton: 'Their aircraft are delivered to them after
preparation to US standards by the American Preparation &
Maintenance Unit at Burtonwood, about which they can't
think of anything bad enough to say. According to Colonel
Dowdy, the CO, Burtonwood have never done a job right on
his Mosquitoes, and their mechanics slide off the wings and
kick their heels through the ply of the flaps.' A total of 131
PR.XVIs were allocated to the USAAF.
(John Edwards, ex-654th BS Photo Lab, via Stuart Howe)

This H2X radar-equipped PR.XVI is probably NS538, seen at Hatfield on 15 July 1944. H2X was developed by the American Rad Lab (under researcher George Valley) as an X-band targeting radar operating in the 3cm waveband. Referred to as 'Mickey' or 'BTO' (Bombing Through Overcast), the USAAF version of H2X was produced by Western Electric and initially fitted to B.17 Pathfinders of the Eighth Air Force. By the end of 1943 USAAF bombing raids led by 'Mickey' Pathfinders were obtaining effective results over cloud-covered targets. H2X was also installed in several USAAF PR.XVIs (the first conversion being MM308/G) operated by the 482nd Bombardment Group and the 25th Bombardment Group (Reconnaissance), the latter employing them on radar mapping sorties with the 654th BS. The objective of these sorties was to obtain a photographic record of radar bombing approaches to high-priority targets deep in Germany, the resulting 'Mickey' target run-ups being used to brief key radar-navigator-bombardiers prior to bombing raids. H2X sets were not particularly reliable and were later encased in pressurised boxes to overcome electrical arcing problems caused by the rarefied air at high altitudes.

As depicted, H2X Mosquito PR.XVIs received substantial nose modifications to accept the radar scanner unit, the amplifier and associated equipment being installed in the nose and ventral bay. The observer's radar scope occupied the rear fuselage forward of the access hatch and to the right of the oxygen bottles. Note the port engine's flame-damping exhaust stubs and the heat-resistant panels on the inboard side cowling. The plate mounted midway down the nose (immediately aft of the radome) incorporated the static vent for the Air Speed Indicator system.

Hatfield-built NS538 was delivered to the USAAF at Alconbury on 4 July 1944 before allocation to the 654th BS of the 25th Bombardment Group (Reconnaissance). The 654th BS operated NS538 (coded 'F') until 2002hrs on 8 September 1944 when it blew up in the air 3 miles south-east of Newmarket. It was on a test flight prior to a sortie, eye-witnesses stating that a severe thunderstorm was in progress when the aircraft exploded. The crew (F/O Russell and Master Sgt Raymond G. Armstrong) were both killed. The inscription on the crew entrance door reads 'BEWARE OF AIRSCREWS'. *(BAE SYSTEMS)*

NF.30 MM746 belongs to the 416th Night-Fighter Squadron USAAF, the only American fighter unit to operate the Mosquito. Previously equipped with Beaufighters, the 416th converted to Mosquitoes at Pisa during December 1944, flying the type until June 1945, when they received Northrop P-61 Black Widows. Merlin 76-powered MM746 was built at Leavesden in July 1944 and delivered to the Mediterranean Theatre two months later. Allocated to the USAAF on 30 November 1944, it was eventually Struck Off Charge in March 1945. Note that the aircraft is fitted with non-louvred exhaust shrouds. *(Stuart Howe collection)*

Canadian pilot George Stewart is seen at Downsview with one of the Mosquitoes used to instruct Chinese Air Force pilots in Canada. For all students of Mosquito history the name George Stewart will be forever linked with the type. A tremendous advocate of the Mosquito, he flew FB.VIs with 23 Squadron during the war before serving as an instructor at 8 OTU. By the time of his demob in July 1945 George had accumulated 581 flying hours on Mosquitoes. In February 1948 he signed a contract with the Chinese Nationalist Government to travel to China and train Chinese Air Force pilots to fly the aircraft. This picture was taken in February 1948 while George was undergoing refresher training to reacquaint himself with the Mosquito. Note that the canopy starboard direct vision quarter window has been slid back to the fully open position. The Canadian instructors departed for China on 22 March 1948. *(George Stewart)*

Following the end of the Second World War civil war broke out in China between the Sino Communists and the Nationalist Government of Chiang Kai-Shek. The Chinese Air Force was reorganised with assistance from the USA, which naturally wished to support any resistance against Communism. The Americans supplied various aircraft types, including Mustangs, Thunderbolts, Mitchells and Liberators. However, reserve forces were required by the Chinese, and in 1947 around 200 Canadian-built Mosquitoes were purchased from the Canadian Government at a reported cost of $12 million. These aircraft were in storage and consisted largely of FB.26s, but also included several T.27s and T.29s. Following overhaul by de Havilland Canada at Downsview, the Mosquitoes were shipped to Shanghai via the Panama Canal. Chinese Air Force pilots initially began their Mosquito conversion training in Canada (using nine refurbished FB.26s/T.29s), but this later switched to Hankow in China.

This photograph was taken at Downsview in February 1948 and depicts one of the FB.26s used for the initial pilot conversion programme. It is not carrying Nationalist Chinese Air Force markings, but wears the emblem of No 1 Bombardment Group on the fuselage side. The letters 'FB' stand for 'Fighter Bomber', the number '4' indicating that this was the fourth FB.26 taken on charge by the Nationalist Chinese Air Force. Chinese Trainer Mosquitoes at Downsview were similarly marked with the prefix 'T'. In China the Mosquitoes wore full Nationalist Chinese markings and serial numbers. *(George Stewart)*

Chinese Nationalist Air Force Mosquitoes undergoing re-assembly at Tazang following shipment from Canada. After overhaul at Downsview, the Chinese Mosquitoes were dismantled and transported by rail (see page 193) to Canadian east coast ports from where they were shipped to China via the Panama Canal. Upon arrival the Mosquitoes were transported to Tazang airfield near Shanghai, where two hangars were used for their assembly. By 12 November 1948 179 Mosquitoes had been assembled before the Nationalist Chinese evacuated Tazang. The aircraft on the left is an FB.26; it has yet to have its machine-guns installed and still bears traces of the original camouflage scheme on its port engine inner side cowling. Note that this aircraft has been jacked into the rigging position, the jacks engaging with jacking pins screwed into fittings on the outboard undercarriage structure. It would appear that the majority of Chinese Mosquitoes were refinished in silver dope prior to departure from Canada. *(George Stewart)*

de Havilland Canada engineer George Smith stands in front of a recently assembled T.27 or T.29 at Tazang. The de Havilland Canada technical support team in China was organised by Fred Plumb (the original foreman at Salisbury Hall during construction of the Mosquito Prototypes) and led by Eddie Jack. In addition to George Smith, the other engineers were Jim Crowe, Bill Hall, Bill Morgan and Les Abyss. The Chinese groundcrews were trained by Bill Mann, Johnny Howlett, Ernie Croydon, Geoff Williams and Ed Slater. Note other newly assembled Mosquitoes in the background, including an FB.26 (third from the left) and two more Trainers, the example on the extreme left still retaining its RAF fin flash. The silver-doped finish seen on these aircraft later gave way to a Nationalist Chinese Air Force scheme of dark green (possibly olive green) upper surfaces and light grey under surfaces. The machine-gun/cannon blanking fairings are well illustrated on the aircraft in the foreground. *(George Stewart)*

Following re-assembly, test-flying and repainting at Tazang, the Chinese Mosquitoes were flown to Hankow where Chinese pilots continued their type conversion training. Pictured at Tazang with three of the initial four Trainer Mosquitoes ferried to Hankow are (left to right) Engineer Les Abyss, flying instructor Jack Turnbull, an unidentified Chinese Nationalist Air Force officer, and engineer Eddie Jack. This picture was taken on 30 March 1948 just prior to departure for Hankow. The newly assembled Mosquitoes were test-flown from Tazang by de Havilland Canada test pilot Fred Offord. Note the Liberator in the background. *(George Stewart)*

This atmospheric shot shows Chinese trainer 'T-19' taxying at Hankow. Hankow was home to No 1 Bombardment Group, Nationalist Chinese Air Force, and became the base for the Mosquito pilot training school. Once the newly assembled Chinese Mosquitoes arrived from Tazang, conversion training (supervised by the Canadian instructors) immediately got under way. Being used to American nosewheel aircraft such as the Mitchell and Boston, many Chinese pilots initially had great difficulty controlling the Mosquito and developed a great fear of it. These difficulties were exacerbated by the Chinese pilots who originally trained in Toronto, as they returned home with horrific tales regarding the Mosquito's handling (they managed to damage several aircraft in Canada). Taxying, take-off and landing accidents were commonplace, and at least sixty aircraft were written off in various training incidents. This Mosquito carries the Nationalist Chinese Air Force serial number 'B-MO19' on the fin upper section ('MO' standing for Mosquito). Within the 'T-19' fuselage code, 'T' stood for Trainer and '19' was an abbreviated form of the aircraft's serial number. Depending on whether the Mosquito was a Trainer or Fighter-Bomber variant, 'T' or 'FB' markings were carried beneath the starboard wing with the serial number repeated beneath the port wing. The rudder is finished in white with light blue stripes. *(George Stewart)*

To speed up the Mosquito pilot training programme, the Chinese insisted on relinquishing control from the Canadian instructors. The end result was an increase in accidents, leading to a much higher attrition rate. This photograph depicts one such casualty, a well and truly destroyed machine that appears to have suffered from a ground loop. Note the oxygen bottles visible within the starboard side of the shattered fuselage. After two months the Canadians resumed control of pilot training in July 1948. The Chinese insistence on urgency was partly understandable due to the worsening civil war situation within their country. (George Stewart)

de Havilland Canada engineer Johnny Howlett examines main spar damage to an FB.26 sustained in a typical 'prang' at Hankow. This aircraft is believed to be FB.26 B-M040 'FB-40'. Chinese groundcrews are preparing to recover the aircraft. *(George Stewart)*

A pilot of No 3 Squadron, No 1 Bombardment Group, Nationalist Chinese Air Force, is pictured with his FB.26 at Hankow in late 1948. Previously equipped with the B.25 Mitchell, No 3 Squadron received its first Mosquitoes in the autumn of 1948. In contrast to the write-offs incurred during the early stages of Chinese Mosquito pilot training, No 3 Squadron had a good safety record and only crashed two aircraft during conversion. Although not displayed on this particular FB.26, No 3 Squadron's aircraft often carried the unit emblem (an eagle releasing a bomb) on the port nose gun bay door. The Trainer and Fighter-Bomber role codes displayed on the training aircraft at Hankow were dispensed with on No 3 Squadron's machines, the latter featuring serial numbers in the '300' range marked on the fuselage and fin ('3' denoting No 3 Squadron). In October 1948 most of No 3 Squadron's Mosquitoes were flown to Peiping before relocating to Formosa two months later. From Formosa the Mosquitoes attacked Communist positions on the Liuchow Peninsula as well as supply depots in Swatow and Canton. With the Communist take-over in 1949 the Mosquito disappeared from Chinese service. The spinners on this FB.26 appear to be either natural metal or finished in silver. Note the Trainer Mosquito in the background. *(George Stewart)*

This dramatic shot depicts an unidentified Chinese Nationalist Air Force T.27 or T.29 'beating up' the aerodrome at Hankow. *(George Stewart)*

Mosquitoes on Film

The Mosquito's wartime exploits and dramatic appeal made it an ideal candidate for appearances on the big screen. The subject of numerous wartime newsreel and documentary productions, the Mosquito went on to star in several postwar feature films including (undoubtedly its most famous outing) the renowned *633 Squadron*. The wartime RAF Film Production Unit 'Gen' newsreels portrayed Mosquito construction in both the UK and Canada, while the 'Airfront' series depicted low-level precision strikes by FB.VIs of the 2nd Tactical Air Force. The National Film Board of Canada produced the excellent documentary *From Spruce to Bomber* (covering Canadian Mosquito production at Downsview) and went on to release *Mosquito Squadron*, the latter featuring Mosquito aircrew training at 36 OTU. Wartime Australian Mosquito manufacture is well covered by the Movietone News feature 'Latest Mosquito planes now made in Australia', which included footage of the Bankstown production line in addition to aerial shots of the first Australian-built Mosquito, FB.40 A52-1. However, the most comprehensive record of Mosquito design, construction and operational use is provided by the Cecil Musk production *de Havilland Presents The Mosquito*. Shot between 1944 and 1945 and directed by Captain P. L. Cecil-Gurney, this has become an established footage source for subsequent documentaries on the aircraft.

One of the earliest postwar film appearances by a Mosquito came in the 1946 production *A Matter of Life and Death*, starring David Niven as Sqn Ldr Peter Carter. Early in the film Sqn Ldr Carter, having been washed up on the coast after baling out of his Lancaster the night before, witnesses a very low flypast by an unidentified Mosquito. Another 1946 release was the French film *Jericho*; directed by Henri Calef, it focused on the Amiens prison raid of 18 February 1944 and featured RAF FB.VIs flying over a mock-up of the prison. The 1954 Rank Organisation/Two Cities film *The Purple Plain*, based on the novel by H. E. Bates, included fine ground and take-off shots of PR.34s RG238 and RG177, both modified to represent SEAC FB.VIs. *The Dambusters* also featured Mosquitoes, including ground shots of PR.35 VR803 and wartime archive footage of 'Highball' trials using modified B.IV Series iis. As an introduction to the film's 'Highball' sequences, TT.35 TH981 (from No 2 CAACU at Langham) was reportedly filmed flying off the Norfolk coast.

Two T.3s (masquerading as FB.VIs) made a brief appearance in the 1956 film *The Man Who Never Was*, but the Mosquito's crowning screen glory came seven years later in the Mirisch Corporation production *633 Squadron*. Employing recently retired No 3 CAACU TT.35s and T.3s, five aircraft were airworthy for the film and provided some spectacular ground and air-to-air sequences that compensated for the film's rather weak storyline. Although three aircraft were destroyed during the filming, the five flyable aircraft exist to this day, although none is currently airworthy.

As a sequel to *633 Squadron*, Oakmont Productions made *Mosquito Squadron* in 1968. By this time airworthy Mosquitoes were more difficult to source, but four were eventually gathered including two previously flown in *633 Squadron*. The budget for *Mosquito Squadron* was considerably less than its predecessor and the film never made an impact at the box office. After 1968 T.3 RR299/G-ASKH, owned by Hawker Siddeley (later British Aerospace), appeared in a number of smaller productions including the Dutch film *Soldat Van Orange*, together with the BBC drama series *Tenko* and *Secret Army*.

Released in 1945, the wartime film *de Havilland Presents The Mosquito* is undoubtedly the ultimate contemporary work on the aircraft. A Cecil Musk production for the Film Producers Guild, the film was shot by Merton Park Studios and directed by Captain Percy Lionel Cecil-Gurney. Introduced as 'a plain narrative of industry and war', this comprehensive 36½-minute production covered the Mosquito's design, construction, development and operational use. Superbly shot and edited, it provides an excellent historical record rarely matched by other contemporary films on famous RAF aircraft types Taken in the winter snow at Hatfield on 11 January 1945, this photograph shows the Merton Park Studios team (left) with de Havilland staff including Public Relations Manager Martin Sharp (believed to be fourth from the right). The aircraft behind them is FB.VI PZ202, which was filmed taxying with four 60lb rocket projectiles beneath the port wing (the FB.VI's full complement of eight rockets described in the film as 'equivalent to the broadside of a 6-inch cruiser'). Note the camera tripod forward of the port tailplane. *(BAE SYSTEMS)*

On Friday 2 June 1944 FB.VIs of 464 Squadron (RAAF) flew into Hatfield for the filming of *de Havilland Presents The Mosquito*. Merton Park Studios required in-flight shots of Fighter-Bomber Mosquitoes armed with 500lb underwing bombs, 464 Squadron despatching three aircraft from its base at Gravesend. Several flights were filmed, but the resulting footage did not feature in the final production. Four days later 464 Squadron was heavily engaged on night intruder operations over the invasion area in northern France. In this shot two of the aircraft are seen over Hatfield, their underwing bombs clearly visible. *(BAE SYSTEMS)*

The 464 Squadron (RAAF) crews who demonstrated their FB.VIs for *de Havilland Presents The Mosquito* are pictured at Hatfield on 2 June 1944. The brand new FB.VIs in the background are PZ199 (right) and PZ173. Four days after this picture was taken PZ199 was delivered to 27 MU before allocation to 418 Squadron (RCAF) on 29 July. Damaged on 30 September, PZ199 had been repaired by 28 December but made a belly-landing while returning from an operational sortie on 19 March 1945. Following repairs it was allocated to 21 Squadron on 7 June 1945, but two weeks later the port undercarriage collapsed in a landing accident at Melsbroek.

This FB.VI passed to the Armée de l'Air in 1946, later being stored at Rennes before sale to Israel in February 1951. After overhaul at Rennes, PZ199 flew to Israel in June 1951, becoming '2107' in Israeli Defence Force/Air Force service. 2107 was eventually written off in a landing accident on 29 January 1953. PZ173 initially served with 21 Squadron before allocation to 487 Squadron (RNZAF). On 22 January 1945 it went missing during a night intruder sortie over Germany. The identities of the crews depicted in this picture are currently unknown. *(BAE SYSTEMS)*

Geoffrey de Havilland Junior taxies W4052 for the cameras during filming of *de Havilland Presents The Mosquito*. This scene was shot at Hatfield on 2 June 1944 during a simulation of W4052's maiden flight from Salisbury Hall (see page 25). Photography for the film was undertaken by A. T. Dinsdale and Jo Jago, with commentary provided by Robert Speight. Eric Spear's music, specially composed for the production, was described at the time as 'sensitively descriptive and captures the spirit of the narrative in a remarkable way'. *(BAE SYSTEMS)*

A mobile crane hauls a Merton Park Studios camera dolly through the Board Room window at Hatfield on 23 May 1944. This was necessary to film scenes of a de Havilland Company Directors' meeting for inclusion in *de Havilland Presents The Mosquito*. These scenes appear early on in the film and feature company founder Captain (later Sir) Geoffrey de Havilland. This is one of the few remaining de Havilland Company buildings on the Hatfield site today. Note the camouflaged exterior. (BAE SYSTEMS)

81 Squadron PR.34As RG238 (right) and RG177 seen at RAF Negombo, Ceylon, in January 1954; both had been detached to Negombo, ostensibly to conduct a photographic survey of Ceylon's airfields. However, it later transpired that they would be assisting in the production of a feature film (produced by the Rank Organisation and Two Cities Films) based on the H. E. Bates novel *The Purple Plain*. As the novel was set in Burma, both Mosquitoes were repainted to represent wartime SEAC FB.VIs, RG238 receiving 'cosmetic surgery' in the process. Throughout the detachment, RG238 and RG177 were maintained by an 81 Squadron groundcrew team led by engine fitter Cpl 'Acker' Paine and comprising airframe fitter SAC Brian 'Wilbur' Wright, engine mechanic Patrick 'Spider' Webb and electrician SAC Ray Jarvis. RG238 has just started its engines, as signified by the groundcrew member wheeling away the trolley accumulator. Note that both aircraft feature PRU blue under surfaces and light grey upper surfaces. *(Former SAC 'Wilbur' Wright, ex-81 PR Squadron)*

Pictured outside the Negombo Fire Section hangar, RG238 begins the initial stage of its 'FB.VI' conversion for *The Purple Plain*. Airframe fitter SAC Brian 'Wilbur' Wright (standing on the steps) and engine mechanic Patrick 'Spider' Webb (inside the nose compartment) are preparing to remove RG238's Perspex nose prior to the installation of a dummy 'machine-gun' nose. Affixed to the fuselage by 6BA nuts and bolts, removal of the nose was an awkward and time-consuming task that was vastly compounded by the sweltering Negombo heat. 'Wilbur' and 'Spider' began work at around 1100hrs, taking it in turns for one man to secure the counter-sunk bolts from the outside while the other slackened off and removed the 6BA nuts from inside the nose compartment. By midday, with

temperatures approaching 98°F, neither man was able to spend more than 20 minutes at a time inside the nose (in total they probably sweated off half a stone!).

Historically, RG238 was a very significant PR.34, having gained the London to Cape Town speed record in 1947 before service with the BEA Gust Research Unit at Cranfield (as G-AJZF) in 1949. This shot emphasises the 'pregnant' appearance of the PR.34's ventral bay doors and clearly shows the camera ports located in their forward sections. Note the aircraft's serial number beneath the starboard wing, interrupted by the drop tank.
(Former SAC 'Wilbur' Wright, ex-81 PR Squadron)

A local worker (attached to Negombo's camp workshops) prepares to paint RG238's new 'fighter' nose, which was manufactured from sheet metal and beaten into shape using the original Perspex nose as a template (thereby rendering the original unit totally useless!). Once fixed in position, the nose was covered over with fabric (to reduce drag) and dummy machine-guns installed through specially designed pre-cut openings. The 'machine-guns' (according to Jack Maxted, Art Director on *The Purple Plain*) were attached to

turned broom handles and cost 25 shillings each! When Jack Maxted came to view the finished 'nose job' at Negombo he viewed it long and hard before announcing, 'Yes, it's very well done, but it's bugging me that those guns wouldn't convince anyone they'd ever been fired in anger – can you get 'em singed a bit with a blowtorch so they look more like the real thing?' This was duly carried out, Jack Maxted being more than happy with the result.
(Former SAC 'Wilbur' Wright, ex-81 PR Squadron)

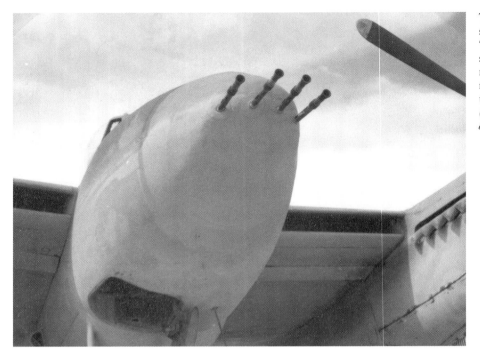

The finished job! This close-up shot shows RG238's new 'fighter' nose. Although somewhat pointed, the new nose was a fairly good representation of that fitted to the FB.VI.
(Former SAC 'Wilbur' Wright, ex-81 PR Squadron)

RG238 photographed at Negombo shortly after preparation for its starring role in *The Purple Plain*. Both RG238 and RG177 were finished in an approximation of the Temperate Land Scheme (Dark Green and Dark Earth camouflaged upper surfaces and Azure Blue under surfaces) originally applied to many SEAC FB.VIs. The paint used was a thick water-based distemper, its crude application described as 'pure vandalism' by SAC Brian 'Wilbur' Wright, the airframe fitter assigned to the care of RG238, who took great pride in

his aircraft. Note the bogus serial number 'FP136' and code letter 'P'; the other PR.34 employed on the film, RG177, became 'VF310', code letter 'F'. Judging by the lack of exhaust stains on the engine cowlings, RG238's engines have yet to be run following the application of this new scheme. The repaint was carried out inside the hangar in the background. Engine mechanic Patrick 'Spider' Webb is standing on the port wing.
(Former SAC 'Wilbur' Wright, ex-81 PR Squadron)

The aircraft and aerodrome shots for *The Purple Plain* were filmed at Sigiriya airstrip, located some 70 miles north of Negombo. It was originally planned to shoot the film in Burma, but that country's unstable political situation made insurers reluctant to cover star Gregory Peck. During the course of filming the RAF detachment remained based at Negombo but flew in to Sigiriya each day. This is the flying control tower at Sigiriya that features in the film and was used to shoot landing and take-off shots of RG238. Built by the RAF in 1942, Sigiriya employed around 1,000 local workers during its construction and featured more than twenty hangars to protect aircraft from Japanese night-bombing raids. Abandoned by the RAF in 1946, Sigiriya is now a Sri Lanka Air Force base. The sign mounted midway up the tower reads: 'FLYING CONTROL – ALL PILOTS REPORT HERE'. *(Former SAC 'Wilbur' Wright, ex-81 PR Squadron)*

RG238 at Sigiriya shortly after filming the opening flying scenes of *The Purple Plain*. During these sequences, Sqn Ldr Forrester, played by Gregory Peck, makes a single-engine landing back at base following action against the Japanese. The 'hangar' structure in the background had no practical purpose and was erected purely as set dressing for the production. All the Mosquito flying sequences in the film were carried out by 81 Squadron pilot 'Chas' Kirkham. Note RG238's feathered starboard propeller. *(Former SAC 'Wilbur' Wright, ex-81 PR Squadron)*

Radio mechanic SAC Geoff 'Lofty' Pownall watches engine fitter Cpl 'Acker' Payne check RG238's port engine coolant tank level during a break in filming at Sigiriya. Note the water-based paint on RG238's engine cowlings, which 'weathered' extremely well for the film. The intake immediately beneath the forward exhaust stub directed air into the spark plug cooling duct. RG238's nose 'machine-guns' are clearly visible beneath the port spinner's lower section. *(Former SAC 'Wilbur' Wright, ex-81 PR Squadron)*

Taken on the film set at Sigiriya, this shot depicts aircraft electrician SAC Ray Jarvis checking the navigation lamp housing on RG238's tail fairing cone. To remove the cone, first the tailwheel under fairing (between tailcone and rear fuselage) was extracted by disengaging its retaining Dzus fasteners. Then the electric cables to the navigation lamp were disconnected by unscrewing a plug located on fuselage bulkhead number seven. Following the disconnection of all bonding leads, three screws on either side of the fairing's forward section, and one attaching the fin fairing to the cone, were also removed. Finally, with the elevators in the down position, the tail fairing cone was withdrawn from the aircraft. Note the hole for the starboard elevator gust locking clamp positioned (inboard) just forward of the elevator trim tab. The streamlined fairing on the cone's starboard upper section shrouded movement of the elevator static balance weight.
(Former SAC 'Wilbur' Wright, ex-81 PR Squadron)

Airframe fitter SAC Brian 'Wilbur' Wright adjusts the jettison pedal on RG238's cockpit entrance door. In the event that the crew needed to abandon the aircraft in flight, the navigator would pull the inner hatch out of its hinge straps (throwing it into the nose compartment) before pressing the jettison pedal to release the outer door. The window at the rear of the door is for the navigator's drift sight. Note the trailing aerial tube positioned forward of the starboard ventral door (both ventral doors had their camera ports painted over for the film). The 81 Squadron groundcrew detachment for *The Purple Plain* spent nearly three months working on the film set at Sigiriya. *(Former SAC 'Wilbur' Wright, ex-81 PR Squadron)*

Gregory Peck, as Sqn Ldr Bill Forrester, is pictured with RG238 on the film set at Sigiriya. He was the Rank Organisation's leading star in *The Purple Plain* and gave an outstanding performance as a suicidal Canadian pilot emotionally scarred by the death of his wife (in the London Blitz) on their wedding night. His character is withdrawn, uncommunicative and prone to anxiety attacks, the majority of his Squadron colleagues regarding him as unbalanced. The Squadron Medical Officer, Dr Harris (played by Bernard Lee), attempts to help Forrester and eventually persuades him to visit local missionary Miss McNab (played superbly by Brenda De Banzie). Here Forrester begins to relax and meets a beautiful refugee nurse called Anna (played by Win Man Than). As their friendship grows Forrester emotionally heals and unwinds, becoming revitalised by his new commitment to Anna. A short while later he makes a routine flight to check out his new navigator (Carrington, played by Lyndon Brook) and to deliver a passenger (his tent mate, Blore, played by Maurice Denham) to a nearby aerodrome. Engine problems force Forrester to make a crash landing in the jungle, where he takes responsibility for the injured Carrington and stubborn Blore. Forrester's survival instinct is reinforced by his bond with Anna and, despite the loss of Blore, eventually gets both Carrington and himself to safety.

Gregory Peck is remembered with great affection by the 81 Squadron groundcrew detachment who recall him as 'a gentleman' and always willing to talk and pose for pictures. The circular panel above the forward section of RG238's entrance hatch provided access to the cabin pressurisation test point. The original PRU blue finish is visible through the film paint under the forward fuselage.
(Former SAC 'Wilbur' Wright, ex-81 PR Squadron)

Photographed on the film set at Sigiriya, director Robert Parrish (right) discusses a forthcoming scene for *The Purple Plain* with Gregory Peck. Born in 1916, Parrish was the son of actress Laura Parrish and began acting as a child, making his film debut in John Ford's 1928 film *Four Sons*. He also starred in *All Quiet on the Western Front* during 1930 and Charles Chaplin's *City Lights* the following year. In 1936 he worked for John Ford as assistant editor on *Mary of Scotland*, becoming sound editor on *Young Mr Lincoln* in 1939. He made his debut as a feature film editor with the 1947 Robert Rossen boxing drama *Body and Soul*, for which he won an Oscar. He began film directing in 1951 with the revenge drama *Cry Danger*, and in addition to *The Purple Plain* also directed *Fire Down Below* (1957), *The Wonderful Country* (1959), *Up from the Beach* (1965) and *Mississippi Blues* (1983). Robert Parrish died in 1995.
(Former SAC 'Wilbur' Wright, ex-81 PR Squadron)

Gregory Peck runs behind a camera vehicle, probably during shooting of the opening sequence of *The Purple Plain*, during which Sqn Ldr Forrester suffers a nightmare and believes his aerodrome is being bombed by the Japanese. He bolts from his tent and runs to his aircraft, waking up groundcrew member Sgt Brown (played by Jack MacNaughton), demanding to know 'Why isn't this aircraft ready to fly?' Sgt Brown slaps Forrester, bringing him back to reality and waking him from the nightmare. These sequences were shot during daylight but specially darkened for the finished production.

During the early 1950s the US Congress passed a law allowing Americans who worked abroad for seventeen out of eighteen months to be exempt from income tax. The law was designed to entice oil workers to remote locations, but the film studios maximised it to their advantage. Many big stars of the day subsequently worked abroad, including Gregory Peck, who, as well as *The Purple Plain*, made several films including *Roman Holiday* (with Audrey Hepburn) and *The Million Pound Note*. *(Former SAC 'Wilbur' Wright, ex-81 PR Squadron)*

In the shadow of RG238's starboard wing, Win Min Than (left), the Burmese actress who played Anna in *The Purple Plain*, sits with her sister on the film set at Sigiriya. Gregory Peck had insisted the part of Anna be played by a Burmese girl, so Robert Parrish travelled to Rangoon to screen-test many young hopefuls. Eventually he settled for the beautiful Win Man Than and flew her to London for further screen-tests. During the tests it became evident she had a habit of moving her head from side to side when speaking. Consequently, for close-up shots Robert Parrish had a special brace, featuring two sharp nails, attached to the back of her neck (the nails would make contact with her head unless she held it absolutely still). The brace had the desired effect, Than later being praised for her quality of 'stillness' by at least one critic. *The Purple Plain* was Win Man Than's only film credit. *(Former SAC 'Wilbur' Wright, ex-81 PR Squadron)*

'Chas' Kirkham taxies RG238 at Negombo prior to taking off for another filming session for *The Purple Plain* at Sigiriya. The marshaller in the foreground is RG238's 'keeper', 81 Squadron airframe fitter SAC Brian 'Wilbur' Wright. One day during rehearsals at Sigiriya, Brian became aware that Robert Parrish and Jack Maxted were deep in conversation while pointing towards him. This led to Parrish announcing, 'He's the right shape and height – he'll do!' Brian was then asked to take the place of bit-part actor Jack MacNaughton (who played the role of groundcrew member Sgt Ralph Brown) who had contracted an overnight fever and was unable to take part in the day's filming. Brian subsequently appears in the film, running in under the port wing before placing a chock behind RG238's starboard wheel. This occurs early on in the production when Sqn Ldr Forrester returns to base with a wounded navigator and a disabled starboard engine. During briefing for his 'starring' role, Brian naturally 'found it highly amusing to have someone telling me how to perform a duty I regarded as part of my life'. *(Former SAC 'Wilbur' Wright, ex-81 PR Squadron)*

This is the crash site of a SEAC FB.VI in the Burmese jungle – or is it? In *The Purple Plain* storyline Sqn Ldr Forrester is forced to make a crash-landing in the jungle following an engine fire. To simulate the 'crashed' Mosquito, a surplus T.3 or FB.VI was purchased from the Air Ministry and transported to Sigiriya. Repainted in RG238's film colour scheme, this engineless aircraft had its flat 'Fighter' windscreen replaced by a mock-up of RG238's 'Bomber'-style 'Vee'-shaped windscreens. As this picture illustrates, the port wing was sawn off and the airframe generally 'butchered' to resemble the effects of a crash-landing. Placed with the starboard wing 'high', the airframe was carefully rigged to hide its supporting props from the camera.

The 'crash site' was close to Sigiriya airstrip in a tract of jungle beneath a large hill. Jack Maxted and Robert Parrish reportedly stood at the hill summit one day surveying the scene for a suitable 'crash' location. The area chosen was

around 300 yards wide and 400 yards long, a team of local workers clearing the trees and levelling the whole site. The wrecked Mosquito was positioned at the end of two arcing trails (to simulate the aircraft's 'landing run'), the latter produced by dragging two large tree trunks behind a bulldozer. Prior to shooting the crash scene, the Mosquito was coated in a special material that created a very convincing fire effect but didn't actually burn the coated surface; nevertheless this aircraft (not surprisingly!) was badly 'scorched' during the shooting of these scenes. Note the fuel tanks propped up against the fuselage and the torn section of port outer engine nacelle lying in the foreground. The strips running along the fuselage were probably connected with special effects for the 'fire' sequence. The cockpit escape hatch is resting on the port wing's inboard trailing edge. *(Former SAC 'Wilbur' Wright, ex-81 PR Squadron)*

The most famous feature film to include Mosquitoes was the 1964 Mirisch Corporation production *633 Squadron*, which was based on a novel by Frederick E. Smith. The story of the film's making has been told many times before, but it is worth noting that the Mosquitoes taking part were former No 3 CAACU TT.35s and T.3s, most of which had recently retired from RAF service. Five aircraft flew for the film (TT.35s TA719, RS709, RS712 and TA639, and T.3 TW117) with four non-airworthy examples (TT.35s RS718, TA642 and TA724, and T.3 TV959) employed for ground scenes, and two fuselages (TJ118 and RS715) for cockpit and close-up shots. The latter six were transported by road to Bovingdon, which became the main base for the film. Here we see one of the non-airworthy TT.35s (probably RS718) about to receive its port 'paddle'-blade propeller during re-assembly at Bovingdon. The fuselage on the lorry in the background is believed to be that of TT.35 RS715. *(Stuart Howe collection)*

The crane used for re-assembly of the non-airworthy *633 Squadron* Mosquitoes passes one of the flyable TT.35s at Bovingdon, in this case TA719/G-ASKC. Constructed at Hatfield as a B.35, TA719 was delivered direct from the factory to 218 MU on 6 July 1945. The following September it entered storage with 44 MU at Edzell, remaining there until transferred to 22 MU in October 1948. Three years later, on 9 August 1951, TA719 underwent modifications and refurbishing at Brooklands Aviation before returning to 22 MU on 26 September. Between 13 August 1953 and 28 January 1954 Brooklands Aviation converted TA719 to TT.35 status, the aircraft afterwards returning to store at 22 MU. It finally entered RAF service on 30 April 1954 when it joined No 4 CAACU at Llandow, the latter unit merging with No 3 CAACU shortly afterwards. TA719 spent the remainder of its service career with No 3 CAACU at Exeter, receiving the code number '56' (worn on both sides of the fuselage just forward of the roundel). Declared Non-Effective Stock on 14 March 1963, TA719 flew to 27 MU Shawbury for storage pending disposal.

On 11 July the same year TA719 was sold to Mr Peter Thomas of the 'Skyfame' Museum at Staverton, who then loaned TA719 to Film Aviation Services for use in *633 Squadron*. The most regularly flown TT.35 during the making of the film, TA719 wore the fictitious serial 'HJ898' together with the unit code letters 'HT-G'. After a somewhat turbulent career as a preserved aircraft, TA719 is now on display at Duxford resplendent in the Target Tug colour scheme shown here. The *633 Squadron* camouflage finish was applied shortly after this picture was taken. The spinners are painted red. *(Stuart Howe collection)*

The fuselage of TT.35 RS715 'HT-P' is seen at Bovingdon on 9 August 1963 during the making of *633 Squadron*. In addition to being used for set dressing, this fuselage was rigged for cockpit shots during the filming and acted as a spares source for the other TT.35s employed on the production. With its painted nose Perspex (and low nose camouflage demarcation line), RS715's fuselage resembles that of a wartime OBOE-equipped Percival-built B.XVI.

An early Airspeed-produced B.35, RS715 was delivered from the Christchurch factory to 27 MU on 25 July 1946. Conversion to TT.35 standard took place at Brooklands Aviation between 6 December 1951 and 14 May 1952, after which RS715 returned to 27 MU. In August 1953 it was assigned to No 4 CAACU at Llandow before returning to store, this time with 38 MU (which was also based at

Llandow). Allocated to the 2nd Tactical Air Force in December 1955, RS715 entered service with the Armament Practice Station at Sylt in January 1956, remaining there until June 1957 when it returned (once again) to 27 MU. Finally, this TT.35 passed to No 3 CAACU at Exeter in November 1959 and was Struck Off Charge on 18 September 1961. It was later broken down into components and remained at Exeter until sold to the Mirisch Corporation two years later. RS715's fuselage eventually ended up at MGM Studios in Borehamwood and was rescued by Tony Agar (for his Mosquito NF.II restoration) in 1973. With no jury strut fitted to the ventral bay, the structural integrity of RS715's fuselage is somewhat precarious! Its fuselage carries the FB.VI serial 'MM398', which was applied for filming purposes. *(J. M. G. Gradidge)*

Preparations for the filming of *633 Squadron* under way at Bovingdon during the summer of 1963. Due to a lack of surviving Fighter-Bomber Mosquitoes, the Mirisch Corporation had to adapt the TT.35s to represent FB.VIs. However, unlike PR.34 RG238 used in *The Purple Plain*, the *633 Squadron* TT.35s had dummy machine-guns fitted to their original Perspex noses, the noses themselves being overpainted. With their two-speed, two-stage supercharged Merlins, enlarged ventral bays and Bomber-style canopies, the TT.35s hardly approximated the FB.VI but they were the only available option in the circumstances (of course, it could be argued that the TT.35s were symbolic of the specially modified aircraft described in Frederick Smith's original novel). The two T.3s (the only available Mosquitoes most closely resembling the FB.VI) were not fitted with dummy machine-guns.

TT.35 RS712 (right) is in the process of being repainted and already wears its film serial 'RF580' and unit code letters 'HT-F'. The aircraft on the left is RS718 'HJ662', with the fuselage of RS715 visible in the centre. The identity of the TT.35 in the middle distance is presently unknown. The colour scheme chosen for the Mosquitoes resembled that of wartime Mosquito Bombers rather than the Fighter-Bombers that the film company was striving to represent. Nevertheless, aside from the rather narrow fin flashes the scheme looked quite authentic. The serial numbers applied to the *633 Squadron* aircraft were genuine wartime Mosquito FB.VI and T.3 registrations (eg MM398, HJ898 and RF580), but the 'HT' unit code letters had never been worn by Mosquitoes. During the course of filming, aircraft registrations and unit code letters were regularly changed. Note the mock-up 'Earthquake' bombs in the foreground. *(Gary Brown collection, via Stuart Howe)*

TT.35 RS718, one of the non-airworthy *633 Squadron* Mosquitoes, photographed at Bovingdon in its film garb, wearing the serial number 'HJ662' and the unit code letters 'HT-C'. Built by the Airspeed Christchurch factory in September 1946, RS718 was delivered to Marshalls on 11 October before allocation to the BTU at West Freugh in early 1947. After suffering a flying accident on 12 July 1947, repairs were undertaken by de Havilland's before RS718 entered storage with 19 MU in April 1948. Five and a half years later it was converted to TT.35 standard by Brooklands Aviation and entered service with No 1 CAACU on 17 May 1954. In February 1957 RS718 began a short period in storage, initially with 27 MU but later with 12 and then 10 MUs. The Target Towing Flight of the Armament Practice Station at Schleswigland took delivery of RS718 in November 1957, the

aircraft remaining with that unit until 9 April 1958, when it returned to 27 MU. Three weeks later it began its final tour of duty when it was assigned to No 3 CAACU at Exeter. Following a flying accident on 31 May 1962, RS718 was Struck Off Charge on 19 June and allotted to 71 MU for disposal as scrap. It probably remained at Exeter before transport to Bovingdon the following year.

Note the mock-up 'Earthquake' bomb (a fictional weapon devised within the storyline to blast an overhanging rock on to a German rocket fuel factory in a Norwegian fjord) positioned beneath RS718's starboard wing. The set dressing department was rather enthusiastic in its application of 'exhaust staining' on the starboard outer side cowling and nacelle! 'HJ662' was originally applied to the prototype FB.VI in 1942 (see Mosquito Fighter-Bombers). *(DHAMT Ltd)*

Airworthy T.3 TW117 (finished as 'HR155' 'HT-M') is seen at Bovingdon during the making of *633 Squadron*. Built at Leavesden in May 1946, TW117 entered storage with 15 MU on 30 May, residing there until 22 July 1947 when it was delivered to the Armament Practice Station at Acklington. Just over two years later it was allocated to the Linton-on-Ouse Station Flight, remaining on charge until July 1951 when it passed to 204 AFS. Following an accident in February 1952, TW117 was repaired by de Havilland's before transfer to 58 Squadron at RAF Benson during late 1953. April 1954 saw TW117 begin a six-year period in storage (passing between 48, 5 and 27 MUs) before entering service with No 3 CAACU in March 1960. Struck Off Charge on 31 May 1963, TW117 was officially transferred from Exeter Airport Ltd (operators of No 3 CAACU) to RAF Henlow for storage as part of the RAF Museum Collection, being flown to Henlow by No 3 CAACU pilot John Oliver on 7 June 1963. By this time TW117 had flown 832hrs 15mins, its last major inspection having been completed at 562hrs 30mins in September 1956.

Shortly after its 'retirement' TW117 was loaned to the Mirisch Corporation to assist with pilot training for *633 Squadron*, John Oliver flying the aircraft back to Exeter on 16 July 1963. No 3 CAACU Chief Pilot Harry Ellis used TW117 (and TT.35 TA719) to check out prospective pilots for the film before John Oliver delivered it to Bovingdon to appear in the production itself. The latter flight took place on 22 July 1963 and marked the last Mosquito sortie of his career. At the conclusion of filming TW117 returned to Henlow, where it was later refurbished prior to going on display at the RAF Museum, Hendon. This Mosquito now forms part of the Norwegian Air Force Museum Collection, where it masquerades as a wartime 333 Squadron FB.VI. Note the Nord 1002 in the background (visible beneath the windsock), one of two examples flown in *633 Squadron* to represent Messerschmitt Bf 109s.
(Gary Brown collection, via Stuart Howe)

633 Squadron TT.35 TA642 ('HJ898' 'HT-G') languishes at Bovingdon on 1 August 1963 following an unscheduled collapse of its port undercarriage. Captain John Crewsdon (of Film Aviation Services) originally intended to perform a high-speed taxi run in TA642 before retracting the undercarriage in front of the cameras. These shots were required to portray the return to base from a precision strike over Bergen of the damaged Mosquito of Wg Cdr Grant (played by Cliff Robertson), but this incident put paid to that. Constructed as a B.35 at Hatfield in April 1945, TA642 entered storage with 27 MU on 14 April where it remained for the next seven years. On 19 May 1952 it was delivered to Brooklands Aviation at Sywell for conversion to TT.35 standard, this work being completed by 9 September. Later that year TA642 was assigned to No 3 CAACU at Exeter, as it was planned to gradually replace the unit's Beaufighter TT.10s with Mosquito TT.35s. TA642 became one of the unit's first TT.35s and in January 1953 Harry Ellis flew the aircraft on a test flight (to prove the target drogue winching system) with Peter Howland as Target Towing Operator (TTO). TA642 spent the remainder of its service career with No 3 CAACU, eventually being Struck Off Charge on 31 May 1963. Note the simulated 'battle damage' to the rudder, rear fuselage and port wingtip. TA642 still retains its cable guard frame forward of the tailwheel. *(London Express News Service)*

The damage to TT.35 TA642 is assessed shortly after the unintentional collapse of its port undercarriage on 1 August 1963. TA642's pilot, Captain John Crewsdon of Film Aviation Services, is sitting on the cockpit canopy. His company undertook and co-ordinated all the flying sequences for *633 Squadron* in addition to negotiating the hire of several airworthy Mosquitoes, including TT.35 TA719. Aside from John Crewsdon, other pilots employed on the film included Peter Warden, Graham 'Taffy' Rich (ex-No 3 CAACU), Flt Lt C. Kirkham (RAF), Flt Lt John Hawke (RAF) and Flt Lt D. Curtis (RAF). The camera aircraft for the aerial shots was North American B.25J Mitchell N9089Z flown by Martin Caidin and Gregg Board. Note that the dinghy box has been removed from its stowage on top of the fuselage. TA642 was later scrapped. *(Francois Prins)*

A *633 Squadron* TT.35 passes low over Bovingdon trailing smoke from an underfuselage-mounted canister. This photograph is believed to have been taken during shooting of the sequence depicting the return of Wg Cdr Grant from a precision strike over Bergen. The identity of this TT.35 (marked up as 'HJ898' 'HT-G) is likely to be TA719. Note the 'battle damaged' rudder and rear fuselage. *(London Express News Service)*

Following the mishap with TA642, another non-airworthy TT.35 was selected to perform the undercarriage collapse scene required by the film-makers. This aircraft was RS718, which Captain John Crewsdon successfully 'bellied in' at Bovingdon on 9 August 1963. RS718's simulated 'battle damage' looked fairly convincing and achieved the desired impression of a shot-up aircraft returning to base. *(London Express News Service)*

In this second view of TT.35 RS718 taken during the undercarriage collapse scene at Bovingdon on 9 August 1963, the figure making a hasty exit from the cockpit is John Crewsdon. Note the paint on the Perspex nose and nose compartment windows, the former fitted with its dummy machine-guns. The smoke behind the wings originated from canisters fitted beneath the fuselage. *(London Express News Service)*

This shot is likely to have been taken at the back of the MGM studios in Borehamwood during the final 'crash' sequence of *633 Squadron*. During these scenes the semi-conscious Wg Cdr Grant is helped from the cockpit of his burning Mosquito by navigator Fg Off Hoppy Hopkinson (played by Angus Lennie) after being shot down over Norway. This scene was quite dangerous to film, as Angus Lennie recalls: 'Cliff and I were strapped in and the aircraft made ready for the scene. The special effects boys had a great cloud of smoke in the cockpit and I was supposed to fling open the emergency canopy and drag Cliff out! Unfortunately, the smoke proved quite dense and my eyes were full of tears from it, and the flames were growing. The aircraft, being wooden, went up quite happily, the cameras were turning and I was fighting to get out. Then I had to try and heave Cliff out – he is quite heavy and eventually I managed it, but it was quite hair-raising! The director thought it was great!' The Mosquito used for this sequence was likely a composite made up from various aircraft destroyed or broken up during the filming. The starboard wing was detached close to the wing root and propped up at an angle. Note the vegetation stuffed in the leading edge of the port wing. *(Francois Prins)*

The box office success of *633 Squadron* led to the production of a sequel in 1968 entitled *Mosquito Squadron*. Produced by Oakmont Productions and released through United Artists, the film's plot was influenced by the Amiens prison raid of 1944 but also incorporated the 'Highball' bouncing bomb. The plot centred around the destruction of a secret underground factory used for production of a new German 'V' weapon. The factory would be destroyed by 'Highball' bombs dropped from Mosquitoes of '641 Squadron'. To complicate matters the factory was located in the grounds of a French chateau housing RAF prisoners of war!

Hamish Mahaddie was initially responsible for gathering aircraft for *Mosquito Squadron* (in addition to acting as the film's technical advisor) but, due to pressure of work on the film *Battle of Britain*, Mahaddie handed over the job to Air Commodore Allen Wheeler. Engineer Leslie Hillman assumed responsibility for aircraft procurement and preparation including liaison with the Air Registration Board. By 1968 airworthy Mosquitoes were more difficult to source, but eventually four were gathered together, as well as a non-airworthy example (TT.35 TA719). The flyable aircraft consisted of TT.35s RS709, RS712 and TA634, and T.3 RR299. RS709 and RS712 had previously starred in *633 Squadron* and were loaned by their owners Peter Thomas (of the 'Skyfame' Museum) and Hamish Mahaddie respectively. TA634 belonged to Liverpool Corporation and hadn't flown since 1963, but Leslie Hillman's team brought the aircraft up to airworthiness at its Speke Airport base. T.3 RR299 belonged to Hawker Siddeley Aviation at Hawarden and was flown throughout the filming by Hatfield-based test pilot Pat Fillingham. Leslie Hillman also inspected T.3 TW117 at Henlow, but subsequently reported that 'a considerable amount of maintenance would be necessary to put it into a flying condition for the production'. Here we see the four airworthy aircraft passing low over Bovingdon during the summer of 1968. The three TT.35s are leading, with T.3 RR299 on the far left. *Mosquito Squadron* is significant for the being the last occasion when four Mosquitoes flew together. *(Bob Tatum collection)*

TT.35 RS712 stands at Bovingdon during the making of *Mosquito Squadron* in July 1968. As with *633 Squadron*, Bovingdon remained the production unit's main base throughout the filming. The 'HT' unit code letters were retained for the second film in order to incorporate sequences from the previous one. RS712 was ready for collection from the Airspeed Christchurch factory on 21 June 1946 and was delivered to de Havilland's at Hatfield the following July. In March 1947 it was allocated to 13 OTU before entering storage with 10 MU at Hullavington the following month. Repair work was carried out by de Havilland's between November 1947 and January 1949, RS712 afterwards entering storage with 27 MU. Selected for conversion to TT.35 standard, RS712 flew to Brooklands Aviation at Sywell on 27 November 1951, the conversion work being completed by 14 May 1952. During its career as a TT.35, RS712 served with No 1 CAACU, the Target Towing Flight of the Armament Practice Station at Schleswigland, and No 3 CAACU at Exeter (coded '50' with the latter unit). Declared Non-Effective Stock on 16 May 1963, RS712 was transferred to the Mirisch Corporation on 11 July and registered G-ASKB for its forthcoming role in *633 Squadron*. After the filming, the aircraft was stored at Henlow prior to taking part in *Mosquito Squadron* five years later.

This aircraft later became part of the celebrated Strathallan Aircraft Collection before sale to American collector Kermit Weeks in 1981. Flown to the USA in 1987, RS712 is currently on display at the EAA Museum, Oshkosh, although it is no longer airworthy. In this picture RS712 retains the film markings 'RF580' 'HT-F', which it previously wore in *633 Squadron*. *(Philip Birtles)*

Taken at Bovingdon during the filming of *Mosquito Squadron*, this photograph depicts Quint Munroe (played by David McCallum) repelling an attack on the '641 Squadron' aerodrome by Luftwaffe fighters. David McCallum was a big star during the late 1960s and is perhaps best known for his role in TV's *The Man from* *UNCLE*. He took the leading role in *Mosquito Squadron*, which also featured Charles Gray (as Air Commodore Hufford), Dinsdale Landen and Suzanne Neave. The Mosquito on the far left is TT.35 TA634 'HT-G', with T.3 RR299 'HT-P' to its right. *(Bob Tatum collection)*

TT.35 TA634 'HT-G' takes off from Bovingdon during the filming of *Mosquito Squadron* in July 1968. Throughout the filming TA634 was flown by test pilot Neil Williams, who had made his first Mosquito solo (in this particular aircraft) the previous month. A former No 3 CAACU TT.35, TA634 had spent the previous five years in storage at Speke Airport, having been delivered there from Aldergrove in 1963. Purchased by the Merseyside Society of Aviation Enthusiasts, it was originally intended for display in the Speke Airport Terminal building, but these plans came to naught.

Engineer Les Hillman inspected TA634 at Speke on 7 May 1968 and reported to the film company: 'After viewing this aircraft, we were of the opinion that it was in very good condition and would prove most useful for the production.' Hillman subsequently offered Liverpool Corporation £1,000 for the use of TA634, which was duly accepted. TA634 was overhauled at Speke by Personal Plane Services and, after being brought up to Air Registration Board standards, was issued with a Certificate of Airworthiness for filming purposes only. Allocated the civil registration G-AWJV, TA634 was test-flown by Neil Williams on 17 June 1968 before delivery to Bovingdon the same day. Between 3 and 6 July TA634 (at times coded 'HT-G') made a total of six flights, three during the first day and one on each of the following days (total flying time 7hrs 50mins). At the

conclusion of filming, Neil Williams returned TA634 to Speke on 16 July on what was to be its last flight. Donated to the Mosquito Aircraft Museum by Liverpool Corporation in 1970, it remains one of the Museum's premier exhibits and underwent a thorough static restoration (by a team of volunteers led by the author) between 1981 and 1990. TA634 currently displays in the markings of a 571 Squadron B.XVI. Note the cable guard frame just forward of the tailwheel, a vestige of TA634's TT.35 conversion and one that distinguished it from RS709 and RS712, the other TT.35s employed for the film's aerial scenes. *(Philip Birtles)*

An unidentified TT.35 flies over Bovingdon during the filming of *Mosquito Squadron* in July 1968.

Within the film's storyline, '641 Squadron' practise dropping 'Highball' bouncing bombs into a mock-up tunnel on a test range, simulating the entrance to the German 'V'-weapon factory located in the grounds of the French chateau 'Charlon'. For this sequence a mock-up tunnel mouth was constructed on Bovingdon aerodrome with distance marker boards positioned to the right of it. The actual 'Highball' release sequences were carried out with aircraft models in the studio, the models being slightly more convincing than those featured in *633 Squadron*! Four pilots were engaged to fly the Mosquitoes for *Mosquito Squadron*, namely Graham 'Taffy' Rich, 'Dizzy' Addicott, Neil Williams and Pat Fillingham. The film's aerial sequences were shot from RAE Shackleton MR.3 WR792 piloted by Tom Sheppard. Former No 3 CAACU pilot 'Taffy' Rich also flew in *633 Squadron* and received approval as a Mosquito type-rated examiner from the Air Registration Board. *(Bob Tatum collection)*

Hawker Siddeley test pilot Pat Fillingham takes T.3 RR299/G-ASKH aloft from Bovingdon during the filming of *Mosquito Squadron*. In order for RR299 to appear in the film, Pat Fillingham had to take leave from his normal duties as a production test pilot at Hatfield. He was involved in Mosquito development and production test flying between 1941 and 1950 and had flown more individual Mosquitoes than any other pilot engaged on the film. Prior to the film RR299 (finished in an immaculate silver dope scheme) had been operated by Hawker Siddeley Aviation as a demonstration aircraft. Camouflaged especially for the film, it wore a variety of unit code letters including 'HT-P' and 'HT-E', the latter retained on the aircraft until its loss in July 1996. Note the dummy machine-guns attached to the nose. *(Philip Birtles)*

Civil Mosquitoes

The first civilian-registered Mosquitoes appeared during the war and were operated between Leuchars and Stockholm by BOAC. The Mosquito's high performance made it the ideal aircraft for this route, as it was the only type that stood a chance of evading German flak and fighters. Diplomatic mail and machine parts regularly featured as BOAC Mosquito cargo, but occasionally special passengers were accommodated in the ventral bay. The Leuchars-Stockholm run took just under 3 hours by BOAC Mosquito, while larger four-engined aircraft took up to twice that time with increased danger of interception.

After the war the Mosquito's excellent range and endurance made it ideal for photographic survey and mapping operations. Several were converted for this role, mainly PR.34s and B.35s, as their two-speed, two-stage supercharged engines delivered the high-altitude performance demanded for this work. The biggest operator of photographic survey Mosquitoes was Spartan Air Services of Canada, which employed nine converted B.35s all over northern and western Canada and from remote bases in the Arctic Circle. Jack Amman Photogrammetric Engineers of San Antonio, Texas, also operated a large fleet of Mosquitoes for photo-survey work, but, unlike the Spartan Air Services Mark 35s, these were mostly converted PR.34s. Lesser quantities of Canadian- and Australian-built Mosquitoes were converted for photo-survey work, the Canadian aircraft featuring Packard Merlin V 1650-9 engines. One Australian civil Mosquito was even fitted with a Magnetometer for oil-searching over the Canning Desert.

The Mosquito's sleek form also caught the attention of the American air-racing scene, two examples being entered for the 1948 Bendix Trophy Race. Both were Canadian-built B.XXVs, one ranking among the fastest and most powerful Mosquitoes ever flown.

Civil-registered Mosquitoes were also employed on research and development, as well as trials work. BEA operated two converted PR.34s between 1948 and 1950 for the purpose of conducting research into clear air turbulence at high altitude. Two NF.XIXs passed to Flight Refuelling in 1949, one being used to film air-to-air refuelling trials. A single NF.36 (G-ALFL) was employed on propeller unfeathering trials in cold conditions, these tests taking place in Norway during 1949.

Several PR.XVIs found their way on to the British Civil Register, two of these later being clandestinely ferried to Israel during the arms embargo. Three others languished at Thruxton aerodrome until they were destroyed in 1960.

Five of the last Mosquitoes to see service use were entered on the British Civil Register during the 1960s. These were aircraft formerly operated by No 3 CAACU at Exeter and comprised four TT.35s and one T.3. The TT.35s later went to Museums, the sole T.3, RR299/G-ASKH, being operated as a display aircraft by Hawker Siddeley/British Aerospace. In addition to being the last airworthy example of its type, G-ASKH was also the world's last active civil-registered Mosquito.

This photograph was taken on 6 August 1944 during a visit by the Merton Park Studios Film Unit (accompanied by de Havilland Public Relations Manager Martin Sharp) to the BOAC base at Leuchars. Merton Park Studios required shots of BOAC Mosquito operations for inclusion in *de Havilland Presents The Mosquito* (see Mosquitoes on Film). In the foreground is Mark VI G-AGGC, one of nine examples delivered to BOAC between April 1943 and April 1944. BOAC had been anxious to obtain Mosquitoes for mail and freight flights between Scotland and Sweden, previous types employed by the airline lacking the performance necessary to evade German flak and fighters. Mosquitoes offered the only real chance of operating in relative safety, so BOAC keenly pressed for examples to be released to it. These efforts bore fruit when PR.IV DZ411 was assigned to the airline in December 1942. Registered G-AGFV, DZ411 began flights to Stockholm on 4 February 1943, being joined at Leuchars by six Mark VIs (registered G-AGGC to AGGH) the following April and May. Prior to delivery from Hatfield, the Mark VIs had their machine-gun and cannon armament removed (the nose louvres being faired over as per the Mosquito T.3), and ballast was installed to compensate for the alteration in the centre of gravity. The Mosquitoes regularly operated between

Leuchars and Sweden, occasionally carrying passengers in the ventral bay (in less than luxurious conditions), until the service ceased on 17 May 1945.

BOAC's first Mark VI, G-AGGC, was constructed at Hatfield as FB.VI HJ680 and passed to BOAC at Bramcote on 16 April 1943. On 18 July 1943, while carrying a passenger in the ventral bay on a flight from Sweden to Leuchars, the aircraft was chased by Luftwaffe fighters but managed to evade its pursuers. G-AGGC continued the Swedish flights until it was withdrawn from use on 30 November 1944, remaining at Leuchars for emergency use only. The longest-serving BOAC Mosquito, G-AGGC was cancelled from the civil register on 4 January 1946 and later passed to 22 MU, eventually being sold as scrap to John Dale on 15 June 1950.

G-AGGC's upper surfaces appear to be finished in Extra Dark Sea Grey and Dark Slate Grey with the under surfaces in Night. Registration letters were applied to the fuselage sides and the top and bottom surfaces of the wings (all underlined with red, white and blue stripes). The BOAC 'Speedbird' logo is visible beneath the cockpit. Note Mark VI G-AGKP (ex-LR296) in the left background. *(BAE SYSTEMS)*

BOAC air and ground crews, including Flt Capt Nigel Pelly (extreme right), pose for the camera at Leuchars on 6 August 1944. Previously based with the BOAC/RAF Communications section in North Africa, Nigel Pelly joined the BOAC Mosquito unit in September 1943, replacing Flt Capt L. A. Wilkins, killed when Mark VI G-AGGF (ex-HJ720) crashed near Invermark Lodge, Angus (overlooking Glen Glee) on 17 August 1943.

The Mark VI Mosquito in the background is either G-AGKO, G-AGKP or G-AGKR, these three aircraft having been acquired by BOAC as attrition replacements for G-AGGD, G-AGGF and G-AGGG. G-AGKO was constructed at Hatfield as FB.VI HJ667 in February 1943 and passed to 10 MU on 8 March. Nineteen days later it was damaged in a flying accident, repairs being completed by 24 December when it entered storage with 27 MU. HJ667 joined BOAC in April 1944, operating on the Leuchars to Stockholm service between 14 June and 30 November. Delivered to 19 MU on 24 July 1945, this Mark VI was Struck Off Charge on 14 December 1945.

G-AGKP was constructed at Hatfield as FB.VI LR296 in November 1943. Equipped with Merlin 21s, it entered storage with 27 MU on 13 November but was damaged in

an accident on 27 January 1944. Following repairs, LR296 remained with 27 MU until 25 April 1944 when it was delivered to BOAC and converted for civil use as G-AGKP. Thirteen days after this photograph was taken the aircraft crashed into the sea 9 miles from Leuchars, killing Capt Gilbert Rae OBE, Radio Officer D. T. Roberts and BOAC Mosquito pilot Capt B. W. B. Orton, the latter travelling as passenger in the ventral bay. G-AGKP was returning from Stockholm and crashed (reportedly due to structural failure) during its descent to Leuchars.

G-AGKR was formerly FB.VI HJ792 and was delivered to 418 Squadron (RCAF) on 26 June 1943. Three weeks later it received battle damage, repairs being carried out by Martin Hearn before the aircraft entered storage with 27 MU on 17 February 1944. Delivered to BOAC on 11 April 1944, G-AGKR operated for only four months before being lost off the Norwegian coast during a flight from Gothenburg to Leuchars on 28 August 1944.

For crew training, BOAC was allocated (at various times) T.3s HJ898 (see Mosquito Trainers), HJ985 and LR524. In this shot the pitot head cover line has been secured to the external current supply plug access panel, located on the port side of the fuselage above the inboard flap. *(BAE SYSTEMS)*

A passenger is led towards the ventral bay of BOAC Mosquito Mark VI G-AGGC. This staged shot was taken at Leuchars during filming of *de Havilland Presents The Mosquito*. The film's commentary describes the scene as: 'Accommodation was not quite up to the standard of the Albatross restaurant service to Paris…' The passenger boarded the Mosquito through the ventral doors of what used to be the bomb compartment, climbing on to a small seat (via the steps seen on the right) located above the former cannon bay access doors. Facing backwards, the passenger reclined on a mattress with his head close to the front spar lower boom. He was provided with a parachute (seen here being carried by the officer on the right), flying suit, oxygen mask and reading lamp, and maintained two-way radio contact with the pilot. Several notable passengers were carried by BOAC Mosquitoes, including the Danish nuclear physicist Niels Bohr. On average, a flight to Stockholm would take around 2¾ hours, the return trip to Leuchars lasting just over 3 hours. As on the standard FB.VI, the rear ventral bay doors were hydraulically

operated, the passenger having to raise his legs to avoid the jacks! G-AGGC's crew are standing on the left.
(BAE SYSTEMS)

PR.IV DK310 under Swiss ownership as 'HB-IMO'. Interned following its forced landing at Belpmoos on 24 August 1942 (see page 271), DK310 was later made serviceable and Swiss national markings painted on the wings (both upper and lower surfaces), fuselage and rudder. Allocated the code 'E-42' (which was not displayed on the aircraft), DK310 flew to Lucerne-Emmen on 6 September 1943 for technical evaluation by the Kreigstechnische Abteilung (KTA). On 3 July 1944, after much negotiation with the British Government, DK310's ownership passed to the Swiss, the Mosquito remaining with the KTA until 13 October, when it was flown to Dubendorf by Swissair pilot Capt Laderach accompanied by Flt Capt Ernst. Swissair planned to use E-42 (loaned from the KTA) on night mail flights, for which purpose the Swiss Federal Civil Authority issued the registration HB-IMO on 19 January 1945 ('HB-IMO' being applied to the wing under surfaces and fuselage sides together with white bands on the nose, rear fuselage and outer wings). Capt Laderach begin training Swissair pilots F. Zimmermann, E. Nyffenegger, H. Ernst, A. von Tscharner, R. Fretz and O.

Heitmanek to fly HB-IMO on 20 March 1945, the aircraft accumulating 2hrs 47mins of flying time in the process. The Swissair night mail flight project was later abandoned, HB-IMO's registration being cancelled on 7 August 1945 when the aircraft returned to KTA charge.

On the same day (having amassed a total flying time of 17hrs 52mins in Switzerland) the Mosquito was handed over to the DMP, the former Air Force Logistics Command, and re-serialled 'B-4'. No further flights are recorded in 1945, but on 10 July 1946 the starboard Merlin 21 was replaced by a zero-houred Merlin (Mark unknown). Following a coolant leak on the right cylinder bank, B-4's port engine was removed in August 1946, the aircraft having by then flown a total of 39hrs 33mins. The Mosquito never flew again, the starboard engine being installed in FB.VI 'B-5' (ex-NS993) on 21 March 1949. Officially withdrawn from service on 1 July 1951, B-4 was later scrapped. Note what appears to be an additional pitot mast mounted on the nose, probably applied during technical evaluation by the KTA.
(Archiv Flieger Flab Museum, Dubendorf)

This postwar shot of Swiss-operated FB.VI 'B-5' shows it following collapse of its starboard undercarriage. 'B-5' was originally 515 Squadron FB.VI NS993, which force-landed at Dubendorf on 30 September 1944. This Merlin 25-powered FB.VI was delivered direct from the Hatfield factory to 13 MU on 24 March 1944 before allocation to 617 Squadron on 11 April. The following month it passed to 515 Squadron, being assigned the unit code letters '3P-T', which were incorrectly applied as 'P3-T' ('P3' being the code letters of 692 Squadron). During a daylight intruder operation on 30 September 1944, NS993 (in company with PZ440), attacked Holzkirchen aerodrome near Munich, but received serious damage from ground fire. With the port engine shut down, NS993 made for the Swiss border, eventually force-landing at Dubendorf, where it remained for nearly five years.

Between 3 March and 18 June 1949 NS993 was overhauled by the Swiss and its port engine replaced with a Merlin 21 from PR.IV 'B-4' (ex-DK310). Officially transferred from the British Government on 20 April 1949, NS993 entered service with the Swiss Army as 'B-5' on 27 June 1949. On 21 March 1950 'B-5' was handed over to Eidg. Flugzeugwerk Emmen for conversion as a flying test-bed for the 'Swiss Mamba' SM-1 turbojet (developed for the Swiss N.20 jet fighter project), conversion work being completed by 4 November. The turbojet was mounted beneath the forward fuselage, 'B-5' making its first flight in this configuration on 8 November 1950. By 31 December 1952 'B-5' had accumulated 34hrs 42mins of flying time during trials work in Switzerland. The flame-damping shrouds on the aircraft's engine side cowlings were later removed and the engines fitted with individual exhaust stubs. Aside from the collapsed starboard undercarriage, damage appears to be relatively minor.
(via Ralph Steiner, DHAMT Ltd)

It is the end of the line for 'B-5', which was declared unserviceable on 31 December 1953 following the discovery of glue failure within the airframe structure. These findings were confirmed by Eidg. Flugzeugwerk Emmen on 15 January 1954, which declared that 'B-5' be withdrawn from service. Three months later technical experts from the DMP (formerly the Air Force Logistics Command) ordered that the aircraft be scrapped, its airframe, as shown here, eventually being burned. The Swiss accumulated a total of 41hrs 14mins of flying time with 'B-5'.
(via Ralph Steiner, DHAMT Ltd)

delivered considerably greater power than the 225. However, de Havilland's also advised: 'An intercooler radiator was always fitted on two-stage Merlins and a rather larger oil cooler. With no intercooling there will be a substantial loss of power and at the lower altitudes the available power may be below that of the Merlin 225.' de Havilland's recommended that N1203V's three-bladed propellers be retained, as the performance gain (at altitude) provided by four-bladed units was negligible. The Aviation Export Company believed that specially equipped Mosquitoes had been able to attain altitudes as high as 47,000 feet, but de Havilland's informed them: 'A height of 45,000 feet is rather beyond the capabilities of the aeroplane.'

Following consultation with Rolls Royce, N1203V's fuel cavitation problems were overcome and the aircraft began to reach altitudes of around 41,000 feet. N1203V's new nose was designed for a pressure differential of 7.65, but at first gave only 2.65 due to leaks around the top hatch. Pressure was provided by a blower driven by a hydraulic motor integrated with the hydraulic system (the whole unit being fitted in the dinghy box stowage aft of the cockpit). The cockpit heating system was removed as the pressurising system provided enough heat. Fuel capacity was increased to 1,320 US gallons, providing N1203V with a range of 3,900 miles.

Dianna Bixby's solo round-the-world record attempt never took place; she was later killed in an air crash, and N1203V was subsequently employed on aerial survey work. Note the extended nose (with the distinctive 'sharkmouth' markings of the Flying Tiger Line) and the lack of intercooler radiator housings on the lower engine cowlings. N1203V's original cowlings were lengthened to accommodate the Packard V1650-9 Merlins, but the aircraft retained the B.XXV's Merlin 225 five-stub exhaust layout. The Aviation Export Company also drew up plans for a passenger-carrying conversion of the Mosquito, N1203V being utilised for research! The aircraft was ultimately written off in 1956. *(Photographers unknown)*

B.XXV N1203V (ex-KA997) at Burbank in 1954 following preparation for a solo round-the-world record flight (sponsored by the Flying Tiger Line and the Aviation Export Company) by Mrs Dianna Bixby. Four years previously N1203V (named 'The Huntress') had been used by Mrs Bixby and her husband Bob for an attempted round-the-world record flight that ultimately proved unsuccessful. Since that attempt, and by the time these pictures were taken, N1203V had been substantially modified by the Los Angeles-based Aviation Export Company. The most significant of these modifications was the installation of a metal pressurised nose (clearly evident here), which increased nose length by 18 inches. Two-speed, two-stage supercharged Packard Merlin V 1650-9 engines were fitted, but without the intercooler radiators featured on production two-stage Merlin Mosquitoes. Initial flight testing proved N1203V to be some 40mph slower than in its original Packard Merlin 225 configuration, altitude performance also proving disappointing. This was thought due to the increase in weight, alteration in the centre of gravity position, fuel cavitation problems, and the lack of four-bladed propellers.

In April 1954 Mr Clare Waterbury, Aviation Export Company President, wrote to de Havilland's at Hatfield for advice in resolving these difficulties. de Havilland's replied the following month stating that the increase in weight was unlikely to be a factor, except at high altitudes where the Merlin V 1650-9

Derelict FB.VI N9909F photographed at Whiteman Air Park, California, on 28 January 1961. Hatfield-built as PZ474 in April 1945, this FB.VI was delivered to 19 MU on 19 April before allocation to 8 OTU on 3 May. The following month PZ474 transferred to 132 OTU, serving until February 1946 when it entered storage with 51 MU. Later sold to New Zealand, PZ474 was delivered to the RNZAF in April 1948, being assigned the RNZAF serial number NZ2384. In 1953 Aircraft Supplies (NZ) Ltd purchased six former RNZAF FB.VIs for export, these aircraft being allocated the New Zealand civil registrations ZK-BCT to ZK-BCY. NZ2384 became ZK-BCV and was later sold to Trans World Engineering Corporation of California as N9909F. Ferried to the USA by Lewis Leach, N9909F was modified to accept a nose-mounted camera in preparation for aerial survey work. However, the aircraft's lack of two-speed, two-stage supercharged engines negated high-altitude survey operations and in 1956 it passed to the Insurance Finance Corporation of Studio City, California. N9909F was next acquired by California Air Charter and leased to an independent operator, the Mosquito reportedly being used for illegal purposes in South America. Following cancellation of the lease, N9909F languished at Whiteman Air Park, its forlorn remains eventually being acquired in 1970 by Jim Merizan. Note the missing starboard wingtip and drop tank. *(Bernard B. Deatrick, via Stuart Howe)*

PR.34 G-AJZF, of the British European Airways (BEA) Clear-Air Gust Research Unit, runs up at its Cranfield base. Prior to the war it was assumed that high-altitude flight would be smooth, with aircraft rarely subject to vertical accelerations caused by turbulence. Wartime and immediate postwar experiences revealed this supposition to be incorrect, as clear-air turbulence had been encountered at high altitude and without visual warning. This would obviously effect future high-flying airliners, so Mr N. E. Rowe of BEA proposed an investigation into the phenomenon.

In December 1947 the Ministry of Supply awarded a contract covering such research work to BEA. At the time little was known about clear-air turbulence, so in order to obtain results with minimum delay, a small BEA Clear-Air Gust Research Unit was formed. Based at Cranfield, it comprised two Mosquito PR.34s, one flying crew (later increased to two) and a resident scientist. Leased from the Ministry of Supply, the Mosquitoes were RG231 and RG238, which received the civil registrations G-AJZE and G-AJZF respectively. TRE Defford and RAE Farnborough installed communications and navigational equipment before the aircraft flew to Cranfield for modifications and the granting of Certificates of Airworthiness in the 'Special' Category. Modifications included removal of the ventral bay fuel tanks and the permanent fixing of 100-gallon drop tanks beneath the wings. Supplies of coolant and hydraulic fluid were stowed in the rear fuselage, together with tools and spares for use at overseas stations. Both aircraft's normal take-off weight was 21,500lb including 739 gallons of fuel.

To facilitate their research role, the Mosquitoes were fitted with a Peravia Type XR 144 recording accelerometer, a Barnes Type B recording accelerometer (to obtain data concerning the rate of build-up of accelerations, as this could not be satisfactorily gathered by the Peravia instrument), a Hathaway V-g recoder, and a Bridge Thermometer (balanced by the Meteorological Office) to record ambient air temperature. 'Kent' flowmeters (of the 'gallons' type) were incorporated to provide a reliable indication of fuel status during any stage of a flight.

The Mosquitoes were maintained by the Cranfield College of Aeronautics Flight Department, which was directly responsible to BEA. Spares (together with most of the ground support equipment) were provided by RAF Maintenance Units. Both PR.34s were finished in light grey overall and serviced by licensed aircraft engineer Don Chapman. As RG238, this Mosquito previously gained the London to Cape Town speed record and went on to play a 'starring' role in the 1954 feature film *The Purple Plain* (see Mosquitoes on Film). Assigned to 81 Squadron in 1952, RG238 was eventually Struck Off Charge in January 1954. Note the BEA 'Keyline' insignia on G-AJZF's nose. *(Don Chapman)*

G-AJZE, the other PR.34 employed by the BEA Clear-Air Gust Research Unit, was photographed at Cranfield by George Kilcoyne. The unit commenced operations in April 1948, continuing until the project was terminated at the close of 1950. Flight crews consisted of pilots Capt T. T. Thomas DFC and Capt D. F. Wilson, together with navigating officers D. L. Jones and H. J. P. Bower.

Destinations were selected to cover a wide range of terrain and weather conditions, with flight plans adopted to maximise the chance of locating turbulence. Flights mainly covered the European area where the existing organisation of BEA would simplify operations (in addition to taking place in regions where future high-flying aircraft would operate). Flight plans were of the 'saw tooth' pattern, whereby aircraft took off, climbed to 37,000 feet, descended to 20,000 feet, climbed to 37,000 feet, descended to 20,000 feet and so on until the destination was attained. Usually three such 'saw teeth' were flown on an overseas flight of average length.

During the twenty-five months from January 1948 to January 1950, a total of 680 hours were flown by the Mosquitoes. Of this figure, 124 hours were on test flying, positioning flights, etc, these including determination of position error correction and compressibility correction to the thermometer for forward speed. The accuracy of wind-finding using GEE was also checked against the radio-sonde winds. The remaining 556 hours comprised gust research work, and were termed 'voyage hours' (each research flight was termed a 'voyage'). Several 'voyages' were aborted due to technical defects, which included four engine failures. The 'voyage' times were calculated 'chock to chock' so that the actual time flown (above the lowest observing altitude) totalled around 320 hours. Overseas flights were made to Lisbon, Gibraltar, Rome and Stockholm, together with a single trip to Iceland. In total, 92,300 miles of research were covered.

As RG231, G-AJZF previously served on trials work at Hatfield and Boscombe Down. Following service with the BEA Clear-Air Gust Research Unit, RG231 was converted to PR.34A standard before allocation to 58 Squadron at Benson. Transferred to Non-Effective Stock in October 1955, RG231 was sold as scrap to Lowton Metals on 27 March 1957. *(G. A. Kilcoyne)*

A truly magnificent Mosquito! Don Bussart's B.XXV N37878 'The Wooden Wonder' is seen at Rosamond Dry Lake, California, prior to the 1949 Bendix Trophy Race. As KB377, this aircraft was constructed in mid-1944, being retained in Canada on RCAF charge until sold to Don McVicar in 1948. Registered CF-FZG, Don prepared KB377 for entry in the 1948 Bendix Trophy Race but starboard engine problems prevented its participation. The aircraft was later sold to Donald Bussart of Illinois and extensively modified by Capital Airways, being fitted with extended engine mountings to accept two-speed, two-stage supercharged Packard Merlin V-1650-7 engines, together with associated alterations to engine and propeller controls. Fuel tankage was also greatly increased, the bomb bay accommodating a 550-gallon tank, which projected beneath the line of the fuselage. To accommodate this tank, both bomb doors were replaced by a streamlined fairing giving the aircraft an under-fuselage profile similar to that of the B.XVI, B.35 and PR.34.

Donald Bussart intended to enter the modified Mosquito in the 1949 Bendix Trophy Race before continuing to New York for an attempt on the Transcontinental Record. If all went smoothly, he would then try and claim the around-the-world speed record. Registered N37878, in its modified form this Mosquito reportedly achieved level speeds exceeding those attained by W4050 with Merlin 77s. However, starboard engine cooling problems prevented it from winning the 1949 race. The aircraft was later sold to the Mark Hurd Mapping Company and modified for aerial photography, eventually being damaged beyond economical repair at MacCarron Field, Las Vegas, in 1952. Like the other American two-speed, two-stage supercharged Merlin Mosquito conversion (N1203V), N37878 did not feature the intercooler radiator of production two-stage Merlin Mosquitoes and retained the five exhaust stacks (permitted by the exhaust 'slots' of its lengthened but original side cowlings) associated with the standard B.XXV engine installation. N37878 is finished dark blue overall with cream spinners and registration letters. The spinners feature three red triangular strips running from the blade roots to the spinner tips. *(Dick Hin, via Stuart Howe collection)*

PR.XVI G-AOCI is seen at Thruxton aerodrome in the late 1950s. This Mosquito was one of six former Royal Navy PR.XVIs purchased by scrap dealer R. A. Short that were flown to Thruxton during May 1956. Three were later sold to the Israeli Defence Force/Air Force, the remainder languishing in the undergrowth until they were burned in 1960. G-AOCI was constructed at Hatfield as NS639 in the summer of 1944 and delivered to RAF Benson on 27 July. Allocated to 544 Squadron on 23 August, it survived an attack by Me262s during a photo-reconnaissance sortie over Germany on 16 September. Despatched to the Mediterranean Theatre in April 1945, NS639 returned to the UK four months later and entered storage with 44 MU. Later transferred to the Royal Navy, the aircraft passed to RNAS Stretton in April 1947, where it remained until flown to de Havilland's at Leavesden during January 1949. Returning to Stretton in July, NS639 spent the remainder of its service life in storage, passing between Stretton, Yeovilton, Culham and Lossiemouth before sale as scrap to R. A. Short on 31 August 1953. Registered G-AOCI on 18 May 1955, NS639 was ferried to Thruxton in May 1956, but never flew again, becoming one of the three aircraft destroyed during 1960. The PR.XVI to NS639's left is G-AOCK, formerly NS753. NS639's airframe is finished in silver dope and features a yellow band on the rear fuselage. Note the Rover saloon car parked beneath G-AOCI's starboard wing. *(John Stride collection)*

CF-HMP of Spartan Air Services awaits overhaul at Derby Aviation's Burnaston base in 1955. A former 139 Squadron B.35, CF-HMP still bears its service colour scheme of light grey upper surfaces and Night under surfaces. As TK648, this B.35 was constructed at Hatfield in March 1946 and delivered to 38 MU on 4 April. It passed to AST Hamble for modifications in August 1947, this work being completed by May 1948 when it was assigned to 15 MU. Five months later TK648 entered service with 230 OCU, remaining with this unit until June 1950, when it was allocated to 139 Squadron at Hemswell. Damage repairs were carried out during September 1952, the aircraft returning to squadron strength the following month. Sold to Spartan Air Services on 8 December 1954, TK648 was overhauled and repainted by Derby Aviation before delivery to Ottawa on 29 October 1955. CF-HMP and its crew were lost in an unexplained crash close to Neepawa, Manitoba, on 10 September 1957. Note the painted-out fuselage roundel and fin flash. The badge on the fin is that of CF-HMP's previous operator, 139 Squadron. *(A. J. Jones, via Stuart Howe collection)*

This nice ground shot is of Spartan Air Services' Mark 35 CF-HMS. Following delivery from the UK, nine of the Spartan Mark 35s were heavily modified in preparation for their new careers as high-altitude aerial survey platforms (the tenth aircraft, CF-HMT, ex-RS711, was broken down for spares). Modifications included the installation of a Wild RC-5 camera in the aft section of the ventral bay (between fuselage bulkheads three and four) and the creation of a camera operator's position in the rear fuselage, aft of bulkhead four. This extremely cramped and claustrophobic crew station received natural light via a single porthole (later increased to two) on the fuselage port side. A clear Perspex panel (visible here) was fitted to the rear access hatch, which also acted as a means of entry and exit for the camera operator. To increase structural integrity, fuselage bulkhead three was infilled to the lower line of the fuselage, reducing the ventral bay length by approximately a quarter and necessitating re-routing of the elevator cables. The Mark 35's 'bulged' ventral bay doors, together with their forward and rear fairings, were removed, being replaced by a detachable plywood under-panel (with their 'flat' bellies, the Spartan aircraft partially resembled the Mosquito B/PR.IX and the PR.XVI). A 65-gallon fuel tank was fitted in the ventral bay, which, coupled with 100-gallon drop tanks, increased fuel capacity to 739 gallons.

Spartan Air Services' Mosquitoes operated all over western and northern Canada, flying from bases in the Northwest Territories such as Yellowknife, Pelly Lake and Sawmill Bay, and from harsh, primitive airstrips within the Arctic Circle, including Resolute Bay and Mould Bay. Their excellent endurance and range permitted survey flights of up to 5½ hours, aircraft often covering more than 1,000 miles.

CF-HMS left the Airspeed factory as B.35 RS700 in March 1946 and immediately entered storage with 274 MU. Eight months later it moved to 37 MU before returning to Airspeed for modifications in April 1947. This work was complete by 5 February 1948, RS700 passing to 9 MU on 11 March. Following two and a half years in storage with 19 MU, RS700 was delivered to de Havilland's for conversion as the first PR.35. This Mosquito went on to serve with 58 Squadron at Benson and Wyton before retirement to 22 MU. On 8 December 1954 it was sold to Spartan Air Services and, following overhaul by Derby Aviation, was delivered to Canada as CF-HMS in July 1956. Following its withdrawal from service in 1963, CF-HMS was bought by a private concern in Calgary before acquisition by the Calgary Centennial Planetarium Museum in 1972. The venturi on top of the fuselage provided suction to the RC-5 camera, ensuring that film remained flat on the platen during exposure. Later cameras fitted to the Spartan Mosquitoes included their own vacuum source, so this venturi was deleted. *(Stuart Howe collection)*

Surrounded by Miles Hawk Trainers, B.35 G-AOSS is seen in the Derby Aviation hangar at Burnaston. Hatfield-built as TK655 in April 1946, this aircraft entered storage with 38 MU at Llandow on 2 May. Between 13 August 1947 and 6 April 1948 it underwent modifications at Marshalls before entering another period of store, this time with 19 MU. Transferred to 48 MU on 8 June 1951, TK655 passed to 27 MU in August 1953, where it was declared Non-Effective Stock on 11 January 1955. This virtually new aircraft was sold to Derby Aviation at Burnaston on 14 August 1956; it was reportedly due for sale (as N9912F) to Jack Amman Photogrammetric Engineers in the USA but this fell through, TK655 later being registered G-AOSS. Derby Aviation began to overhaul the Mosquito in readiness for a record crossing of the South Atlantic by Miss Roberta Cowell. However, largely due to a lack of suitable engines, work on G-AOSS ceased, the aircraft eventually being destroyed at Burnaston during 1960. G-AOSS appears to be finished in silver dope overall. *(Stuart Howe collection)*

B.XXV NX6613 'Miss Martha', probably at Berry Field, Tennessee, in 1948. Constructed in March 1945 as KA984, this B.XXV was retained in Canada by the RCAF and placed in storage for most of its service career. In June 1948, together with B.XXV KB377 (see page 378), KA984 was purchased from the War Assets Corporation by Don McVicar and flown to Montreal early the following month. Shortly afterwards the aircraft was sold to Jessie Stallings of Capital Airways, who entered it for the 1948 Bendix Trophy Race. Registered NX66313, KA984 was prepared at Berry Field, Nashville, receiving an extra fuel tank in the ventral bay together with a streamlined 'solid' nose in place of the original Perspex unit. Completely repainted, NX66313 was christened 'Miss Martha', this name appearing on the port side of the nose (just visible in this picture). It completed the race, later being sold to a new owner who based the Mosquito at Birmingham, Alabama. In June 1951 NX66313 passed to the Mark Hurd Mapping Company, but was written off in a take-off accident at El Paso, Texas, during October 1951. It is finished in white overall with maroon engine cowlings and registration lettering. This aircraft was arguably the most elegant of all racing Mosquitoes. *(Stuart Howe collection)*

Mark 35 CF-HML being test-flown from Burnaston following overhaul and repainting for Spartan Air Services. Constructed as B.35 VR796, this Mosquito was ready for collection from the Airspeed Christchurch factory on 5 December 1947 but remained at Christchurch for modifications before entering storage with 22 MU in June 1948. In November 1954 it was purchased for $1,500 Canadian by Spartan Air Services and ferried to Derby Aviation at Burnaston the following January; there it was overhauled before being repainted in Spartan Air Services' colours and the Canadian civil registration CF-HML applied. The first of ten Spartan Air Services Mark 35s flown to Canada, CF-HML arrived at the company's Uplands Airport (Ottawa) base on 3 May 1955.

Following withdrawal of Spartan's dual-control FB.26 (CF-GKK, ex-KA244) in 1959, CF-HML was fitted with dual controls in order to provide pilot training and check-outs. This modification prevented cockpit access via the conventional under-fuselage hatch, pilots instead entering the aircraft through the canopy roof escape hatch, which was fixed but hinged forward. Spartan Air Services worked CF-HML hard in the photographic survey and training role before the aircraft was withdrawn from use in 1963.

CF-HML remained in Ottawa until December 1966 when it was bought by Don Campbell of Kapuskasing, Ontario, as a restoration project for his 647 Squadron RCAF Air Cadets. The decision was taken to restore CF-HML to flying condition and tremendous strides were made in this regard before the aircraft was transferred to Mike Meeker of Mission, British Columbia, for completion. CF-HML later passed to Ed Zalesky, and is today owned by Bob Jens, who is continuing this Mosquito's restoration to airworthiness. In this pre-delivery shot, CF-HML is finished in silver overall with red spinners and outer wing bands. The fairing on top of the fuselage houses the DF Loop. Note that the tailwheel has not retracted. *(via Philip Birtles)*

Spartan Air Services' Mark 35 CF-HMM is believed to have been photographed at Edmonton. This aircraft was constructed as B.35 TK623 at Hatfield in January 1946. Delivered into storage with 27 MU on 3 March 1946, TK623 passed to 22 MU in December 1948 before suffering accident damage in January 1949. Repairs were carried out by Brooklands Aviation and took more than a year to complete, TK623 then making its way to 22 MU on 9 March 1950. Later sold to Spartan Air Services, it was overhauled by Derby Aviation before delivery to Canada, registered CF-HMM, in August 1955. Note the full-blown single-piece Perspex nose, which was similar to that featured on the PR.34. Spartan replaced the original B.35

Perspex nose on its Mosquitoes to improve visibility during photographic survey operations. The cockpit canopies were also modified for increased visibility and featured a white-painted top section to reduce glare. Aside from Canada, Spartan's Mosquitoes conducted high-altitude aerial survey work in several different countries, including Colombia, Mexico, the Dominican Republic, Argentina and Kenya. CF-HMM crashed at Ciudad Trujillo (Dominican Republic) on 27 March 1960 after experiencing severe engine problems shortly after take-off – pilot Doug Wade and engineer Frank Francis were tragically killed. *(Bill Cottrell, Alberta Aviation Museum Collection)*

PR.XVI G-AOCK out to grass at Thruxton in July 1959. This former USAAF aircraft was constructed at Hatfield in October 1944 as NS753. Delivered to 10 MU on 28 October, it was delivered to the USAAF at Watton on 7 December 1944. The following March it was sent to Martin Hearn for damage repairs, afterwards passing to 44 MU. Transferred to the Royal Navy in December 1946, NS753 flew to Gosport before entering storage at Stretton. 771 Squadron (Fleet Air Arm) at Ford took delivery of NS753 in November 1948, the aircraft later being despatched on squadron detachment to Lee-on-Solent, where it received the unit codes '598/LP'. Overhauled

by Brooklands Aviation at Sywell during January 1949, NS753 later served with the Airwork FRU at Hurn before entering storage at Lossiemouth. Purchased by scrap dealer R. A. Short and registered G-AOCK, NS753 was one of six Mosquito PR.XVIs flown into Thruxton during May 1956 (see page 379). NS753 fell into dereliction at Thruxton, eventually being burned in October 1960. Note that the letter 'C' of NS753's civil registration has been modified to resemble an 'O'. The aircraft to NS753's right is G-AOCI (ex-NS639). *(Stuart Howe collection)*

PR.34A N9870F stands outside the flight test hangar at de Havilland's Hatfield aerodrome on 11 September 1956, while being prepared by the de Havilland Service Department in readiness for collection by its new owner, Jack Amman Photogrammetric Engineers of San Antonio, Texas. N9870F was constructed at Hatfield in May 1945 as PR.34 RG233. Delivered to 27 MU on 25 May, it was stored for the next five years before despatch to the MEAF in June 1950. Following further periods in store (this time with 107 and 109 MUs) RG233 was allocated to 13 Squadron at Fayid on 27 March 1951. Returning to the UK in February 1952, the aircraft was assigned to 19 MU before undergoing conversion to PR.34A standard (by Marshalls) between April and August the same year. Aside from six months undergoing accident repairs, RG233

spent the remainder of its service life in storage before transfer (at 22 MU) to Non-Effective Stock in October 1955. RG233 was sold to Jack Amman Photogrammetric Engineers on 16 August 1956, becoming one of five PR.34As purchased by that company. Modified to accept a camera, together with an operator's position, in the rear fuselage, N9870F was later employed on photographic survey work in Libya. This Mosquito's ultimate fate was to be scrapped at Cambridge airport during 1960. N9870F retains its PRU blue finish and carries the FAA 'RESTRICTED' notice on the ventral bay forward under fairing. Note the enlarged elevator horn balances, 'paddle'-blade propellers and underwing drop tanks. *(BAE SYSTEMS)*

List of Surviving Mosquitoes

Mark and serial number	Owner and location
Prototype W4050	de Havilland Aircraft Museum Trust, Salisbury Hall, UK
NF.II HJ711	Tony Agar, Yorkshire Air Museum, Elvington (composite restoration)
T.3 TV959	Flying Heritage Collection, Washington, USA (stored in UK pending restoration)
T.3 TW117	Norwegian Aviation Museum, Bodo
FB.VI TA122	de Havilland Aircraft Museum Trust, Salisbury Hall, UK (restoration project incorporating a TR.33 wing)
FB.VI TE758	Ferrymead Aeronautical Society, New Zealand (restoration project)
FB.VI TE863	RNZAF Museum, Wigram (restoration project)
FB.VI TE910	John Smith, Mapau, Nelson, New Zealand
FB.VI PZ474	Jim Merizan, Chino, California (restoration project)
FB.VI HR621	Camden Museum of Aviation, Narellan, NSW (restoration project)
PR.IX LR480	South African Museum of Military History, Saxonwold
PR.XVI A52-600 (ex-NS631)	RAAF Museum, Point Cook, Victoria (restoration project)
B.XX KB336	Canada Aviation Museum, Ottawa, Ontario
FB.26 KA114	The Fighter Factory, Suffolk, Virginia (under restoration to flying condition with Avpecs, New Zealand)
NF.30 MB-24 (ex-RK952)	Belgian Army Museum and Museum of Military History, Brussels
PR.34 RG300	Jim Deerborn, California (restoration project)
TT.35 TA634	de Havilland Aircraft Museum Trust, Salisbury Hall, UK
TT.35 TA639	Royal Air Force Museum, Cosford
TT.35 TA719	Imperial War Museum, Duxford
TT.35 TH998	National Air & Space Museum, Washington
TT.35 TJ138	Royal Air Force Museum, London
TT.35 TJ118	de Havilland Aircraft Museum Trust, Salisbury Hall, UK (restoration project)
TT.35 RS709	National Museum of the United States Air Force, Dayton, Ohio
TT.35 RS712/N35MK	Air Venture Museum, Experimental Aircraft Association, Oshkosh, Wisconsin
Mk 35 VR796/CF-HML	Bob Jens, Vancouver International Airport (under restoration to flying condition)
Mk 35 RS700/CF-HMS	Calgary Aerospace Museum
Mk 35 VP189/CF-HMQ	Alberta Aviation Museum
PR.41 A52-319	Australian War Memorial, Canberra
T.43 NZ2305 (ex-A52-1053)	Museum of Transport and Technology, Auckland, New Zealand

Select Bibliography

Anoni, Shlomo *Wooden Wonders – The DH Mosquito in Israeli Service* (*Air Enthusiast*, September/October 1999)

Ashworth, Chris *Chinese Mosquitoes* (*Aviation News*)

Birtles, Philip *Mosquito – A Pictorial History of the DH.98* (Janes Publishing, 1980)
    Mosquito – The Illustrated History (Sutton Publishing, 1999)

Bowyer, Chaz *Mosquito at War* (Ian Allan, 1973)
    Mosquito Squadrons of the Royal Air Force (Ian Allan, 1984)

Bowyer, Michael J. F. and Rawlings, John D. R. *Squadron Codes* (Patrick Stephens Ltd, 1979)

Chorley, W. R. *Royal Air Force Bomber Command Losses of the Second World War – 1945* (Midland Publishing, 2004)

Forslund, Mikael *J.30 de Havilland Mosquito NF. Mk XIX* (Allt OM Hobby AB, 1997)

Franks, Richard A. *The de Havilland Mosquito – A Comprehensive Guide for the Modeller* (SAM Publications, 1998)

Hardy, M. J. *The de Havilland Mosquito* (David & Charles, 1977)

Hislop, G. S. PhD and Davies, D. M. MA 'An Investigation of High-Altitude Clear-Air Turbulence over Europe using Mosquito Aircraft' (HMSO Reports and Memoranda No 2737, 1950)

Howe, Stuart *de Havilland Mosquito – An Illustrated History* (Crécy Publishing, 1999)
    Mosquito Portfolio (Ian Allan, 1984)
    Mosquito Survivors (Aston Publications, 1986)
    China Diary (*Air Enthusiast/Forty Five*)

Lucas, Paul *Combat Colours Number 5* (Guideline Publications, 2002)
    Combat Colours Number 6 (Guideline Publications, 2003)

Malayney, Norman *California Mosquitoes* (Journal of the American Aviation Historical Society, Spring 2002)
    The Bendix Mosquitoes (Journal of the American Aviation Historical Society, Fall 1994)
    The Jack Amman Mosquitoes (Journal of the American Aviation Historical Society, Winter 1994)

'The Mosquito 50 Years On – A Report on the 50th Anniversary Symposium held at British Aerospace Hatfield on the 24th November, 1990' (GMS Enterprises, 1991)

Moyes, Philip *Bomber Squadrons of the RAF and their Aircraft* (Macdonald, 1964)

Pasco, Dennis *Tested – Marshall Test Pilots and their aircraft in war and peace 1919-1999* (Grub Street, 1999)

Rawlings, John D. R. *Fighter Squadrons of the RAF and their Aircraft* (Macdonald, 1969)

Sharp, C. Martin and Bowyer, Michael J. F. *Mosquito* (Faber & Faber, 1967; Crécy Publishing, 1997)

Stitt, Robert M. *High-Flying Exotica – Spartan's Lockheed and de Havilland Aerial Survey Twins* (*Air Enthusiast*, May/June 1998)

Streetly, Martin *Confound and Destroy – 100 Group and the Bomber Support Campaign* (Macdonald & Janes, 1978)

Sturtivant, Ray *The Squadrons of the Fleet Air Arm* (Air Britain)

Sturtivant, Ray, Burrow, Mick and Howard, Lee *Fleet Air Arm fixed wing aircraft since 1946* (Air Britain (Historians) Ltd, 2004)

Taylor, Bill *The Royal Air Force in Germany Since 1945* (Midland Publishing, 2003)

Vincent, David *Mosquito Monograph* (1982)

Index